*The Pre-industrial Consumer in
England and America*

The Pre-industrial Consumer in England and America

CAROLE SHAMMAS

CLARENDON PRESS · OXFORD

1990

Oxford University Press, Walton Street, Oxford OX2 6DP

Oxford New York Toronto
Delhi Bombay Calcutta Madras Karachi
Petaling Jaya Singapore Hong Kong Tokyo
Nairobi Dar es Salaam Cape Town
Melbourne Auckland

and associated companies in
Berlin Ibadan

Oxford is a trade mark of Oxford University Press

Published in the United States
by Oxford University Press, New York

British Library Cataloguing in Publication Data
Shammas, Carole
The pre-industrial consumer in England and America.
1. Consumer goods. Consumption. Social aspects, history
I. Title   306.3
ISBN 0–19–828302–4

Library of Congress Cataloging in Publication Data
Shammas, Carole.
The pre-industrial consumer in England and America / Carole
Shammas.
p. cm.
1. Consumption (Economics)—Great Britain—History—18th century.
2. Consumption (Economics)—United States—History—18th century.
3. Home-based businesses—Great Britain—History—18th century.
4. Home-based businesses—United States—History—18th century.
5. Cost and standard of living—Great Britain—History 18th
century.   6. Cost and standard of living—United States—
History—18th century.   I. Title.
HC260.C6S5   1990
339.4'7'094209034—dc 20   90–31433
ISBN 0–19–828302–4

Typeset by Joshua Associates Ltd, Oxford
Printed and bound in
Great Britain by Bookcraft Ltd
Midsomer Norton, Bath

For
Jeanette Hilland Shammas
and
Nickolas N. Shammas

Acknowledgements

THIS project on consumption in England and America from 1500 to 1800 has been underway since 1974. During the course of the work I received two research fellowships, one from The Philadelphia Center for Early American Studies and the second from the Newberry Library in association with the National Endowment for the Humanities. Closer to home, the Center for Women's Studies and the Social Science Research Facility at the University of Wisconsin–Milwaukee provided valuable support services. Many graduate students in the University of Wisconsin–Milwaukee History Department helped with coding over the years, including Judith De Groat, Joanne Murphy, and Lloyd Velicer.

A number of scholars have generously shared their work with me or, at one point or another, provided much-needed expertise. I wish to thank Margo Anderson, Timothy Breen, Lois Green Carr, James Cronin, Jack Crowley, Thomas Doerflinger, Richard Dunn, Eugene Eisman, Stanley Engerman, Cissie Fairchilds, Robert Fogel, Jack P. Greene, Gloria Main, Mary Beth Norton, Sharon Salinger, Marylynn Salmon, Daniel Scott Smith, Peter H. Smith, Lee Soltow, Lorena Walsh, Jeffrey Williamson, E. A. Wrigley.

Darryl Holter read through the entire manuscript—so any remaining errors are his fault.

Contents

List of Figures

List of Tables

I

The Early Modern Economy and the Pre-Industrial Consumer

WHEN I began this project in 1974, many historians considered 'pre-industrial consumer' to be something of a contradiction in terms. In early modern England, the population was often described as living at subsistence level, and in early America, communities were frequently identified as self-sufficient. With diet, clothing, and shelter at such a rudimentary level in the Old World and with necessities largely home-produced in the New, the study of mass consumption and standards of living seemed to belong to the industrial era.[1]

This is no longer the case, however. Being poor and being a consumer, it turns out, were not mutually exclusive conditions. Scholars now write of early modern Europe's 'peasant demand' and 'hedonistic culture of mass consumption', of the 'birth' and 'development' of a Tudor–Stuart consumer society, and of an 'empire of goods' in British America. They seem fully convinced that the bulk of the population in these places, and not just the upper classes and a small number of urban dwellers, participated in the consumption of market goods.[2] The old Industrial Revolution paradigm has collapsed and its demise has had a very liberating effect on the study of past levels of consumption. Some of the disintegration can be attributed to recent discoveries about the slow rate of British economic growth during the closing decades of the eighteenth century and the first quarter of the nineteenth century—a place and a period that previously had enjoyed a reputation for unparalleled acceleration in development.[3] But even more of a threat to the notion of a neat pre-industrial–industrial dichotomy, separated by a transforming revolution, has been the discovery of how the rural household economy functioned in the early modern West.

Early in this century, the work of R. H. Tawney drew attention to the sixteenth-century decline in English manorial agriculture and the large number of households excluded from arable cultivation. Clearly, few early modern households in England could have been self-contained production and consumption units.[4] Tawney's work, of course, did not go unchallenged, and debates continue into the present over the reasons for landlessness—was it caused by the wealthy enclosing land and adopting other profit-maximizing tactics, as Tawney believed, or was it more the result of demographic pressures and of burdens placed on the economy by the state? Also, opinions differ sharply as to whether the rural industry that emerged should be considered proto-industrialization, and whether what the working classes experienced was proletarianization.[5] These controversies should not obscure the fact that there are some substantial areas of agreement about economic developments in England between 1500 and 1800 that are highly relevant to the study of consumption.

To a surprising extent, the early modern English population depended on wages, and this income came from both agricultural work and rural manufacturing. For some, manufacturing was a by-employment, while for others it was a full-time job. Yet another group were those with dual occupations, having a craft as well as agricultural holdings. There were many industrial villages throughout England where a large proportion of households relied on the production of one basic commodity for their livelihood. In some cases, small independent artisans made the products and sold to a middleman, but in other cases those who fashioned the commodity worked more or less for a wage. They might labour in a workshop or in their houses through the outwork system. More often than not these rural workers produced consumer items—cloth, stockings, caps, buttons, cutlery, and a multitude of other commodities for personal and household use. Obviously, if these enterprises employed so many people there must have been a mass market for the commodities produced. This is what Joan Thirsk concluded after surveying the new goods being produced in various parts of the English countryside in the seventeenth century.[6]

The study of the consumption of durables in early modern society has now begun in earnest with probate inventories being, so far, the favoured source. In most European countries and in America, local appraisers have evaluated, often item by item, the personalty (all property aside from realty) of the deceased. Although there are biases and shortcomings in these kind of data, inventories probably do provide a more complete record of what households possessed in the way of durables than any other single source, and there are a growing number of studies using them to measure the distribution of consumer goods.[7]

Also influential in promoting the study of early modern consumption has been work documenting the establishment of a world system of trade and the concomitant rise of chattel slavery.[8] While the studies of rural industries have drawn attention to the importance of consumer durables, the research on world trade has highlighted the significance of another area of consumption, non-European foodstuffs. What led to the voluntary and forced mass migration of people from Europe and Africa to the New World and to wars among Europeans for control of American real estate and Atlantic–Pacific waterways? Whatever way one looks at it, the demand for tobacco, sugar products, and caffeine drinks—what contemporaries referred to as groceries—has to be a big part of the answer. This change in consumption had an enormous impact on the nature of post-1500 international relations, European national politics, and the social structure of American colonies.

Given the new consensus that the trend in pre-1800 consumption is more than just a flat, horizontal line, what are the major issues that need to be addressed concerning that consumption? This book deals with three subjects—demand, standards of living, and distribution. The exact form of the questions asked of these subjects emerged from combining economic theories about consumption with recent historical interpretations of early modern economic structures and processes. I studied both England and America because their respective inhabitants shared the same trading network and many of the same cultural values, but their material situation (e.g. land availability, population density, social structure, natural resources) differed substantially. This kind of variation is useful when testing theories about how shifts in consumption take place.

In the first part of this book, I explore the way the household mode of production generated demand for consumer goods. Jan de Vries, more than a decade ago, put forward the interesting proposition that in early modern peasant society not only might changes in production and higher crop prices have resulted in specialization and increased reliance on consumer commodities, but the reverse could also have occurred. Households might have altered modes of production in order to buy goods less primitive than those made in the home or to purchase items unavailable from local producers.[9] Two implications of De Vries's suggestion made it especially noteworthy. First, it meant that those studying economic development had to consider not just a household's strategies for market production, but also its consumer preferences. Second, it implied that any explanation for the transformation of peasants from producers to consumers ought to take account of more than just lack of access to land. Although that must be an important element in any discussion of demand and material well-being, total reliance on land availability as an explanation tends to represent the labouring classes as nothing more than the dupes of crafty landlords. It also tends to glorify the living conditions of those practising peasant agriculture. Moreover, the dispossession thesis fails rather miserably as an explanation for American colonial consumers.

The availability of land in America and the dominant position of agriculture would lead one to believe that households there would have had few reasons to consume market goods. In plantation colonies, however, settlers producing the new groceries tied the economy to world-wide trade from the beginning. The shortage of labour and the great returns on sale of staple crops may have made it desirable for plantation owners to put all servants and slaves into fieldwork and buy cheap clothing and other necessities.[10] The self-sufficient plantation household with spinning-rooms and craftshops appears to have been largely a post-colonial development designed to employ slaves no longer needed to cultivate a declining staple.[11]

Of course, the situation in the northern colonies was very different, because staple crops for export to the Old World constituted a much smaller part of their economy. Some historians have argued that the New England family farm was a nearly self-contained production and consumption unit, and that neighbourhood exchange and bartering supplied whatever else the household lacked. Most economic historians, however, are sceptical about this depiction of the family economy, arguing that only the affluent had the resources to even aspire to self-sufficiency.[12] Tenancy existed in all regions of America, including New England, and poor soil meant even small farmers who owned their land had to supplement their incomes with paid work.[13] Moreover, in the middle colonies, wheat eventually developed into a staple crop, tying family farms into a world system of trade and making the region a major consumer of bound labour as well as market goods.[14]

In Part I, I examine the ability of households to produce their own consumer goods in different regions of England, in plantation America, and in New England, and compare this ability with trends in the consumption of market goods, paying attention to whether consumers were being pushed into the market due to the declining ability of their household or their locality to provide the goods. I also investigate the extent to which demand was driven by greater personal wealth, lower prices, demographic shifts, changes in the occupational structure, urbanization, and educational level.

A second objective in writing this book has been to evaluate the impact of changes in early modern diet, housing, and ownership of durables on the population of England and America. These are the subjects of Part II. Most of the work that has been carried out on standards of living has been associated with the debate as to whether the Industrial Revolution of the late eighteenth and nineteenth centuries served to benefit or worsen the lot of the working class.[15] Now that industrialization is seen less as a sudden, cataclysmic event, and it is realized that mass production could go on in rural locales without power-driven machinery, it seems artificial to restrict discussions about the relationship between economic development and living standards to the years after 1790.

Research on mortality and nutritional status has also directed attention to earlier times. In *The Population History of England*, E. A. Wrigley and R. S. Schofield have found that the positive correlation between grain prices—an important indicator of cost of living—and mortality is very, very weak and ends altogether in the first half of the eighteenth century.[16] Nevertheless, the English do not compare favourably with other groups when indicators of health and general vigour, such as average height, are examined. The heights recorded for British and American soldiers from the 1760s on reveal the former as being, on average, 3.5 in. shorter than the latter (64.7 in. compared to 68.1 in.). Other work suggests that certain portions of the late eighteenth-century population of London could properly be described as stunted. Major increases in height in England may not have occurred until the end of the nineteenth or even the twentieth century. In America, too, the story is not simply a matter of onward and upward. In the mid-nineteenth century, white native-born men had much higher mean heights than the British, but on average, they were not as tall as their late-colonial forebears.[17]

How dietary changes during the early modern period may have affected the health of the population is not well understood, partially because very little is known about how much and what people actually ate and drank. Previous standards of living studies have concentrated more on cost of living indices than on nutritional measures.[18] Although beneficial commodities such as rice and potatoes first made their appearance in the Western diet during the early modern period, so did a long list of other products—sugar, tobacco, tea, coffee, chocolate, strong alcoholic drinks, adulterated white bread—that today lead the list of dietary substances considered to have detrimental effects. Unfortunately, there are few detailed studies of food intake by class and what it implies about people's health.[19] Records are a problem here. Probate inventories are of limited use because perishables were not normally listed. Modern dietary studies depend upon aggregate production figures or household budget surveys, neither of which are very plentiful prior to 1850. It is necessary, therefore, to utilize a variety of sources of information to estimate the proportion of expenditure devoted to food and drink as well as the composition and caloric content of what was consumed.

More has been written on housing and consumption of durables. Most notably, scholars studying vernacular architecture have hypothesized that England, during the early modern period, experienced a great rural rebuilding. According to this argument, English families replaced impermanent dwellings lasting less than a generation or two with sturdier houses equipped with chimneys, second storeys, stairways, glass windows, and additional rooms.[20] In colonial America, researchers have been more impressed with the continuing under-investment in housing. One hundred years after settlement, even affluent Chesapeake planters still lived in quite small and impermanent dwellings; and in northern communities, all-wooden houses with one- to three-room floor plans seem to have been the norm for most income classes.[21] Is the English picture too rosy? Or did colonists settle for a lower standard of housing in America—and if so, was this due to the rapid population growth or the shortage of skilled labour, or to other factors?

As regards household furnishings, colonial historians have found evidence in probate inventories of a widespread rise after 1730 in the ownership of amenities (linen, tableware, books, clocks, and so forth), particularly those connected with the taking of meals.[22] There are fewer relevant studies in England, but the most comprehensive survey published to date argues that the growth in the possession of new tableware items and other household consumer goods went no further than the affluent middle class.[23] Unfortunately, probate coverage in England falls off sharply in the second quarter of the eighteenth century, just at the time when the situation began to change in the colonies. The question is, therefore, whether an Old World–New World difference exists, or whether the divergence is simply a result of the records stopping earlier in England.

The reasons why an increase in the ownership of such household goods as ceramic dishes or knives and forks could be viewed as important are less apparent and more in need of explanation than is the case with shifts in diet and shelter. For much of the work on material culture to have meaning, it has to be set alongside research on family social relations and changing patterns of household labour.[24] Also the histories of diet, housing, and consumer durables have tended to proceed on separate tracks, with those engaged in research on one of the subjects making little reference to the other two. By looking at general consumer trends, there will be an opportunity to examine the interrelationships and also comment on the overall trend in material well-being.

Part III of this book deals with the system of distributing consumer goods in societies with few urban areas and a high proportion of the population engaged in agricultural activities. One of the relatively well-researched areas of economic history has been the activities of early modern merchants in the trading cities of Europe and America. Their wealth and class characteristics, the organization of their firms, and their overseas transactions have been carefully documented and analysed. Less well known is how their merchandise ultimately reached customers who lived primarily in rural communities. The stagnation of so many of the smaller cities and towns in Western Europe during the seventeenth and much of the eighteenth century has made it difficult for historians to conceptualize how an increasing volume of international goods could have been traded in the early modern era, so dependent are we on the notion that urbanization, specialization, and mass consumption are inseparable phenomena. In England, London grew rapidly, and until the mid-eighteenth century accounted for most of the increase in the total percentage of persons living in urban areas. Many traditional regional centres even failed to keep pace with the population growth in the nation as a whole.[25] When confronted with the evidence of more and more consumer goods being distributed throughout England and the colonies, one has a reaction very similar to that of demographers studying the nineteenth-century decline in fertility—how *did* they do it?

England had market towns, and clearly one must start any investigation of internal trade there with these centres. Of course, market towns go back to the medieval period, and if anything were probably more important in the thirteenth century than the sixteenth.[26] Either something changed in the towns or they were displaced. Chapter 7 discusses how market towns fit into a hierarchically structured system of distribution in which consumer goods were channelled through masters, employers, and heads of households before reaching the ultimate consumer. What contemporaries pointed to as new in the early modern period was the proliferation of retail shops, but estimating their numbers and their volume of business is not easy. Because provincial retailers are the least likely kind of merchant to have extant accounts, it is necessary to rely on trade tokens and tax records to measure their prevalence.[27]

Whether the retailing network in which they participated operated through market towns or was in competition with the older system is one issue. To what extent did they replace the local great man who had served as a go-between earlier? Another question concerns the importance of itinerant traders in spreading goods among the rural population. Did peddling and village shops grow together, or were they in competition, with one waxing while the other waned?

No formal market-town system developed in America, although certain cities organized market-days and held fairs. Retailing in the colonies did not follow the English pattern. In some regions, the same merchants who handled the staple crops also sold consumer goods. The most sophisticated version of this trade occurred in the Chesapeake. There eighteenth-century Scottish merchants actually established chain stores to provide planters with manufactured goods, groceries, and whatever else they wanted in exchange for their tobacco.[28] What rural shopkeepers sold, and to whom they sold under what terms, however, have only been studied in a few instances, and their suppliers and their links to importers in major cities are only partially understood.[29] Given the comprehensive stock handled by the general storekeeper, diversification rather than specialization may be the key to understanding how the system operated.

There are two conflicting tendencies in the writings on consumption in the past. One is to view consumers as alienated from the means of production, pushed into the market-place, and force-fed market goods until, through merchandizing and advertisements, they become hooked on a culture of consumption. The other tendency is to interpret the accumulation of all new commodities as an unequivocal sign of general societal advancement and well-being. I have tried to avoid adopting either position in this book. One has to leave open the possibility that trends over a long period of time may be other than linear and that not all types of consumption change in the same way.

Chapter 1

1. See Chap. 5 on the tendency to assume that pre-modern English households spent 80% or more of their income on diet. On American self-sufficiency see Carole Shammas, 'How Self-Sufficient was Early America', *Journal of Interdisciplinary History*, 13 (1982), 247–72. See also the articles by Rothenberg, Pruitt, and Breen referred to below.

2. Jan De Vries, 'Peasant Demand Patterns and Economic Development: Friesland, 1550–1700', in William N. Parker and Eric L. Jones (eds.), *European Peasants and their Markets: Essays in Agrarian Economic History*, Princeton, 1975,

pp. 205–66; Chandra Mukerji, *From Graven Images: Patterns of Modern Materialism*, New York, 1983, p. 1; Joan Thirsk, *Economic Policy and Projects: The Development of a Consumer Society in Early Modern England*, Oxford, 1978; Neil McKendrick, John Brewer, and J. H. Plumb, *The Birth of a Consumer Society in Early Modern England*, Bloomington, Ind., 1982; and T. H. Breen, 'An Empire of Goods: The Anglicization of Colonial America, 1690–1776', *Journal of British Studies*, 25 (1986), 467–99.

3. C. Knick Harley, 'British Industrialization before 1841: Evidence of Slower Growth during the Industrial Revolution, 1780–1860: A Survey', *Journal of Economic History*, 42 (1982), 267–89; N. F. R. Crafts, 'British Economic Growth, 1700–1831: A Review of the Evidence', *Economic History Review*, 36 (1983), 177–93; and Jeffrey G. Williamson, 'Why was British Growth so Slow during the Industrial Revolution?', *Journal of Economic History*, 44 (1984), 687–712.

4. R. H. Tawney, *The Agrarian Problem in The Sixteenth Century*, London, 1912; A. J. Tawney and R. H. Tawney, 'An Occupational Census of the Seventeenth Century', *The Economic History Review*, 5 (1934–5), 25–64.

5. Many scholars, both Marxist and non-Marxist, view the centuries from 1500 to 1800 as a period of transition from a pre-capitalist to a capitalist society, and consider England to have been furthest advanced in this transition. Consequently, there has been a constant reworking and a re-analysis of the problems Tawney dealt with many years ago. For some recent examples, see Robert Brenner, 'The Agrarian Roots of European Capitalism', *Past and Present*, no. 97 (1982), 16–113, J. R. Wordie, 'The Chronology of English Enclosure, 1500–1914', *Economic History Review*, 36 (1983), 483–505, Richard Lachmann, *From Manor to Market: Structural Change in England, 1536–1640*, Madison, 1987, and J. A. Goldstone, 'The Demographic Revolution in England: A Re-examination', *Population Studies*, 49 (1986), 5–33. To more traditional English historians the 'transition' people go too far when they use the terms proto-industrialization and proletarianization to describe the development of rural industries and changes in the social structure. On this debate see Joan Thirsk, 'Industries in the Countryside', in F. J. Fisher (ed.), *Essays in the Economic and Social History of Tudor Stuart England*, Cambridge, 1961, pp. 70–88; Franklin Mendels, 'Proto-industrialization: The First Phase of the Process of Industrialization', *Journal of Economic History*, 32 (1972), 241–61; David Levine, *Family Formation in an Age of Nascent Capitalism*, New York, 1977; Peter Kriedtke, Hans Medick, Jurgen Schlumbohm, *Industrialization before Industrialization*, Cambridge, 1981; D. C. Coleman, 'Proto-industrialization: A Concept too Many', *Economic History Review*, 36 (1983), 435–48; Charles Tilly, 'Demographic Origins of the European Proletariat', in David Levine (ed.), *Proletarianization and Family History*, Orlando, 1984, pp. 1–86; Rab Houston and K. D. M. Snell, 'Proto-industrialization? Cottage Industry, Social Change, and the Industrial Revolution', *Historical Journal*, 27 (1984), 473–92.

6. On the extent and nature of agricultural wage labour and service see Alan Everitt, 'Farm Labourers', in Joan Thirsk (ed.), *The Agrarian History of England and Wales*, iv, *1500–1640*, Cambridge, 1967, pp. 396–465; Keith Wrightson and David Levine, *Poverty and Piety in an English Village: Terling, 1525–1700*, New York, 1979; Ann Sturm Kussmaul, *Servants in Husbandry in Early Modern*

England, Cambridge, 1981; K. M. D. Snell, *Annals of the Labouring Poor: Social Change and Agrarian England, 1660–1900*, Cambridge, 1985, Chap. 1; Carole Shammas 'The World Women Knew: Women Workers in the North of England during the late Seventeenth Century', in Richard S. Dunn and Mary Maples Dunn (eds.), *The World of William Penn*, Philadelphia, 1986, pp. 99–116. On rural industry see D. G. Hey, *The Rural Metalworkers of the Sheffield Region*, Leicester, 1972; Thirsk, *Economic Policy and Projects*; Pat Hudson, 'From Manor to Mill: The West Riding in Transition', in Maxine Berg, Pat Hudson, and Michael Sonenscher (eds.), *Town and Country before the Factory*, Cambridge, 1983, pp. 124–46; and John T. Swain, *Industrialization before the Industrial Revolution: Northeastern Lancashire c.1500–1640*, Manchester, 1986.

7. For references to this work see Ad Van Der Woude and Anton Schuurman (eds.), *Probate Inventories*, in *AAG Bijdragen*, 23 (1980); Mark Overton, *A Bibliography of British Inventories*, Newcastle-upon-Tyne, 1983; Hildegard Mannheims and Klaus Roth (comps), *Nachlassverzeichnisse: Internationale Bibliographie*, Munster, 1984; and Peter Benes ed. *Early American Probate Inventories* in *The Dublin Seminar for New England Folklife Proceedings* XII, Boston, 1989. Many articles in these collections concern methods, because probate inventories are very complicated sources to use. The late Alice Hanson Jones (*Wealth of a Nation to Be: The American Colonies on the Eve of the Revolution*, New York, 1980) was a pioneer in the systematic analysis of American inventories.

8. Immanuel Wallerstein, *The Modern World System*, i, *Capitalist Agriculture and the Origins of the European World-Economy in the Sixteenth Century*, New York, 1974, and ii, *Mercantilism and the Consolidation of the European World-Economy, 1600–1750*, New York, 1980.

9. *The Dutch Rural Economy in the Golden Age*, New Haven, Conn., 1974, and 'Peasant Demand Patterns'.

10. Over the past fifteen years, there have been a number of fine books and dissertations on the colonial plantation economy and its labour system, including: Richard S. Dunn, *Sugar and Slaves: The Rise of the Planter Class in the English West Indies, 1624–1713*, Chapel Hill, 1972; Russell Menard, 'Economy and Society in Early Colonial Maryland', unpublished Ph.D. dissertation, University of Iowa, 1974; Carville V. Earle, *The Evolution of a Tidewater Settlement System*, Chicago, 1975; Edmund Morgan, *American Slavery, American Freedom*, New York, 1975; Philip David Morgan, 'The Development of Slave Culture in Eighteenth-Century Plantation America', unpublished D. Phil. thesis, University of London, 1977; Gregory A. Stiverson, *Poverty in a Land of Plenty: Tenancy in Eighteenth-Century Maryland*, Baltimore, 1977; Lorena Seebach Walsh, 'Charles County, Maryland, 1658–1705: A Study of Chesapeake Social and Political Structure', unpublished Ph.D. dissertation, Michigan State University, 1977; Paul Clemens, *The Atlantic Economy and Colonial Maryland's Eastern Shore*, Ithaca, 1980; David Galenson, *Indentured Servitude in America*, Cambridge, 1982; Gloria L. Main, *Tobacco Colony: Life in Early Maryland 1650–1720*, Princeton, 1982; Darrett B. Rutman and Anita H. Rutman, *A Place in Time: Middlesex County, Virginia, 1650–1750*, New York, 1984; and Allan Kulikoff, *Tobacco and Slaves: The Development of Southern Cultures in the Chesapeake, 1680–1800*, Chapel Hill, 1986. On the role of demand in the

colony see John McCusker and Russell Menard, The *Economy of British America*, Chapel Hill, 1985, ch. 13, and Charles Wetherell, 'Boom and Bust in the Colonial Chesapeake Economy', *Journal of Interdisciplinary History*, 15 (1984), 210. Jack P. Greene, *Pursuits of Happiness: The Social Development of Early Modern British Colonies and the Formation of American Culture*, Chapel Hill, 1988, ch. 8 and epilogue, discusses the centrality of these plantation societies—particularly those in the Chesapeake—to the development of early American culture.

11. Lois Green Carr and Lorena S. Walsh, 'The Planter's Wife: The Experience of White Women in Seventeenth-Century Maryland', *William and Mary Quarterly*, 3rd ser. 34 (1977), 542–71; Carole Shammas, 'Black Women's Work and the Evolution of Plantation Society in Virginia', *Labor History*, 26 (1985), 5–28; Lois Green Carr and Lorena S. Walsh, 'Economic Diversification and Labor Organization in the Chesapeake, 1650–1820', in Stephen Innes (ed.), *Work and Labor in Early America*, Chapel Hill, 1988, pp. 144–88.

12. Winifred B. Rothenberg, 'The Market and Massachusetts Farmers, 1750–1855', *Journal of Economic History*, 41 (1981), 283–314, and Bettye Hobbs Pruitt, 'Self-sufficiency and the Agricultural Economy of Eighteenth-Century Massachusetts', *William and Mary Quarterly*, 3rd ser. 41 (1984), 333–64, discuss the self-sufficiency literature and offer an alternative view of how the New England economy functioned.

13. On tenancy in New England see Stephen Innes, *Labor in a New Land: Economy and Society in Seventeenth-Century Springfield*, Princeton, 1983, and for Pennsylvania, see Lucy Simler, 'Tenancy in Colonial Pennsylvania: The Case of Chester County', *William and Mary Quarterly*, 3rd ser. 43 (1986), 542–69.

14. James T. Lemon, *Best Poor Man's Country: A Geographical Study of Early Southeastern Pennsylvania*, Baltimore, 1972; James Shepherd and Gary M. Walton, *Shipping, Maritime Trade, and the Economic Development of Colonial North America*, Cambridge, 1972; and McCusker and Menard, *Economy of British America*, pp. 71–88 and 189–208.

15. A. J. Taylor (ed.), *The Standard of Living in Britain in the Industrial Revolution*, London, 1975; P. K. O'Brien and S. L. Engerman, 'Changes in Income and its Distribution during the Industrial Revolution', in Roderick Floud and Donald McCloskey (eds.), *The Economic History of Britain since 1700*, Cambridge, 1981; Peter H. Lindert and Jeffrey G. Williamson, 'English Workers' Living Standards during the Industrial Revolution: A New Look', *Economic History Review*, 36 (1983), 1–26; Joel Mokyr, 'Is There Still Life in the Pessimist Case? Consumption during the Industrial Revolution, 1790–1850', *Journal of Economic History*, 48 (1988), 69–92.

16. E. A. Wrigley and R. S. Schofield, *The Population History of England, 1541–1871: A Reconstruction*, London, 1981, p. 399.

17. Kenneth L. Sokoloff and Georgia D. Villaflor, 'The Early Achievement of Modern Stature in America', *Social Science History*, 6 (1982), 453–81, and Roderick Floud and Kenneth W. Wachter, 'Poverty and Physical Stature: Evidence on the Standard of Living of London Boys, 1770–1870', *Social Science History*, 6 (1982), 422–52. Joel Mokyr and Cormac O'Grada, 'Living Standards in Ireland and Britain, 1800–1850: The East India Company Army Data', paper presented at the meeting of the Social Science History Association,

St Louis, 16–19 Oct. 1986, found that the British did not compare favourably with the Irish, either. On 19th-cent. American trends see Robert W. Fogel, 'Nutrition and the Decline in Mortality since 1700: Some Additional Preliminary Findings', *National Bureau of Research, Working Paper Series*, 1802 (1986), 88.

18. See, for example, Elizabeth Gilboy, *Wages in Eighteenth Century England*, Cambridge, Mass., 1934; E. H. Phelps-Brown and Sheila V. Hopkins, 'Seven Centuries of the Price of Consumables, Compared with Builders' Wage-Rates', in E. Carus-Wilson (ed.), *Essays in Economic History*, ii, New York, 1962, pp. 179–96; Donald Woodward, 'Wage Rates and Living Standards in Preindustrial England', *Past and Present*, 91 (1981), 28–46; and Paul A. David and Peter Solar, 'A Bicentenary Contribution to the History of the Cost of Living in America', *Research in Economic History*, 2 (1977). The most intense scrutiny of cost of living indices, of course, has been in conjunction with the debate on the impact of the Industrial Revolution (see references below).

19. The surveys are J. C. Drummond and Anne Wilbraham, *The Englishman's Food*, London, 1957, and Richard Osborn Cummings, *The American and his Food: A History of Food Habits in the United States*, Chicago, rev. edn. 1941. For more detailed studies of particular places and times See Sarah F. McMahon, 'Provisions Laid up for the Family: Toward a History of Diet in New England, 1650–1850', *Historical Methods*, 14 (1981), 4–21, and Billy G. Smith, 'The Best Poor Man's Country?: Living Standards of the "Lower Sort" in Late Eighteenth-Century Philadelphia', *Working Papers from the Regional Economic History Research Center*, 2 (1979).

20. W. G. Hoskins, 'The Rebuilding of Rural England, 1570–1640', *Past and Present*, 4 (1953), 44–59; R. Machin, 'The Great Rebuilding: A Reassessment', ibid. 77 (1977), 33–56; and M. W. Barley, 'Rural Housing in England', in Joan Thirsk (ed.), *The Agrarian History of England and Wales*, v. 2, *1640–1750*, Cambridge, 1985, pp. 653–4.

21. Abbott Lowell Cummings, *The Framed Houses of Massachusetts Bay, 1625–1725*, Cambridge, Mass., 1979, p. 23; Cary Carson and Lorena Walsh, 'The Material Life of the Early American Housewife', paper delivered at the Conference on Women in Early America, 5 Nov. 1981, Williamsburg, Va.; and Cary Carson, Norman F. Barka, William M. Kelso, Garry Wheeler Stone, and Dell Upton, 'Impermanent Architecture in the Southern American Colonies', *Winterthur Portfolio*, 16 (1981), 135–67.

22. Lois Green Carr and Lorena S. Walsh, 'Changing Life Styles and Consumer Behavior in the Colonial Chesapeake', Tables 1.A–1.F, in Ronald Hoffman and Cary Carson (eds.), *Of Consuming Interest*, Charlottesville, forthcoming. See also their 'Changing Life Styles in Colonial St Mary's County', *Working Papers from the Regional Economic History Research Center*, 1 (1977), 96–9, and Gloria L. Main and Jackson Turner Main, 'Standards and Styles of Living in Southern New England, 1640–1774', *Journal of Economic History*, 48 (1988), 27–46.

23. Lorna Weatherill, *Consumer Behaviour and Material Culture in Britain, 1660–1760*, London, 1988.

24. Carole Shammas, 'The Domestic Environment in Early Modern England and America', *The Journal of Social History*, 14 (1980), 1–24.

25. Jan De Vries, *European Urbanization, 1500–1800*, Cambridge, Mass., 1984, ch. 4, and E. Anthony Wrigley, 'Urban Growth and Agricultural Change: England and the Continent in the Early Modern Period', *Journal of Interdisciplinary History*, 15 (1985), 688, 693.

26. R. H. Hilton, 'Medieval Market Towns and Simple Commodity Production', *Past and Present*, 109 (1985), 4–23, and Alan Everitt, 'The Marketing of Agricultural Produce', in Thirsk (ed.), *Agrarian History*, iv. 446–592.

27. The most thorough studies of merchandising in early modern England are T. S. Willan, *The Inland Trade*, Manchester, 1976; S. Ian Mitchell, 'Urban Market and Retail Distribution, 1730–1815', unpublished D.Phil. thesis, Oxford University, 1974; Margaret Spufford, *The Great Reclothing of Rural England: Petty Chapmen and their Wares in the Seventeenth Century*, London, 1984; and Hoh-cheung and Lorna Mui, *Shopping and Shopkeeping in Eighteenth-Century England*, London, 1987.

28. J. H. Soltow, 'Scottish Traders in Virginia, 1750–1775', *Economic History Review*, 12 (1959), 83–98.

29. Margaret E. Martin, *Merchants and Trade of the Connecticut River Valley, 1750–1820*, Smith College Studies, 24, Northampton, Mass., 1938–9; Wilbur C. Plummer, 'Consumer Credit in Colonial Philadelphia', *Pennsylvania Magazine of History and Biography*, 56 (1942), 385–409; and Robert D. Mitchell, *Commercialism and Frontier: Perspectives on the Early Shenandoah Valley*, Charlottesville, 1977.

I

DEMAND

2

Household Production in Early Modern England

AN obvious first step in a study of early modern consumption is to determine which products households were most likely to produce for themselves and which they were most likely to buy. Research on enclosure, rural industries, and overseas commerce all suggest that some important changes in English household production took place during the early modern period, long before industrialization. The decline in manorial agriculture and the enclosure of common land lowered the probability that a given household would cultivate its own land and raise livestock. Growth in manufacturing and trade implies more non-agricultural employment, and also a rise in consumer demand. What confuses the situation somewhat is that these developments occurred while most English families continued to live in the countryside far removed from major distribution centres.[1]

Tax lists and contemporary occupational surveys have been the main sources used to describe what was happening economically to households in the early modern period. One of the earliest tax lists, the Lay Subsidy of 1524, indicates that in that year the proportion of rural people without property (those who had to be assessed on their wages because they had neither land nor goods) ranged from 20% to slightly over 33%, depending on the county. These percentages can be contrasted with figures in the famous 1688 occupational tables of Gregory King, where he estimated that labourers, cottagers, servants, and vagrants constituted about 65% of English households, a proportion very similar to that found in surveys made a hundred years later.[2] Figures such as these have prompted scholars such as Charles Tilly and David Levine to argue that at a relatively early date rural proletarianization overtook the English peasantry. According to Tilly, households went from a situation where they 'exercised considerable control over their means of production, however meagre those means' to a dependence on paid work and, presumably, market commodities.[3]

Early modern tax lists and occupational surveys, however, can only take one so far into the problem of how control over capital and house-hold production patterns evolved in England. Many of those in the Tudor subsidy list who had land and goods to be assessed may have had insufficient resources to produce much for either the market or home consumption. Conversely, those labelled in occupational surveys as labourers may in fact have had some agricultural capital. As A. J. and R. H. Tawney wrote many years ago in regard to the occupational census they were analysing, 'the attempt [in using these documents] to draw a sharp line between wage-earners and independent producers is for the early seventeenth century—and indeed, much later—an anachronism.'[4] They went on to note that for many, perhaps most, occupations, paid work was an 'occasional or subsidiary expedient'. Trades, moreover, cause problems for anyone trying to measure the size of the proletariat as well as for those studying household production. Some crafts, such as weaving, shoemaking, certain kinds of woodworking, required so little capital outlay that their practitioners, almost always poor, could be classed as proletarians. Nor does the practice of a craft, particularly in a rural area, give much hint as to the degree of agricultural activity going on in the household, because of the dual or multiple employments of people in pre-industrial times.

Inventories as a Source

In investigating control over the means of production in these years and the degree to which households made what they consumed, probate inventories listing the actual goods that people owned are indispensable evidence, and they will be used extensively throughout this book to shed light on both home production and the consumption of market goods.[5] This type of source has its shortcomings too, of course. Although Parliament passed a statute in 1529 requiring that inventories of personalty (all property except land, buildings, and improvements) be taken as part of the probate procedure, in most areas it is not until at least mid-century that sizeable numbers of inventories appear. Coverage for England is heaviest during the seventeenth century. In the 1700s, English inventories fall off sharply in number and detailed enumerations become exceedingly rare. Contested wills produced most of the inventories after the first third of the eighteenth century. Consequently, inventories are most helpful for the study of household production over a period of about two hundred years.

Even in the centuries when coverage is good, these documents contain omissions and biases. The appraisals excluded real estate, both land and buildings, although leases and crops growing in the fields are usually listed. While inventories enumerate credits owed to the decedent, seldom do they reveal the debts he or she owed to others. Inventoried wealth, therefore, is actually the gross value of the personal estate. Then there are the problems arising from the fact that the probate population is not the same as the general population. The estates of affluent people more frequently went through probate than the estates of poor householders; consequently they are over-represented in the inventory samples. Those with estates under £5 could legally escape probate altogether. The inventoried were older than the wealthholders in the general population. Also, in early modern times, women surrendered their personalty to their husbands when they wed, and consequently the authorities only had a wife's goods appraised in extraordinary circumstances. Yet another problem, if one is comparing inventories from different times and places, is the effect of inflation and of fluctuations in currency exchanges.

These omissions and biases limit the conclusions that can be drawn from the raw data in inventories. For example, if one wanted to calculate per capita wealth in a particular community, one would have to make estimations of realty holdings and debts. One would also have to turn the richer and older probate population into a better reflection of the living population by increasing the weight given to the wealth of younger and poorer decedents in the per capita figure. If very little is known about a community's social structure, however, it is difficult to assign weights.

Fortunately, to answer many questions, such elaborate adjustments of inventories prove unnecessary. If one wants to know the trend in ownership of certain goods over a period of time or wants to make comparisons between communities at one point in time, one can do so as long as similar biases exist in all of the samples. The absolute percentages are not correct, but the trend or the ranking of communities will be. If there is some reason to believe that the biases are not similar and that some samples have many more decedents with a characteristic that sharply increased or decreased the likelihood of owning a good, then one would have to control for that characteristic by dividing the sample communities. For example, samples that had primarily urban decedents might own very different kinds of production and consumer goods than those where most of the inventoried lived in villages. The urban and rural decedents would be put into different categories in tables, and when doing multivariate analysis, urban location would be one of the independent variables.

Wealth, as regression analysis indicates, is by far the most important determinant of whether or not a person owns a particular good or of the value of the consumer good owned. Consequently, in this book, wealth is always controlled or adjusted for unless the process might introduce more bias into the results than would occur if the sample remained untouched. When the monetary value of a good or class of goods over time is being analysed, yet another type of adjustment is needed. The values must be deflated to reflect the prices in some base year.

Household Production by Time Period and Region: A Summary

Many collections of inventories have been published by English historical and genealogical societies, and I have made use of these along with inventories I gathered myself in preparing Table 2.1, which covers rural household production, and 2.2, which relates to household production in cities and towns. In Table 2.1, I have distinguished between data from the North and the South of England. Although pockets of rural industry existed throughout the country, early modern commercial growth was more closely associated with the South. Also, much more of the North was pastoral, and therefore the impact of the enclosures and other agricultural alterations was different. The South encompasses the south-eastern and western Midlands, the West Country, East Anglia, and the South-east. The North includes the Pennines and the north-eastern Midlands as well as the North proper.[6]

I selected only those inventory collections that covered the entire probated population and had full enumeration of goods. Because inventories in both England and America are not filed in one central repository but are found in a combination of regional and local record offices, obtaining a national random sample would be very time-consuming and expensive. Consequently, most investigators choose one or more local offices and take all inventories proved there for a set period or periods of time when it seems the coverage is the most complete. That was how the samples in Tables 2.1 and 2.2 were gathered. None except the Worcestershire and East London samples I collected and the Frampton Cotterell sample compiled by John S. Moore include the very rich, those whose estates were probated in the Prerogative Courts of Canterbury or York rather than in the locality. Still, all the samples have a bias towards the affluent, because it was their estates that were more

TABLE 2.1 Household production in rural England, 1550–1739 (% of inventories showing crops, livestock or equipment)

Rural area	No. of inventories[a]	Field crops	Cows	Pigs	Sheep	Poultry	Cheese/butter-making	Brewing/cider-making	Spinning-wheels
LATE SIXTEENTH CENTURY									
North									
Abbotside, Yorks, 1570–99	16	6.3	100.0	6.3	80.0	6.3	33.3	0.0	12.5
Chesterfield Hamlets, Derby, 1550–99	86	72.3	83.7	66.7	66.3	57.0	14.1	11.8	10.5
Southwell, Notts, 1550–68	66	65.2	90.9	80.3	65.2	66.7	30.3	34.8	21.2
South									
Oxfordshire, 1550–90	165	56.3	83.2	61.1	60.5	50.9	10.9	15.7	13.9
Yetminster, Dorset, 1576–99	16	25.0	75.0	56.3	37.5	25.0	43.8	25.0	18.8
Devonshire, 1550–99	25	52.0	60.0	68.0	60.0	16.0	39.1	21.7	26.1
EARLY SEVENTEENTH CENTURY									
North									
Durham & Northumberland, 1600–49	26	72.0	65.4	46.2	65.4	34.6	36.0	24.0	16.0
Abbotside, Yorks, 1600–59	29	10.3	79.3	17.2	64.5	24.1	41.2	17.6	17.6
West Riding, Yorks, 1600–49	52	35.2	74.1	25.9	40.7	29.6	40.4	7.7	38.5
South									
Banbury Hamlets, Oxon & Northants, 1600–49	73	31.5	53.4	46.5	37.8	28.8	38.4	19.2	21.9
Clifton, Glos., 1609–57	84	31.0	51.2	52.4	45.2	38.1	34.5	7.1	13.1

TABLE 2.1 (cont.)

Rural area	No. of inventories[a]	Field crops	Cows	Pigs	Sheep	Poultry	Cheese/butter-making	Brewing/cider-making	Spinning-wheels
Frampton, Glos., 1600–50	63	35.9	49.2	44.4	22.2	30.2	41.3	11.1	14.3
Devon, 1600–59	124	49.3	58.1	62.9	46.8	30.6	29.3	28.5	22.8
Bedfordshire, 1617–20	160	40.6	60.0	51.9	38.8	38.8	35.0	9.4	31.9
King's Langley, Herts, 1610–59	47	27.7	36.2	40.4	34.0	17.0	4.2	6.4	19.1
Mid Essex, 1630–59	26	57.7	46.2	42.3	34.6	30.8	46.2	23.1	30.8
Sedgley, Staffs, 1650–9	23	43.5	78.2	30.4	30.4	43.4	52.2	4.3	56.5
LATE SEVENTEENTH CENTURY									
North									
Abbotside, Yorks, 1660–89	52	9.6	86.5	3.8	40.4	15.4	31.0	2.7	36.3
South									
Sedgley, Staffs, 1660–99[b]	70	54.2	74.2	48.6	27.1	18.6	45.7	8.5	45.7
Telford, Salop., 1660–99[b]	350	38.0	66.8	n.a.	31.4	20.0	25.1	n.a.	17.4
S. Worcestershire, 1669–70	223	56.1	61.4	59.6	35.4	17.9	30.8	15.8	10.9
Clifton, Glos., 1660–99	90	18.9	42.2	40.0	35.6	5.5	34.4	24.4	1.1
Frampton, Glos., 1660–99	133	32.1	60.2	54.1	18.0	8.3	49.6	21.1	0.8
Yetminster, Dorset, 1660–99	78	29.5	65.3	47.4	25.6	3.8	41.0	39.7	6.4
Devonshire, 1660–99	48	50.0	50.0	60.4	50.0	16.6	23.4	34.0	19.1
Mid-Essex, 1660–99	156	54.0	59.0	62.8	58.3	6.4	58.3	47.4	21.2

South

Sedgley, Staffs., 1700–39	21	23.8	52.3	57.1	4.8	4.8	38.1	38.1	47.6
Telford, Salop, 1700–39[b]	432	28.2	56.7	n.a.	16.8	1.2	21.2	n.a.	20.8
S. Worcestershire, 1720–1	225	49.3	51.1	48.4	42.7	11.6	35.1	23.9	12.8
Clifton, Glos., 1700–39	42	9.5	28.6	26.2	26.2	2.9	26.2	28.6	0.0
Frampton, Glos., 1700–39	151	24.0	41.7	35.1	9.2	0.7	33.8	37.7	2.6
Yetminster, Dorset, 1700–39	20	15.0	30.0	40.0	30.0	0.0	25.0	20.0	10.0
Mid-Essex, 1700–39	55	52.9	54.5	50.9	50.9	5.5	43.6	74.5	9.1

[a] The number of observations for various categories may vary slightly due to missing information for certain kinds of goods in the inventories.

[b] Taken from totals supplied by editors, because not all the inventories are printed.

Sources: *Abstracts of Abbotside Wills, 1552–1688*, ed. Harley Thwaite, Yorkshire Archaeological Society Record Series, 130 (1968); *Chesterfield Wills and Inventories 1521–1603*, ed. J. M. Bestall and D. V. Fowkes, Derbyshire Record Society, 1 (1977); *Nottinghamshire Household Inventories*, ed. P. A. Kennedy, Thoroton Society Record Series, 22 (1963); *Household and Farm Inventories in Oxfordshire, 1550–1590*, ed. M. A. Havinden, London, 1965; *Probate Inventories and Manorial Excepts of Chetnole, Leigh, and Yetminster*, ed. R. Machin, Bristol, 1976, mimeo.; *Devon Inventories of the Sixteenth and Seventeenth Centuries*, ed. Margaret Cash, Devon and Cornwall Record Society, n.s. 11 (1966); *Wills and Inventories from the Durham Registry*, pt. iv., ed. Herbert Maxwell Wood, Surtees Society, 142 (1929); *Wills ... Court of the Manor of Crossley ...*, ed. William E. Preston, Bradford Historical and Antiquarian Society, 1 (1929); *Sedgley Probate Inventories, 1614–1787*, ed. John S. Roper, Dudley, n.d. mimeo.; 'Jacobean Household Inventories', ed. F. G. Emmison, *Bedfordshire Historical Record Society*, 20 (1938), 1–143; *Life and Death in King's Langley: Wills and Inventories, 1498–1659*, ed. Lionel M. Munby, King's Langley, 1981; 'Banbury Wills and Inventories, 1621–1650', *Banbury Historical Society*, 13 (1985) and 'Banbury Wills and Inventories, Part One, 1591–1620', ed. E. R. C. Brinkworth et al., *Banbury Historical Society*, 14 (1976); *Clifton and Westbury Probate Inventories, 1609–1761*, ed. John S. Moore, Bristol: Avon Local History Association, 1981; *The Goods and Chattels of our Forefathers: Frampton Cotterell and District Probate Inventories, 1539–1804*, ed. John S. Moore, London, 1976; *Farm and Cottage Inventories of Mid-Essex, 1635–1749*, ed. Francis W. Steer, Colchester: Essex County Council, 1950; *Yeomen and Colliers in Telford: Probate Inventories for Dawley, Lilleshall, Wellington, and Wrockwardine, 1660–1750*, eds. Barrie Trinder and Jeff Cox, London, 1980. See Appendix 1 for a description of the Worcestershire inventories collected by the author.

TABLE 2.2 Household production in English cities and towns 1550–1739 (% of inventories showing crops, livestock or equipment)

Cities and towns	No. of inventories	Field crops	Cows	Pigs	Sheep	Poultry	Cheese/butter-making	Brewing/cider-making	Spinning-wheels
LATE SIXTEENTH CENTURY									
Ipswich, Suffolk, 1583–99	29	6.9	6.8	6.9	10.3	3.4	10.0	12.9	16.1
Oxfordshire towns,[a] 1550–90	80	27.5	33.7	41.3	20.0	26.3	11.3	32.5	25.0
Chesterfield, Derby., 1550–99	79	16.5	56.9	58.3	27.8	11.1	33.3	44.4	33.3
Dudley, Worcs., 1550–99	45	17.8	77.8	57.8	57.8	37.8	13.3	6.7	17.8
EARLY SEVENTEENTH CENTURY									
Ipswich, Suffolk, 1600–31	39	0.0	2.6	2.6	0.0	2.6	5.1	17.9	17.9
Banbury, Oxon., 1600–49	224	4.5	6.7	17.4	5.4	4.9	6.7	26.3	25.0
Devonshire towns,[a] 1600–59	25	20.0	28.0	32.0	20.0	28.0	20.0	12.0	16.0
Stockport, Ches., 1600–10	45	15.6	42.2	37.7	22.2	17.8	11.1	33.3	20.0
Lichfield, Staffs, 1600–59	36	29.4	44.4	41.7	16.7	22.2	16.7	52.7	19.4

LATER SEVENTEENTH CENTURY

East London, 1661–4	129	0.0	3.1	1.6	0.0	0.0	0.0	0.0	1.6
Worcester, Worcs., 1669–70	33	6.1	3.0	9.1	3.0	1.9	0.0	0.0	3.0
Lichfield, Staffs., 1660–79	105	21.2	21.9	37.1	7.6	2.9	11.4	55.2	21.9
S. Worcestershire towns,[a] 1669–70	19	31.6	31.6	57.9	21.1	5.3	10.5	5.3	5.3

EARLY EIGHTEENTH CENTURY

East London, 1720–9	172	0.0	2.9	3.5	1.2	0.0	1.2	8.1	4.7
Worcester, Worcs., 1720–1	61	8.2	8.2	13.1	4.9	0.0	8.2	31.1	6.6
S. Worcestershire towns, 1720–1	19	26.3	21.1	26.3	10.5	0.0	0.0	42.1	15.8

[a] Oxford towns include Banbury, Bicester, Bloxham, Burford, Charlbury, Chipping Norton, Deddington, Dorchester, Henley, Islip, Watlington, Witney, Woodstock; Devonshire towns include Barnstaple, Crediton, Dartmouth, Exborne, Okehampton, Teignmouth, Totnes; and South Worcestershire towns include Evesham, Pershore, and Droitwich.

Sources: The Ipswich Probate Inventories, 1583–1631, ed. Michael Reed, Suffolk Records Society, 22 (1981); Household and Farm Inventories in Oxfordshire 1550–1590, ed. M. A. Havinden, London, 1965; Chesterfield Wills and Inventories, 1521–1603, ed. J. M. Bestall and D. V. Fowkes, Derbyshire Record Society, 1 (1977); Dudley Probate Inventories, 1544–1603, ed. John S. Roper, Dudley, 1965; Devon Inventories of the Sixteenth and Seventeenth Centuries, ed. Margaret Cash, Devon and Cornwall Record Society, n.s., 11 (1966); Banbury Wills and Inventories, ed. E. R. C. Brinkworth et al., Banbury Historical Society, 13 (1985) and 14 (1986); Probate Inventories of Lichfield and District, 1568–1680, ed. D. G. Vaisey, Staffordshire Record Society, 4th ser. (1969); Stockport Probate Records, 1578–1619, ed. C. B. Phillips and J. H. Smith, Record Society of Lancashire and Cheshire, 124 (1985). See Appendix 1 for information about East London and Worcestershire samples collected by the author.

likely to be probated. The substantial yeoman or tradesman is over-represented, and the cottager and labourer under-represented.

As mentioned above, there are a few instances where the distortions produced by adjusting for biases—in this case, differences in wealth between communities—outweigh the benefits to be derived from the adjustments. The data in Tables 2.1 and 2.2 fall into that category. Ideally, each sample would have been divided into high- and low-wealth groups as in most of the other tables, but that would have involved deflating each inventory in each sample, regardless of region, by the price index number for the year in which the estate was probated. That procedure, it was felt, relied excessively on the year by year accuracy of an historical price index, and unjustifiably assumed that the index applied to the North of England when it was based on data only from the South. The decision not to use wealth groups with these samples, however, means that the percentages in these two tables can only show trends and regional contrasts, not the actual proportion of a community's households owning a particular good.

What household production goods listed in inventories are of interest? For early modern households to meet their principal consumption needs, they would have had to grow crops, raise livestock, and possess certain tools. Food was paramount, and from what is known of the English diet, cereals constituted the single most important item, providing bread, meal, fodder, and the principal drink, beer. Legumes, primarily peas and beans, were grown along with the grain and served the same purpose as cereals. Inventories do not list land, but they do give information on crops in the barn and in the fields and also enumerate field equipment. Meat and dairy products, sometimes referred to as whitemeat by contemporaries, were next in importance. Special milling, cooking, malting, brewing, butchering, and dairying equipment was needed to process these foodstuffs. Clothing was the other major area of household production. English dress in this period consisted mainly of articles made from wool, flax, hemp, and leather. Apart from livestock and a small patch of land, spinning-wheels, looms, dyeing, fulling, tanning, and sewing equipment were required for manufacturing and finishing the goods.

Previous research, including the conclusions reached in the introductions to the English inventory collections themselves, indicates that from the beginning of the early modern period, and in some cases even earlier, ordinary families seldom performed important steps in the preparation of food and the manufacture of clothing. These tasks were the preserve of specialized craftsmen or of servants in the households of the rich. Almost no family did its own milling of grain for bread. The making of malt for beer was also a process most households left to professional maltsters or to the affluent, as it required space, time, and skill. A 1709 law actually forbade private households not in the trade from engaging in another craft, candlemaking. As regards clothing, only spinning could be considered in any way a common household task. Weaving, fulling, dyeing, sewing, the making of shoes, hats, and gloves were almost always undertaken by craftsmen. Next to agriculture, these specialized occupations constituted the largest category of employment, sometimes engaging about a quarter of the male workforce. Only a tiny percentage of inventories listed looms, and the possessors were almost always identified as weavers or clothiers. If they wanted new clothing, especially woollen garments, householders turned to tailors and seamstresses, perhaps because the cloth was too valuable to risk a cutting error. Accessories—gloves, caps, hats, stockings—were, of course, a mainstay of the outwork system and the workshops of industrial villages. By the sixteenth century, few regional differences in English dress remained.[7] Consequently, producers with the resources could sell on a national or even international level.

In addition, there are a couple of household functions that inventories are poor at revealing. The baking of bread is one. Ovens in chimneys would not be listed because chimneys were part of the building and thus realty rather than personalty. In inventory collections where there was careful enumeration and little lumping together of the wooden utensils, kneading-troughs sometimes merit mention, but their presence might simply indicate that dough was prepared at home and then taken to a baker's oven. For baking at home, those preparing the bread would need moulding-boards to shape the loaves and peels to remove them from the oven. Some of course may have baked by simply turning a pot over on top of a griddle or bakestone to make an oven.[8] Trying to understand how bread was prepared is further complicated by the fact that references to baking often just meant cooking. The words were not well differentiated in the early modern period. Regular household baking in an oven may have been largely a nineteenth-century phenomenon. Slaughtering and preparing of meat is another problem area. Households may have butchered and salted their own meat, but the equipment involved was not specialized or expensive enough to earn separate and distinct enumeration in many inventories.

To make the most of the limited information available concerning diet and clothing, each inventory in every sample was checked for evidence that the deceased cultivated a field crop, owned cows, sheep, pigs, and poultry, and possessed cheese and/or buttermaking equipment, brewing utensils, and spinning-wheels. The three types of equipment were chosen because they were connected with processes most frequently performed by 'non-specialist' households. Also, appraisers found these items sufficiently distinctive to justify more consistent enumeration than such utensils as powdering-tubs for salting meat or troughs for the preparation of dough.

Let us begin with the South of England, which had a greater share of the population than the North, and with the cultivation of grain (essentially wheat, barley, oats, rye), beans, and peas. In most areas, cultivators would have grown both cereals and legumes as part of a field rotation system. It is not possible, of course, to know whether the farm families used these crops for human or livestock consumption. What is most striking is that even in the sixteenth- and early seventeenth-century samples, less than half of the rural inventoried decedents cultivated field crops. As the more affluent people tended to be over-represented among those inventoried, a percentage has to be reduced by between 50% and 25% to make it representative of the whole population. Areas showing 40% of the inventoried growing field crops may well have had only 20–30% of the total households actually engaged in arable cultivation.

Also, there was a decline over time. By the early eighteenth century, in Telford, Shropshire, 28.2% of the inventories showed indications of field cultivation—a drop of 10% from the percentage for the late seventeenth century. In Sedgley, Staffordshire and Frampton, Gloucestershire, the figures for the early eighteenth century were just below 25%, again marking a decline. Sedgley had shown a fairly high percentage of cultivators, 54.2%, in the late seventeenth century. In Yetminster, Dorset and Clifton, Gloucestershire, even fewer, 15% and 9.5% respectively, were recorded in the early eighteenth century as showing signs of crop cultivation. In every case where there were inventories covering two or more periods, a decline occurred in crop cultivation over time. By the early eighteenth century, cultivators constituted between 10% and 25% of those inventoried. Only in southern Worcestershire, which included very good arable land, and in the Essex communities of Writtle and Roxwell did the proportions as high as 50% persist into the 1700s.

In the North of England, there were areas such as Abbotside in Yorkshire where practically no arable land existed. On the other hand, in communities where the land could be used for grain cultivation, the growing of it in the sixteenth and early seventeenth century tended to be much more widespread than in the South. For the later periods, however, there is only one sample, so it is impossible to know if this situation continued.

Presumably, many rural inhabitants without land worked in the fields of those who did. But what did people do in the villages where little grain cultivation took place? Rural industry occupied households in some of these areas. The manufacturing of woollen cloth had been important since medieval times in the West Riding of Yorkshire communities that had little arable land. Sedgley inhabitants worked at dressing and spinning flax. Further south, there were the feltmakers and hatters of the Frampton district of Gloucestershire; mining also employed a significant number of the population. In the Banbury hamlets, workers specialized in the making of gloves and other leather goods. In by no means all of the communities, however, could one identify a particular industry. The Clifton area, like that of Frampton Cotterell, was near Bristol, but no particular kind of manufacturing system seemed to dominate. Instead, the proximity to a major port produced a population of shipbuilders, mariners, and publicans. In other places, there was much pastoral activity—dairying, the grazing of sheep, and livestock fattening—and many people with dual occupations, people who owned livestock but whose occupation was listed as carpenter, or weaver, or smith.

At the beginning of the early modern period, livestock-holding was much more ubiquitous than cultivation of field crops. In the sixteenth century in the North and, to a slightly lesser extent, in the South nearly everyone seemed to have a cow, percentages of ownership ranging from 60% to over 90%. Sheep were also common, but only in the South did many of the deceased own pigs. Poultry-keeping cropped up more frequently during this period than later. Its relative rarity, especially in later times, has led some students of inventories to conclude that poultry were often missed or excluded by appraisers, but that does not explain why they should be more often missed in the last half of the early modern period than they were in the first half.

In the early seventeenth century, the growing population created an increased demand for grain. Perhaps this explains why the percentage of the inventoried deceased holding all forms of livestock declined everywhere. In the later seventeenth century, livestock-holding revived somewhat, and it is tempting to connect this with the population stagnation and the falling prices of cereals. The ubiquity of cow ownership, however, did not return, at least in the South. Nor did sheep-raising recover fully, which may in part be explained by the fact that wool prices declined sharply during this period. In 1614 the government prohibited the export of wool in order to aid the textile industry, and this ban continued throughout the rest of the early modern period.[9]

The general pattern of livestock possession in the South of England during the eighteenth century was again one of decline. Cow ownership by those inventoried ranged between 57% and 29%, and pig ownership had also become less common in most places. The ownership of these two animals was related because pigs could be fed on the waste from the dairy. Sheep-owning also continued to decrease, almost dying out in several locations. Only a small proportion of those inventoried in the various communities were recorded as having poultry. What remains to be investigated is whether all economic groups experienced this decline in livestock ownership, or whether it occurred mainly among low-wealth groups.

In urban areas (see Table 2.2), grain cultivation and livestock-holding depended largely on population size. In the metropolis of London or even in a provincial city of 5,000 or more, such as Ipswich or Worcester, inhabitants did not engage in arable husbandry. Smaller towns with significant amounts of industrial activity, such as Banbury, left field cultivation to their hamlets. But in other towns and market centres of not more than a few thousand inhabitants—for example, in Lichfield—grain was grown in the borough or immediately outside the town by a certain number of residents throughout the late seventeenth and early eighteenth century. These part-time farmers, of course, were a gradually decreasing minority of a town's citizenry. There was a more dramatic drop among the smaller urban communities in the keeping of cows, pigs, and sheep. The first two were very common in the late sixteenth and even the early seventeenth century. But in the seventeenth century, at the time when the percentage of people holding livestock in rural England was recovering somewhat, urban cow-keeping continued to decline and sheep-raising became a rarity. Apparently pigs were the last livestock to die out in towns, but by the early eighteenth century, their numbers, too, had fallen off.

It is interesting to compare rural and urban areas in terms of their possession of processing equipment. Utensils for brewing (furnace and mashing-vat) or cidermaking (press), buttermaking (churn) and cheese production (press, vat), and spinning-wheels (the small flax wheel or the larger wool wheel) were far from universal in either town or country. Somewhat surprisingly, in the first part of the early modern period, the inventories of town residents indicate that as much or more brewing and spinning went on in their dwellings as took place in rural households. This was true with brewing because a large proportion of those who brewed did it for a living. The alewife and the poor alehouse-keeper served the countryside, while even more alehouses, along with inns and taverns, clustered in and around the towns. During the Elizabethan period, it has been estimated that there was one licensed drinking establishment for about every 120 people, and therefore, assuming household size at five, one for every twenty-four families. Unlicensed sellers and brewers also have to be taken into account. Consequently, it is likely that out of the percentage recorded as having brewing or cidermaking equipment in each community, 5 or more of the percentage points can be attributed to those making a living from the activity. Cities of the size of Worcester or larger tended to have the lowest percentages of the population owning brewing equipment, because there big brewers supplied the victuallers.[10]

At the end of the seventeenth and particularly during the early eighteenth century, however, a change occurred. Table 2.2 shows percentages so high, frequently in the range of 33% to over 40%, that it would seem that more than just the rich and those in the trade must have been participating. The making of drink in the household seems to have increased in both rural and urban areas. In every community where inventories exist for both eras, the percentages for the early eighteenth century exceed those of the late seventeenth. This increase took place despite the fact that brewers became more important as suppliers, thus presumably shrinking the ranks of the pubkeepers who brewed their own.[11] Also, West Country inventories reveal growing numbers of the deceased possessing cidermaking equipment. To understand the significance of this, one needs to know if the rising incidence occurred among medium-wealth groups, or among poorer people who might well be alehouse-keepers.

The inventories bolster an earlier assertion that few English households in this period manufactured all their own cloth. The presence of spinning-wheels does not appear to have been very closely correlated with the keeping of sheep. Those communities that had higher percentages of sheep-raising did not necessarily have a lot of households with spinning-equipment. In fact, towns or good arable areas with little proto-industry seem to have been the most likely places to find spinning-wheels. Nor was there an association between the ownership of spinning-wheels and of looms. Although they do not appear in the two tables, looms were counted; but it was found that only weavers had looms, and, in all but two of the samples, weavers constituted just a few percentage points of all households.

Three areas had a substantial proportion of weavers or clothiers: one rural, the West Riding of Yorkshire manors near Bradford, and two urban, the clothmaking towns of Devon and Stockport in Cheshire. In the West Riding, 25% of those inventoried in the early seventeenth century had looms, with 33% of them owning two or three. These Bradford area weavers produced kersey woollen cloth for the market. About half of them had spinning-wheels, while only 36.4% of the spinners had looms, not a vastly higher incidence than among the inventoried as a whole. Spinners were no more likely to own sheep than non-spinners. The percentage of all those inventoried owning sheep (40.7%) was smaller than in any other inventoried area in the North. In the Devon towns, 28% of households had looms for woollen cloth while only 16% had spinning-wheels, half of which belonged to weavers, leading to the assumption that most yarn was spun in the countryside. In Stockport, which in the early seventeenth century manufactured Stockport cloth, those who spun were also different from those with looms. In only one case did an inventory with a spinning-wheel also list a loom. The richest people involved with the Devon cloth industry were those who organized the various processes but did not have looms or spinning-wheels themselves. These people seem to be absent from the West Riding. That may be an indication that the industry there was less stratified than it was in Devon. But it should also be noted that the West Riding sample did not include any substantial towns, the kinds of places in which the cloth entrepreneurs tended to live.[12]

A recent study of sixteenth- and early seventeenth-century woollen manufacture in the Colne area of north-eastern Lancashire furnishes much information about how the industry operated in a place where there were many small producers.[13] Colne specialized in a low grade of kersey cloth. The small producer tended to be one with probated wealth over £40 and some agricultural holdings. While he did the weaving, he obtained most of his wool from a merchant, and relied not only on yarn spun at home but also on some provided by poorer households, whose clothmaking activities seemed largely confined to carding and spinning. As Colne offered very little in the way of fulling facilities, much of the cloth was finished and sold to middlemen in Yorkshire towns such as Hepstonstall and Halifax. Thus, even when weavers had control over their own looms and cloth, some stratification existed in the production process.

Because most inventories did not describe the spinning-wheels they appraised, it is usually impossible to know if wool, flax, or hemp was being spun. From evidence about the kinds of homespun cloth available, however, a few general conclusions can be suggested. Probably most of the spinning of wool done in poorer households was part of an outwork system. Affluent households with plentiful female labour—for only women spun—would be the principal locale where spinning for home consumption might take place, and the spinning is likely to have been of hemp or flax to send to a weaver. Linen was the most important manufactured import coming into England. Continental, Scottish, and Irish linen was common in the shops, but most of the English linen production, until later in the eighteenth century, was, according to N. B. Harte, mainly for the 'bumpkin trade'. It was spun at home, woven locally, and either consumed by the makers or distributed by pedlars and at fairs. To know whether in a given community the percentages that appear in the spinning-wheel column in Tables 2.1 and 2.2 represent spinning that went on mainly for home purposes or the market would require knowing whether it was households with servant labour who undertook the work, or poor households involved in the outwork system.[14] Whatever the case, the only places where more than 30% of those inventoried owned spinning-wheels were locations like Yorkshire and Sedgley, Staffordshire, where we know that some production for more than a local market was taking place. In Yorkshire, of course, this comprised the manufacture of woollen cloth, and in Sedgley, the dressing and spinning of flax.

Butter and cheesemaking equipment, linked as it was to the keeping of cows, always showed up more frequently in rural inventories. Still, the proportion of the sixteenth-century probated deceased who owned churns or cheese-presses was surprisingly low, considering the much higher proportion who had cows. In the seventeenth and eighteenth centuries, however, cow-ownership declined, while the possession of equipment increased in most communities, bringing the two percentages closer together. Possibly those with one cow only had enough milk to drink or put in porridges immediately, and not enough to store in the form of cheese and butter. Perhaps some owners of cows used makeshift means to produce a low-quality cheese. Occasionally, in urban areas, one comes across household inventories in which no cows appear but a churn or cheesemaking equipment is listed. In some dairying areas in the West

Country, the discrepancy between cow-ownership and the possession of processing equipment can be explained by the practice of leasing cows. At death the lessee would have the equipment, but no animals.[15]

A More Detailed Study: The Midlands and Household Production

I ignored wealth—an obvious factor of importance in determining the scope of household production—in summarizing the contents of the inventories, because of the problems in deflating all the samples. To investigate its effect and examine more closely the workings of the household economy, the sixteenth-century Oxfordshire sample and the two southern Worcestershire samples I collected will be analysed more closely. Three points in time are covered: 1550–90, when inventories first began to appear in large numbers; the 1720s, the last decade in which they exist in quantity; and a point midway between, 1669–70. Why did I choose these Midland communities? I originally collected inventories in the southern half of Worcestershire because it seemed that if in any place in England many households would be engaged in a wide variety of home-production activities, it would be there. A big enough area was covered to include both arable and pastoral sections. Such a mix would have been harder to find in the West Country. In addition, during the period being studied, there were still substantial tracts of common land: the area was not totally enclosed. It also had fewer large farming units than counties in the East. Finally, it was far enough from London and from the large English ports to escape total domination by their economies. The Oxfordshire sample collected by Michael Havinden has most of the same characteristics, so when it became clear that this study of consumption and household production would have to be taken back to the sixteenth century, it made sense to use that collection rather than gathering another Worcestershire sample.[16]

Sixteenth-century Oxfordshire, as can be seen in Table 2.1, had comparatively high levels of livestock ownership and grain cultivation. In Table 2.3, the Oxfordshire estates are divided into two groups, a low-wealth group and a medium- to high-wealth group. £20 of total personal wealth was the dividing line. This was very near the median, and below it fell mainly labourers, husbandmen, and practitioners of the lower-paying crafts such as shoemaking and weaving.[17] The late sixteenth century was a time of great inflation, so it is somewhat difficult to define precisely

TABLE 2.3 Household production by wealth group, sixteenth-century Midlands: Oxfordshire 1550–1590 (% of inventories showing crops, livestock, or equipment)

Wealth group	No. of inventories	Field crops	Cows	Pigs	Sheep	Poultry	Cheese/ butter- making	Brewing/ cider- making	Spinning- wheels
Rural									
Low wealth[a]	78	30.8	70.5	32.1	48.7	32.1	2.6	1.3	13.9
Medium and upper wealth	89	78.7	94.4	86.5	70.8	67.4	18.4	28.4	9.2
City and towns[b]									
Low wealth	47	10.6	12.8	23.4	8.5	12.8	2.1	8.5	29.8
Medium and upper wealth	40	42.5	57.5	60.0	35.0	40.0	23.1	41.0	27.5

[a] Those in the low-wealth group are the deceased with inventoried personal estates at or below the median of £20. Those with wealth above that amount are in the medium- and upper-wealth category. See text and Appendix 1 for explanation of cut-off point.
[b] The city and towns represented are Oxford, Bampton, Banbury, Bicester, Bloxham, Burford, Charlbury, Chipping Norton, Deddington, Henley-on-Thames, Thame, Watlington, Witney, Woodstock.

Source: data set derived from inventories printed in *Household and Farm Inventories in Oxfordshire, 1550–1590*, ed. M. A. Havinden, London, 1965.

what £20 could buy. Perhaps some idea can be conveyed however, by noting that in the inventories a cow, or a half-dozen sheep, or enough cereals to feed one adult for a year, or brewing equipment, a loom, or a good flockbed with sheets and covering might each be appraised at about £1.

It is clear from Table 2.3 that wealth made a great difference in household production. This was particularly true as regards grain cultivation. Fewer than one out of three of the inventoried rural decedents in the low-wealth category grew any grain, while almost four out of five in the medium- and high-wealth group did. With livestock, great differences also emerge in the proportion owned by the two wealth groups, although poorer households were much more likely to have a cow (70.5%) or sheep (48.7%) than they were to produce cereals. Pigs, the animal most often associated with the poor, actually appeared less often in the inventories of low-wealth decedents than did cows or sheep. Just 32.1% owned them, the same proportion as owned poultry. Only among the better-off group were pigs ubiquitous (86.5%). It seems that during the sixteenth century and, in the North, the early seventeenth century as well, sheep were particularly popular. In some places the ewes were milked.[18] It was not the case that those rural poor who lacked sheep had pigs or vice versa. Among those in the low-wealth category owning sheep, 50% also had pigs, while of those who had no sheep, only 15% had a pig; 43.6% had neither (see Table 2.3).

Needless to say, few of the inventoried decedents had vast holdings of livestock. If an average-sized family were to meet all of its milk, cheese, and butter needs itself all year long, it would probably require two cows; yet less than 50% of all those inventoried and fewer than 25% of the low-wealth group owned two or more.[19] Only 20 per cent of the sample had more than 20 sheep, and as Michael Havinden has noted, that probably meant their animals were part of common herds.[20]

As far as equipment for the processing of grain and animal products was concerned, these items show up more frequently among the wealthier estates, except in the case of spinning-wheels. Possession of woollen or linen wheels was not all that widespread; only 19% of the entire sample had them. They were found most often, however, among town residents in the low-wealth group (29.8%), suggesting that the rural outwork system was not yet well developed, and that spinning was for income rather than exclusively for home use. Only 9.2% of the more affluent in the countryside had wheels. Clearly, one is not dealing here with many households that, after shearing their sheep, spun the wool, or that grew flax, and then wove it into cloth. Of those with spinning-wheels 67% had no sheep, a higher proportion than in the sample as a whole, and the four inventoried decedents who owned looms had no spinning-wheels. Hemp, a rough fibre for the making of coarse fabric, was mentioned in about 5% of inventories, but again the association between it and wheels was not strong.

Brewing equipment, particuarly furnaces, cost a fair amount of money, so it is not too surprising that few in the low-wealth group (other than alehouse-keepers) engaged in home brewing. Brewing was also much more common in the towns than in the rural areas, perhaps because urban dwellers had better access to maltsters. The one utensil related to beer that cropped up frequently in the Oxfordshire inventories and continued to be a popular item in the Worcestershire samples discussed below, was the malt mill. It shows up when neither malting paraphernalia nor brewing equipment was listed. It appears that many households bought their malt, ground it to their liking, and then had it brewed elsewhere.

When it comes to butter- and cheese-making equipment, the Oxford-shire inventories mirror those we looked at at the beginning of this chapter. Despite the widespread ownership of cows among all wealth groups, the documents record limited numbers of churns or cheese moulds and presses. The vast majority of these Oxfordshire households either drank all of their cows' yield, sold it, or processed it without the aid of specialized dairy utensils.

It seems fairly certain, then, that for those inventoried in this late sixteenth-century Midlands county, farming activities had principally revolved around their small livestock holdings, particularly their cows and sheep. Much of household production for home consumption consisted of obtaining meat and edible by-products from these animals. For the manufacture of leather goods and textiles, most families went outside their own households. Cloth of course was a widely traded international commodity, and while few Tudor husbandmen regularly frequented the shops of drapers and mercers, it seems safe to assume that the fabrics they wore, slept, and ate on were not obtained exclusively from their own village. The inventories also indicate that only a minority of households cultivated their own grain crops, and that the processing of cereals, whether for bread or beer, occupied few households not specializing in the function. On the whole, home production was stronger in the county towns than in the villages, and except for spinning, wealthier households were more likely than poorer ones to engage in it.

How do the two Worcestershire samples from the late seventeenth and early eighteenth centuries compare with the situation of Oxfordshire? The southern half of Worcestershire, the area from which the inventories were drawn, includes some excellent arable land, much of it still in common-field strips, and also some good pasturage for livestock-raising and dairying. The proportion of late seventeenth-century rural households who cultivated their own crops, however, appears to have been nearly identical to the modest percentages observed in Oxfordshire eighty years earlier. Nor did the 1720s bring much change in the trend. What did change was the ownership of livestock by the low-wealth group. It dropped sharply (see Table 2.4). A little over one in three owned a cow in the 1669–70 sample, and less than one in five by the 1720s. For sheep the percentages were surprisingly low 17.3 and 18.6 respectively. Pig ownership held its own at 38.5% in the 1669–70 period, but then fell to under 20% by the early eighteenth century. The raising of poultry appears to have been almost non-existent.[21]

On the other hand, livestock ownership by the wealthier rural group remained high. Table 2.5 illustrates what happened with cattle and sheep. Among those who owned livestock, the size of their herds and flock increased; and the mean number of animals per person inventoried increased for sheep while staying nearly constant for cattle.[22]

The wealthier group also moved to the forefront when it came to the processing of animal by-products and grain. Spinning does not appear to have been a widespread activity in southern Worcestershire, but when wheels did surface they were more likely to be in the households of the more affluent. With no group in either period having more than 15% ownership, it is obvious that medium- and upper-wealth groups did not routinely manufacture their own cloth. Nor, in this part of the county, does a very extensive outwork system seem to have operated among poorer households. The distribution of wheels suggests a more or less equal division between the two activities, with the former being reflected in the rural medium-wealth households with spinning-wheels, and the latter in the percentages of the low-wealth group in towns and elsewhere with wheels. As in Oxfordshire earlier, owners of sheep, wheels, and looms did not overlap to any extent.

A substantially higher percentage of the medium- and high-wealth group from rural Worcestershire owned butter and cheesemaking equipment than among their counterparts in sixteenth-century Oxfordshire or their poorer contemporaries in their own county, who almost never possessed such utensils. Ownership, moreover, increased for the

TABLE 2.4 Household production by wealth group, seventeenth- and eighteenth-century Midlands: Southern Worcestershire, 1669–1670 and 1720–1721 (% of inventories showing crops, livestock or equipment)

Wealth group	No. of inventories	Field crops	Cows	Pigs	Sheep	Poultry	Cheese/butter-making	Brewing/cider-making	Spinning-wheels
SOUTHERN WORCESTERSHIRE, 1669–1670									
Rural									
Low wealth[a]	104	30.8	36.5	38.5	17.3	5.8	9.7	7.8	6.8
Medium and upper wealth	119	78.2	83.2	78.2	51.3	28.6	49.2	22.0	14.4
City and towns[b]									
Low wealth	27	7.4	7.4	22.2	3.7	0.0	0.0	0.0	0.0
Medium and upper wealth	25	24.0	20.0	32.0	16.0	4.0	8.0	4.0	8.0
SOUTHERN WORCESTERSHIRE, 1720–1721									
Rural									
Low wealth[a]	97	23.7	18.6	19.6	18.6	2.1	6.2	9.3	9.6
Medium and upper wealth	128	68.7	75.8	70.3	60.9	18.8	57.6	35.2	15.7
City and towns[b]									
Low wealth	30	6.7	3.3	10.0	0.0	0.0	0.0	10.0	15.4
Medium and upper wealth	50	16.0	16.0	20.0	10.0	0.0	10.4	49.0	6.7

[a] The cut-off point for the low-wealth group is £40 for the 1669–70 data set and £45 for the 1720–1 inventories. See text and Appendix 1 for fuller explanation.
[b] The city and towns represented are Worcester, Evesham, Pershore, and Droitwich.

Sources: Worcestershire Consistory Court and Peculiar Court probate files, Herefordshire and Worcestershire Record Office, St Helens, Worcester; and Prerogative Court of Canterbury Probate files, Public Record Office, London. See Appendix 1.

TABLE 2.5 Mean number of cattle and sheep in Southern Worcestershire inventories, seventeenth and eighteenth centuries

	1669–70	1720–1
Total no. of inventories	275	305
Cattle mean	4.3	4.5
No. of inventories of cattle-owners	144	124
Cattle mean for owners	8.2	11.0
Sheep mean	9.4	14.1
No. of inventories of sheep-owners	84	101
Sheep mean for owners	30.7	42.7

Source: see Table 2.4.

group from the late seventeenth to the early eighteenth century, perhaps reflecting a more vigorous dairy market. Finally, by the eighteenth century brewing had become very popular among the more affluent rural group, as it had been earlier among those of a similar wealth level in towns.

Residents of all wealth levels in the market towns and the provincial centre of Worcestershire began to behave at this time more as one might expect in an urban centre, and curtailed their grain cultivation and livestock holding. Table 2.2 indicates that this was a general trend in provincial towns after the mid-seventeenth century.

Household Production and Proletarianization

What emerges from the summary of English household production activities and the more detailed analysis of areas in the Midlands is that a decline in what was produced for home consumption did occur among the one-half to two-thirds of the population that probably fell into the low-wealth group, as defined here. This was not, however, a result of a loss in rights to arable land. Even in the sixteenth century, many English households did not grow their own field crops. In some areas, most notably large parts of the North, there was virtually no arable land from which to be excluded. People there survived largely through animal husbandry and rural industry. Elsewhere there was land, but a lack of capital made it difficult for many low-wealth families to supply themselves with their own grain. Their toil in the field was done as labourers, not proprietors. Whatever change in the rights to arable land took place during the early modern period happened gradually—a slow decline in field cultivation right across the wealth spectrum, most noticeably in areas near towns and cities and sites of rural industry.

There is, of course, some question as to when the bulk of the English population ever had much say over the growing of field crops, especially a cash crop such as wheat. The medieval common field system was designed to give a maximum number of mature male household heads rights over arable land, but custom and the lord of the manor relieved them of much of the decision making on land use and crops. Lords, lay or monastic, had rights over milling and sometimes over the ovens for baking bread. They also held the charter for the market towns where peasants bought and sold grain and other commodities.[23] The villein was no free-wheeling farmer, and his powers over the means to produce grain had never been great.

A more dramatic transformation in these centuries seems to have been the sharp decline in livestock-holding among the less wealthy segment of the rural population and among all households in towns. As far back as the eleventh century it can be documented that possession of livestock was nearly universal among English villeins. The principal animal, though, was the sheep, requiring as it did less in the way of provision than cattle.[24] The rise of the cow to be the most commonly held animal was apparently a late medieval or early modern development, and turned out to be relatively short-lived as well. The loss of livestock by the working portion of the population has often been associated with the Parliamentary enclosures of the late eighteenth century.[25] In a very thorough investigation of the inventories of peasant labourers (labourers and poor husbandmen) in the period 1560–1640, however, Alan Everitt found that ownership of animals, particularly cattle, was declining in all regions of England. The figures assembled here and the analysis of the Midlands data bear out Everitt's findings about the working class and suggest that the fall in livestock ownership continued into the eighteenth century.[26] It was a long steady decline, with cow and pig ownership in the South of England perhaps as low as 20% in many rural communities, and sheep ownership even lower at the point when the inventory samples end. Poor householders in the North may have held on to livestock longer, although by the time Frederick Eden and David Davies made their household surveys in the late eighteenth century, most had relinquished their animals.[27]

For rural households of medium wealth and above, however, livestock ownership remained high. The pattern apparently was one of an early seventeenth-century decline as the demand for grain increased, a late seventeenth-century recovery, and then a modest fall in the early eighteenth century. Those who continued to own livestock seem to have possessed larger flocks and herds, and frequently combined arable cultivation with their animal husbandry. Household production among the more affluent also seemed to pick up in the areas of butter- and cheese-making and brewing; the former may have been mainly for market sales, but the latter seems to have been more exclusively for home consumption. While their home production activities, then, may have actually increased, they had the resources to buy many market commodities, too.

So, in short, what forced husbandmen and peasant labourers into a category that some historians today would describe as a proletariat appears to have been the loss of livestock. This had the potential to change household consumption, as dairy goods and meat, to mention only the two main products derived from the animals, would have to be purchased on the market. But why was this happening?

Charles Tilly has recommended that we 'cherchez le capitaliste', and that seems a suggestion worth pursuing.[28] After all, enclosure, the outwork system, and the growth in overseas trade cannot be characterized as worker-led movements. It has recently been argued that the seventeenth century witnessed the greatest number of enclosures.[29] If so, the greatest impact was apparently on common grazing rights. The large proportion of sixteenth-century householders with livestock, yet not engaged in arable husbandry, suggests that there were many people living in leased cottages, which gave them, apart from gardens, grazing rights on common land.[30] As those with capital pushed for more enclosures, fewer and fewer communities could support these rights. Alternative employment in rural industry or in the commercial world of the city and the colonies also depended on the investment decisions of those with capital.

Working men and women, however, had some choices—rather circumscribed to be sure, but choices none the less. It is difficult to believe that, for most, concern about losing control over the means of production exceeded anxiety of an even more basic nature about living standards. The importance of possessing cattle, sheep, and pigs can certainly be overestimated. Presumably, mature villagers with grazing rights did not want to surrender their way of life. But for young people contemplating the future, livestock investment and the traditional pastoral life had its drawbacks. First, it was risky. The husbandman whose only capital resided in a small flock of sheep and/or a few cows could easily have his wealth wiped out by the death of several animals. Second, because of the cost involved, in hard times husbandry could further delay marriage, and the seventeenth century, particularly, was a period of hard times for the maritally minded. Age at marriage rose in many communities. Furthermore, it is now estimated that 20% of the English population during the seventeenth century never married, compared to about 5% in the sixteenth century and 12% in the early eighteenth.[31] Third, the quantity and quality of the animal products obtained from household livestock might be inferior to what could be purchased on the market. Here the issue of market supply was crucial, as was alternative employment.

What kinds of alternatives existed for these people? They could relocate in cities, and a number of them did migrate to London. The metropolis increased in size from 2.25% of the English population in 1520 to 11.5% in 1700, and there it stayed for the rest of the eighteenth century. The situation in provincial capitals was the reverse. Cities with populations of 5,000 or more grew quite sluggishly, rising slowly from 3% of the total population in 1520 to no more than 5.5% in 1700, but they then tripled their proportion of the population by 1800. Trends in smaller provincial centres and market towns are less certain, although there is little indication that they increased their population share prior to 1700.[32]

Those opposed to relocation could stay in a village environment but practise a non-agricultural trade. According to estimates made by E. A. Wrigley, the proportion of the total population in rural non-agricultural employment grew about as fast as the increasing percentage represented by London between the sixteenth century and 1700, and about as fast as that of provincial cities of 5,000 and more in the eighteenth century. Thus urban areas and rural industries each absorbed about equal amounts of the 40% of the rural population that allegedly left agriculture between 1520 and 1800.[33] Those living in hamlets and communities near major trading centres might be engaged in some sort of manufacturing activity, such as the feltmakers and hatters of the Frampton Cotterell district. That option probably did not exist for villagers in more traditional farming areas. In the Midlands samples from Oxfordshire and southern Worcestershire, where arable and mixed husbandry prevailed, inventories identified an increasingly large proportion of the rural male deceased as craftsmen, either by specifically mentioning a trade or by listing tools in the appraisal. Also, more agriculturalists owned equipment indicating a trade: this is the group I have referred to as having dual occupations. Table 2.6 gives the percentages following various occupations. The upper half of the table covers all the rural male probates, while the bottom half focuses on the low-wealth group. Clearly a growing proportion of poorer rural males took up a trade. In the sixteenth century, they tended to be husbandmen and labourers; in the seventeenth and eighteenth century, they progressively had less to do with agriculture. Those in a trade constituted over one-third of the low-wealth deceased in the Worcestershire sample from the 1720s, more than the husbandmen and labourers categories combined. Those with dual occupations, on the other hand, who had the bulk of their capital in agriculture, were not necessarily poor. What this occupational breakdown seems to show is that not only did the employment in rural industries grow, but the corps of artisans who furnished basic goods and services to their neighbours expanded as well. Butchers, masons, carpenters, thatchers, smiths, weavers, tailors, shoemakers—these were the type of crafts one finds increasingly among those inventoried in rural communities.[34]

There was, of course, a third alternative. Perhaps the truest measure of how much villagers valued agricultural endeavours and animal husbandry is the proportion of them who emigrated to America in the seventeenth and eighteenth centuries, hoping to establish their own farm households. Most poor Englishmen went to America as indentured servants. Studies of the servant trade to the colonies do not furnish comprehensive information on the exact numbers of English men and women involved. It is known, however, that males usually predominated by a ratio of about 8:2. that they tended to be under the age of 30, *and* that the demand always seemed to exceed the supply. Using some highly speculative estimates of emigration from England, it seems likely that the height of the exodus occurred in the mid-seventeenth century during the Revolutionary period. Just taking the group of males aged 15–30, probably the highest proportion of Englishmen of that group who permanently left the country during any one decade was one out of fifteen. By the end of the seventeenth century, it was more like one in forty per decade.[35] Thereafter, English servant emigration consisted largely of convicts more or less forced to make the trip. Merchants turned to African slaves and Irish and German servants to meet the colonial demand. It seems few women and a declining proportion of men found

TABLE 2.6 Male occupational structure in areas of the Midlands (% in various occupations)

Occupational status	Rural Oxfordshire, 1550–90	Rural S. Worcestershire 1669–70	Rural S. Worcestershire 1720–1
All inventoried estates			
Gentlemen/professional	3.7	14.6	3.3
Yeoman	0.7	53.0	44.9
Husbandman/farmer[a]	68.4	13.2	19.7
Labourer/servant	16.9	3.3	3.4
Dual occupation	0.7	—	13.5
Tradesman/craftsman	9.6	15.9	15.2
Total no. of inventories	136	151	178
Low-wealth estates[b]			
Gentleman/professional	—	8.9	3.5
Yeoman	—	37.5	26.3
Husbandman/farmer[a]	48.4	21.4	15.8
Labourer/servant	35.5	5.6	8.8
Dual occupations	—	—	10.5
Tradesmen/craftsman	16.1	26.8	35.1
Total no. of inventories	62	56	57

[a] This category includes those inventoried decedents identified as husbandmen and those whose property clearly indicated that they were engaged in agricultural production, although their exact status—yeoman, husbandman, farmer—could not be ascertained.
[b] Low wealth is total personal estate valued £20 or under in 1550–90, £40 or under in 1669–70, and £45 or under in 1720–1. See text and Appendix 1 for explanation of cut-off points.
Sources: See Tables 2.3 and 2.4.

the promise of a yeoman's life a great enough enticement to outweigh the risks and disadvantages of migration and servitude.[36]

In the next chapter, I will consider the household production patterns established by those who did emigrate. These settlers were transplanted into a colonial environment that possessed quite different physical and economic characteristics from those that existed in the Old World, so one might well expect quite different forms of household production.

Chapter 2

1. On English city and town population in the early modern period see Jan De Vries, *European Urbanization, 1500–1800*, Cambridge, Mass., 1984, p. 39; Peter Clark (ed.), *The Transformation of English Provincial Towns, 1600–1800*, London, 1984, p. 13; and E. Anthony Wrigley, 'Urban Growth and Agricultural Change: England and the Continent in the Early Modern Period', *Journal of Interdisciplinary History*, 15 (1985), 686–8.

2. Alan Everitt, 'Farm Labourers', in Joan Thirsk (ed.), *The Agrarian History of England and Wales*, iv, 1500–1640, Cambridge, 1967, pp. 396–400; Peter Lindert, 'English Occupations, 1670–1811', *Journal of Economic History*, 40 (1980), 685–712; Peter H. Lindert and Jeffrey G. Williamson, 'Revising England's Social Tables, 1688–1812', *Explorations in Economic History*, 19 (1982), 385–408; Lindert and Williamson, 'Reinterpreting Britain's Social Tables, 1688–1913', ibid., 20 (1983), 94–109; and Peter Mathias, *The Transformation of England*, New York, 1979, pp. 171–89.

3. Charles Tilly, 'Demographic Origins of the European Proletariat', in David Levine (ed.), *Proletarianization and Family History*, Orlando, 1984, pp. 1–86, and David Levine, 'Production, Reproduction, and the Proletarian Family in England, 1500–1851', in ibid., pp. 87–128. The quotation from Tilly is taken from p. 1.

4. A. J. Tawney and R. H. Tawney, 'An Occupational Census of the Seventeenth Century', *Economic History Review*, 5 (1934–5), 48.

5. For a guide to British inventory research, see Mark Overton, *A Bibliography of British Inventories*, Newcastle-upon-Tyne, 1983.

6. For the counties that comprise these regions, see E. A. Wrigley and R. S. Schofield, *The Population History of England, 1541–1871*, London, 1986, p. 44.

7. See the introductions to the inventory collections listed as sources for Tables 2.1 and 2.2. On the candle tax see *Probate Inventories and Manorial Excepts of Chatnole, Leigh, and Yetminster*, ed. R. Machin, Bristol, 1976, p. 9. On the percentage of clothworkers see Tawney and Tawney, 'Occupational Census', 47, 55 ff. See Margaret Spufford, *The Great Reclothing of Rural England: Petty Chapmen and their Wares in the Seventeenth Century*, London, 1984, pp. 118–46, on tailors and home sewing. On the goods manufactured rurally see Joan Thirsk, *Economic Policy and Projects: The Development of a Consumer Society in Early Modern England*, Oxford, 1978. On the lack of regional differences in

dress, see Keith Thomas, 'Social Differences in Early Modern England: Dress', a paper delivered at the Newberry Library, Chicago, 10 Apr. 1989.

8. For the overturned-pot method of baking see *Probate Inventories and Manorial Excepts*, ed. Machin, p. 10, and *Devon Inventories of the Sixteenth and Seventeenth Centuries*, ed. Margaret Cash, Devon and Cornwall Record Society, n.s. 11 (1966), p. xvii. Machin believes the Dorset villagers he studied replaced his primitive method of home baking with a village bakery in the seventeenth century, because utensils begin to disappear from the records then (p. 12). *Farm and Cottage Inventories of Mid-Essex, 1635–1749*, ed. Francis W. Steer, Colchester, 1950, which has well-enumerated inventories, shows 131 estates out of 245 with kneading-troughs, but other baking equipment had far fewer mentions—moulding board to form the loaves: 6; peel to pull the bread out of the oven: 30; slice to clear out ashes in the oven: 11; boulting-troughs to separate out bran from the flower: 4; flour boxes: 2; meal: 3. Flour itself was not even listed once. Ian Mitchell, 'The Development of Urban Retailing, 1700–1815', in Peter Clark (ed.), *The Transformation of English Provincial Towns, 1600–1800*, London, 1984, claims (p. 272) that in Chester the traditional role of bakers was to bake dough prepared by citizens at home.

9. Joan Thirsk (ed.), *The Agrarian History of England and Wales*, v. 2, 1640–1750, Cambridge, 1985, pp. 1–5, 363–6.

10. Peter Clark, *The English Alehouse: A Social History, 1200–1830*, London, 1983, pp. 42–3. Alan D. Dyer, *The City of Worcester in the Sixteenth Century*, Bristol, 1973, pp. 82, 139–40, discusses Elizabethan brewers in the city.

11. Clark, *English Alehouse*, p. 213, says the following about the growth in home brewing: 'influential was the rising price of alehouse beer (due to the excise), the wider dissemination of basic brewing skills through the publication of technical manuals, and more speculatively perhaps, the increase in the proportion of servants living in the masters' houses.' The latter refers to Ann Kussmaul's argument that with the decline in cereal prices and the cost of living, households once again more frequently hired live-in servants in husbandry rather than relying on labourers (*Servants in Husbandry in Early Modern England*, Cambridge, 1981, 97ff.). Peter Mathias, *The Brewing Industry in England, 1700–1830*, Cambridge, 1959, p. 377, shows from tax records that the proportion of home brewing stayed relatively steady from 1710 to the 1770s, comprising nearly two-thirds of all brewing. After that it declined.

12. Cash (ed.), *Devon Inventories*, pp. xii–xxiii and Stanley D. Chapman (ed.), *Devon Cloth Industry in the Eighteenth Century*, Devon and Cornwall Record Society, n.s. 23 (1978), pp. vii–xiv, discuss cloth-making in Devon. In the 18th cent. the Bradford area switched to worsteds and was one of the first to mechanize. See Pat Hudson, 'From Manor to Mill: The West Riding in Transition', in Maxine Berg *et al.* (eds.), *Town and Country before the Factory*, Cambridge, 1983, pp. 124–46. On the spread of cloth-making into rural areas generally, see Joan Thirsk, 'Industries in the Countryside', in F. J. Fisher (ed.), *Essays in the Economic and Social History of Tudor and Stuart England*, Cambridge, 1961, pp. 70–88. On the division of labour in the industry see G. D. Ramsay, *The Wiltshire Woollen Industry in the Sixteenth and Seventeenth Centuries*, 2nd edn. London, 1965, and D. C. Coleman, 'Textile Growth', in N. B. Harte and K. G. Ponting (eds.), *Textile History and Economic History*, Manchester, 1973, p. 8.

On the different organizational forms for textile production in the 18th cent., see John Styles, 'Implementing Visual Design in Eighteenth-Century English Manufactures', unpublished paper, Nov. 1988, pp. 8–12.

13. John T. Swain, *Industrialization before the Industrial Revolution, Northeastern Lancashire c.1500–1640*, Manchester, 1986, pp. 108–62.

14. Paul Slack (ed.), *Poverty in Early-Stuart Salisbury*, Wiltshire Record Society, 31 (1975), 84, includes a project for relief of the Salisbury poor in 1613. In it the projector alleges that the chief reason 'clothmen' sought spinners in the country-side was the deceit of city spinners. The usual assumption about why spinning was done in rural areas, however, has been that it was cheaper. It is not unusual to find spinning-wheels in inventories of very little worth where there is no other indication of how the person made a living. Victor Skipp, *Crisis and Development: An Ecological Case Study of the Forest of Arden, 1570–1674*, Cambridge, 1978, p. 58, notes that in the area he studied there was almost a doubling of spinning-wheel ownership over the course of the 16th cent. among those of below average wealth, indicating an expansion of this activity as a rural by-employment. On linen, see N. B. Harte, 'The Rise of Protection and the English Linen Trade', in Harte and Ponting (eds.), *Textile History and Economic History*, pp. 74–112.

15. On the leasing of cows see *Probate Inventories and Manorial Excepts*, ed. Machin, pp. 18–21. Cases where the imbalance between the possession of cows and of cheese and buttermaking equipment seems to indicate renting out are in the two Gloucestershire inventory collections edited by John Moore and in the Telford, Shropshire inventories (see note to Table 2.1).

16. On the agricultural characteristics of Oxfordshire and Worcestershire see Thirsk (ed.), *Agrarian History*, iv. 4, 66, 99–109, and v. 2, 161–72, 317–26; M. A. Havinden (ed.), *Household and Farm Inventories in Oxfordshire, 1550–1590*, London, 1965, introduction; John Walter, 'A "Rising of the People"? The Oxfordshire Rising of 1596', *Past and Present*, 107 (1985), 108–9; James Yelling, 'The Combination and Rotation of Crops in East Worcestershire, 1540–1660', *Agricultural History Review*, 17 (1969), 24–43; and J. A. Yelling, *Common Field and Enclosure in England, 1450–1850*, London, 1977, pp. -63–9.

17. The median is the midpoint in the distribution: thus the median for personal wealth in the Oxfordshire sample was £20.2, meaning that half the sample left less than £20 and the other half left more. Considering that inventories are biased towards the more affluent, it is likely that much more than half of the living population had wealth below £20. Alan Everitt's discussion of labourers' wealth in the late 16th cent. ('Farm Labourers', pp. 420–1), indicates that a £20 limit would include the entire group he studied, together with some husbandmen and artisans. In the Chesterfield, Derbyshire inventories used in my survey of household production, 41% of the 1550–90 estates possessed less than £20 in wealth (*Chesterfield Wills and Inventories, 1521–1603*, ed. J. M. Bestall and D. V. Fowkes, Derbyshire Record Society, 1 (1977), p. xx). In the 1590s, after the Oxfordshire sample ends and in a decade of high inflation, the median value of estates in the Yetminster area of Dorset (also in my survey) was £27 (*Probate Inventories and Manorial Excepts*, ed. Machin, p. 4). Thus Oxfordshire's median of £20 does not seem atypical.

18. Alan Everitt also notes the scarcity of pig ownership among labourers in the first half of the early modern period ('Farm Labourers', p. 416). On using sheep for milk see ibid., pp. 53 and 453. See also Richard Carew, *Survey of Cornwall*, London, 1602, p. 66, for contemporary comment.

19. This assumes an average annual output per milking cow of 200 gallons (Thirsk (ed.), *Agrarian History*, v. 2, 109) and a family intake of 365 gal.

20. Havinden (ed.), *Inventories in Oxfordshire*, p. 38.

21. The cut-off point between low and medium–high wealth groups is £40 for 1669–70, double the £20 figure for 16th-cent. Oxfordshire, a difference accounted for by inflation during the 1590s and the first half of the 17th cent. The price of consumables doubled between 1550–90 and 1660–74 (E. H. Phelps Brown and Sheila V. Hopkins, 'Seven Centuries of the Prices of Consumables, Compared with Builders' Wage-Rates', in E. M. Carus-Wilson (ed.), *Essays in Economic History*, ii, New York, 1962, pp. 194–5). As with the Oxfordshire data, the cut-off point of £40 was very near the median of wealth. 48% of this Worcestershire 1669–70 sample had estates of £40 or less. Other studies of probated wealth at this date indicate medians that are not dissimilar. Of estates probated in Cambridgeshire and the West Midlands in the years 1669–70, 51.7% and 48.5%, respectively, had estates of £50 or less. See Peter Lindert, *Appendices to Lucrens Angliae: The Distribution of English Private Wealth since 1670*, Working Paper Series, 19, Agricultural History Center, University of California–Davis, 1985, pp. 258–60. Cambridgeshire in the 1660s had a median wealth figure of £40, while Lincolnshire's in 1669 was a little higher at £57: H. M. Spufford, 'The significance of the Cambridgeshire Hearth Tax', *Proceedings of the Cambridge Antiquarian Society*, 55 (1961), 63. J. P. P. Horn, 'Distribution of Wealth in the Vale of Berkeley, Gloucestershire, 1660–1700', *Southern History*, 3 (1981), 101, found that 45.0% of the Gloucestershire estates probated between 1670 and 1679 were appraised at under £50, and he further estimated that if the poor were included the percentage would actually be between about 60% and 70%. For the 1720–1 Worcestershire sample I increased the low wealth cut-off to £45. The Phelps Brown and Hopkins index does not rise between 1669–70 and 1720–1, but that may be because it is heavily dependent on cereal prices, which were declining. As other prices, e.g. for livestock, were modestly rising, an increase of £5 (12.5%) in the low wealth cut-off point seemed reasonable. 42% of the Worcestershire 1720–1 sample had wealth of £45 or under. In the first decade of the 18th cent., the median probated wealth for tradesmen, husbandmen, and labourers in the entire diocese of Worcester (which included most of the county of Worcester and part of Warwickshire) was £63, £50, and £12, respectively: J. A. Johnston, 'The Vale of Evesham, 1702–1708: The Evidence from Probate Inventories and Wills', *Vale of Evesham Historical Society Research Papers*, 4 (1973), 88.

22. These trends coincide with what is believed to have been occurring nationally—a growth in sheep stocks and a stagnation in the number of cattle being raised for meat—during the late 17th and the early 18th cent. See Thirsk (ed.), *Agrarian History*, v, part 2, 445.

23. R. H. Hilton, 'Medieval Market Towns and Simple Commodity Production', *Past and Present*, 109 (1985), 13 ff. On the manorial system and the rights of lords, generally, see George Caspar Homans, *English Villagers of the Thirteenth*

Century, New York, 1968 (reprint of 1941 (edn.). On the necessity for early modern labourers to purchase meal at local markets see Everitt, 'Farm Labourers', pp. 450–1.

24. B. H. Slicher van Bath, *The Agrarian History of Western Europe*, London, 1963, pp. 68 and 108; Maurice Bereford and John G. Hurst (eds.), *Deserted Medieval Villages*, London, 1974, p. 139; and Kathleen Biddick, 'Medieval English Peasants and Market Involvement', *Journal of Economic History*, 45 (1985), 830.

25. K. D. M. Snell, *Annals of the Labouring Poor: Social Change and Agrarian England, 1660–1900*, Cambridge, 1985, pp. 174ff.

26. 'Farm Labourers', pp. 412–18. A study of over 1,800 inventories from south Staffordshire from 1560 to 1720 reveals a trend in livestock ownership almost identical to that for the rural South of England shown in Table 2.1. See Pauline Frost, 'Yeomen and Metalsmiths' Livestock in the Dual Economy in South Staffordshire, 1560–1720', *Agricultural History Review*, 29 (1981), 35. Cattle ownership began at 89.6% and dropped to 58.6% by the end of the period. For sheep the figures were 74.4% and 31.3%. Swine started lower at 66.8% and fell less to 42.3%. Both cattle and swine ownership dropped most in the early 17th cent. and stayed there at about the same levels until 1680, dropping again in the period 1681–1720. Ownership of sheep declined steadily in all periods.

27. David Davies, *Labourers in Husbandry*, 1795 and Frederick Eden, *The State of the Poor*, 3 vols., 1797. Of course, short-term regional trends could be missed with our periodic cross-sectional data. Also, by postulating a long secular decline, I do not preclude the possibility that those late 18th and 19th cent. communities that experienced rural depopulation might well have seen a subsequent resurgence in livestock ownership.

28. Tilly, 'Demographic Origins of the Proletariat', p. 53.

29. J. R. Wordie, 'The Chronology of English Enclosure, 1500–1914', *Economic History Review*, 2nd ser. 36 (1983), 483–505.

30. See e.g. the cottagers in Myddle, Shropshire: David G. Hey, *An English Rural Community: Myddle under the Tudors and the Stuarts*, Leicester, 1974, p. 165.

31. Roger Schofield, 'English Marriage Patterns Revisited', *Journal of Family History*, 10 (1985), 9. See also David Weir, 'Rather Never than Late: Celibacy and Age at Marriage in English Cohort Fertility, 1541–1871', ibid., 9 (1984), 341–55.

32. Wrigley, 'Urban Growth and Change', p. 688; see also de Vries, *European Urbanization*, pp. 39 and 124. On smaller towns see chapters on marketing by Alan Everitt and John Chartres in Thirsk (ed.), *Agrarian History*, iv and v. 2 (respectively).

33. Wrigley, 'Urban Growth and Change', pp. 688, 700.

34. R. V. Jackson, 'Growth and Deceleration in English Agriculture, 1660–1790', *Economic History Review*, 2nd ser. 38 (1985), 333–51.

35. These calculations are based upon the net emigration figures calculated by Henry A. Gemery in 'Emigration from the British Isles to the New World, 1630–70', *Research in Economic History*, 5 (1980), 179–231, and 'European Emigration to North America, 1700–1820: Numbers and Quasi-numbers', *Perspectives in American History*, n.s. 1 (1984), 283–342, and on the population and age structure information in E. A. Wrigley and R. S. Schofield, *The Population*

History of England, 1541–1871, London, 1981, pp. 574 and 576. Gemery estimates net migration was about 70,000 per decade in the mid-17th cent. Males aged 15–30, perhaps 25% of the male population, would have numbered about 610,500. If 60% of the emigrants were from that group, then about 6.9% of the group was lost during a decade, or 1 in 14 or 15. Wrigley and Schofield show (pp. 185–7) the role this loss played in the stagnation of the English population during this period.

36. On servants, see David W. Galenson, *White Servitude in America: An Economic Analysis*, New York; 1981, Farley Grubb, 'Redemptioner Immigration to Pennsylvania: Evidence on Contract Choice and Profitability', *Journal of Economic History*, 46 (1986), 407–18; A. Roger Ekrich, *Bound for America: The transportation of British Convicts to the Colonies, 1718–1775*, New York, 1987; and Sharon Salinger, *'To Serve Well and Faithfully': Labor and Indentured Servants in Pennsylvania, 1682–1800*, New York, 1987.

3

Household Production in Colonial America

THERE are several good reasons for assuming that colonial households produced more of their own goods than did households in the Old World. First of all, households were bigger in America, averaging between six and nine persons on the mainland and sometimes reaching thirty or forty in households on the sugar islands of the West Indies. English communities, on the other hand, seldom had a mean household size of over five persons.[1] The difference is not difficult to explain. Plantation colonies recruited unfree labour, so indentured servants and slaves swelled the size of their 'families'. In some areas of the North, notably Pennsylvania, servants also increased mean household size, but more often in the non-plantation colonies it was higher fertility that was responsible.[2] With more workers in the household and with more members to feed and clothe, it seems logical to suppose that more home production would have taken place.

Second, the colonies tended to have more affluent households. The labourers and cottagers that populated the villages of England were not so much in evidence in America, thanks to the unfree labour system. Those in the seventeenth century who migrated to establish plantations had to have a certain amount of capital, otherwise they would have been forced to join other people's households as indentured servants. When slaves came to replace servants, the capital demands increased further, and those without the necessary resources moved elsewhere. Slaves, the working class of the eighteenth-century plantation colonies, were, of course, permanent members of their masters' households. One of the important characteristics of the Puritan migration to New England, besides the fact that it was family-based, was that both the richest and the poorest elements were absent.[3] If, as was the case in England, household production tended to flourish in wealthier households, the more generalized affluence of American households should have promoted more of this kind of activity.

Third, the colonies were overwhelmingly rural, and the plentiful land for grazing and the rich soil and warm climate for growing crops should have encouraged household production for consumption. Interestingly enough, over the course of the colonial period, America actually de-urbanized, with a smaller proportion of the population living in towns at the time of the Revolution than had lived there at the end of the seventeenth century.[4]

To see if these suppositions are correct, let us turn to inventories from America in the colonial era.

Household Production in Plantation and Non-plantation Colonies

The population of British America on the eve of the American Revolution was about evenly split between plantation and non-plantation areas.[5] The total in the thirteen colonies, about 2.5 million, was approximately a third of the population of England and Wales. In Table 3.1 inventories from one of the larger plantation areas and one of the larger non-plantation settlements, the Chesapeake (Virginia and Maryland) and Massachusetts, respectively, are used to demonstrate the prevalence of certain types of household production activities in the late seventeenth century and again about a hundred years later, in the Revolutionary period. Because of the peculiar pattern found in seventeenth-century Chesapeake, an additional sample for the 1720s was taken.[6]

What immediately catches the eye in Table 3.1 is the small percentage of late seventeenth-century Virginia inventories showing grain cultivation, livestock ownership, and equipment for household production. Only in the possession of cows and pigs did these colonists equal or exceed the ownership levels of their contemporaries in English rural communities. Moreover, changes occurred slowly. In the 1720s, while sheep-raising and spinning did dramatically increase, only a quarter of estates showed signs of field crops, and almost none contained equipment for the making of cheese, butter, beer, or cider. Not until the Revolutionary-era sample did the Chesapeake figures begin to resemble the profile that might be expected for colonial households. By then field crops and sheep-raising appeared in half of the inventories, while cow and pig ownership continued to be more or less universal. In all of these activities, the ownership levels of the colonial deceased exceeded those of the deceased in most of the English probate samples. Spinning-wheels also reached levels unseen in England.

The Chesapeake was a tobacco-producing region, and wheat, maize,[7] beef, and pork did not become important exports until the second

TABLE 3.1 Household production in Colonial America (% of inventories showing crops, livestock or equipment)

Colony and time period	No. of inventories[a]	Field crops[b]	Cows	Pigs	Sheep	Poultry	Cheese/butter-making	Brewing/cider-making	Spinning-wheels
Plantation									
Virginia, 1660–76	134	13.8	77.6	65.2	9.0	1.5	5.3	6.0	1.0
Virginia, 1724–9	299	25.4	86.2	72.9	44.5	15.1	1.0	4.0	43.1
Virginia & Maryland, 1774	141	43.7	88.0	75.4	51.2	19.1	9.4	14.4	71.4
Non-plantation									
Essex Co., Massachusetts, 1660–73	300	47.0	75.7	65.7	33.3	0.7	16.3	6.0	29.0
Rural Massachusetts, 1774	164	58.5	71.2	57.9	48.7	15.9	43.6	5.5	63.3
Urban Massachusetts, 1774[c]	116	2.6	25.0	18.1	0.9	0.0	9.5	4.3	23.7

[a] The number of observations for the different categories may vary slightly due to missing information about certain classes of goods in the inventories.
[b] Grain crops. Tobacco crops not counted.
[c] All towns in the sample that had over 500 houses in the 1765 census; these include Boston and Salem.

Source: See Appendix 1.

quarter of the eighteenth century. Undoubtedly the percentages of grain cultivation are underestimations. The most common grain, maize, was grown more like a garden crop, without a plough or team of horses or oxen. Consequently, there are fewer potential indicators of cultivation to be found in the inventories. Still, if most households produced cereals on a scale where the yield met all their human and animal needs, then crops should have surfaced more in the probate documents than they do.

Other studies confirm what Table 3.1 suggests about grain cultivation in the early Chesapeake. An examination of plantation inventories from the 1660s and 1670s in All Hallows Parish, Maryland reveals only 24% with corn and 3% with wheat. Charles County, 1658–80, registered even lower percentages. Another study of six counties in Maryland indicates that a mere 5% of plantation families owned ploughs in the last half of the seventeenth century, although among the more affluent as many as 44% owned them. This all changed of course, when wheat and corn became big export crops. In the Piedmont area of Virginia, during the mid-eighteenth century, 30% to 40% had ploughs, but several decades later, at the time of the Revolution, that percentage had doubled.[8]

The poor state of arable husbandry in the seventeenth century affected another area of household production as well—brewing. Tea, rum, and cider came to replace beer as the principal drink of the population, presumably because it was easier to buy tea and rum or grow fruit than cultivate barley. Signs of cider consumption abound in inventories, but equipment does not. Cider presses were not as prevalent in the colonies as were brewing utensils in early eighteenth-century England.

More puzzling was the near absence of cheesemaking equipment and the very low level of butter utensils among Chesapeake households in all time periods. Perhaps the problems with cooling and drying butter and cheese affected production in the South, and the plentifulness of milk and meat made the 'storing' of calcium and protein as cheese unnecessary.[9]

In certain areas of household production, however, the plantation colonies did distinguish themselves. The decline in the proportion of households owning livestock, the most noticeable trend in early modern England's communities, cannot be identified in the New World data. A wealth breakdown of the American data has not been presented yet, so it would be wrong to assume that all income levels failed to experience a drop in livestock ownership. Still, ownership percentages for cattle and pigs are so consistently high that it seems unlikely that the kind of declines seen in England could have occurred in the Chesapeake. With sheep the pattern also varied from that in England, but in a different way.

Sheep had been the most common animal owned by villagers in medieval England. That primacy was lost in the fifteenth or sixteenth century to the cow, and ownership percentages steadily fell throughout the early eighteenth century. In the Chesapeake, sheep ownership was rare in the late seventeenth century, but by the 1720s the animal was much more common, and at the time of the Revolution about half of the inventories listed them. Ownership of sheep, however, continued to be less widespread than that of cattle and pigs. A Virginia pamphleteer writing in 1765 alleged about sheep that there was 'no dumb creature taken so little notice of' in the colony.[10]

The trend in the possession of spinning-wheels initially paralleled the pattern in sheep ownership. From seldom being listed in the late seventeenth century, wheels became more common than in England by the 1720s, and finally became almost universal by the time of the Revolution. Spinning, of course, was not just of wool but of flax and hemp as well.

Switching to the northern colony of Massachusetts, one sees a rather different pattern in the late seventeenth century from that in the Chesapeake. Sectarian Massachusetts, so anxious to set itself apart from the Mother Country in its laws and institutions, looked remarkably like her in terms of general patterns of household activity in the 1660s and 1670s. Differences of course existed. Maize predominated over wheat in the fields, less brewing took place, and cow ownership stood about 10 percentage points higher than in most areas of late seventeenth-century England. Still, the profile was one that was much closer to England than to the plantations. A hundred years later, though, that was not the case. By the time of the Revolution, Massachusetts shared the high level of livestock ownership, the paucity of drink-processing equipment (beer having given way to cider and rum in New England as well), and the ubiquity of spinning-wheels with the Chesapeake. Only in the possession of dairy equipment did Massachusetts resemble England rather than the southern colonies.

Of course, unlike the plantation colonies, pre-revolutionary Massachusetts had a significant urban component. Over one in four inhabitants lived in towns with a population above 2,500, the standard measure of urban status.[11] Predictably, Table 3.1 shows that those in urban areas engaged in almost no grain cultivation and had much smaller holdings of livestock. One in four of those inventoried in urban areas had cows, less than one in five owned a pig, and sheep-holding was virtually non-existent. While their ownership of livestock exceeded the percentages found in English cities and towns, they were behind eighteenth-century urban households of the Mother Country in the making of drink and in the ratio of urban to rural spinners.

The Wealth Factor

With the English inventories, the most interesting findings emerged when I applied wealth controls, and split samples into low-wealth and medium- or high-wealth groups. Doing the same for the colonies (see Table 3.2) produces a more complicated pattern than the long-term decline in livestock ownership observed among those in the English low-wealth groups.

In the plantation colonies of the late seventeenth-century Chesapeake, wealth seems to have made only a small difference to levels of household production. In both the low-wealth and the medium- or high-wealth group, percentages for grain cultivation, sheep-raising, and poultry-keeping were low, cow- and pig-holding very high, and equipment for the manufacture of butter, cheese, drink, and yarn almost non-existent. Even in the 1720s, differences were not all that great. Livestock ownership was about 10 points higher for each type of animal in the wealthier group, but both groups enjoyed comparatively high rates of ownership.

Some divergence, however, is apparent by the time of the Revolution. By that point, it appears, the low-wealth group had lost ground. The incidence of grain cultivation and livestock ownership was lower than for their counterparts in the 1720s. Those in the more affluent group, however, had higher percentages in every category than their earlier counterparts. Grain cultivation, sheep-raising, and drinkmaking equipment especially increased dramatically. In England the one type of household activity that poorer households participated in more frequently or as frequently as richer ones was spinning, whereas in the plantation colonies the wealthier households had a much higher proportion with spinning-wheels than the low-wealth group. Presumably this difference can be explained by the absence of an outwork system in the South.

In Massachusetts, a sharp disparity between low- and higher-wealth groups, as in England, had existed from the beginning, and it increased over time as the livestock-holding of the low-wealth group declined and that of the high-wealth group rose. In the case of both Massachusetts and the Chesapeake, the decline in animal ownership experienced by poorer households was masked in Table 3.1's total percentages by the rise in ownership by the more affluent. In comparison with England, of course,

TABLE 3.2 Colonial household production by wealth group[a] (% of inventories showing crops, livestock or equipment)

Colony and time period	No. of inventories	Field crops[b]	Cows	Pigs	Sheep	Poultry	Cheese/butter-making	Brewing/cider-making	Spinning-wheels
LOW-WEALTH GROUP									
Plantation									
Virginia, 1660–76	67	11.1	67.2	63.6	0.0	1.5	4.4	0.0	0.0
Virginia, 1724–9	152	22.4	77.0	64.5	30.3	11.8	0.0	0.0	30.9
Virginia & Maryland, 1774	71	17.9	59.2	58.6	29.9	18.3	5.6	4.2	56.3
Non-plantation									
Essex Co., Massachusetts, 1660–73	151	24.5	60.1	53.6	16.6	0.0	9.3	2.0	19.2
Rural Massachusetts, 1774	83	31.3	50.6	34.9	26.5	13.2	26.5	0.0	57.8
Urban Massachusetts, 1774	61	1.6	11.5	8.2	0.0	0.0	1.6	0.0	14.5
MEDIUM- AND HIGH-WEALTH GROUP									
Plantation									
Virginia, 1660–76	66	16.1	88.1	66.7	17.9	1.5	6.1	0.0	1.0
Virginia, 1724–9	147	28.6	95.9	81.6	59.2	18.4	2.0	8.2	55.8
Virginia & Maryland, 1774	70	66.7	97.1	92.6	72.0	20.0	13.2	25.0	87.0
Non-plantation									
Essex Co., Massachusetts, 1660–73	149	69.8	81.0	77.9	50.3	1.3	23.5	10.1	37.6
Rural Massachusetts, 1774	81	86.4	92.5	81.5	71.6	18.5	61.3	11.1	68.9
Urban Massachusetts, 1774	55	3.6	40.0	29.1	1.8	0.0	18.2	9.1	33.9

[a] The two groups were divided at the median. For the cut-off points see Appendix 1.
[b] Grain crops. Tobacco crops not counted.

Source: See Appendix 1.

the poorer households were still animal-rich. More similarity existed between Old World and New when it came to arable husbandry. In both, the poorer segment of the rural population did not often cultivate their own field crops.

The results from an analysis of the 1771 Massachusetts tax valuation list of 37,000 taxpayers parallel the findings from the 1774 probate inventories. Bettye Hobbs Pruitt, who has analysed that list, found that 44% of the taxpayers could not be considered farmers because they did not own any improved land and livestock. An additional 9 had no tillage land. Thus the proportion of taxpayers who had the resources to cultivate grain was less than 50%, and only 50% of those produced enough for self-sufficiency. Of the poorer 50% of farmers (ranking based on acreage), nearly all had at least one cow, two out of three had pigs, but only 27% produced cider.[12]

The Main Characteristics of Colonial Household Production

The uniformly high levels of colonial household production for consumption envisioned at the beginning of this chapter due to household size, wealth and agrarianism did not materialize. First of all, the inventories from the plantation colony of Virginia in the late seventeenth century indicate that, despite much open land and widespread ownership of livestock, very few households engaged in certain processing activities that were necessary to produce goods for home consumption. Other studies done on counties in Maryland point to the same conclusion.

Detailed analysis of the labour force on early Virginian plantations shows that while household size might have been large, most of the labour was devoted to production of the very profitable tobacco staple. Also the high male to female ratio among whites and the use of black women for fieldwork meant a shortage of females available for doing the labour that was traditionally defined by the English as women's work, and that was indispensable for the furnishing of goods and services for home consumption—dairying, brewing, baking of bread, poultry-keeping, spinning, and so forth. A rise in household production in the mid-eighteenth century, as indicated by both inventoried goods (see Table 3.1) and also by the increase in the proportion of slaves given occupational designations relating to household work, coincided with a decline in the staple and the emergence of a demographically more mature black population with many children and older women. These two groups formed the core of the domestic workforce. The self-sufficient plantation with large spinning- and weaving-rooms and numerous outbuildings for good-processing only existed among the wealthy and, in the Chesapeake, turned out to be more characteristic of the late eighteenth and early nineteenth century than of earlier periods. During the seventeenth century, plantation colonies were usually the least self-sufficient areas in the English-speaking world.[13]

There was one area of household activity in which the plantation settlements, as well as communities in the North, consistently excelled throughout the colonial period—animal husbandry. They only concentrated on certain types of livestock products, however. Mainly these were beef, pork, and milk.

Cow and pig ownership was just about universal among rural medium- or high-wealth groups and was commonly in the 50% to 60% range among the rural low-wealth groups, although in both regions the proportion owned by the latter had declined by the time of the Revolution. Sheep ownership, on the other hand, surfaced mainly among the wealthier groups, and in the Chesapeake even those in that category did not routinely own sheep until the eighteenth century. Low levels of ownership in the early years of settlement have been attributed to the problem of protecting sheep from wolves. Even after sheep ownership became as widespread in America as it was in England the size of the flocks seldom attained the levels found in the Old World. In New England, the average number held by farmers and rural taxpayers in a community usually stayed below 10, and in the Middle Colonies and the South below 15. Where in England it was common to see rural inventories with one or two pigs and a flock of sheep, the reverse was often true in American inventories. According to one source, farmers were reluctant to set aside much fodder for sheep during the winter.[14] This disinterest might be linked to the poor export potential for mutton, which could not be preserved through smoking or salting, and the Woollen Act of 1699, which prohibited Americans from selling wool or woollens outside the borders of their own colony.

As already suggested, the availability of beef and pork as well as large quantities of milk may have made it less necessary to preserve milk in the form of cheese and butter. However, although milk may have been the primary beverage, the thirteen colonies were actually net importers of cheese and butter before the Revolution due to deficits in all regions except New England. The southern disinclination to make dairy products continued well into the nineteenth century. The 1850 agricultural census revealed that the northern states produced at least fifty times as many pounds of cheese and made about twice as much butter per cow as did farmers in the South.[15] The initial pattern established in the seventeenth century, probably as a result of the shortage of English women in the colonies, apparently resulted in a more or less permanent change in household tasks and possibly some alteration in dietary habits. Milk, meat, and animal fat may, to some extent, have replaced cheese and butter.

Colonial household production also distinguished itself from that of England by the growth in domestic cloth production during the eighteenth century. At the time of the Revolution 71.4% of the Chesapeake inventories and 63.3% of those from rural Massachusetts listed spinning-wheels, and unlike the situation in the Old World these wheels were more likely to be in the wealthier than in the poorer estates, suggesting that much of the spinning was for home consumption rather than part of an outwork system. Also looms were not as exclusively the tool of weavers as they had been in the Mother Country. Still, the vast majority of households only had equipment for the making of yarn, not for the weaving and finishing of cloth. Table 3.3 shows the proportion of estates in the 1774 Massachusetts sample owning spinning-wheels, and also the percentage owning both woollen and linen wheels, looms, sheep,

TABLE 3.3 Percentage of Massachusetts 1774 inventories containing materials and equipment for cloth-production

County	No. of inventories	% with spinning-wheel(s)	% with linen and woollen wheels, loom, sheep, flax
Suffolk	98	27.4	2.1
Essex	95	49.0	6.1
Plymouth	25	64.0	8.0
Worcestershire	39	74.3	5.1
Hampshire	27	74.1	14.8
Total and average	284	48.9	5.7

Source: See Appendix 1.

and flax. The figures are broken down by county. Spinning-wheel ownership became much less common as one moves toward the coast and near major urban centres such as Boston and Salem. Households in the interior counties of Worcester and Hampshire had much higher levels of ownership, but relatively few of them had all the materials for the production of woollen and linen cloth—5.1% in Worcester and 14.8% in Hampshire. Considering both the relative complexity of eighteenth-century colonial clothing and the scarcity of weavers, fullers, dyers, and the like in frontier areas, these percentages suggest not only that few households made their own cloth but also that the scale of local production was low and meant to supplement imported cloth when that was unavailable or too expensive.

The Reliance on Imports

Americans may have been the people of plenty as far as land was concerned, but trade statistics suggest that New World households may have depended more than their English counterparts on imports from overseas or other colonies. Reliance of colonials on imports of three types—grain products, drink, and cloth and clothing—is particularly striking.

By the later eighteenth century, most of the colonies in British America imported more flour, wheat, or maize than they exported. The West Indies, of course, and the Canadian maritime colonies brought in large amounts of grain products. For a variety of reasons, a majority of the thirteen colonies did the same. In the case of Pennsylvania and New York, wheat was purchased to mill into flour for re-export. Pennsylvania's wheat purchases exceeded in value every other coastal import in the 1770s. Flour was the colony's staple. Five of the thirteen colonies, Georgia, South Carolina, Rhode Island, Massachusetts, and New Hampshire, were net importers of flour and bread, and the New Englanders had deficits in wheat and maize as well.[16]

Massachusetts, with its poor soil and large urban population, purchased the lion's share of these commodities. The colony had always imported some grain, but by the 1760s the coastal trade in flour from Pennsylvania and wheat and maize from the Chesapeake had assumed impressive dimensions. This can be indicated by estimating the proportion of the colony's population whose basic grain consumption could be satisfied by what was shipped in. There are two dates for which we have figures, 1761–5 and 1768–72. The annual amount of flour and grain imported at these dates would have fed between 25% and 28% of the population. While it could be argued that the figures are an overestimate because some of the maize sent in would have been to feed livestock, there is some doubt as to whether many New Englanders would have used this relatively costly import for animals. It is more likely, though, that the percentages are an underestimate because they do not include the grain that travelled into Massachusetts by inland routes.[17] Whatever the exact amount imported, it seems indisputable that the nearly two-thirds of Massachusetts residents that lived in the maritime counties along the seaboard were no strangers to shop-bought flour and cereals.

Imports inundated another area of food consumption, which affected all the colonies. Earlier, I noted the relatively small number of households that owned utensils for brewing or cidermaking. It appears that much of the reason for these low percentages had to do with the growth in the consumption of rum and tea.

In a detailed study of the rum trade in the colonies, John McCusker has calculated that in the year 1770 the colonists consumed 7,518,000 gal. of the spirit.[18] Even if all adults, male, female, free, and unfree are considered eligible as drinkers, per capita consumption would have been 2.5 oz. a day. In fact, rum was given to labourers in America as beer had been provided in England as a source of energy while performing hard manual work. Women and slaves also consumed the alcoholic drink in these pre-temperance days. Probably most of it, however, found its way into the cups of white free men. If drinkers are limited to them, then they must have imbibed a startling 7 oz. daily or the near equivalent of five 1.5 oz. measures. This level of consumption would provide about a quarter of the calories needed daily for an active adult male.[19]

Beverages containing sugar were difficult to escape in America. Ironically, the comparatively small amount of brewing that did go on in the colonies in the eighteenth century tended to use molasses as a base. Sugar flavoured the increasingly popular caffeine drinks, mainly tea, the commodity that began the American Revolution. The two plantation commodities became so closely linked that Joseph Massie, in a polemic against the sugar lobby in Parliament, chose to demonstrate the high usage of the sweetener by estimating the frequency of tea drinking in Britain.[20]

Unfortunately Massie did not work on the statistics for the colonies. Sketchy figures are available for consumption in the 1760s and 1770s, a period when wars, non-importation agreements against British taxation, and smuggling wreaked havoc on trade figures. A contemporary in 1773 set annual consumption on the American continent at 2.5 lb. of tea per person, more than enough for people to consume the drink daily. Modern historians have placed the figure lower, more like 0.75 lb. per capita, but that level of intake still would have allowed at least two-thirds of white adults to have had tea every day.[21]

In terms of volume, water, milk, and cider were clearly more important drinks than rum and tea. Yet in terms of frequency of consumption and number of consumers, these two drinks, both of which had addictive qualities, competed well with the others. Americans derived nearly as much of their alcohol intake from rum as from the less potent cider.[22] Colonials' allegiance to caffeine drinks can be measured by the amount of equipment—tea kettles, teacups, tea tables, coffee and chocolate pots—they bought to accompany their consumption.[23] The dietary and social changes associated with these beverages will be discussed in later chapters.

Another area of imports, textiles and clothing, comprised the main class of commodities exported from Britain to America. Historians studying the seventeenth century have been amazed at the substantial proportion of the household budget that colonials devoted to cloth purchases for clothing and household uses. One careful study of an ordinary planter household in the Chesapeake in the 1650s and 1660s revealed not only the heavy reliance of settlers on imports—55% of expenditure went on imported items—but the large chunk of money laid out for cloth and clothing. These devoured one-third of total expenditure. As discussed above, more households, as time went on, engaged in spinning, and in very large plantation households and in some frontier areas weaving was sometimes undertaken. Evidence for these activities, however, can be somewhat misleading because neither in their households nor locally were Americans anywhere near self-sufficient in cloth production. Few colonists concentrated on sheep-raising, and most grew flax for the seed that could be exported. Both the South and the Middle colonies imported flax. Apparently also, proper processing of linen was something of a mystery to many Americans.[24]

The British government may have had many failures in America, but they did manage to prevent the emergence of an American cloth and clothing industry. Probably nowhere else in the 'civilized' world did inhabitants produce their own fabric in such a primitive fashion and manufacture such a small amount of the textiles and the clothing they consumed.[25]

The millions of yards of material and thousands of wardrobe items from all over the world delivered by ships from England and Scotland every year successfully retarded textile manufacturing in America. During 1768–72, colonists spent an estimated 9% of their per capita income on textile products from Great Britain, and if haberdashery items and accessories not counted as textiles are added, it must have been at least 10%. It is unlikely that what Americans purchased locally or made at home in the way of clothing and household linens could have equalled that amount. Overseas products satisfied an amazing percentage of consumer needs. For example, the British sent over nearly enough men's stockings in a year to put a pair on every adult male's feet. And at the rate beaver hats poured into the colonies it would have taken only six years of imports to put one on every adult male's head.[26]

To summarize the whole trade situation, the major commodity imports coming in legally from each of the main trading areas—the coastal trade, the West Indies, Southern Europe, and England—1768–72 appear in Table 3.4. Slaves and shipping were not included in the statistics. The commodities were almost all consumer goods: grain, sugar, and drink from other colonies, and cloth and drink—tea and wine—from England and Europe. Well over half the goods exported from England to the colonies were textile products. Wool and linen comprised 53.1%, and cotton and silks (subsumed under the rubric 'Other' in the table) probably added a few per cent more. Except for sailcloth and sacking, nearly all the cloth commodities served a personal or domestic purpose. Among other imports, wrought iron could mean nails and tools, but it also included housewares. It seems, then, that at least 75%, and probably more, of the total commodities legally entering the colonies went to meet consumer needs. In addition, the prime goods smuggled in—sugar, molasses, spirits, and tea—were all consumer commodities.

Because of the way goods were split up by those compiling the statistics and because of smuggling, the tremendous change in early modern consumption wrought by 'groceries' (sugar, caffeine drinks, spices, and tobacco), a subject that will be returned to in later chapters, does not emerge as clearly as perhaps it should in Table 3.4. It is known that in England imports of these commodities increased from under 17% of total imports in 1700 to nearly 36% by 1772. America may not have been too far behind the Mother Country in this regard, considering the importance of sugar products and the volume of groceries entering illegally. For example, the tea coming in from England is shown as being

TABLE 3.4 Most important commodities exported legally to the Thirteen
Colonies, based on annual average, 1768–1772

Origin and nature of exports	% of total value
Exports from other parts of the	
Thirteen colonies	
(total value = £715,000[a])	
Rum and molasses	25.7
Flour and bread	19.0
Cereals	13.7
Meat	6.1
Other	35.5
Exports from England	
(total value = £2,526,804[b])	
Woollens	37.0[c]
Linens	15.8
Wrought iron	6.6
Tea	2.9
Goods of 'several sorts':	
paper, glass, etc.	12.3
Other	25.4
Exports from the West Indies	
(total value = £771,000[d])	
Rum and molasses	61.8
Sugar	16.5
Cotton	2.4
Other	19.3
Exports from Southern Europe	
and the Wine Islands	
(total value = £68,000[e])	
Wine	67.9
Salt	32.1

[a] This is the estimated value of 79 out of a total of 118 commodities in the record. Shepherd and Williamson ('Coastal Trade', p. 799) calculate that these commodities comprise 90% of the value of all commodities in the customs records.

[b] This is the 'official value' of all exports and re-exports sent out from England. See US Bureau of the Census, *Historical Statistics*, p. 1176.

[c] Shepherd and Walton (*Shipping, Maritime Trade* ..., p. 182) estimate that woollens constituted 35–40% of all exports in the years 1768–72.

[d] Estimated value from Shepherd and Walton, *Shipping, Maritime Trade* ..., p. 104.

[e] Estimated value from Shepherd and Walton, *Shipping, Maritime Trade* ..., p. 104.

Source: Calculations made from numbers in James F. Shepherd and Samuel Williamson, 'The Coastal Trade of the British North American Colonies, 1768–1772', *Journal of Economic History*, 32 (1972), 798, 808; US Bureau of the Census, *Historical Statistics of the United States, Colonial Times to 1970*, Washington DC, 1975, p. 1176; and James F. Shepherd and Gary M. Walton, *Shipping, Maritime Trade, and the Economic Development of Colonial North America*, Cambridge, 1972, pp. 104, 180–6, 228–30.

under 3% of the value of total imports, whereas if the contraband trade was included, the percentage would probably be nearer 10%.[27] It is actually possible to make some estimate of the percentage of their income that Americans devoted to goods coming from outside their own colony, goods which, as we have seen, were almost entirely for personal consumption. Most imports, of course, came from England. Because of the revenue that it generated, overseas trade became the first area of the economy for which the British Crown collected annual statistics. Figures for imports from England into the thirteen colonies begin in 1697. Table 3.5 shows the per capita unadjusted value of these legal imports from England. Despite the growth of colonial crafts and manufactures, the full-scale entry of the Scots into American commerce, a series of trade-disrupting wars, and a growth in the percentage of the colonial population constituted by slaves, the per capita value did not exhibit a downward trend. And when Scottish totals, which are available from 1740 on, are added, there is a steady rise, reaching £1.20 by *c*.1770.[28]

After adding the figures from the coastal, West Indian, and Southern European trades to those for England and Scotland, some further adjustments have to be made in order to estimate the percentage of per capita income spent on imports. Smuggling flourished in the Land of the Free.

TABLE 3.5 Per capita unadjusted 'official' value of English imports into the Thirteen Colonies[a]

Decade	£ per capita
1701–10	0.92
1711–20	0.86
1721–30	0.86
1731–40	0.84
1741–50	0.82
1751–60	1.14
1761–70	0.96

[a] The imports included goods of English and Irish manufacture as well as re-exports such as tea. The average annual import value for each decade was divided by an average of the population at the start of that decade and at the end.

Source: US Bureau of the Census, *Historical Statistics of the United States, Colonial Times to 1970*, Washington, DC, 1975, pp. 1168 and 1176.

Also the official values of the British trade and the estimated value of the other trades are wholesale not retail figures that exclude merchants' profits, some transportation and distribution costs, and customs and excise taxes.[29]

After making suitable adjustments, I arrived at the figure of £3.66 for the average annual per capita expenditure on imported goods by colonists *c*.1768–72.[30] This is a very conservative estimate, and, if anything, too low. It is not that far off, however, from the £4 that a Cape May, New Jersey shopkeeper believed to be the amount of foreign goods consumed by each individual in his county at the end of the 1750s.[31]

Alice Hanson Jones has calculated per capita income in 1774 to be in the range of £10.7 to £12.5. Even assuming a figure of £12, each American would still have spent 30.5% of his or her budget on imports from outside his or her colony of residence.[32]

More Consumption of Home-produced Goods in the Colonies?

At the beginning of this chapter, I listed some reasons why consumption of home-produced goods might have been greater in the colonies than in Britain. It turns out, though, that certain conditions that should have promoted home manufacturing did not always work out in the expected way.

The heads of large seventeenth-century plantation households directed the labour of their unfree, mainly male, workers into staple production. Only slowly did grain cultivation and housewifery activities—dairying, drink-making, spinning—develop. Some tasks such as brewing and cheesemaking never did become widespread.

Affluence also turned out to be a two-edged sword. Those in the colonies who had the resources and labour to engage in household production also had the most direct access to market commodities. A lot of commodities consumed daily or on a regular basis—especially grain, drink, and textile products—were bought.

Plentifulness of land did enable more colonists of modest wealth to own livestock than was the case with their English counterparts. A surprisingly large number of households in both plantation and non-plantation colonies, however, did not cultivate much grain. Also, the possession of livestock did not mean that the processing of their by-products—butter, cheese, wool—necessarily flourished.

The supply of meat and milk afforded by the ownership of livestock in combination with the institutions of slavery and indentured servitude, which shrank the proportion of low-income households in the population, clearly meant more of the New World than the Old World diet was home-produced. The grain trade and the merchandising of rum, caffeine drinks, and sugar, however, suggests the degree of American self-sufficiency in food has been exaggerated. In cloth and clothing, the value of what was imported may have equalled or perhaps in many places exceeded the worth of what was made in the home or manufactured locally. Textile products poured into America from Britain decade after decade. Like groceries, they were part of a complex worldwide trade network. The ubiquity of spinning-wheels in the households of many late eighteenth-century American communities testified to the absence of a local cloth industry, not to household self-sufficiency in fabrics.

Plantation and non-plantation colonies had contrasting trends in home production. In the former, there was probably an increase over time as the ratio of men to women dropped, meaning more women were available for housewifery activities, and as declines in the profitability of some staples, such as tobacco, resulted in more grain production. The plantation economy went from being peculiarly dependent on the market to being, in some areas, peculiarly independent of it. On the other hand, in the northern coastal region, especially in New England, the increases in the grain and drink trade seem to indicate that over time more households moved away from certain types of home consumption. The Revolution may have arrested this development for a while. Home production of corn whiskey and homespun were the great material achievements of the break with Britain. It took a major war, however, to accomplish this about-face, and it was not permanent.[33]

Chapter 3

1. Robert V. Wells, *The Population of the British Colonies in America before 1776: A Survey of Census Data*, Princeton, 1975, pp. 299–300.
2. On the demographic characteristics of the colonies see Daniel Scott Smith, 'The Demographic History of Colonial New England', *Journal of Economic History*, 32 (1972), 165–83; 'A Malthusian-Frontier Interpretation of United States Demographic History before c.1815', in Woodrow Borah, Jorge Hardoy, and Gilbert A. Stelter (ed.), *Urbanization of the Americas: The Background in Comparative Perspective*, Ottawa, 1980, pp. 15–24; John J. McCusker and Russell R. Menard, *The Economy of British America, 1607–1789*, Chapel Hill, 1985, pp. 226–30, and the works they cite in their notes to these pages.

3. For example, see the description of the New England migration in John J. Waters, 'Hingham, Massachusetts, 1631–1661: An East Anglian Oligarchy in the New World', *Journal of Social History*, 1 (1968), 359, and in T. H. Breen and Stephen Foster, 'Moving to the New World: The Character of Early Massachusetts Immigration', *William and Mary Quarterly*, 3rd ser. 30 (1973), 198–9.

4. Smith, 'Malthusian-Frontier Interpretation', p. 18.

5. This is true if one looks at all the British colonies including settlements in the West Indies and other islands, Florida, and Canada, or if only the territory covered by the thirteen colonies that revolted against Britain in 1776 is considered. See US Bureau of the Census, *Historical Statistics of the United States, Colonial Times to 1970*, Washington DC, 1975, p. 1168, and McCusker and Menard, *Economy of British America*, pp. 103, 112, 136, 154, 172, and 203.

6. On the sources for the inventory samples and the method of collecting and processing them see Appendix 1.

7. David C. Klingaman, *Colonial Virginia's Coastwise and Grain Trade*, New York, 1975, pp. 98–125.

8. Carville V. Earle, *The Evolution of a Tidewater Settlement System: All Hallow's Parish, Maryland, 1650–1783*, University of Chicago Dept. of Geography, Research Paper 70, Chicago, 1975, pp. 122–3; Lorena Seebach Walsh, 'Charles County, Maryland, 1658–1705: A Study of Chesapeake Social and Political Structure', unpublished Ph.D. dissertation, Michigan State University, 1977, pp. 268, 282–4; Gloria L. Main, *Tobacco Colony: Life in Early Maryland, 1650–1720*, Princeton, 1982, pp. 75–6; and Robert D. Mitchell, *Commercialism and Frontier: Perspectives on the Early Shenandoah Valley*, Charlottesville, 1977, p. 115.

9. Main, *Tobacco Colony*, p. 221.

10. John Wily, *A Treatise on the Propagation of Sheep, the Manufacture of Wool, and the Cultivation and Manufacture of Flax*, Williamsburg, 1765, p. 5. The pattern of cattle being the most frequently owned, pigs second, and sheep third exists in all the Chesapeake local studies using inventories (Earle, *Evolution of a Tidewater Settlement*, p. 122; Walsh, 'Charles County, Maryland', p. 282; Philip David Morgan, 'The Development of Slave Culture in Eighteenth Century Plantation America', unpublished Ph.D. dissertation, University of London, 1977, pp. 36ff.; Main, *Tobacco Colony*, p. 67), with sheep being seldom owned through most of the 17th cent. and growing in popularity in the 18th. Research on faunal remains (animal bones) indicates that frequency of consumption followed the same order: Henry M. Miller, 'Meat, Bones, and Colonists: An Archaeological Perspective on Diet in the 17th Century Chesapeake', paper presented at 'Maryland: A product of Two Worlds', a conference at St Mary's City, Md., 19 May 1984, and William M. Kelso, *Kingsmill Plantations, 1619–1800: Archaeology of Country Life in Colonial Virginia*, Orlando, Fla., 1984, pp. 181–5. On New England and New York see the contributions of Michael and Sophia Coe, Roberta Wingerson, and Joanne Bowen, *Foodways in the Northeast: Dublin Seminar for New England Folklife*, ed. Peter Benes, Boston, 1984.

11. In the 1765 Massachusetts census, 26.7% of inhabitants lived in towns of 2,500 or more. While the population in towns was probably more spread out than in England, the figure is still impressive.

12. Bettye Hobbs Pruitt, 'Self-Sufficiency and the Agricultural Economy of

Eighteenth-Century Massachusetts', *William and Mary Quarterly*, 3rd ser. 41 (1984), 335–9.

13. See Carole Shammas, 'Black Women's Work and the Evolution of Plantation Society in Virginia', *Labor History*, 26 (1985), 5–28 for the evidence behind these generalizations. My 'How Self-Sufficient Was Early America?', *Journal of Interdisciplinary History*, 13 (1982), 247–72 contains a more extensive discussion of what work was involved in producing various goods for household consumption.

14. Main, *Tobacco Colony*, p. 63, suggests the presence of wolves in tidewater Maryland discouraged sheep-raising before 1680. Robert Gross, 'Culture and Cultivation: Agriculture and Society in Thoreau's Concord', *Journal of American History*, 69 (1982), 57, James T. Lemon, *The Best Poor Man's Country: A Geographical Study of Early Southeastern Pennsylvania*, Baltimore, 1976, p. 162, and Earle, *Evolution of a Tidewater Settlement*, p. 124, list mean sheepholding for the areas they studied. Wily, *Treatise on Sheep*, p. 5, complained of the lack of fodder being set aside for sheep in Virginia.

15. On imports of butter and cheese see George Max Schumacher, *The Northern Farmer and his Markets during the Late Colonial Period*, New York, 1975, pp. 130 and 171. On the continuation of these trends into the 19th cent., see Richard Lyle Power, *Planting Corn Belt Culture*, Indianapolis, 1953, pp. 97–100. I owe this latter reference to Anne Firor Scott. On northern dairying, see Joan M. Jensen, *Loosening the Bonds: Mid-Atlantic Farm Women, 1750–1850*, New Haven, 1986, pp. 79–113, and Elinor F. Oakes, 'A Ticklish Business: Dairying in New England and Pennsylvania, 1750–1812', *Pennsylvania History*, 47 (1980), 195–211. On the frequency with which cheese and buttermaking equipment appears in Chester County, Pennsylvania inventories, see Mary Schweitzer, *Custom and Contract: Household Government and the Economy in Colonial Pennsylvania*, New York, 1987, p. 83.

16. David C. Klingaman, 'Food Surpluses and Deficits in the American Colonies, 1768–1772', *Journal of Economic History*, 31 (1971), 558, using figures in Schumacher, *The Northern Farmer*, and James Shepherd and Samuel Williamson, 'The Coastal Trade of the British North American Colonies, 1768–1772', *Journal of Economic History*, 32 (1972), 808.

17. David C. Klingaman, 'The Coastal Trade of Colonial Massachusetts', *Essex Institute Historical Collections*, 108 (1972), 231, using naval lists estimates that in the period 1761–5 Massachusetts imported annually an average of 38,000 barrels of flour and bread, 250,000 bushels of grain, and 3,500 casks of rice. The 1768–72 customs lists shows a net amount of 3,263 tons of flour and bread, 45,046 bushels of wheat, and 187,356 bushels of maize brought in yearly on average (Schumacher, *The Northern Farmer*, p. 152). If we count all the bread and flour as flour (flour heavily predominated where there were separate breakdowns of exports available; and as 1 lb. of bread contained more calories than 1 lb. of flour, we are actually underestimating how many could be fed), and if we assume that there were 196 lb. of flour in a barrel, that per capita cereal needs were 300 lb. of flour a year, with 75% of the population consuming 340 lb. and 25%, mainly infants and small children, consuming half that amount, then about 24,827 people could have been fed. The grain imported, assuming it was mostly corn, as was the case in the 1768–72 period, would have furnished 35,714

people with a yearly supply of cereals. This assumes a per capita consumption level of 7 bushels: 8 bushels of corn allotted to 75% of the population, and half that to the remaining 25%. The number of bushels of wheat needed for per capita yearly consumption was even lower (somewhat over 6 bushels for 75% of the population and 3 bushels for the rest), so 7 is probably a generous figure. When the 60,541 that could be fed by the imported flour and grain is divided by 220,000, the population of Massachusetts proper (Maine's grain imports were calculated separately in the sources used here), then 27.5% of the people were being supplied by imported grain products. If one adds the number that could be fed from the 3,500 casks of rice (525 lb. each), that is, 5,742, then 30.1% of the population would have been provided for. Using the 1768–72 estimates of imported flour, wheat, and maize and dividing by the per capita figures for annual consumption of 300 lb., 5.3 bushels, and 7 bushels respectively, then 59,628 people could have been fed, about 25% of the 235,000 population. On the conversions and yearly estimates of needs see the sources cited in James F. Shepherd and Gary M. Walton, *Shipping, Maritime Trade, and the Economic Development of Colonial North America*, Cambridge, 1972, p. 206; Schumacher, *The Northern Farmer*, p. 26; Pruitt, 'Self-Sufficiency', pp. 343–4; and Peter Bowden, 'Agricultural Prices, Farm Profits, and Rents', in Joan Thirsk (ed.), *The Agrarian History of England and Wales*, iv, Cambridge, 1967, p. 658.

18. John James McCusker, jun., 'The Rum Trade and the Balance of Payments of the Thirteen Continental Colonies, 1650–1775', unpublished Ph.D. dissertation, University of Pittsburgh, 1970, ch. 8.

19. On the use of rum by labourers, women, and slaves, see W. J. Rorabaugh, *The Alcoholic Republic: An American Tradition*, New York, 1979, p. 13; Michael D. Coe and Sophie D. Coe, 'Mid-Eighteenth Century Food and Drink on the Massachusetts Frontier', in Peter Benes (ed.), *Foodways in the Northeast: Dublin Seminar for New England Folklife, Annual Proceedings*, Boston, 1984, p. 45; Daphne Derven, 'Wholesome, Toothsome, and Diverse: Eighteenth Century Foodways in Deerfield, Massachusetts', ibid., pp. 49–50; Michael A. Bellesiles, 'World of the Account Book: The Frontier Economy of the Upper Connecticut River Valley, 1760–1800', paper presented at the 1986 Organization of American Historians meeting, New York; and Historical Society of Pennsylvania, *The Thomas Scully Daybook*, Christiana Bridge, Del., 1773.

20. Joseph Massie, *Reasons Humbly Offered against Laying any further Tax upon Malt and Beer*, London, 1760.

21. Samuel Wharton, 'Observations Upon the Consumption of Teas in North America, 1773', *Pennsylvania Magazine of History and Biography*, 25 (1901), 140, and Benjamin Labaree, *The Boston Tea Party*, New York, 1964, p. 7. Labaree calculates that about 75% of tea was smuggled in.

22. Rorabaugh, *Alcoholic Republic*, pp. 232–3.

23. See Chap. 6.

24. Schumacher, *The Northern Farmer*, pp. 44–5, gives the information on flax importation. Despite its title, Wily's *A Treatise on Sheep* contains a substantial section on linen, but when he came to describe the bleaching of the cloth (p. 50), he had to admit that he himself had never seen it done! The book was published in Williamsburg.

25. Shoes were the only clothing item of note in the pre-Revolutionary coastal trade, and there were no textiles listed: Shepherd and Williamson, 'The Coastal Trade', pp. 788–9. Export of woollens and hats was prohibited by Parliamentary statute, as was the manufacture of hardware. Even before the prohibitions, however, the colonial cloth and clothing industry seems to have had a hard time finding a niche for itself, because of the sophistication of the British and European trade. On the complexity of the average mid-18th-cent. English cloth 'factory', see Richard Rolt, *A New Dictionary of Trade and Commerce*, London, 1756, 1002ʳ. On America, see William R. Bagnall, *The Textile Industries of the United States*, i, Cambridge, Mass., 1893, pp. 1–65; Victor S. Clark, *History of Manufactures in the United States*, New York, 1929, i, 22 ff.; Main, *Tobacco Colony*, p. 184; Linda R. Baumgarten, 'The Textile Trade in Boston, 1650–1700', in Ian M. G. Quimby (ed.), *Arts of the Anglo-American Community in the Seventeenth Century*, Charlottesville, 1975, p. 220; and Gary B. Nash, 'The Failure of Female Factory Labor in Colonial Boston', *Labor History*, 20 (1979), 165–88. A rosier view of the effectiveness of American household cloth production appears in Rolla Milton Tryon, *Household Manufactures in the United States, 1640–1860*, Chicago, 1917, *passim*, and Alice Morse Erle, *Home LIfe in Colonial Days*, New York, 1898. The only occupational lists where I have seen large numbers of weavers are those for Chester County in the period 1720–55. See Schweitzer, *Custom and Contract*, p. 72.

26. The figures for stockings and shoes are based on an average of what was imported during the years 1760, 1765, and 1770 as listed in Elizabeth Boody Schumpeter, *English Overseas Trade Statistics, 1697–1808*, Oxford, 1960, pp. 66 and 69. Beaver hats were often not made of beaver but of some cheaper imitation. The 9% figure was obtained by assuming that 55% of English exports 1768–72 were textile products (£1,389,742), and that an estimated 50% of Scottish exports were also (£151,047—for Scottish import figures see US Bureau of the Census, *Historical Statistics of the United States, Colonial Times to 1970*, Washington DC, 1975, p. 1177: note switched headings for cols. 227 and 228), and that these sums should be increased to account for merchant costs and mark-ups (see n. 30, below). Dividing by the population in 1770, 2,148,076, produces a figure of £1.08, which is 9% of £12, the per capita income of colonists in 1774 (see n. 32, below).

27. This would be the percentage if, as Labaree has calculated (*Boston Tea Party*, pp. 7 ff. and 267), only 25% of the tea brought in from England entered legally, and if the contraband tea was valued at the same rate as the legal tea.

28. McCusker and Menard, *The Economy of British America*, p. 280.

29. See T. S. Ashton's introduction to Schumpeter, *English Overseas Trade Statistics*, pp. 1–14; Shepherd and Walton, *Shipping, Maritime Trade*, Appendix II; George N. Clark, *Guide to English Commercial Statistics, 1696–1782*; Thomas C. Barrow, *Trade and Empire: The British Customs Service in Colonial America, 1660–1775*, Cambridge, Mass., 1967, 134–50; and John McCusker, 'The Current Value of English Exports, 1697 to 1800', *William and Mary Quarterly*, 3rd ser. 28 (1970), 607–28.

30. To arrive at the figure of £3.66 as the average annual expenditure per capita for the thirteen colonies in the years 1768–70, I made the following calculations and assumptions.

A. The total per capita value of goods legally exported into the thirteen colonies amounted to approximately £1.95. The sub-totals are listed by area of origin below.

1. The £ sterling value of legal exports per capita from England = £1.18. (Total export figure given in Table 3.4, divided by 1770 population of 2,148,076.)
2. The £ sterling value of legal exports per capita from Scotland = £0.14. (1768–72 average of £302,095 divided by the 1770 population figure.) See US Bureau of the Census *Historical Statistics of the United States*, p. 1177, as corrected by Jacob Price in 'Communication', *William and Mary Quarterly*, 3rd ser. 34 (1977), 517.
3. The £ sterling value of legal exports per capita from the West Indies = £0.35. (Total export figure in Table 3.4, divided by 1770 population.)
4. The £ sterling value of legal exports per capita from Southern Europe and the Wine Islands = £0.03. (Total export figure in Table 3.4, divided by 1770 population).
5. The £ sterling value of legal exports per capita from the coastal trade of the thirteen colonies = £0.25. To get this figure several corrections had to be applied. First, the figure in Table 3.4 does not include the value of all commodities. Shepherd and Williamson, 'Coastal Trade', p. 799, estimate it is about 90% of the total, which would make the total trade about £794.000. Thus total trade when divided by the 1770 population would amount to £0.37. This figure includes some duplication, however (e.g. rum imported from the West Indies and then sold by New Englanders to another colony). To allow for this, the £0.37 figure has been reduced by one-third to £0.25.

B. Smuggling, especially of tea and sugar products, was not insignificant. In 1768 the colonies were supposedly paying duties on enumerated articles shipped from one colony to another. In 1770, the repeal of the Townshend Duties still left duties on tobacco, wine, sugar, molasses, and tea. Tea was certainly the star of the pre-Revolutionary contraband trade, as molasses had been earlier. It has been estimated that 75–90% of the tea consumed in America was from non-East India Company sources and thus illegal (Labaree, *Boston Tea Party*, p. 7). When the smuggling of sugar products from the non-English West Indies is added to this, plus some smuggling of wine, tobacco, and so forth, it is likely that the illegal trade constituted at least 20% of the total value of exports. So the total per capita figure moves up to £2.44.

C. Mercantile mark-ups also have to be taken into account. The value of British goods did not include all of the transportation costs. Also, English commission merchants often added something to the price of items apart from their 2.5% fee, and colonial merchants marked up the goods by 20% or more to cover costs of freight, insurance, and factorage, and to make a profit. Shopkeepers or pedlars who usually sold the goods to the consumer also had to make a profit and cover the costs of inland transportation. Thus a 50% mark-up on the £2.44 seems sufficiently conservative, and this results in a total average annual expenditure per capita of £3.66 on goods from outside one's own colony. On merchant mark-ups see Jacob Price, *Capital and Credit in British Overseas Trade: The View from the Chesapeake, 1700–1776*, Cambridge, Mass., 1980, pp. 149–

50; Margaret E. Martin, *Merchants and Trade of the Connecticut River Valley, 1750–1820*, Smith College Studies, 24, Northampton, Mass., 1938–9, pp. 138–9; and Arthur Jensen, *The Maritime Commerce of Colonial Philadelphia*, Madison, 1964, pp. 103–6. Jensen's book contains complaints by colonists about English commission merchants raising the prices of the goods they bought from wholesalers. If the wholesaler or retailer in America had to offer credit to his customer, as he often did, then the mark-up would be higher, and some commodities provided a larger margin of profit than others. Total mark-ups could be as high as 100%. Shepherd and Walton, *Shipping, Maritime Trade*, pp. 58–9, suggests that the distribution costs on British products sold to colonial consumers declined substantially during the 18th cent.

31. Quoted in Schumacher, *The Northern Farmer*, p. 141.

32. Alice Hanson Jones, *Wealth of A Nation to Be*, New York, pp. 61–4. The figure of 30.5% is slightly higher than the percentage in my article, 'How Self-Sufficient Was Early America?', pp. 265–6, where I used the year 1768 for most of the estimates, rather than the average for the years 1768–72.

33. On the tremendous push to produce yarn and cloth during the Revolutionary era in order to show independence from Britain see Tryon, *Household Manufactures*, pp. 106 ff.; Rita Susswein Gottesman, comp., *The Arts and Crafts in New York, 1726–76*, New York, 1938, pp. 249–69; and Mary Beth Norton, *Liberty's Daughters: The Revolutionary Experience of American Women, 1750–1800*, Boston, 1980, pp. 155–67.

4

Changes in Consumer Demand

IT is one thing to know what early modern households produced themselves and what they purchased on the market, and quite another to explain changes in those purchases. What I want to investigate in this chapter is demand for two types of goods: groceries and consumer durables—goods for which it is generally conceded that some change in demand occurred during the early modern period. The magnitude of the change and how one explains it, though, are open questions that are best answered, in my opinion, by combining certain modes of analysis favoured by economists with the historian's interest in the substance, rather than the form of consumer demand. We want to know if rising incomes, falling prices, or a switch in the way the household budgetary pie was divided accompanied new demand for a category of expenditure, but we also need to know, specifically, *who* consumed *what* particular good and *when*, in order to know what exact change we are explaining and what its implications are for the standard of living.[1]

Sugar products, caffeine drinks, and tobacco became objects of mass consumption long before 1800, against the objections of contemporary social critics who considered working-class consumption of products formerly classified as luxuries a shameful waste of money. Because most groceries were imports, it is possible to consult trade statistics, which exist from the late seventeenth century on, about the growth in the popularity of these commodities in both England and the thirteen colonies.

Consumer durables, however, were more often manufactured within the country, and so probate inventories, the sources used to study household production, provide the best information. Such goods were, of course, not new in the early modern period, but a certain subgroup of durables, according to available research, did first enjoy a mass market at this time.[2] Interestingly enough, the majority of these goods might be classified as semi-durable, in the sense that, if routinely used, they would require early replacement. Pottery, glassware, paper products, and, in clothing, cheaper linens, cottons, and thin woollen weaves were unlikely to last as long as items made of wood, iron, brass, pewter, skins, fine linens, and heavy woollens. Ironically, as housing—if we are to believe scholars who have looked at vernacular building in this period[3]—grew more sturdy and permanent, furnishings may have become more disposable. What will be focused upon here are the long-term trends in grocery and durables consumption and also, in the case of the latter, the nature of the change in expenditure on durables and the characteristics of those households that altered their demand for that category of good. Did the availability of the new products result in a structural change in expenditure, cutting into spending on production goods or into savings? Or did changes in prices and real wages, as well as substitution of cheaper commodities for dearer ones, account for the difference? If there was a structural change, what can we find out about the household character-istics associated with it?

The Consumption of Groceries in England and America

Probably the most striking development in consumer buying during the early modern period was the mass adoption by the English and the colonials of certain non-European groceries. Table 4.1 documents the

TABLE 4.1 Imports of groceries as a percentage of the total value of imports into England and Wales, 1559–1800

Year	% in groceries
1559[a]	8.9
1663–9[a]	16.6
1700	16.9
1750	27.6
1772	35.8
1790	28.9
1800	34.9

[a] Calculated from Port of London figures, assuming that London's imports represented 80% of the total for the country, and that 5% of the value of imports in the outports were groceries in 1559 and that 10% were in 1663–9.

Sources: Joan Thirsk, *Economic Policy and Projects*, Oxford, 1978, Appendix 1; Ralph Davis, 'English Foreign Trade, 1660–1700', *Economic History Review*, 2nd ser. 7 (1954), Appendix; Elizabeth Boody Schumpeter, *English Overseas Trade Statistics, 1697–1808*, Oxford, 1960, p. 11.

growth in the importation of these commodities into England and Wales between the 1550s and 1800. In 1559 groceries constituted less than 10% of the value of all imports. Pepper was the major mass-consumed grocery. The value of imported dried fruits exceeded that for sugar. No tobacco, tea, coffee, or chocolate came into London at all. In the later seventeenth century the percentage increased to 16.6%, and by the 1770s it amounted to 35.8%. This gain is particularly impressive when it is realized that the prices of the main groceries—tobacco, sugar products, and caffeine drinks—all fell sharply during the period. In fact, the temporary absence of any gain between 1663–9 and 1700 can probably be explained by the big drop in the cost of sugar and tobacco.

Literary evidence abounds about courtiers and London trend-setters smoking tobacco and drinking tea. The question is when did usage of the various grocery products spread beyond the élite and the citizens of the metropolis, and how sustained was the growth over the three centuries under study? For a good to be considered a mass-consumed commodity in any given place, two conditions must be fulfilled. It must be bought by people of varied income levels, and they must be buying it on a more or less regular basis. In this book, a grocery item will be considered to be mass consumed if enough was imported to allow 25% of the adult population to use it at least once daily.[4] In most cases, of course, more than 25% would have used the item, but not every day.

It is appropriate to look first at tobacco, because chronologically it was the first of the new mass-consumed groceries. As it was a crop grown primarily in the thirteen colonies, no accurate records of consumption exist for America, although all the evidence points to it becoming a mass-consumption item almost immediately after becoming a staple. Colonial consumption of the product, it is believed, averaged between 2 lb. and 5 lb. per capita during the eighteenth century.[5]

Large-scale shipments of the plant into England began with the settlement of the Chesapeake. It was also grown, of course, in many other colonies and, despite government laws to the contrary, in England itself until the end of the seventeenth century. The first column in Table 4.2 reports the annual average of pounds per capita of legal imported tobacco retained for home consumption. The figures suggest that at some time in the mid-seventeenth century tobacco, by the standard adopted in this book, became a mass-consumption item. By c.1670, per capita consumption had reached 1 lb.; 2 lb. of tobacco a year would probably allow enough for every person to have a pipeful a day, and so the total imports could furnish 2,700,000 people, or 50% of the total

TABLE 4.2 Tobacco imports for home consumption, England and Wales, 1620–1799ᵃ

Years	Legal imports, lb. per capita (annual average)	Years	Estimated total of legal and illegal lb. per capita (annual average)
1620–29	0.01		
1630–1	0.02		
1669	0.93		
1672	1.10		
1682, 1686–8	1.64		
1693–9	2.21	1698–1702	2.30
1700–9	2.23	1703–7	1.56
1710–19	1.57	1708–12	2.23
1720–9	1.83	1713–17	1.80
1730–9	1.00	1718–22	2.62
1740–9	0.96	1723–7	2.13
1750–9	1.65	1728–32	2.23
1760–9	1.37	1733–7	2.00
1770–9	0.65	1738–42	1.65
1780–9	1.43	1743–7	1.56
1790–9	0.87	1748–52	1.94

ᵃ For the years 1620–94, when only total imports without indication of amount re-exported are available, it was assumed that one-third of the total was retained.

Sources: US Bureau of the Census, *Historical Statistics of the United States, Colonial Times to 1970*, Washington, DC, 1975, pp. 1190–1; Schumpeter, *English Overseas Trade*, pp. 61–2; and Robert C. Nash, 'The English and Scottish Tobacco Trades in the Seventeenth and Eighteenth Centuries: Legal and Illegal Trade', *Economic History Review*, 2nd ser. 35 (1982), 367.

populace with that ration. The actual number of regular smokers fell far below that, yet there was too much tobacco around in 1670 for it to have been all consumed by an élite group. For most of the nineteenth century, per capita figures for British tobacco consumption did not exceed the 1620 level.[6]

If full information on imports and domestic production were available, it might actually turn out that mass consumption began prior to 1650, in the 1630s or 1640s when producer prices dropped to a quarter or less of the original selling-price. During the late 1630s, London alone received an average of 1.8 million lb. legally, enough for 25% of the adult population to smoke 2 lb. annually; much of that was exported, however. Still, allowing for outport totals and domestic production, which was at its height, the total could conceivably have come near to mass-consumption levels. The Stuart government, always on the look-out for a new revenue source, slapped a licensing fee on retailers in 1633, indicating the existence of a nationwide trade.[7]

While tobacco enjoyed the most rapid diffusion of any commodity being studied here, desire for it seemed to wane in the next century. From the figures in the first column of Table 4.2, the reader might well conclude that tobacco usage peaked at the beginning of the eighteenth century at around 2 lb. per capita and turned sharply downward thereafter. Before jumping to that conclusion, however, smuggling must be considered.

The import duties on tobacco were very high in England, exceeding the initial cost of the commodity. After a sizeable increase in duties in 1685, it became particularly worth the while of English traders to evade the tariffs.[8] According to contemporary accounts, they bribed customs officers to declare merchantable tobacco 'damaged', or to enter the weights of hogsheads below their true poundage. Scotland, it appears, engaged in more than its fair share of this type of manœuvring and surreptitiously exported much of the contraband into England. Finally there was the re-exporting of American tobacco to offshore islands or abroad and then smuggling it back for duty-free sale. Re-landing, frequently done via the coast of France, proved difficult during the wartime years 1689–1713, which may explain why the drop in legal imports retained for home consumption did not occur earlier. In the 1730s, the British government considered tobacco smuggling to be such a problem that they sent out troops to deal with those in the trade and proposed changing the import duty to an excise. Public outcry, however, was so enormous that the politicians backed off from making the substitution.[9]

The effects of smuggling and other fraud on per capita consumption figures have been estimated by Robert Nash for the period 1698–1752 and appear in the last column of Table 4.2. His corrections suggest neither a big drop nor an increase during the first half of the eighteenth century, but rather a rate of consumption fluctuating around 2 lb. per capita.

The trend that needs explaining, then, instead of decline, is one of no growth in per capita consumption during the eighteenth century, or at least up to the American Revolution. Without data on individual consumption patterns, however, explanations are not that easy to give. Demographic changes, especially an increase in the proportion of the population aged under 15, would depress per capita figures, but that development would have had little effect until the last few decades of the eighteenth century. The fact, though, that smoking remained largely the preserve of adult males certainly put limitations on its continued growth. In addition, pipe smoking, the primary means of taking tobacco in early modern England, was closely associated with the alehouse. Almost from the beginning, publicans had been the main retailers of both tobacco and pipes, and they offered easy access to affordable amounts of the narcotic. The pipeful became another of the refreshments connected with alehouse social life. When in the later eighteenth century the alehouse fell into decline,[10] it is hard to believe this did not affect smoking habits, too. It is interesting to note that British tobacco consumption only began to rise above early modern levels in the twentieth century with the marketing of the cigarette, a product that attracted many new customers, especially among the female population.

The first of the new mass-consumed groceries, then, gained acceptance almost immediately, but demand for it soon reached a plateau. Sugar, on the other hand, had a slower start, yet once it took off demand continued to grow right into the modern age. The English population was quite familiar with sugar long before the sixteenth century. Their acquaintanceship, however, took the form of small lumps received as gifts or as special treats. High prices, reflecting limited supplies, kept sugar out of the daily life of most people. Even in the sixteenth century, when New World sources caused the real price of the product to drop by two-thirds, 1 lb. of sugar still cost over 1 s., as much as a labourer's wage for two days' work. Over the course of the seventeenth century, the price dropped by half, and between 1700 and 1750 the price went down by another third.[11] Although sugar never became cheap, it eventually furnished nearly as many calories per penny as did meat or beer (see Chapter 5, below).

Table 4.3 gives an indication of the trend in sugar consumption. The earliest figures are for the 1660s and they show annual consumption at about 2 lb. per capita. Probably for a person to be regularly sweetening food or drink with sugar required about 24 lb. a year. *Per capita* consumption actually reached those levels by the third quarter of the eighteenth century. It is not necessary for per capita figures to be that high, however, to consider sugar mass-consumed. By the end of the seventeenth century sugar imports per head were at 4 lb., which would supply nearly 900,000 people, about 25% of the adult population, with

TABLE 4.3 Sugar and rum imports for home consumption, England and Wales, 1663–1799

Years	Sugar, lb. per capita (annual average)	Rum, gal. per capita (annual average)
1663, 1669	2.13	n.a.
1690, 1698–9	4.01	n.a.
1700–9	5.81	<0.01
1710–19	8.23	<0.01
1720–9	12.02	0.02
1730–9	14.90	0.06
1740–9	12.73	0.08
1750–9	16.94	0.14
1760–9	20.20	0.15
1770–9	23.02	0.22
1780–9	21.14	0.17
1790–9	24.16	0.24

Sources: Richard B. Sheridan, *Sugar and Slavery: An Economic History of the British West Indies, 1623–1775*, Baltimore, 1974, pp. 22, 404, 493, and Schumpeter, *English Overseas Trade*, pp. 60–2.

24 lb. Again, in reality, probably a small group consumed more than 24 lb., and most consumed less. Still, the amounts present seem to indicate that sugar was a constant presence in the lives of a significant number of English men and women before 1700. Growth rates per decade during the eighteenth century were over 40% before 1730, spurts that are often attributed to the rising popularity of tea (see below), although tea clearly needed sugar more than vice versa. If tea and other caffeine drinks had not been available, the sweetener probably would have been combined with some other substance.

Much of the imported sugar was consumed in a form other than brown sugar. Some was refined, during which process not only whitened sugar emerged but also molasses, which in turn could be consumed, often by those unable to afford sugar, or made into rum. Then there were the West Indian molasses and rum imports. Apparently little molasses was brought into England after 1720, instead English refiners manufactured it. But rum was another matter. Increasingly large quantities were shipped over the course of the eighteenth century, and traders smuggled in additional amounts to avoid paying duties.[12] Rum was very popular with sailors, and rum punch enjoyed great popularity among the general population. Table 4.3 shows the volume of *legal imports* of rum consumed; by the end of the century it amounted to almost 2 pt. per capita, and that was not counting the rum made from sugar imports or entering as contraband.

The year by year trend in the consumption of sugar products by Americans is not known. Apart from the record of refined sugar imported from England, comprehensive records of West Indian sugar, molasses, and rum importation are not available for the thirteen colonies, and even if they were, the considerable smuggling of sugar and molasses from non-British areas of the Caribbean would have to be taken into account. What can be done is to compare the 1770 consumption of sugar products in England and Wales with the intake in the thirteen colonies, because there are estimates of American consumption for that year. As it happened, the English imported more sugar per capita, 23.7 lb. to America's 14.2, but the latter's much greater intake of rum, as measured by imports of rum and molasses, made the per capita consumption of the thirteen colonies much higher than that of the Mother Country. Americans brought in an estimated 1.7 gal. of rum and 3 gal. of molasses per capita. Meanwhile the per capita drinking of rum by the English, even if they smuggled in an amount of rum equal to the 0.2 gal. they legally imported and imported as much molasses as 0.2 gal., was less than 25% that of the colonists, and their consumption of molasses less than 7%. If all the sugar products consumed are converted into calories, the estimated imports of England yielded 140 calories per capita daily while those of the thirteen colonies totalled 260, almost double the English figure.[13]

Finally there is tea, the most popular of the caffeine drinks among the English in the early modern period. The East India Company began importing Chinese tea in the 1660s, but shipments were sporadic and often of relatively small amounts, because the Company had no direct access to China. Then in 1713 they established trade with Canton, and imports became more regular and voluminous.[14] Of course at no time prior to 1784 did English men and women depend solely on legally imported tea. With duties on the average doubling the net cost of the drink, alternative vendors, mainly the trading companies of other European countries, found a ready market. In some years the tea of the East India Company may have represented as little as 25% of the total imported. The colonies had even less compunction about evading the duties, particularly after the tea duty became embroiled in the general rebellion against British commercial regulation and taxation.[15]

Table 4.4 displays what is known about the amount of tea legally imported into England and America for consumption. The trend in both places is onward and upward, except for the war years in the 1770s. The amounts for most of the years, however, are below what would be expected if tea was being mass-consumed. Thus we need to make some estimate of the level of smuggling.

There were substantial numbers of Londoners consuming tea by 1700, but, given the uncertain supply of even legal tea prior to 1713, the 1720s was probably the first decade in which mass consumption nationwide could have taken place. If it took 2 lb. of tea annually per capita to have a cup a day, and an average of 580,800 lb. of tea were imported each year legally, then less than 300,000 people were supplied. For there to be enough tea to meet the standard of 25% of the adult population being constant consumers, then over three times that number, or 951,000 people, needed a total of 1,902,000 lb., and around two-thirds would

TABLE 4.4 Tea imports for home consumption, 1700–1799 (annual average)

Years	England and Wales		Thirteen Colonies	
	Legal lb. per capita	Estimated legal and illegal lb. per capita	Legal lb. per capita	Estimated legal and illegal lb. per capita
1700–9	0.01	n.a.	n.a.	n.a.
1710–19	0.05	n.a.	n.a.	n.a.
1720–9	0.10	n.a.	n.a.	n.a.
1730–9	0.17	0.50	n.a.	n.a.
1740–9	0.29	1.00	n.a.	n.a.
1750–9	0.49	1.10	0.11	0.43
1760–9	0.81	1.60	0.19	0.80
1770–9	0.70	1.40	0.13	n.a.
1780–9	1.26	2.00	n.a.	n.a.
1790–9	2.00	2.10	n.a.	n.a.

Sources: Schumpeter, *English Overseas Trade*, pp. 60–1; W. A. Cole, 'Trends in Eighteenth-century Smuggling', *Economic History Review*, 2nd ser. 10 (1958), 395–409; Hoh-Cheung Mui and Lorna H. Mui, *The Management of Monopoly*, Vancouver, 1984, pp. 12–14; and Benjamin Woods Labaree, *The Boston Tea Party*, New York, 1964, p. 331 and *passim*.

have had to be smuggled in. During 1720–3, the authorities believed that much of the smuggling involved re-landing of exported cargo. East India Company tea was sold and re-exported to get the customs duty refunded and was then secretly brought back in. In 1724 the government changed the customs duty to an excise or sales tax to thwart this scheme, and sure enough re-exports plunged. In that year the English retained about 1,200,000 lb. After that, foreign companies mobilized to supply duty-free tea to the English. It seems likely that in this decade total imports for consumption were in the area of 1–1.5 million lb., or 3.2 oz. per capita annually. All classes in London and surrounding counties and in major provincial centres may have been regular consumers. It seems, though, that for there to have been a more generally diffused mass consumption throughout England, smuggling in the last five years of the decade would have had to have been on a scale only associated with the 1730s and 1740s, by which time it appears that mass consumption certainly had taken hold throughout much of the country.[16]

In 1745 the government, again re-assessing its duties on tea in the light of rampant smuggling, concluded that in the period 1742–5 about 3 million lb. of tea had been smuggled in. At that point, legal tea may have represented only 25% of the whole, and per capita consumption may have been near 1 lb.

Some hint of what it would have been possible to smuggle in comes from the statistics on what the European companies imported: 8.7 million lb. in 1749–55, 6.8 million lb. during the Seven Years War, 10.3 million lb. in 1763–9, and 13.4 million lb. in 1770–84.[17] It is believed that most of this tea went to English consumers in the British Isles and in America. These amounts probably pushed English consumption per capita up to 2 lb. before the British government removed most of the duty from tea in 1784. Although step by step they reintroduced taxes as the conflict with France developed in the late 1780s and 1790s, by then the high price of foreign tea and wartime conditions made smuggling of little consequence.

In the 1750s, per capita legal imports of tea into the thirteen colonies resembled those into England in the 1720s, but because of a higher ratio of illegal to legal tea, the true level may have been nearer to the total illegal and legal consumption in England during the 1730s, 0.5 lb. per capita—high enough for the colonists to be considered mass consumers of the product. What seems to indicate that substantial smuggling was being carried out is the suspiciously small amount of tea recorded as going into New York and the ports of Pennsylvania. One Philadelphia merchant even admitted that as long as Great Britain imported so little Pennsylvanian wheat, the colonists would continue to seek out Dutch and other European markets and smuggle in foreign supplies of tea on return voyages.[18] The New Englanders, having no such commodity to trade, relied more heavily on the East India Company for supplies. Coffee of course was more popular than tea on the Continent, and it is not difficult to see how after the break with Great Britain, coffee may have become more accessible than tea, especially in the post-1784 period when the English market for smuggled tea collapsed.

Behind the story of rising consumption of both legal and illegal tea during the eighteenth century was a falling real price for the commodity. At the time of the American Revolution, English consumers paid half of what they would have expended in the 1720s for legally imported tea, despite higher duties. After the removal of the tariffs in 1784, the price was halved again. As with sugar, consumers seemed to react to lower prices, although once tea was firmly entrenched in the diet, they did not cut back when prices rose.

The new groceries—tobacco, sugar, and caffeine drinks—seemed to offer something for everyone. Big profits for planters and merchants, relatively light weight for shippers, and cheap energy and relaxation for consumers. In Chapter 5, exactly how the early modern diet in England and America changed as a consequence of this new demand will be examined more closely.

Consumer Durables in England and America

Most of those who write of a revolution in consumption during the early modern period have been more interested in consumer durables than in groceries. Their eye has been caught by the proliferation of small haberdashery items, clothing accessories such as caps and stockings, linens and cottons, and tableware of various sorts in customs records, shopkeepers' accounts, and probate inventories.[19] One has the sense that there must have been a continual increase in spending on these items. It is a little disappointing, therefore, to look at the £ sterling amounts and percentages in Table 4.5 and discover that the trends are not quite as clear-cut as might be desired.

The table shows the percentage of total personal wealth in consumer goods and their mean and median value as revealed in probate inventories from the Midlands and London in England and from the Chesapeake and Massachusetts in America. Both the unadjusted means

TABLE 4.5 Inventoried wealth in consumer goods, England and the Colonies, 1551–1774

Place and years	No. of inventories	Mean wealth constant £[a]	% wealth in consumer goods constant £[a]	Consumer goods mean		Consumer goods median
				Current £[a]	Constant £[a]	Constant £[a]
Oxfordshire, 1551–90	254	67.2	28.0	9.4	18.8	10.4
S. Worcestershire, 1669–70	275	103.8	28.0	29.1	29.1	17.0
S. Worcestershire, 1720–1	305	153.4	19.9	30.5	30.5	17.0
East London, 1661–4	129	72.0	33.6	24.2	24.2	14.0
East London, 1720–9	177	1,293.1	5.6	72.0	72.0	32.0
Virginia, 1660–76	134	139.4	18.7	26.1	26.1	14.3
Virginia, 1724–9	299	104.3	27.1	28.3	28.3	18.3
Virginia & Maryland, 1774	141	310.0	10.7	33.3	25.0	15.0
Essex Co., Massachusetts 1660–73	300	105.2	33.0	34.7	34.7	27.5
Massachusetts, 1774	299	142.8	21.4	39.6	29.8	17.3

[a] All constant and current values are in £ sterling. The base years for the constant values are 1660–74 (England). For method of adjustment see Appendix 1.

Source: See Appendix 1.

and those after correction for inflation over time or for colonial currency (on these adjustments see Appendix 1) are given. Total personal wealth is all wealth except realty. Livestock, crops, merchant stock, financial assets, equipment are considered producer goods. Consumer goods are primarily housewares, furniture, and clothing. Transportation vehicles such as carriages and even a horse are counted if the horse seemed to be kept solely for the conveyance of people. Small stocks of food and pocket money are occasionally included because some inventories simply say 'all the stuff in the kitchen' or 'in the parlour' or 'apparel and purse'. Primarily, though, consumer goods comprised bedding, clothing, linens, brass and pewter, and plate and jewellery. These goods (as Table 4.6 shows, below) made up from 50% to 75% of the total value of consumer goods.

The first measure of consumer demand given in Table 4.5 is that of the percentage of total aggregate personal wealth in consumer goods. As quickly becomes apparent, there is really not a consistently upward trend. First of all, those areas which had a group of very wealthy people—the rich industrialists and financial magnates of East London in 1720–9 and the slaveholders of the Chesapeake in 1774—show a small percentage of wealth in consumer goods, not because they did not have a lot of consumer durables, but because their producer wealth was so great. Cities such as London always produce peculiar results unless wealth is controlled, due to the high concentrations of poor and rich in urban environments and lower per capita rates of leaving probate records. For example, in the 1660s East London (i.e. the East End) appears to have been very poor. In fact it was still very poor in the 1720s, and the only reason for the greater wealth shown in the figures for the 1720s was the increase in the number of very rich individuals, who are disproportionately represented in the sample. If any generalization can be made it is that in most places an average of about 25% of inventoried wealth was devoted to consumer goods. Before 1700 the proportions tended to be somewhat higher than that, and after 1700 they were somewhat lower. Because the post-1700 samples were wealthier than the earlier samples, this trend is not too surprising. All modern consumption studies show richer households spending a smaller proportion of their income on consumption and more on savings. Whether the increase in wealth was real, or an artefact of who left an inventory and who moved in or out of an area, requires a separate study. Suffice it to say that much of the difference in means can be attributed to such factors.

Comparing the changes in wealth with the changes in the proportion in consumer goods within each area indicates that only in the Midlands between the late sixteenth and the late seventeenth century did a rise in mean wealth result in no drop in the proportion of wealth in consumer goods. Everywhere else a drop occurred, although in some areas the decline was not as great as the rise in wealth. All in all, however, there is little confirmation of the theory that the supposed transformation of many producers to consumers led to a dramatic increase in the proportion of wealth devoted to consumer goods. Rather, in the first three-quarters of the seventeenth century, English households kept up the proportion 'invested' in durables when their wealth increased; afterwards it fell. It is interesting to compare the proportions with current data. In a 1979 survey of household wealth in America, survey researchers found 12.3% of wealth devoted to household goods and vehicles. If real estate is subtracted from total wealth in order to make the data comparable to the inventories, the percentage doubles, making it about 25%—very similar to early modern figures on consumer goods.[20]

In some ways, the means and medians, despite the inflation problem, are a more reliable guide to how accumulation of consumer goods was progressing. The means are reported in both current £ sterling and in constant terms, after adjustments for inflation. There appears to have been a considerable increase in the real amount spent on consumer goods between the late sixteenth and the late seventeenth century, although that is based on only one sixteenth-century sample. In Oxfordshire in the period 1551–90, the mean adjusted amount spent on consumer goods was £18.8, whereas in Worcestershire and elsewhere at *c*.1670 it rose to between £24.2 and £34. But there it seemed to stay during the eighteenth century apart from the idiosyncratic figure for East London. Because, as in that case, a few high values often distort means, it seemed advisable to look at medians as well. The trend, though, is essentially the same. The sixteenth-century median is still noticeably lower, while there is little difference between those for the late seventeenth and the eighteenth century. The median falls between £14 and £18 in seven of the samples. East London's is higher (£32), but not as spectacularly so as when means are used. The median for the Massachusetts inventories of the 1660s to 1670s (£27.5) also exceeds that range. This Essex County sample is a great deal more homogeneous than the rest. Among the Puritan immigrants there were few poor, not many rich, and not many single decedents. They had quite substantial holdings of household wares (one-third of their wealth was in consumer goods), perhaps as a protection against uncertain supply. Another study of consumption patterns in

TABLE 4.6 The value of major categories of inventoried consumer goods, England and the Colonies, 1551–1774

Place and years	Bedding			Linen			Apparel		
	No. of inventories	Mean	Median	No. of inventories	Mean	Median	No. of inventories	Mean	Median
Oxfordshire, 1551–90	254	4.8	2.4	253	2.8	2.4	196	2.4	1.4
S. Worcestershire, 1669–70	267	6.9	5.0	265	2.3	1.0		2.8	2.0
S. Worcestershire, 1720–1	260	6.8	4.0	262	2.8	1.0	31	3.2	2.0
East London, 1661–4	123	5.5	3.0	123	2.1	1.0	87	3.6	1.9
East London, 1720–9	61	8.2	4.0	94	5.3	1.0	71	6.6	3.0
Virginia, 1560–76	128	7.5	5.1	132	1.2	1.0	94	3.2	2.0
Virginia, 1724–9	298	7.9	5.8	297	0.8	0.0	297	1.9	0.8
Virginia, 1774	138	9.8	7.5	138	1.0	0.0	94	5.2	2.3
Essex Co., Massachusetts, 1660–73	285	9.2	7.5	291	3.9	2.5	276	5.8	5.0
Massachusetts, 1774	290	6.3	4.5	290	2.0	0.8	282	5.0	3.0

Place and years	Pewter & Brass			Plate & Jewellery			Total of means for all 5 categories	% all 5 categories constitute of consumer goods mean
	No. of inventories	Mean	Median	No. of inventories	Mean	Median		
Oxfordshire, 1551–90	252	2.2	1.4	252	0.8	0.0	13.0	69.1
S. Worcestershire, 1669–70	266	2.4	2.0	270	1.3	0.3	15.7	54.0
S. Worcestershire, 1720–1	253	2.4	1.6	260	1.1	0.0	16.3	53.4
East London, 1661–4	123	2.5	1.0	124	2.5	0.3	16.2	66.9
East London, 1720–9	87	1.6	1.0	145	23.8	1.0	45.5	63.2
Virginia, 1660–76	133	1.6	1.0	132	0.9	0.1	14.4	55.1
Virginia, 1724–9	295	2.4	1.7	296	1.7	0.0	14.7	51.9
Virginia, 1774	139	1.0	0.8	141	1.7	0.0	18.7	74.8
Essex Co., Massachusetts, 1660–73	292	2.1	1.7	300	0.4	0.0	21.4	61.7
Massachusetts, 1774	293	1.4	0.8	295	4.4	0.0	19.1	64.1

[a] All values are in constant £ sterling, base years 1660–74.

Source: See Appendix 1.

colonial Massachusetts also finds that in this period the amount was greater than in subsequent decades.[21]

A glance at the amounts invested in the main categories of commodities comprising consumer goods (Table 4.6) provides some insight into the reason the total failed to increase during the late seventeenth and the eighteenth century. The adjusted means and medians suggest that although the money put into bedding (mattress, pillows, curtains, blankets, and coverlets as well as the bed frame) and clothing may have been increasing, the other goods, bed and table linen, brass and pewter, and plate and jewellery, show no positive movement, particularly in the eighteenth century. The decline in brass and pewter is quite marked. With plate and jewellery the means hold up but the medians fall. With bed and table linen the median amounts spent by Oxfordshire decedents in the late sixteenth century were not surpassed except by seventeenth-century Essex County Massachusetts wealthholders, and in most cases the medians and the means moved lower. Some appraisers lumped bed linen in with bedding, but this was done throughout the period under study, so it should not affect the trend.

There are several possible explanations for the pattern of spending on durables found in Tables 4.5 and 4.6. One is that there is something the matter with the data. American probate records do not begin until the mid-seventeenth century and the English inventories become scarce by the 1730s. A lot of different places are used in charting the trend. Also, errors could creep into the adjustments for inflation and different currencies.

The trouble with that explanation is that most of the other researchers who have used inventories to analyse trends in the consumption of durables have come up with similar findings. A study of rural Pennsylvania from 1690 to 1735 reports that the average proportion of wealth in consumer goods during this period varied between 25% and 30%, with little clear direction up or down. Lois Green Carr and Lorena Walsh report a continual rise in the number of Chesapeake consumer goods that could be called amenities, yet no increase in the amount of money devoted to consumer durables. Table 4.7 shows the mean amount invested in consumer goods in three colonial areas—rural Pennsylvania, Massachusetts, and Maryland—and these figures also parallel the results recorded in Tables 4.5 and 4.6. In both the northern colonies, where in the beginning religious dissidents with some property constituted a large portion of the population and family migration generally prevailed, the value of consumer goods started out very high. In the 1690s, a decade after the founding of Pennsylvania, inventoried decedents held an average of £29.9 in consumer goods, and in Massachusetts in the period 1656–75 the mean reached £33, the same as reported in Table 4.5 for Essex County alone. By contrast, inventories from a Maryland, plantation colony, like those from Virginia, started out with a low amount, not quite £19. In the following decades there was a rise, just as there was a fall in the amounts registered in Pennsylvania and Massachusetts, until there was something of a convergence. The trend over time in the eighteenth century, however, is not clear at all. Nor do series for Massachusetts and Maryland that stretch into the middle and late eighteenth century give any firmer indication of direction.[22]

There are no comparable studies for England in the early modern period that follow the trend in the mean amount devoted to consumer goods from the seventeenth to the eighteenth century in the same area. One study covering four villages in north Warwickshire during the seventeenth century furnishes the percentage of wealth devoted to consumer goods in various decades. In contrast to what has been found in colonial America, this study supports the hypothesis that the percentage of wealth in consumer goods rose sharply over the century. Consumer goods constituted 27% of wealth at the beginning of the period, and a surprisingly high 48% at the end. A larger study of the domestic goods of English peasant labourers found a much smaller rise (10%) between 1560 and 1640.[23] Also, for this impoverished group, the mean value of wealth in domestic goods increased only slightly over what can be attributed to inflation. One might speculate that the increase in the percentage of wealth devoted to consumer goods in peasant labourers' inventories reflects the reduction in livestock holdings. Producer goods became a smaller proportion of total wealth and consumer goods a greater part. The waged work that replaced livestock-holding and agricultural production generated credits that should have compensated for the disappearance of animals from the inventory. Credits, however, were very poorly reported in comparison to other assets. The slightly higher figures, therefore, could be a result of a shift from producer to consumer, or simply an artefact of the measurement error in the financial assets component of total wealth.

If one looks at the means found in other inventory studies of particular areas and/or more limited periods of time where all the inventoried deceased were included, not just labourers, they are more in keeping with those found in the English Midlands areas I sampled. In Bedfordshire during the second decade of the seventeenth century, the unadjusted mean was £14.9, right between the mean for Elizabethan Oxfordshire (£9.4) and that for Worcestershire in 1669–70 (£28.0). Samples from all over England in the period 1675–1725 give a mean for household goods of £23. The amount does not, it seems, include clothing. If £5 were added to compensate for the omission of clothing, the mean would be £28, very near the figures given in Table 4.5 for rural areas in the 1660s–70s and the 1720s.[24]

So although it is always possible that the data for one reason or

TABLE 4.7 Other studies of mean inventoried wealth in consumer goods, the Colonies, 1650–1753

Years	No. of inventories	Mean (£ sterling)
Rural Pennsylvania		
1690–9	64	29.9
1700–4	73	20.8
1705–9	70	25.1
1710–14	82	24.2
1715–19	124	23.2
1720–4	91	19.1
1725–9	122	22.6
1730–4	157	21.0
Massachusetts, estates of young fathers		
1650–66	33	31.3
1667–75	33	35.5
1676	31	25.9
1677–82	32	29.8
1683–9	35	24.8
1690–2	32	42.9
1693–6	38	28.3
1697–1702	30	30.4
1703–8	33	26.5
1715–18	33	29.7
1719–24	38	46.6
1725–8	34	37.2
1729–32	33	37.9
1733–5	34	34.8
1736–40	35	27.4
1741–5	34	21.1
1746–50	33	35.1
1751–3	41	43.8

cont.

Massachusetts and Maryland[a]

1656–75	Massachusetts	33.0
1656–75	Maryland	18.8
1676–96	Massachusetts	27.5
1676–96	Maryland	23.2
1697–1702	Massachusetts	28.5
1697–1702	Maryland	26.6
1703–12	Massachusetts	33.3
1703–12	Maryland	28.4
1713–19	Massachusetts	22.7
1713–19	Maryland	26.7

[a] Weighted to approximate wealthholding population.

Sources: Jack Michel, ' "In a Manner and Fashion Suitable to their Degree": A Preliminary Investigation of the Material Culture of Early Rural Pennyslvania', *Working Papers from the Regional Economic History Research Center*, 5 (1981), 11; Gloria L. Main, 'The Standard of Living in Colonial Massachusetts', *Journal of Economic History*, 43 (1983), 105, and 'The Standard of Living in Maryland and Massachusetts, 1656–1719', unpublished paper, tables 2 and 3.

another are distorted, the weight of the evidence tends to buttress the arguments that the proportion of wealth in consumer goods did not move steadily upwards during the early modern period, and that after some rise in the sixteenth and early seventeenth century, the mean amount in consumer goods did not show much upward movement either, and in some areas might even have turned slightly downwards.

A second possibility is that there was in fact no boom in consumer durables as there was in groceries. Again, though, the sheer number of studies of English and American inventories that show higher consumption after 1660 of a whole array of textile, paper, metal, and pottery products (see Chapter 6), not to mention the work on the growth of rural manufacturing, makes this hard to believe.

Two other possible and not mutually exclusive explanations remain. One is that inventories are a poor source for discovering growth in many of the new durables, because of the latter's semi-durable nature. Inventories only record goods still owned by the person at death. They cannot measure the rate of turnover in goods over a lifetime. Many of the new consumer goods were of a more ephemeral nature than earlier products. The textiles were lighter, whether made of the new draperies, linen, or cotton. Chapbooks and other paper products might not last for many years. Pottery could be destroyed much more readily than wood or brass and pewter. Also small items such as needles, combs, and the like might be too insignificant to be inventoried, and were easily lost. There is a tendency to think of the twentieth century as the time when disposable products came into being, but the early modern population may have experienced at least as big a shift to impermanent objects. The problem with this line of argument is that it is not easily provable with the evidence available. None the less, it merits further consideration.

An explanation that *can* be investigated is the possibility that the cost of goods declined, enabling consumers to buy more and yet invest no more—or even, in some cases, less—in durables or semi-durables. There are two ways that this could have happened, and again, they are not mutually exclusive. The first is that the price of the same manufactured good may have dropped over the course of the early modern period, just as we know that the price of some groceries did; and the second is that consumers may have substituted new, cheaper goods for the products they have formerly used.

To try to understand what might have been happening to prices, let us look at the appraisals of the most important semi-durable, cloth, in the inventories of retailers (shopkeepers and pedlars) during the early modern period.[25] Establishing the prices of textiles is an extremely tricky business, because usually one cannot be sure of the grade of the material. Also the width of the bolts could vary. The trends I found, however, were so consistent among all the fabrics that it seemed impossible for them to be simply the result of quality or size differences.

Table 4.8 shows both current prices (the actual prices appearing on the inventory at the time) and constant prices (the deflated prices) in England from the late sixteenth century to the early eighteenth for wools, linens, cottons, and blends. The woollens are of two basic types, the older, heavier draperies—broadcloth, kerseys, and friezes—and the lighter woollens, the new draperies—serge, baize, flannels, and stuffs—that tended to be less expensive. Very limited kinds of linens or linen-like materials (whether made from flax, cotton, nettles, or of some blend) were available in the sixteenth century, but the varieties, particularly of cheaper grades, greatly increased thereafter. As Table 4.8 indicates, neither blue linen nor Scotch cloth, both very inexpensive fabrics, show up in sixteenth-century retailers' inventories, but they constantly appear in subsequent periods.

It can be seen from Table 4.8 that in England, all fabrics dropped in price between the late sixteenth and the late seventeenth century, with the sole exception of frieze. Even if one converted back to current prices, very few of the textiles were as costly in the late seventeenth century as

TABLE 4.8 Average prices of select textiles in retailers' inventories, England, 1578–1738

Type of cloth	Constant prices (base 1660–99) in pence (*d.*) per yard[a]			
	Late 16th cent.	Early 17th cent.	Late 17th cent.	early 18th cent.
Woollens				
Heavy broadcloths	138	72	56	54
Kerseys	55	41	21	25
Frieze	17	15	22	21
Serge	41	24	24	19
Baize	36	34	18	10
Flannel	17	11	10	15
Stuffs	n.a.	13	9	9
Linens, etc.				
Fine Holland	83	46	41	32
Linen	24	22	11	13
Blue linen	n.a.	13	10	10
Osnaburg	10	10	8	8
Fustian	31	13	8	10
Calico	28	13	12	24
Scotch cloth	n.a.	17	13	10

[a] To obtain current prices for textiles in late 16th century (1560–99) divide constant price by 1.72, for early 17th century (1600–59) divide by 1.1. The average of Phelps Brown and Hopkins price index for early 18th century (1700–39) is nearly identical to the average for the late 17th century (1600–99), so no correction has been made to that column to obtain constant prices. There are 12 pence to a shilling, 20 shillings to a pound.

Sources: Retailers' inventories in *Durham Wills and Inventories*, comp. William Greenwell, pt. 2, Surtees Society, 38 (1860); *Wills and Inventories from the Archdeaconry of Richmond*, comp. James Raine, Surtees Society, 26 (1854); Margaret Spufford, *The Great Reclothing of Rural England*, London, 1984; *Chesterfield Wills and Inventories, 1521–1603*, ed. J. M. Bestall and D. V. Fowkes, Derbyshire Record Society, 1 (1977); C. B. Phillips and J. H. Smith, *Stockport Probate Records, 1578–1619*, Gloucester, 1985; J. J. Bagley, 'Matthew Markland, A Wigan Mercer: The Manufacture and Sale of Lancashire Textiles in the Reigns of Elizabeth I and James I', *Lancashire and Cheshire Antiquarian Society*, 68 (1958), 45–68; D. G. Vaisey, 'A Charlbury Mercer's Shop, 1623', *Oxoniensia*, 31 (1966), 107–16; *Probate Inventories of Lichfield and District, 1568–1680*, ed. D. G. Vaisey, Stafford, 1969; *Sedgley Probate Inventories, 1614–1787* ed. John S. Roper, Dudley, n.d. mimeo; *Yorkshire Probate Inventories, 1542–1689*, ed. Peter C. D. Brears, Yorkshire Archaeological Society, 134 (1972); *Newmarket Inventories, 1662–1715*, ed. Peter May, Newmarket, 1976; *Yeomen and Colliers in Telford: Probate Inventories for Dawley, Lilleshall, Wellington, and Wrockwardine, 1660–1750*, ed. Barrie Trinder and Jeff Cox, London, 1980; *Farm and Cottage Inventories of Mid Essex, 1635–1748*, ed. Francis W. Steer, Chelmsford, 1950; *Devon Inventories of the Sixteenth and Seventeenth Centuries*, ed. Margaret Cash, Devon and Cornwall Record Society, n.s. 11 (1966).

they had been at the end of the sixteenth. Most of the declines were quite dramatic: the price of broadcloth fell by about 50% between the late sixteenth and early seventeenth century, and then by another 20% by the late seventeenth century; the price of baize was down 50% by the late seventeenth century, and that of flannel fell only a little less sharply. The prices of non-woollens behaved similarly. By the late seventeenth century, the price of fustian (a linen and cotton blend) had plummeted to 26% of its sixteenth-century value in constant terms, and that of calico had declined by 57%. Considering that we know that the amount of money invested in consumer goods also rose considerably during the same hundred-year period, most households would have had no trouble in greatly increasing their consumption of textile products.

What happened in England between the late seventeenth and early eighteenth century is less clear. A few of the fabrics—serge, baize, and Scotch cloth, plus fine Holland linen—continued to drop in price. Calico, because of British policy limiting the importation of printed cotton cloth, soared in price, while the cost of the remainder of the textiles stayed constant or rose only slightly. The biggest development in the English textile trade at the turn of the century was the appearance of ready-made garments in the stock-in-trade of retailers.[26] Prior to 1700, finished textile goods were limited to accessories such as stockings and hand-kerchiefs. Few shopkeepers' inventories listed coats, suits, breeches, shirts, petticoats, gowns, and so forth. After 1700 they become more common, however (at least in the inventories of English retailers in the South of England), and they are priced generally cheaper than the same articles listed under clothing in personal inventories from earlier periods. The appearance of these finished goods and the fact that there seem to have been more retailers stocking the cheaper materials leads one to suspect that still further accumulations of textile products by individuals in the first quarter of the eighteenth century.

Because English inventories more or less cease after the 1730s, the records of the estates of later retailers are not available. The situation in the colonies can throw some light on what may have occurred, however. Table 4.9 compares prices in inventories from Essex County, Massachusetts in 1660–73 and in 1774. Because of distance from markets and primitive mercantile links, many seventeenth-century Massachusetts families stockpiled an assortment of cloth—something that occurred much less often in England. Consequently the prices for 1660–73 come from the inventories of both retailers and ordinary citizens. For the 1774 prices, though, only the retailers' inventories were used. The drop in

TABLE 4.9 Average prices of select textiles in Colonial inventories, Essex County, Massachusetts, 1660–73 and 1774

Type of cloth	Constant prices (base 1660–69) in pence (*d.*) per yard[a]	
	1660–73	1774
Woollens		
Heavy broadcloths	133	109
Kerseys	58	27
Serge	55	27
Baize	45	12
Penistone	38	12
Flannel	28	10
Stuff	25	11
Linens, etc.		
Linen	20	14
Osnaburg	16	5
Fustian (all cotton/linens)	25	8
Calico	18	15
Homemade	28	8

[a]Values in English pence as in Table 4.7. Base years in that table cover more of the later 17th century because prices go up to 1699. To obtain current Massachusetts prices multiply 1660–73 prices by 1.2; and multiply 1774 prices by 1.33 to get current £ sterling prices, and by 1.33 again to obtain Massachusetts current prices.

Source: See Appendix 1.

prices between the two periods is even more dramatic than that seen in the English evidence. Obviously some of the high cost of cloth in the late seventeenth century can be attributed to Massachusetts being on the fringe of the commercial world. Still, homemade cloth in current as well as constant prices was also expensive compared to prices in 1774. Furthermore, the extent of the drop suggests more was at work than better trade networks and lower transaction costs. The lower prices of many fabrics in 1774 compared to English prices in the early eighteenth century indicate prices may have fallen further in the middle of the century.

Clearly, the evidence on the prices of textile products in Tables 4.8 and 4.9 suggests that part of the reason consumers could own more new goods without raising the percentage of wealth in consumer goods or the amount of real £ sterling invested in them is that they had to pay less for these commodities than did earlier generations. Prices declined, and the popularity of thinner, less expensive fabrics—lighter wools, linens, and cottons—and in the eighteenth century, read-made garments, also brought the costs down. What remains to be investigated is the extent to which other commodities shared this price history. It is known that the glass and pottery tableware people substituted for heavy metals such as pewter cost much less per piece—anywhere from a half to one-twelfth the price—and therefore the value of tableware in the inventories would be substantially lower, even if the cost over the lifetime of the individual might be the same or higher.[27]

The Economic and Social Characteristics of Early Modern Consumers

Up to this point I have considered trends in consumption, but I have not paid much attention to the characteristics of those doing the consuming. What type of people spent more on consumer goods? Because probate records contain a lot of information about those leaving estates, it is possible to evaluate the role of a number of economic and social factors that affected the consumption of durables by individuals.

When economists look at current consumer demand on the individual or micro level, they usually focus on the relationship between income or total expenditure on the one hand and spending on consumer goods on the other. They measure the rate at which consumer expenditure goes up or down as family income varies. This figure is known as the 'income elasticity of demand'. An elasticity of 1.00 (unity) implies that both income and consumer expenditure are rising or falling at the same rate; elasticities over 1.00 denote consumer demand increasing or decreasing at a faster rate; and elasticities under 1.00 indicate increases or decreases in consumer demand at a slower rate. Because in the long run it is impossible for households to spend more than they make, the income elasticity of total consumer expenditure is under 1.00, although certain categories of goods might exceed unity.[28]

Inventories, because they measure wealth rather than expenditure, cannot furnish figures that are directly comparable to income elasticities. They list stocks rather than flows, and perishable goods (most notably food) are generally excluded.[29] Still, this source can provide some important information about the demand for consumer durables. First, inventories can reveal the degree to which wealth determined the level of consumption, and to what extent other variables came into play. Besides just measuring the effect of wealth, though, something can also be learned about the form the relationship took. The notion that the pre-industrial consumer was not much of a consumer at all, that the peasantry had a 'traditional' outlook on expenditure and after basic needs were met showed very little proclivity towards further investment in consumer durables, can be expressed in diagrammatic form and tested with the inventory data.

Figure 4.1 displays the three possible forms—horizontal, linear, and proportional—that the wealth–consumer durables relationship could take. The top diagram *a* corresponds to the putative behaviour of the 'traditional consumer'. At a certain point, additional wealth stops raising

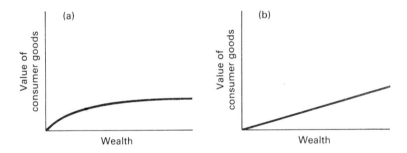

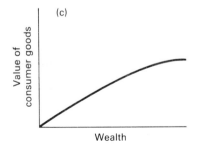

FIG. 4.1. Possible relationships between wealth and value of consumer goods

the value of consumer goods. Diagram *b* shows a linear relationship: with each increment in wealth, the value of consumer goods rises by the same amount as it rose from the previous increment. Not even modern consumers are believed to indulge in that much consumption, because it would violate the notion that the affluent put a higher percentage of their wealth into investment. The third possible relationship is one in which the value of goods continues to climb with increasing wealth, but with a lower rate of growth than that of wealth. Progressively, more additional money is spent on producer goods or savings as wealth levels climb. For example, a family with a total wealth of £10,000 might hold £9,000 in consumer goods, but if, suddenly, their wealth shot up to £20,000 through a bigger salary increase or a legacy, the amount of that increment diverted to consumer goods might not reach £18,000 or 90% of total wealth. A greater proportion of the increment might be put into savings. What might stay constant, however, is the percentage increase in the value of consumer goods. So the £9,000 devoted to consumer goods might increase by 90%, making the value of consumer goods rise to £17,100 or 85.5% of total wealth. Furhter increments would keep the value of consumer goods increasing by 90%, but the proportion of wealth devoted to consumer goods would progressively shrink. Such a relationship can be expressed as the curved line in diagram *c*, and this is assumed to be the modern form. Of course, empirical tests of this modern relationship have been made with income and expenditure data, not stocks of wealth.

In order to see which of the models best describes the relationship between the value of consumer goods and wealth in the English and colonial inventories, three bivariate regressions must be run for each sample. The first is a simple linear regression of the two variables, diagram *b* in Figure 4.1. The second is what is known as a semi-log transformation, where wealth is logged and, if the data actually resemble diagram *a*, the transformation should provide the best fit. If instead the relationship in the data is that of diagram *c*, then a double log transformation where both variables are logged should conform to the contours of the data.

Table 4.10 gives the R^2 values, the measure of goodness of fit, for the three forms of the regression.[30] None of the samples show the semi-log form of the traditional consumer giving the best fit. The highest values are, with a couple of exceptions,[31] the double log form, meaning that consumer durables tended to keep increasing as people got wealthier, but the percentage of their wealth devoted to consumer goods tended to be

TABLE 4.10 A comparison of three forms of the regression of wealth on the value of consumer goods

Place and years	No. of inventories	R²			Elasticities	
		Linear	Semi-log	Double log	Semi-log	Double log
Oxfordshire, 1551–90	254	0.816	0.333	0.601	0.333	0.68
S. Worcestershire, 1669–70	275	0.566	0.398	0.624	0.398	0.66
S. Worcestershire, 1720–1	305	0.582	0.334	0.571	0.334	0.62
East London, 1661–4	129	0.895	0.454	0.575	0.454	0.67
East London, 1720–9	177	0.451	0.334	0.587	0.334	0.56
Virginia, 1660–76	134	0.450	0.582	0.680	0.582	0.73
Virginia, 1724–9	299	0.629	0.528	0.793	0.528	0.82
Virginia & Maryland, 1774	141	0.481	0.411	0.618	0.411	0.59
Essex Co., Massachusetts, 1660–73	300	0.262	0.508	0.665	0.508	0.71
Massachusetts, 1774	299	0.214	0.383	0.667	0.383	0.62

Source: see Appendix 1.

less. What in modern studies of consumer behaviour most often is the relationship between income and consumer expenditure also turns out to describe best the relationship between wealth and consumer goods in the early modern period.

Table 4.10 also demonstrates the strength of the relationship between wealth and consumer goods. The R^2s for the double log form indicate that in most of the places sampled, whether in the colonies or in England, and whether in Tudor times or in the eighteenth century, from 60% to 67% of the variation in the value of consumer goods could be attributed to wealth. This might seem like common sense, except that it would not be the case if the traditional consumer model was the true one. In fact, the R^2s for all the samples are so similar to one another that only the statistic for Virginia in 1724–9, 0.793 (indicating that 79.3% of the variation in the value of consumer goods could be attributed to wealth) requires any special discussion. Probably the reason why even more of the variation in consumer goods can be accounted for by wealth in that sample is that the inventories used have poor coverage of financial assets, which seem often to have less of a relationship to consumer goods than do other kinds of producer goods.[32]

Also included in Table 4.10 are the elasticities for the double log form of the regression equation. For the most part they fall (when rounded off) between 0.6 and 0.7. That is, as wealth rose by 1%, the value of consumer goods rose by 0.6% or 0.7%.[33] There is not any clear-cut variation over time. Mainly the differences seem related to the wealth distribution in the samples. The East London sample of 1720–9 included such a group of wealthy estates that the gap between wealth increases and consumer goods increases was wider. The result is a lower elasticity figure. With Virginia in the 1720s the elasticity is high (0.8 rounded off), for the same reason that R^2 was high, the omission in the inventories of most wealth in financial assets. As regards long-term trends though, the figures give no indication of a rise in the elasticity.

While it is clear that wealth is by far the most important determinant of the value of consumer durables, modern theories of consumption, historical descriptions of economic behaviour, and the R^2s of the bivariate regressions themselves suggest that other factors may have been involved as well. 30% to 40% of the variation has not been explained by wealth. What else might have increased the amount people spent on consumer goods in the early modern period?

In the budget studies done by economists, household size is usually the most important variable after income in predicting consumer behaviour.

In the expenditure studies, it tends to have a positive effect on food expenditure and a negative effect on spending on some durables.[34] The inventory data on wealth stocks, however, cannot furnish information about consumer preferences for food versus durables. Rather this source distinguishes between the amount of wealth in consumer goods versus the investment in producer goods including financial assets. One would expect an increase in family size to have raised the amount of consumer durables, because more household goods would be required to meet the needs of additional children, servants, and relatives.

Market accessibility—whether a person lived in a frontier area or a remote country village as opposed to a market town or city—is believed by many historians and development economists to have had a big effect on consumer expenditure.[35] Households in out-of-the-way places would be less tied to market commodities and more self-sufficient, which would have the effect of boosting their stocks of producer goods, while lowering the value of consumer goods they possessed. Scholars have sometimes overestimated the self-sufficiency of rural householders. None the less, household production in village and town did assume different forms.

Related to these theories, but not identical to them, are ideas about the role of social class and occupational status. Sociologists and social historians have been inclined to posit an effect for social class beyond that caused by income or wealth differences, although unfortunately they do not always hold the latter constant before making claims for the former. Economists tend to be less enamoured of social class explanations and look more exclusively at income. Still, one finding regarding occupation has consistently emerged out of economic research: the comparatively small percentage of income devoted to consumption by twentieth-century farmers.[36] Occupation, therefore, does deserve consideration as a possible influence on consumer expenditure.

Finally, there is the question of the impact of education on consumption. Current research argues that education makes for more efficient consumers, which implies, other things being equal, that this variable should decrease the amount spent on consumer goods.[37] On the other hand, it might well be argued that in the early modern period education aided people in market transactions and whetted the appetite for consumer goods.

Tables 4.11 and 4.12 present the results of the multiple regressions run on the English and colonial data, respectively, to test these various theories. The coefficients, significance levels, and the R^2s for all the variables in all the samples are shown. (The means, standard deviations,

TABLE 4.11 Determinants of the amount of inventoried wealth in consumer goods[a] for England (OLS Regression Coefficients[b])

	Oxfordshire, 1550–90	S. Worcestershire, 1669–70	S. Worcestershire, 1720–1	East London, 1661–6	East London, 1720–9
No. of inventories	247	217	219	120	161
Variables[c]					
Wealth (ln)	0.490	0.517	0.483	0.548	0.378
	(0.000)	(0.000)	(0.000)	(0.000)	(0.000)
Household size (ln)	0.606	0.472	0.610	0.381	0.592
	(0.000)	(0.000)	(0.000)	(0.000)	(0.000)
Town residency	0.072	0.083	0.084	n.a.	n.a.
	(0.401)	(0.426)	(0.358)		
Occupational status élite	n.a.	0.123	0.196	0.036	0.752
		(0.413)	(0.337)	(0.889)	(0.002)

				n.a.	n.a.
farmer	-0.074	-0.382	-0.291		
	(0.530)	(0.000)	(0.030)		
tradesman	0.087	-0.241	-0.208	0.149	0.232
	(0.494)	(0.066)	(0.089)	(0.328)	(0.105)
widow	0.112	-0.157	-0.153	0.085	0.246
	(0.382)	(0.182)	(0.186)	(0.623)	(0.144)
Book-owner	0.503	0.029	0.026	0.149	0.332
	(0.119)	(0.576)	(0.807)	(0.096)	(0.014)
Constant	0.871	0.237	0.047	0.099	0.066
Adjusted R²	0.753	0.722	0.731	0.626	0.705

[a] The dependent variable, the £ sterling amount in consumer goods, is in natural log (ln) form.

[b] The numbers in parentheses are significance levels (t test).

[c] The independent variables town residency and book-ownership are dummy variables coded 1 and 0. The categories of the variable occupational status are also dummied with 1, 0 codes, with labourers and those whose status was missing constituting the reference category. For means, standard deviations, and correlations, see Appendix 2.

Source: see Appendix 1.

TABLE 4.12 Determinants of the amount of inventoried wealth in consumer goods[a] for the Colonies (OLS Regression Coefficients[b])

	Virginia, 1660–76	Virginia, 1724–9	Virginia & Maryland, 1774	Essex Co., Massachusetts, 1660–73	Massachusetts, 1774
No. of inventories	129	299	139	263	269
Variables[c]					
Wealth (ln)	0.548	0.713	0.438	0.587	0.450
	(0.000)	(0.000)	(0.000)	(0.000)	(0.000)
Household size (ln)	0.392	0.298	0.329	0.393	0.506
	(0.000)	(0.000)	(0.000)	(0.000)	(0.000)
Town residency	n.a.	n.a.	−0.000	0.015	0.433
			(0.853)	(0.811)	(0.000)
Occupational status élite	n.a.	−0.194	0.608	−0.041	0.089
		(0.248)	(0.038)	(0.846)	(0.458)

	(1)	(2)	(3)	(4)	(5)
farmer	−0.010	−0.130	0.142	−0.161	−0.138
	(0.748)	(0.279)	(0.544)	(0.089)	(0.175)
tradesman	−0.159	0.041	0.598	−0.210	−0.054
	(0.322)	(0.756)	(0.019)	(0.089)	(0.556)
widow	n.a.	0.109	0.543	−0.122	0.258
		(0.412)	(0.041)	(0.291)	(0.045)
Book-owner	0.174	0.114	0.336	0.142	0.174
	(0.000)	(0.071)	(0.009)	(0.023)	(0.009)
Constant	−0.186	−0.348	−0.185	0.526	0.211
Adjusted R^2	0.793	0.821	0.693	0.725	0.799

[a] The dependent variable, the £ sterling amount in consumer goods, is in natural log (ln) form.

[b] The numbers in parentheses are significance levels (t test).

[c] The independent variables town residency and book-ownership are dummy variables coded 1 and 0. The categories of the variable occupational status are also dummied with 1, 0 codes, with labourers and those whose status was missing constituting the reference category. For means, standard deviations, and correlations, see Appendix 2.

Source: see Appendix 1.

and zero order correlations appear in Appendix 2.) Proxies for certain of the variables had to be used. To obtain household size, the number of beds was multiplied by 2, after counting zero beds as 0.5, and then it was logged. As is the case with household size and income in modern consumer expenditure surveys, wealth and number of beds were positively correlated. The levels, however, were not so high as to make it impossible to run them both in the equations.[38] Book-ownership was used as a proxy for education. The other variables are more straight-forward representatives of the factors discussed above.

Between areas and over time periods the similarities are on the whole more striking than the differences, and wealth clearly drowned out most of the other variables. Explained variation fell between about 70% and 80% (except for the London 1661–4 sample, where it came out at 62.6%), and of that variation, about 90% can be attributed to wealth and most of the remainder to the proxy for household size. Accessibility to markets as measured by town residency or, in the case of the 1774 Chesapeake sample, coastal county residency was not significant in any sample except that for late eighteenth-century Massachusetts.[39] In most cases, town residency was positively correlated with the amount in consumer goods, but once wealth (the probated deceased from towns tended to be wealthier than those in rural areas) and occupational variables were accounted for, the effect disappeared. In the English Midlands, for example, no significant urban effect from living in a provincial town remained after controlling for other variables. Nor did a difference show up in the 1774 Chesapeake sample. However, using larger samples with a larger number of urban observations, Lois Green Carr and Lorena Walsh found significant urban–rural contrasts in York County, Virginia and Anne Arundel County, Maryland.[40] The implication to be drawn from these contrasting results is the none too surprising one that access to consumer durables was a larger problem in the colonies than in provincial England.

Occupational status did not have a very big impact on the amount devoted to consumer goods, once wealth was held constant. Farmers consistently invested less in durables than did other groups, although only in Worcestershire, not in Oxfordshire or the colonies, was the difference significant at an acceptable level. Did a gap between the durables consumption of farmers and non-farmers emerge in the Midlands during the early modern period? If so, it appears less than it would due to those in trades and crafts, whose coefficients were nearer to those of farmers than to those of other groups: namely, labourers (who along with some cases of unknown occupation made up the reference category for occupational status), the élite (those with an honorific title, or professionals), and women (who were included as a separate group under occupational status because in inventories they were designated by their marital status, not their occupation). Part of the reason farmers and tradesmen appear so similar in terms of consumption of durables may be that the trades category included those deceased who had had dual occupations. Still, the contrast between those in agriculture and those who are not seems less pronounced than it is in modern data.[41]

The theory that literacy or education promotes consumption seems to work better for the colonies than for England, although the distribution of books was so limited in sixteenth-century Oxfordshire that it is not much of a test there, and lower levels of ownership in Worcestershire during the 1720s than in 1669–70 suggest that the less-detailed 1720s inventories may have buried books under general rubrics such as 'household stuff' or 'lumber'. The fact, therefore, that only in the East London sample for the 1720s does English book-ownership show up as significant should not be made too much of until further research has been carried out.

Evaluating Consumer Demand in the Early Modern Period

During the early modern period, the demonstrable changes that occurred in consumer demand transpired within each of the two major consumer categories, perishables and durables, rather than between them. That is, the evidence available offers no support for arguing that a long-term change occurred in the proportion of household income or wealth going to either. Within the perishable or food category, a whole group of new commodities appeared with a presumed impact on diet. Between about 1650 and 1750, tobacco, sugar products, and caffeine drinks became items of mass consumption, meaning 25% or more of the adult population regularly used them. Because as demand for these groceries grew the price also fell, and because, for a good part of the later seventeenth and eighteenth centuries, the cost of other foodstuffs declined as well, the percentage of a budget taken up by diet need not have increased.

Similarly, inventory evidence does not indicate that the growth in ownership of semi-durables—lighter-weight fabrics, paper products, glassware, and pottery—increased the proportion of wealth in all consumer goods (durables and semi-durables) at the expense of producer goods or savings. Rather, the proportion stayed the same or fell because of substitutions of cheaper goods for more expensive ones, falling prices, and perhaps in some periods increased wealth. There seems to have been a sharp rise in the real amount of wealth put into consumer goods between the end of the sixteenth century and the later seventeenth century, but the mean and median values in consumer goods stayed fairly constant thereafter. A combination of falling prices and substitutions of less permanent goods for more durable ones probably disguises most of the increased accumulation of consumer goods in the eighteenth century. (There is a problem, as we have seen, in that inventories only measure stocks of wealth at death, and if less durable goods replaced articles with more permanence, then outlays of consumer products over a lifetime could have been greater.)

Nor, in looking at the determinants of money 'invested' in consumer goods, does one see a very clear, consistent role for variables such as occupational status, education, or market accessibility over time.[42] Once wealth and household size are entered into the analysis, these other factors tend to wash out or show relatively minor effects. Of course, if the value of different types of goods is analysed, the results might be different.

A dramatic change in budget proportions has distinguished consumer demand in many Western societies at the end of the nineteenth and in the earlier twentieth century: beginning in the period 1920–40, a sharp drop occurred in the percentage families spent on food, and a notable rise in expenditure on consumer durables.[43] These are not the changes perceived in early modern consumer demand. From the evidence presented here, increases in wealth, substitutions, and lowered prices may have kept proportions more or less the same despite major changes in diet and in material possessions. There are shifts in demand that need explanation, but they are *within* the traditional consumption categories of food and durables. Just what those changes meant nutritionally and in terms of domestic well-being will be the subject of the next two chapters.

Chapter 4

1. The comparative neglect of consumption by economic historians can be traced to the popular conviction that economic change is 'to be sought first and foremost in supply, not demand related processes'. For an articulate expression of this view, see Joel Mokyr, 'Demand vs. Supply in the Industrial Revolution', *Journal of Economic History*, 37 (1977), 1005.

2. Joan Thirsk, *Economic Policy and Projects: The Development of a Consumer Society in Early Modern England*, Oxford, 1978; Margaret Spufford, *Small Books and Pleasant Histories*, London, 1981, and *The Great Reclothing of Rural England*, London, 1984; Lorna Weatherill, 'The Growth of the Pottery Industry in England, 1660–1815', unpublished Ph.D. thesis, University of London, 1981; and Lois Green Carr and Lorena S. Walsh, 'Inventories and the Analysis of Wealth and Consumption Patterns in St. Mary's County, Maryland, 1658–1777', *Historical Methods*, 13 (1980), 81–104.

3. W. G. Hoskins, 'The Re-building of Rural England, 1570–1640', *Past and Present*, 4 (1953), 44–59, and R. Machin, 'The Great Rebuilding: A Reassessment', ibid. 77 (1977), 33–56.

4. 25% of the adult population means that more than just adults in London and among the élite would have to be consuming an item for it to be counted as a mass-consumption good. For consumer durables, the family is a better unit to count than the individual. Unfortunately, most of the available data count individuals or the property of wealthholders rather than households. Some of the inventoried deceased do not have their own households. Thus using inventories to indicate the percentage of people having access to a particular household good underestimates its availability, just as the greater wealth of inventoried decedents overestimates the possession of most articles. Specifying the adult population (i.e. aged 15 and over) exerts some control over the variation over time in the proportion of children, which during the early modern period ranged from 28% to 37% (E. A. Wrigley and R. S. Schofield, *The Population History of England, 1541–1871*, London, 1981, pp. 528–9). In the first third of the nineteenth century, it reached 40%. Some of the stagnation in per capita consumption figures in groceries that one sees from 1770 to 1840 may be partially due to the youthfulness of the population. There is very little historical research on the rate of diffusion of consumer goods. See D. S. Ironmonger, *New Commodities and Consumer Behavior*, Cambridge, 1972, pp. 131–44.

5. US Bureau of the Census, *Historical Statistics of the United States from Colonial Times to 1970*, Washington, DC, 1976, p. 1162.

6. Joan Thirsk, 'New Crops and their Diffusion: Tobacco-growing in Seventeenth-Century England', in C. W. Chalklin and M. A. Havinden (eds.), *Rural Change and Urban Growth, 1500–1800*, London, 1974, pp. 76 ff. On Nineteenth-century per capita tobacco consumption see B. R. Mitchell and Phyllis Deane, *Abstract of British Historical Statistics*, Cambridge, 1971, pp. 355–7.

7. On prices in the Chesapeake for tobacco see US Bureau of the Census, *Historical Statistics*, p. 1198. For the 1633 tax on tobacco retailers, see Peter Clark, *The English Alehouse: A Social History, 1200–1830*, London, 1983, p. 134. He writes, 'the lists of licensees confirm our picture of a nation-wide trade, though with some bias towards London and the West Country.'

8. Robert C. Nash, 'The English and Scottish Tobacco Trades in the Seventeenth and Eighteenth Centuries: Legal and Illegal Trade', *Economic History Review*, 2nd ser. 35 (1982), 354–72. On average, Chesapeake planters in the late 17th cent. received 1 d. per lb. for their tobacco (*Historical Statistics*, p. 1198), but the duty came to be four times that amount (Nash, 'English and Scottish Tobacco Trades', p. 369).

9. On the excise, see Paul Langford, *The Excise Crisis: Society and Politics in the Age of Walpole*, Oxford, 1975, pp. 26–7.

10. Clark, *English Alehouse*, ch. 11. Nash, 'English and Scottish Tobacco Trades', pp. 355–6, discusses the theories put forward by Jacob Price and others as to why the tobacco market failed to expand. The fact that, as Price points out, the rise of gin and the fall of tobacco are inversely correlated gives added credence to the notion that the retailing of tobacco and beer were intertwined.

11. In the early 17th cent. brown sugar sold at 13*d*. to 14*d*. per lb. and white at 20*d*. or so. At the end of the century, brown could be purchased for 6*d*. to 7*d*. and white at 10*d*. to 12*d*. By the mid-18th cent. the prices had fallen to 5*d*. and 8*d*. to 9*d*., respectively. See Noel Deerr, *The History of Sugar*, ii, London, 1950, pp. 528–9; G. N. Johnstone, 'The Growth of the Sugar Trade and Refining Industry', in *The Making of the Modern British Diet*, ed. Derek Oddy and Derek Miller, London, 1976, p. 62; and Barrie Trinder and Jeff Cox (eds.), *Yeomen and Colliers in Telford*, London, 1980, p. 42.

12. Richard B. Sheridan, *Sugar and Slavery. An Economic History of the British West Indies, 1623–1775*, St Lawrence, Barbados, 1974, pp. 344–9.

13. Ibid.; Elizabeth Boody Schumpeter, *English Overseas Trade Statistics, 1697–1808*, Oxford, 1960, pp. 60–2; and John James McCusker, jun., 'The Rum Trade and the Balance of Payments of the Thirteen Continental Colonies, 1650–1775', unpublished dissertation, University of Pittsburgh, 1970, *passim*.

14. K. N. Chaudhuri, *The Trading World of Asia and the English East India Company, 1660–1760*, Cambridge, 1978, pp. 385–406.

15. Benjamin Woods Labaree, *The Boston Tea Party*, New York, 1968, chs 1–3, and Samuel Wharton, 'Observations upon the Consumption of Teas in North America, 1773', *Pennsylvania Management of History and Biography*, 25 (1901), 139–41.

16. W. A. Cole, 'Trends in Eighteenth-Century Smuggling', *Economic History Review*, 2nd ser. 10 (1958), 395–409.

17. Hoh-Cheung Mui and Lorna H. Mui, *The Management of Monopoly: A Study of the East India Company's Conduct of its Tea Trade, 1784–1833*, Vancouver, 1984, p. 12.

18. Wharton, 'Observations', 140–1.

19. Thirsk, *Economic Policy*; Lois Green Carr and Lorena S. Walsh, 'Inventories and the Analysis of Wealth and Consumption Patterns in St. Mary's County, Maryland, 1658–1777', *Historical Methods*, 13 (1980), 81–104; Carole Shammas, 'The Domestic Environment in Early Modern England and America', *Journal of Social History*, 14 (1980), 1–24; Spufford, *Great Reclothing*; and Lorna Weatherill, 'Consumer Behavior and Social Status in England', *Continuity and Change*, 1 (1986), 191–216.

20. Robert B. Pearl and Matilda Frankel, 'Composition of the Personal Wealth of American Households at the Start of the Eighties', in Seymour Sudman and Mary A. Spaeth (eds.), *The Collection and Analysis of Economic and Consumer Behavior Data*, Urbana, 1984, p. 24.

21. Gloria L. Main, 'The Standard of Living in Maryland and Massachusetts, 1656–1719', paper presented at the Conference on the Chesapeake, May 1984, St Mary's College, St Mary's Md., table 3. She also finds that the Massachusetts

means exceeded those of Maryland partly because clothing was more consistently included.

22. Jack Michel, ' "In a Manner and Fashion Suitable to Their Degree": A Preliminary Investigation of Material Culture of Early Rural Pennsylvania', *Working Papers from the Regional Economic History Research Center*, 5 (1981), 11; Gloria Main, 'The Standard of Living in Colonial Massachusetts', *Journal of Economic History*, 43 (1983), 105; Carr and Walsh, 'Inventories and the Analysis of Wealth', fig. 4, pp. 89 and 91; Carter Hudgins, 'Exactly as the Gentry Do in England: Culture, Aspirations, and Material Things in the Eighteenth Century Chesapeake', unpublished paper, 1984, table 6; and Lois Green Carr and Lorena S. Walsh, 'Changing Lifestyles and Consumer Behavior in the Colonial Chesapeake', in Cary Carson, Ronald Hoffman, and Peter Albert (eds.), *Of Consuming Interests: The Style of Life in the Eighteenth Century*, Charlottesville, forthcoming 1990. The lack of direction pertains to rural areas. Lorena Walsh finds that investment in consumer goods in Chesapeake towns did rise after 1730, although it is not clear whether that was due to an increase in wealth, or whether an increase in the percentage of wealth devoted to consumer goods also occurred ('Urban Amenities and Rural Sufficiency: Living Standards and Consumer Behavior in the Colonial Chesapeake, 1643–1777', *The Journal of Economic History*, 43 (1983), 112–13).

23. Christopher Husbands, 'Standards of Living in North Warwickshire in the Seventeenth Century', *Warwickshire History*, 4 (1981), 211. On peasant labourers see Alan Everitt, 'Farm Labourers', in Joan Thirsk (ed.), *The Agrarian History of England and Wales*, iv, 1500–1640, Cambridge, 1967, p. 421. The unadjusted mean amount for England 1560–1600 was £2.25 and for 1601–40, £4.5.

24. Bedfordshire mean calculated from data in F. G. Emmison, 'Jacobean Household Inventories', *The Bedfordshire Historical Record Society*, 20 (1938), 45–6. Samples from various areas in England in Lorna Weatherill, 'A Possession of One's Own: Women and Consumer Behavior in England, 1660–1740 ', *Journal of British Studies*, 25 (1986), 134–5.

25. Carr and Walsh ('Inventories and the Analysis of Wealth', pp. 91–4 and 100) have been the only ones to examine price trends of manufactured goods in inventories. From their analysis of the Maryland data they concluded in 1980 that 'explanations [for the stagnation in investment in consumer goods] which hinge on . . . a general fall in the price of European imports clearly will not do.' Since then they have found a decline in the price of manufactured goods up to 1740 in Maryland and 1760 in Virginia: personal communication, Lois Green Carr, 30 Jan. 1989. This still does not explain how the amount of consumer goods owned could have continued to increase after 1760 when the amount expended on them did not. There are several possible explanations. One has to do with the commodities used for the index of consumer manufactures. Carr and Walsh used the prices of two metals, pewter and silver plate, for half of the index and, for the other half, the prices of three linens—osnaburg, canvas, and dowlas. Only osnaburg was used after 1721. It is very difficult to find commodities that continue to be listed for over two centuries and that also have both price and quantity recorded. The metals were probably chosen because their valuation by the pound and the ounce allowed some standardization from one inventory to the

next. But as shown in Table 4.6, plate and pewter expenditures were declining in the 18th cent. Although traditionally they had been the commodities consumers had stocked up with almost as a form of savings, by the 18th cent. they were not what was stimulating consumer buying. One wonders if it was the price behaviour of these metals, which were of declining importance and of which the prices may have been somewhat idiosyncratic, that kept the index from registering a decline. The price of linens—at least, of osnaburg and dowlas—seems to have gone down in the English and Massachusetts inventories examined for this study.

26. Spufford, *The Great Reclothing*, pp. 123–5.

27. On the changeover from the older to the new draperies, and the rise of linens and calicoes or cottons, see G. D. Ramsay, *The English Woollen Industry, 1500–1750*, London, 1982; Spufford, *The Great Reclothing*, and Chandra Mukerji, *From Graven Images: Patterns of Modern Materialism*, New York, 1983, chs. 5 and 6. Tables 4.7 and 4.8 show how much more expensive broadcloth and even kersey remained in comparison with most lighter fabrics. Weatherill, 'Growth of the Pottery Industry', ch. 3, compares the prices of pewter and pottery tableware.

28. Total consumer expenditure always has an income elasticity under 1.00 because savings are much more likely than consumer expenditure to be affected by changes in income. Often though, in consumption studies savings are removed and total expenditure replaces income. In that case expenditure on certain consumer durables frequently rises above unity, because it is more elastic than most expenditures on food. This is known as Engels' Law, and has been modified over the years by contemporary and historical studies of household expenditure. See Daniel B. Suits, 'The Determinants of Consumer Expenditure: A Review of Present Knowledge', in Daniel B. Suits *et al*. (eds.), *Impacts of Monetary Policy*, Englewood Cliffs, New Jersey, 1963, pp. 1–57; H. S. Houthakker, 'An International Comparison of Household Expenditure Patterns, Commemorating the Centenary of Engels' Law', *Econometrica*, 26 (1957), 532–51; Jeffrey G. Williamson, 'Consumer Behavior in the Nineteenth Century: Carroll D. Wright's Massachusetts Workers in 1875', *Explorations in Entrepreneurial History*, 4 (1967), 98–135; and Trevor J. O. Dick, 'Consumer Behavior in the Nineteenth Century and Ontario Workers, 1885–1889', *Journal of Economic History*, 46 (1986), 477–88.

29. See Appendix 1 for a discussion of the limitations of probate inventories as a source and the particular characteristics of each of the data sets used here.

30. R^2 records the amount of variation in the dependent variable (in this case the natural log of £ value in consumer goods) 'explained' by the independent variable or variables (wealth, occupational status, etc.). R^2 is measured on a scale of 0 to 1.00, the higher the score, theoretically, the more the behaviour of the dependent variable is influenced by the independent variables. The size of the R^2, however, can be affected by a number of factors including outliers and errors of measurement. Consequently, it is important to look at the behaviour of the dependent variable and independent variable in a scatter diagram. See Carole Shammas, 'Consumer Behavior in Colonial America', *Social Science History*, 6 (1982), fig. 2.

31. As mentioned above, R^2 of a linear regression is influenced by outliers. In Table 4.9 the linear form in several of the samples is so much higher because of a few

very large probated estates. Logging has the effect of converting biased wealth of income distribution into more normal distributions, and thus moderates the influence of outliers.

32. In the Virginia samples, slaves constituted one of the biggest categories of producer 'goods'. Financial assets were always undervalued in Virginia because a certain amount of investment and credits was with overseas merchants, most of which was never counted. Reporting was particularly poor in the 1720s sample.

33. A fuller example of elasticities is in Shammas, 'Consumer Behavior in Colonial America', p. 74. (There is a typographical error in the second paragraph: 4.25% should read 0.425%.)

34. Williamson, 'Consumer Behavior in the Nineteenth Century', pp. 118–19.

35. E.g. Dorothy Brady, 'Consumption and the Style of Life', in Lance E. Davis *et al.*, *American Economic Growth: An Economist's History of the United States*, New York, 1972, pp. 61–89, centres her analysis on the differences between farm, village, and city families.

36. See e.g., W. Lloyd Warner, *Yankee City*, New Haven, 1963, abridged edn., pp. 90–104; and Sandra J. Coyner, 'Class Consciousness and Consumption: The New Middle-Class During the Weimar Republic', *Journal of Social History*, 10 (1977), 310–31.

37. Robert T. Michael, 'Education and Consumption', in F. Thomas Juster (ed.), *Education, Income, and Human Behavior*, New York, 1975, pp. 239–40.

38. The correlations between the natural log of wealth and the natural log of household size (as measured by number of beds times 2, with zero beds recorded as 1) ranged between an R of 0.444 to 0.620.

39. I used towns rather than coastal counties for the 1774 Massachusetts regression, because the Essex County 1660–73 regression used towns. In Shammas, 'Consumer Behavior in Colonial America', p. 76, I used county level proxies. The coastal counties of Suffolk, Essex, and Plymouth, in that order, had a higher £ value in consumer goods than did the inland counties of Hampshire and Worcester.

40. Carr and Walsh, 'Changing Lifestyles and Consumer Behavior', tables A1 and A4.

41. The information on occupational status in the 1774 Virginia and Maryland sample is rather confusing because the category of farmer is not significant and the other categories are. This is because both labourers and farmers (other variables held constant) had similar amounts of £ sterling in consumer goods, while the élite, tradesmen, and women all had significantly more. So actually, the pattern for farmers is the same as in the other colonial samples, except that the labourer category in this instance had a little less than the farmers. That is why the farmer category has a positive coefficient, though an insignificant one. For a discussion of the measurement errors, in early modern occupational categories see Keith Wrightson, *English Society, 1580–1680*, London, 1982, ch. 1.

42. For an articulation on the theory that over time, as people have more discretionary income, taste (e.g. changes in values due to differences in class, education, urban living, etc.) should play a larger role in determining consumer behaviour, see Ruth P. Mack, 'The Conference on household Production and Consumption: A General Comment', in Nestor E. Terlecky (ed.), *Household Production and Consumption*, New York, 1975, pp. 647–51.

43. See ch. 5 for information on modern food expenditures. On changes in the percentage spent on consumer durables in the first half of the 20th cent. see Martha Olney, 'Consumer Credit Availability and Changes in the Demand for Consumer Durable Goods, 1900–1940', a paper delivered at the 1986 Social Science History Association Meeting, St Louis.

II

TRENDS IN CONSUMPTION AND THE STANDARD OF LIVING

Food Consumption, New Commodities, and the Transformation in Diet

PROBABLY no area of consumption changed as much over the course of the early modern period as that of food. It is now believed that by the mid-seventeenth century mortality crises directly traceable to famine had disappeared in northern and southern England, and that an increasingly weak relationship existed between variations in grain prices and mortality.[1] By the eighteenth century no direct correlation can be detected at all. Apart from the very earliest settlers, those who migrated to America had even less experience with famine. This situation contrasts sharply with the plight of populations in Ireland, on the Continent, and in Asia during this time, and there has been some speculation as to the reasons for these differences. Historically, it seems that effective state intervention has been crucial to the prevention of famine. When food shortages arose in Tudor and early Stuart England, research has shown that men and women expected the government to act, and it usually did. Those proto-bureaucrats who dragged their heels would be reminded of their obligations by a timely food riot. Neither the 'common sort' nor their 'betters', it seems, believed that they lived in a subsistence economy where nothing could be done other than to appeal to the Almighty when prices soared. The assumption of welfare payments by local government in the Elisabethan era provided additional safeguards against starvation.[2]

The early modern period was also the time when non-European commodities became ensconced in the English diet.[3] The introduction of the 'bad' groceries has already been discussed. However, more nutritional foodstuffs—rice, maize, and potatoes—entered the diet of a large number of Westerners at this time as well. In terms of ingredients, the English and American menu has changed comparatively little since.

Of course, the elimination of widespread famine and the introduction of new foods does not mean people were well nourished. Robert Fogel has recently argued that the intervention of the English government during times of food shortage reached an apogee in the first half of the seventeenth century. The Civil War resulted in the dismantling of the mechanisms to control prices and distribute food, and it took two hundred years before the government once again took responsibility for ensuring a steady food supply for everyone. Prices soared from time to time and created hardship. Moreover, one important indicator of health status, average height, suggests a significant proportion of the English population, while not dying from famines, may have suffered from chronic malnutrition. Analysis of the heights of late eighteenth-century British soldiers and colonial miltia men shows that the latter grew nearly as tall as their mid-twentieth-century counterparts, but that the former registered remarkably low mean heights. It has been hypothesized that diet accounted for much of this difference. Some historians have argued that nutrition declined in Europe during the seventeenth century. A combination of population increases and poor harvests drove up grain prices and, it is believed, forced a drop in the consumption of meat and other animal products that did not reverse itself until the late nineteenth century. This supposed decline, however, has never been well documented for England, nor has it been clear how the new commodities may have affected the situation.[4]

America was not completely free from dietary distress, either. Researchers have attributed the short stature of slave children to the poor diets provided on plantations for unfree pregnant women and boys and girls not yet in the labour force. At later ages, perhaps after joining the work crews, slaves experienced some catch-up growth, but still failed to attain adult heights comparable to those of their white contemporaries. Much of this explanation, though, rests on conjecture, because only a very limited amount is known about plantation diets. Finally, in the nineteenth century, heights for the white male population dip slightly, although the assumption is that a higher incidence of disease rather than a deterioration in diet was to blame.[5]

Did the English have a nutritional problem, and if so, why? How much better was the diet in America? Clearly some additional yardstick of dietary welfare, apart from mortality, that stretches back further than the data on height is needed to indicate changes over time in early modern England and America. One commonly used measure for later periods has been the proportion of a household's budget spent on food and drink. According to 'Engel's Law', named after Ernst Engel, the nineteenth-century pioneer in budget studies, as total family expenditure rises the percentage devoted to food purchases should decline. Poor people and poor countries spend more of their resources and time feeding themselves than do richer ones. A higher percentage of total outlay spent on food suggests a meagre diet and little money left over for clothing, rent, fuel, medical care, and other consumer needs.[6] While there are obvious problems involved in trying to estimate food expenditure in predominantly agricultural societies where products could be homegrown, there were many early modern labourers in rural as well as urban England and America who lacked the means to produce their own food. The idea of pre-industrial expenditure on food is not a historical fiction, but a fact of life.

Household Expenditure on Food

Today, households in most Western countries spend between 20% and 33% of their disposable income on diet. It is assumed that the percentages for early modern times were much higher. One frequently cited estimate of the household expenditure of English families from the fifteenth century to World War I shows the same proportion (80%) spent on diet over the entire 500-year period![7] These hard-to-believe estimates can be blamed, at least in part, on the inadequacy of sources. Statisticians did not begin conducting budget surveys in a systematic fashion until the later nineteenth century. A few contemporaries on the scene during the early modern period, however, made computations and even circulated questionnaires about the spending patterns of the working classes that invite comparisons with modern household budget data.

Table 5.1 shows the percentage of household expenditure devoted to diet at sixteen different periods of time from 1688 to 1978. The first column of percentages is for all households in the survey, while the second column is for that category of household having the lowest income. The earliest figures, those for 1688 and 1695, are from estimates made by Gregory King.[8] The next five surveys were inquiries conducted on a small scale by social reformers or public officials during the late eighteenth and early nineteenth centuries. The first major survey on British family expenditure was undertaken in 1890 by the United States Commissioner on Labor for comparative purposes.[9]

Although many of the percentages are high, nowhere does it appear that 80% of expenditure went for diet. From what is known about rent, clothing costs, fuel purchases, and the number of sundries required to live in previous centuries, it would seem literally impossible for families over prolonged periods to have spent 80% of their earnings on food. At the same time no very clear trend surfaces until the twentieth century, when the proportion declines from 55% to about 25% for average households,

TABLE 5.1 Percentage of English household expenditure devoted to diet: 1695–1978

Year	Household group covered	No. in sample	% expenditure on diet by all households	% expenditure on diet by poorest category of household
1688	All English families	n.a.	50.4	n.a.
1695	All English families	n.a.	60.7	74.1
1787–93	English agricultural labourers	127	72.2	70.1
1794–6	English agricultural and urban labourers	86	74.3	69.0
1836	Manchester working class	19	55.0	
1841	Manchester working class	19	69.3	
1837–8	English agricultural labourers	54	72.2	
1883	British working men's families	16	51.3	
1890–1	'Normal' British industrial families	455	48.8	50.1

1904	United Kingdom working class	1,944	61.0	67.0
1914	Birmingham working class	40	54.5	59.4
1929	Merseyside working class	154	47.0	50.6
1937–8	British industrial workers	8,905	39.5	45.4
1953–4	Cambridgeshire families	3,000	25.5	33.2
1971	United Kingdom families	7,239	26.0	30.0
1978	United Kingdom families	7,001	28.0	35.0

Sources: 1688—Richard Stone, 'Some Seventeenth Century Econometrics: Consumer Behaviour', *Cahiers du Département d'Économetrie, Université de Genève*, 87.08 (1987), 22. 1695—'A First Draft of Gregory King's "Observations" from his Notebook, 1695 and Journal', in *Seventeenth-Century Economic Documents*, ed. Joan Thirsk and J. P. Cooper, Oxford, 1972, pp. 767–8, and Gregory King, 'A Scheme of the Income and Expense of the Several Families of England Calculated for the Year 1688', ibid., pp. 780–1. 1787–93—David Davies, *The Case of Labourers in Husbandry*, Bath, 1795, and George Stigler, 'The Early History of Empirical Studies of Consumer Behavior', *The Journal of Political Economy*, 62 (1954), 97. 1794–6—Frederic Morton Eden, *The State of the Poor*, ii and iii, London, 1797, and Stigler, 'History of Consumer Behavior', p. 97. 1836, 1841—William Neild, 'Comparative Statement of the Income and Expenditures of Certain Families of the Working Classes in Manchester and Dukinfield, in the years 1836 and 1841', *Journal of the Royal Statistical Society*, 4 (1841), 320–35. 1837–8—Frederick Purdy, 'On the Earnings of Agricultural Labourers in England and Wales, 1860', ibid. 24 (1861), 328–73. 1883—[Massachusetts] Bureau of Statistics of Labor, *Fifteenth Annual Report*, Boston, 1884, p. 465. 1890–1—United States, *Seventh Annual Report of the Commissioner of Labour 1891*, Washington DC, 1892, pp. 2000–7. 1904—Augustus D. Webb, *The New Dictionary of Recent Statistics of the World to the Year 1911*, Leipzig, 1911, p. 157. 1914—Peter R. Shergold, *Working-Class Life: The 'American Standard' in Comparative Perspective, 1899–1913*, Pittsburgh, 1982, pp. 179–80. 1929—D. Caradog Jones, *The Social Survey of Merseyside*, i, Liverpool, 1934, p. 32. 1937–8—*The Ministry of Labour Gazette*, 48 (Dec. 1940), 300–5, and J. L. Nicholson, 'Variations in Working Class Family Expenditure', *Journal of Royal Statistical Society*, ser. A (general), 112. 4 (1949), 394. 1953–4—Dorothy Cole and J. E. G. Utting, 'Estimating Expenditures, Savings, and Income from Household Budgets', ibid., 119, 4 (1956), 321–87. 1971—Great Britain, Central Statistical Office, *Social Trends*, 3 (1972), 100. 1978—ibid. 11 (1981), 113.

and from 67% to 33% for the poor. During the 1970s, the percentages begin to creep up again, suggesting the beginning of a reversal.

There are problems, of course, with accepting all these figures at face value. One major difficulty is that in many of the surveys not all types of miscellaneous expenditure were included, making the total expenditure figure too small and inflating the percentage accruing to food. This problem clearly affected the large United Kingdom working-class survey of 1904. Only a few expenses apart from clothing, rent, and fuel were calculated, so that a mere 4% of the budget, compared with 18.5% in the 1890 survey, fell into the miscellaneous category.[10] To a lesser extent, all the earlier surveys suffer from omissions of this sort.

They also have another problem. In the years before offices were established to compile statistics on a regular basis, investigators seldom gathered figures except in times of crisis. In 1695, Gregory King wanted to alert the government to the disastrous impact of the war with France on the working population.[11] Another war at the end of the eighteenth century and sky-rocketing food prices prompted the household budget surveys undertaken by David Davies and Frederick Eden. Likewise the economic crises of the late 1820s and 1840s spurred local and House of Commons investigations. The percentage of expenditure devoted to food in these years was probably uncommonly high.

Some indication of how the percentages could see-saw within the space of a few years is provided by comparing the pre-war 1688 food expenditure estimates of King with what he calculated people had to spend in 1695. King's numbers add up to an average of 50.4% of expenditure being spent on food by the entire English population in 1688, and 60.7% seven years later. Then there are the two entries for Manchester in 1836 and 1841. In the latter year, the mayor, William Neild, had a survey taken of the expenditure by nineteen working-class households in his city and in nearby Dukinfield to illustrate the effects of the depression on people in the area. The analysts found diet absorbed 69% of the workers' weekly outlay. They then figured what it would have cost in 1836 to buy the same goods, and arrived at the much lower figure of 55%. In other words, during one of these bad spells food expenditure percentages could climb abruptly—in this case, by 14%. It seems possible, therefore, that the percentages in the high sixties and low seventies recorded for labourers during the late seventeenth and late eighteenth centuries might have been in the low fifties in better years.

Taking these biases into consideration, Table 5.1 suggests that the proportion spent by the working class prior to 1850 averaged about 60%

and demonstrated no clear trend. From 1850 to 1914, working-class households cut the proportion to 50%, and a much more dramatic fall to under 30% occurred in the subsequent forty years.

The scarcity and shortcomings of English budget data for the period before the late nineteenth century suggests the need to look elsewhere for material on food expenditure in order to learn something about trends *within* the early modern period. One possible source is wage assessments, those schedules approved by Parliament and, after 1563, set by the local justices of the peace.[12] Assessments fixed the maximum wage that could be paid to artisans, agricultural workers, and servants. For those wages paid on a daily basis, usually two figures were promulgated—one with diet furnished by the employer, and one without diet being provided. By subtracting the wage with diet from the wage without diet and dividing the difference by the wage without diet, one obtains the percentage of the wage that the authorities assumed would be spent on food and drink. Assessments are far from ideal documents to use for this purpose. Some counties, such as Middlesex, did not alter their rates much for over a century. Enforcement was undoubtedly lax at times, and masters would pay more than the set amounts. Estimates after the mid-eighteenth century are few and far between, because employers stopped the practice of providing meals for their day workers. Furthermore, the wages were daily rates for male individuals, not family budgets. Were workers supposed to feed a wife and several children on this pay? Probably not. Labourers' families would have to find additional sources of income from self-employment, secondary workers, and the parish poor rates.[13] According to the figures furnished by David Davies and Frederick Eden in the 1780s and 1790s, the earnings of a household head in the majority of cases constituted less than 67% of a working-class household's total expenditure. The food allowance in wage assessments, therefore, is an indication of the value of the diet employers furnished to a male worker. It cannot be multiplied by some estimated annual number of work days to arrive at yearly household income.[14] Of course, in terms of changes over time and variations between regions— and that is what I am most interested in here—it matters little whether it is a labourer's wage or a family's expenditure that is represented. Table 5.2 gives the proportion of wages allowed for food and drink, arranged by time period and region. Because assessments from the eastern and western sections of the South of England differed so much in the later seventeenth century, I calculated them separately. Percentages for two types of workers are shown: labourers (mainly agricultural, but some

TABLE 5.2 Percentage of wage devoted to diet: England, 1420–1780

Year	North	South-west	South-east	All[a]	Real wage index
Labourers					
1420–1514	—	—	—	43.4	897[b]
1560–1600	61.7	51.7	52.2	55.0	559
1601–40	62.8	53.4	51.2	55.3	411
1641–80	56.7	53.1	47.6	51.9	473
1681–1720	58.3	54.0	47.9	52.9	553
1721–60	52.7	53.0	48.2	51.0	658
Master Carpenters					
1420–1514	—	—	—	31.9	897[b]
1560–1600	48.1	43.9	41.4	44.1	559
1601–40	47.1	49.0	48.2	48.1	411
1641–80	50.0	50.2	43.5	47.5	473
1681–1780	45.8	45.8	43.4	44.8	615

[a] Percentage obtained by a weighted average of North (30%) South-west (30%), South-east (40%).
[b] The real wage is an average of 1499–1514 only, 1500 = 1,000.

Sources: 1420–1514—Coventry, 1420, 1444 statute, 1445 statute, 1495–6 statute, 1514 statute; Ellen M. McArthur, 'A Fifteenth-Century Assessment of Wages', *English Historical Review*, 13 (1898), 299–302; Victoria County History, *Warwickshire*, London, 1908, ii, 180; Frederic Morton Eden, *The State of the Poor*, London, 1797, i, 65, 74–5, 81, ii, p. lxxxix.
1560–1600—North: Lincolnshire, 1563, Rutland 1563, York, 1563, Lincoln 1563, Hull 1570, Doncaster 1577, Yorkshire East Riding 1593, Lancashire 1595; West: Exeter 1564–95, Salisbury 1595, Devonshire 1594–5; East: Northamptonshire 1560, 1566, 1595, Buckinghamshire 1561, Kent 1563, 1565, 1589, Berkshire 1563, London 1563–80, Canterbury 1576, 1594, Colchester 1583, Hertfordshire 1591; B. H. Putnam, 'Northamptonshire Wage Assessments of 1560 and 1667', *Economic History Review*, 1 (1927–8), 124–34; *Tudor Royal Proclamations*, eds. R. H. Tawney and E. Power, New Haven, 1969, i–iii, *passim*.
1601–40—North: Rutland, 1610, Lincolnshire 1621, Derbyshire 1634; West: Wiltshire 1603–34, 1635, Merioneth 1601, Staffordshire 1607, Gloucester 1632, Herefordshire 1632; East: Sussex 1606–36, Middlesex 1608–40, Norfolk, 1610, Essex 1612, Suffolk 1630, Hertfordshire 1631; Walter Davies, *General View of the Agriculture and Domestic Economy of North Wales*, London, 1813, pp. 500–1; William Cunningham, *The Growth of English Industry and Commerce in Modern Times*, Cambridge, 1929, pt. 2, pp. 887–93; J. C. Tingey, 'An Assessment of Wages for the Country of Norfolk in 1610', *English Historical Review*, 13 (1898), 522–7: Great Britain, Historical Manuscript Commission Reports, no. 15, *Report on Manuscripts in Various Collections*, i, London, 1901, pp. 160–75; ibid., no. 12, Appendix, pt. 4, *Manuscripts of the Duke of Rutland*, i, London, 1888, pp. 450–2; W. A. J. Archbold, 'An Assessment of Wages for 1630', *English Historical Review*, 12 (Apr. 1897), 307–11; James E. Thorold Rogers, *A History of Agriculture and Prices in England*, Oxford, 1887, vi, *passim*; W. E. Minchinton (ed.), *Wage Regulation in Pre-industrial England*, Newton Abbot, 1972, p. 203; N. M. Hindmarsh, 'The Regulation of Wages in England Under the Statute of Artificers, 1563–1700', unpublished Ph.D. thesis, University of London, 1932, *passim*.
1641–80—North: Yorkshire West Riding 1647–70, Yorkshire North Riding 1658, Yorkshire East Riding 1669; West: Wiltshire 1654, 1655, Gloucestershire 1655, Somerset 1651–3, 1666, 1668–70, 1671–2, 1673, Worcestershire 1663, Herefordshire 1666, 1667, 1668–80, Warwickshire 1672; East—Essex 1651, 1661, Middlesex 1641–80,Northamptonshire 1667; Cunningham, *Growth of English Industry*, pp. 887–93; Great Britain, Historical Manuscript Commission Reports, No. 15, *Manuscript*

urban) and master carpenters, the former representing those at the bottom of the working-class hierarchy and the latter representing those near the top.

What can be said about the trends in these series? Certainly the strikingly lower percentage of wages devoted to diet in the fifteenth and early sixteenth centuries, an average of 43.4% for labourers and 31.9% for carpenters, and the rise thereafter offer further evidence of the dramatic effects of population pressure on food prices during the Tudor–Stuart period. The post-1560 data reveal from 47.6% to 62.8% allotted for labourers and 43.4% to 50.2% for carpenters, depending upon time and region. The proportions, in other words, never do return to their early sixteenth century levels, even in the eighteenth century.

Why they do not revert to the earlier levels is partially explained by the trend in the real wage index, also reported in Table 5.2. As discussed above, the cost side of this index is almost entirely (80%) a reflection of food and drink prices, and is therefore a particularly good companion to the trends in the percentage allotted for diet. The wage index shows that earnings never do recover sufficiently for people to buy the diet they bought in the fifteenth century without increasing the proportion of their budget devoted to food and drink.

in *Various Collections*, i, 160–75, 323; Rogers, *History of Agriculture and Prices*, vi, *passim*; Putnam, 'Northamptonshire Wage Assessments', pp. 124–34; Roger Kelsall, 'Two East Yorkshire Wage Assessments, 1669, 1679', *English Historical Review*, 52 (1937), 283–9; Eleanore Trotter, *Seventeenth Century Life in the Country Parish*, Cambridge, 1919, pp. 161–2; A. W. Ashby, *One Hundred Years of Poor Law Administration in a Warwickshire Village*, Oxford, 1912, pp. 170–83; H. Heaton, 'The Assessment of Wages in the West Riding of Yorkshire in the Seventeenth and Eighteenth Centuries', *Economic Journal*, 24 (1914), 218–35; Minchinton (ed.), *Wage Regulation*, pp. 160–1, 203.

1681–1720—North: Yorkshire West Riding 1703–20; West: Wiltshire 1685, Warwickshire 1684, 1710, Somerset 1680–5, Herefordshire 1680–2, 1684, 1702, 1703–6, 1707 and 1711, 1708–10, 1712–20, Devonshire 1700–20; East: Middlesex 1681–1720, Bedfordshire 1684, Suffolk 1682; Rogers, *History of Agriculture and Prices*, vi and vii, *passim*; Victoria County History, *Warwickshire*, iii, 180; Cunningham, *Growth of English Industry*, pp. 887–93; Elizabeth W. Gilboy *Wages in Eighteenth Century England*, Cambridge, Mass., 1934, p. 88; Minchinton (ed.), *Wage Regulation*, pp. 160–1, 203; T. S. Willan, *A Bedfordshire Wage Assessment of 1684*, Bedfordshire Historical Record Society, 25 (1943), 129–37.

1721–80—North: Yorkshire West Riding 1721–32, Nottingham 1723, Lancashire 1725, Lincolnshire 1754; West: Devonshire 1721–32, 1733–78, Herefordshire 1732, 1733–62, Warwickshire 1730, Shropshire 1732–9; East: Middlesex 1721–5, Kent, 1724; Rogers *History of Agriculture and Prices*, vi, *passim*; J. D. Chambers, *Nottinghamshire in the Eighteenth Century*, New York, 1966 (1st edn. 1932), pp. 280–4; Eden, *State of the Poor*, iii, pp. cvi–cix; Victoria County History, *Lincolnshire*, ii, London, 1906, pp. 345–6; Minchinton (ed.), *Wage Regulation*, p. 204; Gilboy, *Wages*, p. 88; Ashby, *One Hundred Years*, pp. 171–83; F. A. Hibbert, 'The Shropshire Wages Assessment of Easter 1732', *Economic Journal*, 4 (1894), 516–17; Elizabeth Waterman, 'Some New Evidence on Wage Assessments in the Eighteenth Century', *English Historical Review*, 43 (July 1928), 398–408; Cunningham, *Growth of English Industry*, pp. 887–93.

The real wage index is in E. A. Wrigley and R. S. Schofield, *The Population History of England 1541–1871*, London, 1981, pp. 642–3. 1500 = 1,000.

What is especially surprising, though, is the sluggish response of the dietary share in the assessments to both the big drop in real wages during the sixteenth and seventeenth centuries, and to the partial recovery from the later seventeenth century on. In the south-east of England, the dietary percentages for both labourers and carpenters achieved their highest levels in *c*.1600, although the increase was not commensurate with the loss in real wages. While the percentage dropped once in the period 1641–80, it did not fall any further in the two subsequent periods, despite continued improvement in the real wage. In south-west England, the rise in the dietary percentage is also modest compared to the drop in the real wage, but once the percentage rose it never went down again, at least for labourers. Only in the North does one see both an appreciable jump in the late sixteenth and early seventeenth centuries and also an appreciable drop by the mid-eighteenth century. That it should be the North that has this closer correspondence between the two series is rather ironic, since the real wage index was largely based on South of England data.[15] Even in the North, though, the rise in the percentage spent on diet did not completely compensate for the real wage decline. If all these series are correct, households would have had to have been buying smaller quantities of food or food of poorer quality. There was, in other words, some elasticity to food budgets. In the North, where wages were lower and famine-related mortality crises continued during the 1620s, it was impossible to cut back as much as in the South, so the dietary percentage for labourers reached 62.8% in the early seventeenth century. Still, this would mean less real expenditure. This elasticity is also demonstrated by the way an improvement in real wages did not generate a comparable drop in the percentage allowed for labourers' diet in the wages set during the eighteenth century.

According to consumption theory, food is inelastic compared to other goods. People have to eat, so in hard times the 'real' amount spent on diet remains constant, although the nominal amount and the food expenditure proportion might go up because of higher prices, lower wages, or both. In good times when higher wages prevail, the amount spent will not increase proportionately because people can only eat so much. Consequently, the percentage of the total budget devoted to diet will go down. But with the wage assessments, the percentages do not fluctuate to the degree one might assume, implying that the amounts expended did move up and down and that diet expenditures were somewhat more elastic among the working-class population in the early modern period than theory would lead us to believe.

Interestingly enough, food expenditure by the working classes in household budgets from the late eighteenth century also exhibits more elasticity than theory would predict. When the cross-sectional data gathered by Eden and Davies is analysed, it shows that the higher the income the higher the percentage devoted to food and drink, while the percentages spent on clothing, rent, and fuel go *down* as total resources climb. The income elasticity for diet is over unity.[16] Late nineteenth- and very early twentieth-century surveys of the working class that give income-group breakdowns do not show as dramatic a reversal as the Davies and Eden data. One often sees traces of the phenomenon, however, where the lowest income group spends a smaller proportion on food than the income group directly above.[17]

Engel's law and the theory that has been built up around it came into being at a time of steadily falling food prices and some drop in the proportion of household expenditure devoted to food. These 'laws' may not apply to all parts of the income distribution in all time periods. As Table 5.1 shows, the percentages in the 1970s have begun to rise again. Some of the increase may be attributed to falling real wages, but there may be other reasons as well: more meals taken outside the home, for example, as female employment patterns change. Similarly, more than just Engel's law is needed to illuminate the early modern situation, where the food expenditure patterns have some of the characteristics usually, and probably improperly, associated with 'luxury' spending.

The suspicion that high elasticities among working-class English households may indicate a dietary problem is reinforced by other measures of nutritional status and by comparisons with the American colonies. As alluded to earlier in the chapter, analysis of the heights recorded for British and colonial soldiers around the time of the American Revolution shows the former to have been on average about 3.5 in. shorter than the latter (64.7 in. to 68.1 in.), after corrections for biases in the source. Furthermore, the stunted growth of poor boys in late eighteenth-century London suggests a degree of malnutrition among certain segments of the British population that had no parallel in early America.[18] What exists in the way of household budget data and wage assessments for America supports the height studies and the traditional impression that Americans had more ample diets.

Table 5.3 presents American household budget data from 1762 to the present. Before the twentieth century the percentages devoted to food were routinely 10% lower than those in England. Only the Massachusetts 1874–5 budgets show food absorbing more than 55% of

TABLE 5.3 Percentage of American household expenditure devoted to diet: 1762–1973

Year	Household groups covered	No. in sample	% expenditure on diet by all households	% expenditure on diet by poorest category of household
1762	Philadelphia workers	n.a.	51.4	54.2
1830	US cities	n.a.	—	48.8[a]
1874–5	Massachusetts wage-earners	397	58.0	64.0
1883	Massachusetts	19	49.2	n.a.
1886	Kansas	471	47.8	n.a.
1888–91	US 'normal' families	2,562	41.0	49.8
1901	US 'normal' families	11,156	43.1	50.8
1917–19	US white city workers	12,096	40.7	46.3
1934–6	US city workers	14,469	34.7	39.4
1950	US city wage-earners	7,007	30.7	32.0
1960–1	US families	13,728	24.5	29.0
1972–3	US families	20,000	19.3	20.6

[a] This assumes that rent and fuel took up 25% of the budget (see Paul A. David and Peter Solar, 'A Bicentenary Contribution to the History of the Cost of Living in America', *Research in Economic History*, 2 (1977), 47).

Sources: 1762—Billy G. Smith, 'The Best Poor Man's Country: Living Standard of the "Lower Sort" in Late Eighteenth-Century Philadelphia', *Working Papers from the Regional Economic History Research Center*, 2 (1979), 53, and Billy G. Smith, 'Struggles of the Independent Poor', unpublished paper, 1979; 1830—Dorothy Brady, 'Consumption and the Style of Life', in *American Economic Growth: An Economist's History of the United States*, ed. Lance E. Davis et al., New York, 1972, p. 79; 1874–5, 1888–91, 1901, 1917–19, 1934–6, 1950—US, Bureau of Labor Statistics, *How American Buying Habits Change*, Washington, 1959, pp. 34–56; Massachusetts 1883—[Massachusetts] Bureau of Statistics of Labor, *Fifteenth Annual Report*, Boston, 1884, p. 465; Kansas 1886—Kansas, *Second Annual Report of the Bureau of Labor*, Topeka, 1887, pp. 305–6; 1960–1—US, Bureau of Labor Statistics, *Handbook of Labor Statistics*, Washington, 1967, p. 245; 1972–3—ibid, Washington, 1980, pp. 365, 371.

expenditure, and in that instance insufficient allowance was made for sundries.[19]

Unfortunately, continuous colonial wage-assessment schedules are not available to supplement the figure from household budgets. The existing remnants of salary regulations, though, also indicate that Americans, even in the early years, spent less of their income on foodstuffs than did the English. In five out of the six wage rates shown in Table 5.4, expenditure on diet constituted about 33% of labourers' wages and 25% or less of craftsmen's pay. These percentages are nearly 20% lower than those recorded for their counterparts in the Mother Country. Only the Massachusetts rates, set during the chaotic settlement period, approach those in the Old World. Cheaper food and higher wages are presumably the main reasons for the differences between England and America. Total family income may not have been greatly superior in America, however, because of slavery, more limited access to relief outside the workhouse, and fewer employment opportunities for white children and married women.

TABLE 5.4 Percentage of wage devoted to diet: Colonial America, 1621–1777

Year	Place	Labourers	Craftsmen
1621	Virginia	33.3	25.0
1633	Massachusetts	55.0	41.6
1750s	Maryland–Delaware[a]	30.0	n.a.
1750s	Philadelphia[b]	34.2	21.4
1776	Charleston, SC	34.8	11.8
1777	Providence, RI	34.2	n.a.

[a] Male agricultural labourer wage of 30d. and board of 9d. per day.
[b] Labourers including seamen averaged 3.5s. in Pennsylvanian currency, with an average of 1.2s. board per day.

Sources: Virginia, Massachusetts, Rhode Island—Richard B. Morris, *Government and Labor in Early America*, New York, 1946, pp. 59, 87, 97; Maryland–Delaware—Donald R. Adams, jun., 'One Hundred years of Prices and Wages: Maryland, 1750–1850', *Working Papers from the Regional Economic History Research Center*, 5 (1982), 101, 106; Philadelphia—Billy G. Smith, '"The Best Poor Man's Country": Living Standards of the "Lower Sort" in Late Eighteenth Century Philadelphia', ibid., 2 (1979), 38 and 70; South Carolina—Richard Walsh, *Charleston's Sons of Liberty*, Columbia, 1959, p. 144.

Calorific Intake and Diet

The proportion of a budget devoted to food can indicate crisis or non-crisis times and allows for comparisons between regions and time periods, but it tells us little about nutritional standards and dietary change. For that information, it is necessary to look at the actual food items bought. Only one group of pre-1800 household budgets for English working-class families exist (the Davies and Eden surveys of the 1780s and 1790s), and nothing is available for America. Consequently, workhouse menus and accounts will be used to fill in the picture. It should be emphasized that these institutional sources reveal the dietary levels of the poorest part of the population. The poor were a minority, but a significant one in these societies. In America the situation is further complicated by the institution of slavery. Black women and men were certainly at the bottom of the social hierarchy in colonial America, but they are not covered by the poorhouse records.

Considering the superior quality of the late eighteenth-century household budget material, it is probably best to start with it and then move back in time using the poorhouse sources. Out of the 193 household budgets in Davies and Eden that could be used to study budget allocations, only 22 budgets covering 141 people had enough information on family composition and quantities of food consumed to allow calorific levels to be estimated. Among these working-class English families living in the lean years of the late 1780s and 1790s, a clear North–South contrast appears. The North in the late eighteenth century, unlike in the preceding century, does much better than both eastern and western portions of the South in terms of calorific intake. The calories per day per capita work out at 2,352 in the North and 1,734 in the South. These numbers, of course, must be adjusted to reflect differing requirements according to age and sex. Initially I estimated that children would have 0.75 of the needs of adults, and thereby came up with an adult equivalent calorific value of 2,823 in the North and 2,109 in the South. If one estimates that the figure for the North, which had increased its share of the population, represented 33% of the population, and the South 67%, then the national average would be 2,349. I did not make any allowance for sex, because so many of the women in the budgets were either pregnant or lactating, which pushed up their calorific requirements near to those of adult males.[20]

Recently Robert Fogel has re-estimated the adult equivalency figures using the computation system of the World Health Organization. In that system, all calories are calculated as per equivalent adult male aged 20–39. The calorific consumption rates are broken down by 5 to 10-year age-groups and by sex, adult women on average are assumed to consume about 73% of the calories of men of the same age. Using this system, Fogel has come up with revised figures which yield a national average of 2,826 in 1790.[21]

The problem is that to get the correct totals of calories, one must know the age structure of the consumers. Fogel took the age structure in Wrigley and Schofield. The Eden and Davies budgets used for the calorie counts, however, had a very different age structure because they were interested in surveying families with many children. Therefore, I recalculated Fogel's numbers using the World Health Organization system and the actual age and sex structure of the people in the budgets. The results are not much different, as the paucity of older adults compensates for the over-representation of children. The figures come out at 3,408 per adult male equivalent in the North, and 2,375 in the South, amounting to a national average of 2,716. As I consider the 0.73 calorific ratio of women aged 20–39 to men aged 20–39 too low (because of childbearing demands on this eighteenth-century population), I then played around with the conversion factors, making men and women of that age-group equal in their need for calories. That change reduced the national average to 2,586. Also, because of the heavy reliance on child labour after the age of 10, I experimented with giving children aged 10–19 higher conversion factors, and those along with counting women aged 20–39 the same as men, brought down the calories to 2,520.[22] In short, the calorie estimates range from the low 2,500s to the low 2,700s in terms of adult male equivalent units.

Nutritionists today estimate that an average adult male requires approximately 2,700 calories daily and a female 2,000, unless she is pregnant or lactating in whch case her needs jump to about 2,500. The manual labour performed by early modern men and women would have raised the optimum considerably. 3,500 to 4,000 calories are recommended for those engaged in heavy physical work. Also, children from the age of 10 on demand greater amounts than their elders in order to grow. In this context the 2,500 to 2,700 range per equivalent male adult that we have hypothesized would mean that either hard labour, or the growth of children and foetuses, or the health of adults, or all of the above would suffer. Assuming a slightly higher national figure for England of 2,800 per male equivalent and a log normal distribution of these calories among the various income classes, Fogel has estimated that the bottom

20% of the population could not have done more than 6 hours of light work or 65 minutes of heavy work a day.[23]

Apart from the issue of calorie levels, there is the question of nutritional balance and the impact of the new commodities on diet. The working-class households in the Davies and Eden surveys relied heavily on a market-bought diet. About 33% of the families surveyed had gardens. Far fewer had livestock, 15% being owners of pigs and only a couple of households possessing cows. Poultry and eggs were rarely mentioned.

Table 5.5 shows the percentage of total food expenditure taken up by each food category in the Davies and Eden surveys. In both the North and South, the largest expenditure, predictably enough, went on cereals—bread, flour, meal—although there were substantial differences by region, with a higher proportion of expenditure on cereals in the South than in the North. Expenditure on dairy products, on the other hand, was higher in the North, and the North also spent somewhat more on potatoes and vegetables—although the presence of gardens makes this percentage more open to question in both areas than are those for the other categories. Meat consumption in these bad times was low (12% of the budget). Spending on treacle, sugar, and tea constituted over 10% of

TABLE 5.5 Percentage breakdown of annual food expenditure by English labouring families 1787–1796 (No. = 193)

Food category	North	South
Cereals	50.3	66.0
Meat	12.1	12.4
Dairy products and eggs	16.0	5.2
Potatoes and vegetables	7.9	2.6
Sugar, treacle, tea, etc.[a]	11.2	11.3
Beer	2.4	2.5
TOTAL	100.0 = £22.0	100.0 = £23.8

[a] This category also includes small amounts of other grocery items in addition to sweeteners and tea because sometimes the milk put in tea or some butter or salt was included in the price. It is doubtful whether these additional commodities amounted to more than 1% of the 11%. In the observations where the amount spent on tea and sugar alone was clear, these two items constituted 75% of the amount spent on groceries.

Sources: Eden, *State of the Poor*, ii and iii; Davies, *Labourers in Husbandry*.

the money laid out for meals, testifying to the impact made on the English diet by the new commodities.[24]

Middle-class reformers of the period constantly urged the working class to abandon sugar and tea, consume more wholemeal and non-wheat cereals, and grow potatoes. As one such critic of the poor wrote, 'instead of two meals a day of hasty-pudding [oatmeal based], beer, and milk ... the labouring people, in general, have substituted the less substantial food of tea, sugar, wheaten bread and butter; which cost double the sum.'[25] Indeed, the calories per penny of the former clearly exceeded the units provided by the latter, as Table 5.6 reveals. Sugar with its quick energy rush and caffeinated drinks undoubtedly reduced the total calorie intake for most labouring households everywhere in England. That calorific superiority of the North can be explained primarily by its greater expenditure on oatmeal, milk, and potatoes at a time when the South spent its money much more exclusively on wheaten bread. The reasons for these differences, however, are probably more complicated than the reformers would admit. Market availability, facilities for food preparation, as well as physical reaction to certain combinations of ingredients all could have been involved.

Household consumption of meat was very low. Once it was orthodoxy in dietary research that the major cause of malnutrition world-wide was inadequate amounts of protein. More recently, it has been argued that men and women can just about live on bread alone, if there is enough of it. The proponents of this view contend that in

TABLE 5.6 Calories per penny, *c*.1794–1795

Commodity	Calories per penny	Price per lb./pt.
Wheaten bread	384	3*d*.
Oatmeal	880	2*d*.
Potatoes	1,000	0.4*d*.
Meat	192	5*d*.
Cheese	320	5*d*.
Milk	448	0.7–0.5*d*.
Butter	320	10*d*.
Beer	200	1*d*.
Sugar	192	9*d*.
Tea	0	3*s*.

Source: derived from prices in Eden, *State of the Poor, passim*.

malnourished populations a calorie rather than a protein gap exists, because when sufficient energy units are available, so are proteins. This reasoning is based upon the fact that grains—maize, rice, millet, wheat—are the basic component of diets in most poor nations, and when these cereals are consumed in large quantities a considerable amount of protein is also provided. Other researchers, though, continue to maintain that animal proteins are vitally necessary, particularly for growth among adolescents. They also point to the bulkiness of a diet where cereals comprise the only source of protein and the difficulty small children would have digesting it.[26] I mention this debate here because it makes an unequivocal statement about the harm produced by these families' very low consumption of meat (probably no more than about 1 oz. a day) more difficult.

More worrisome are the low levels of milk and cheese consumption.[27] The amount of high-grade animal protein one could obtain from a penny's worth of meat, cheese, or milk is roughly the same, but as Table 5.6 demonstrates, compared with meat, milk had over 100% more calories per penny, and cheese had 50% more. Even more importantly, both dairy products possess large quantities of an indispensable mineral that meat almost entirely lacks—calcium. Calcium is required in greater amounts by children and pregnant or lactating women. For these groups, the recommended daily allowance of milk (or its equivalent in cheese) is 1.5–2 pts. That amount would provide 75–100% of calcium needs for mothers and children, and nearly all the protein, as well as contribute 670 calories to the diet.

It is possible to estimate the milk and cheese consumed by many of the families in the Davies and Eden survey and then divide that amount by the number of children and lactating or pregnant women in the families. Table 5.7 shows the result. In the North, less than 10% of the households obtained sufficient amounts of milk or cheese to provide the children or women in the family with 2 pts. or more a day, while in the South even fewer (2.3%) did. The only other important source of calcium among the foods commonly eaten by the families was cereals. Assuming that children and the mother each ate 1 lb. of bread a day or its equivalent, that amount would furnish about 33% of the calcium requirement. If other foods added a little bit here and there as well, then it is quite possible that 1 pt. of milk a day would be enough. As Table 5.7 indicates, however, consumption by 50% of families in the North and 90% in the South fell below even that amount. These figures, moreover, also assume that all the milk in the family would go to the children and mothers,

TABLE 5.7 Milk or milk equivalent[a] consumption by children aged 2–16 and pregnant or lactating women in English labouring families, 1787–1796

Quantity of milk or milk equivalent	% of families in North (No. = 54)	% of families in South (No. = 128)
2 pt. and over	9.3	2.3
1 pt. and over	40.7	7.8
0.5 pt. and over	31.5	27.3
Under 0.5 pt.	16.7	36.7
None	1.9	25.8
TOTAL[b]	100.0	100.0

[a] Milk equivalent in cheese: 2.6 oz. cheese has approximately the same amount of calcium and protein as 1 pt. of milk.
[b] Rounding up of figures may result in totals which are not precisely 100.
Sources: Eden, *State of the Poor*, ii and iii; Davies, *Labourers in Husbandry*.

when in fact there is no indication that special allotments were reserved for them. Indeed, evidence exists that more milk and more ounces of cheese usually went to grown men who were to receive 'substantial food', while women and children had to content themselves with small amounts of milk added to tea and porridge and lesser portions of other dairy products. The medieval population had considered milk and cheese to be 'peasant food', and apparently households had little trouble obtaining adequate supplies. At the end of the eighteenth century, however, as shortages became chronic, the working class could not count on these items being a part of their meals. It took almost a century before lower-income households could afford to consume regularly 'white meat', the old term for dairy products and eggs.[28]

As we have seen, the Davies and Eden budgets provide evidence that calorific intake was low, regular usage of new commodities widespread, and consumption of foods contributing to growth in children, infants, and foetuses very low among families of the working class. The dietary situation in the populous South was more critical than that in the North. Of course, the late 1780s and 1790s were recognized as an especially bad time for workers with inflation, wars, and urbanization all taking their toll. The question is what about pre-1780 England, and how did those English who migrated to the colonies fare by comparison?

One source for discovering something about the diet of working-class households over time is the menus and accounts of poorhouses in England and America.[29] As with household budget surveys, there are problems. The quality of the commodities is impossible to determine. Many institutions, like households, had gardens which supplied them with vegetables not listed in the accounts. Inmates sometimes purchased their own food to supplement the institutional fare. Generally, however, these figures are an over-estimate of inmates' calorific intake. When menus are the source, one is relying on what institutions want the public to believe about their diets. When amounts are the source, no allowance has been made for spoilage or misappropriation. These shortcomings should be kept in mind when evaluating the information provided in Table 5.8 about food consumption in English institutions from 1589 to 1796, and in the New York Almshouse in 1738 and Philadelphia's Almshouse and Workhouse in 1769. The two pre-1650 poorhouse diets show a somewhat higher level of calories per inmate than do many of the later figures, but the evidence is too skimpy to base generalizations upon. More striking is the consistency in the figures over time, especially when age is taken into account and the similarity with the calorie estimates from household budgets.[30] Throughout the early modern period, workhouses seem to have offered a daily diet in the mid- to high 2,000s in adult male equivalent terms. Hospitals, where less work was done but illness consumed calories, did better by their inmates. The New York Poorhouse in the 1730s provided more than the English institutions, but the Philadelphia Workhouse level of 2,593 in 1769 was not particularly impressive. These institutions do not seem to have catered to children. The poorhouse offering the best calorific situation, New York in 1738, had only one non-adult inmate, and one of the smallest allotments, even after adjusting for male adult equivalency, was offered by the Bristol children's workhouse.

If the often expressed view, that poorhouse inmates fared better than families on the outside, was true, then those on the outside had a problem, particularly those who were expected to do 10–12 hours of work, have a baby, or grow. In adult male equivalency terms, none of the averages, whether from household budgets or workhouse accounts, reach 3,500 or above. Frederick Eden's enthusiastic endorsement of a diet for manual labourers that adds up to a little less than 2,900 calories suggests that dietary standards for the working class remained low throughout the early modern period.[31]

In terms of nutritional balance in these institutional diets, some long-term changes were apparent. The percentage of expenditure devoted to cereals rose perceptibly during the eighteenth century, as might be expected. Over time there was quite possibly a decline in the consumption of animal proteins, although it is not particularly noticeable if one looks only at meat. Throughout the early modern period, English institutions commonly offered less than 0.25 lb. of meat or fish a day, while American institutions provided about double that amount, 0.45 in the New York Poorhouse and 0.43 at Philadelphia's. The colonial figures closely correspond to other estimates made of American meat consumption in the eighteenth century.[32] More clear-cut is the decline in milk and cheese consumption. All four pre-eighteenth-century English poorhouse diets show at least 1 pt. of milk or its equivalent in cheese per inmate daily. In the eighteenth-century diets, only four out of twenty show as much as 1 pt. or more, and all of these were either in the North or the West of England. The decline, moreover, occurred earlier than the 1780s and 1790s. It was apparent by the second quarter of the century, a relatively affluent period. Cheese consumption seems to have dropped off in all regions, as consumption of butter, which contains almost no protein or calcium, increased. In the 1780s and 1790s, some poorhouses gave up serving cheese altogether. The use of milk in porridge also declined in many places, particularly in the South of England.

In the two colonial poorhouses, the milk and cheese consumption was also below 1 pt. Very small quantities of cheese appear in the 1738 New York accounts, and none surfaced in those for Philadelphia in 1769. Meat consumption, of course, could take care of any possible protein shortage, but the calcium requirements of children would not be satisfied.

As a relatively small number of people spent long periods of time in poorhouses, what we want to know is whether the decline in milk and cheese consumption apparent in the institutional records occurred outside the poorhouses as well. What is known about the ownership of cows by labourers and husbandmen suggests that this could well have been the case in England, but in America the poorhouse figures probably do not reflect the situation for the non-urban family. As mentioned in the chapter on home production, the possession of cows by cottagers in the South of England began declining in the early seventeenth century, and continued to drop thereafter. In contrast, during the Tudor period nearly every rural household had 'kyne', and that continued to be pretty much the situation in America throughout the eighteenth century. Cheese was

TABLE 5.8 Poorhouse diets: 1589–1795

Year	Place and kind of source	Daily calories per inmate	Daily calories per male adult equivalent[a]	Cereals as % of expenditure	Daily amount of meat and fish (lb.)	Daily amount of milk or milk equivalent (pt.)	Sugar and caffeine drinks as % of expenditure[b]	Maize	Rice	Potatoes
ENGLAND										
1589	Bury Poorhouse—menu	2,884	n.a.	n.a.	0.29	1.57	no mention	no	no	no
1632	Norwich Children's Hospital—menu	2,581[c]	n.a.	n.a.	0.16	1.18	no mention	no	no	no
1687	Bartholomew's Hospital—menu	2,323	n.a.	n.a.	0.23	1.00	no mention	no	yes	no
1699	Bristol Childrer's Workhouse—menu	1,768	2,357	n.a.	0.16	1.00	n.a.	no	no	yes
1725	St Albans Workhouse—accounts	2,032	2,709	16.5	0.30	1.29	3.7	no	yes	no
1725	Greenwich Workhouse—accounts	2,191	n.a.	26.9	0.47	0.77	n.a.	no	yes	no
1732	St Andrew Holborn Workhouse—accounts	1,814	n.a.	31.4	0.27	0.64	4.5	no	yes	no
1732	Clerkenwell Workhouse—menu	2,331	n.a.	n.a.	0.21	0.89	n.a.	no	yes	no
1743	Northants Hospital—menu	2,704	n.a.	n.a.	0.39	0.32	n.a.	no	yes	no
1773	Norwich Hospital—menu	2,431	n.a.	n.a.	0.14	0.66	n.a.	no	yes	yes
1782	Tiverton Hospital—menu	2,415	n.a.	n.a.	0.11	1.90	n.a.	no	no	yes
1783	Norwich New Workhouse—accounts	2,490	n.a.	58.7	0.22	0.50	1.5	no	no	yes
1783	Norwich Old Workhouse—accounts	2,120	n.a.	55.2	0.23	0.32	1.8	no	no	no

Year									
1787	Norwich New Workhouse—accounts	2,202	n.a.	54.2	0.13	0.09	2.7	no	no	yes
1787	Norwich Old Workhouse—accounts	2,073	n.a.	57.2	0.08	0.19	2.3	no	no	yes
1794	Wight Workhouse—accounts	1,795	2,393	44.2	0.13	0.30	2.6	no	yes	yes
1795	Kettering Workhouse—menu	2,339	n.a.	n.a.	0.21	0.59	n.a.	no	no	yes
1795	Melton, House of Industry—menu	2,164	n.a.	n.a.	0.18	0.39	n.a.	no	no	no
1795	Liverpool Workhouse—accounts	2,477	n.a.	42.3	0.26	1.04	2.7	no	no	yes
1795	All Saints, Derby, Workhouse—accounts	2,376	3,168	42.5	0.43	0.49	2.6	no	no	yes
1795	St Peter's, Derby, Workhouse—accounts	2,080	2,773	35.8	0.49	0.70	0.2	no	no	yes
1796	Hull Workhouse—menu	2,395	n.a.	n.a.	0.14	1.36	n.a.	no	no	yes
COLONIES										
1738	New York Poorhouse	2,886	3,395	27.6	0.45	0.60	13.8	yes	no	no
1769	Philadelphia Workhouse and Almshouse	1,945	2,593	23.7	0.43	0.29	18.6	yes	yes	yes

[a] Only calculated when source gave some age and sex information about inmates.

[b] 'n.a.' indicates that sugar was included in the diet, but the amount spent on it cannot be ascertained.

[c] My calculation. US Bureau of the Census, *Historical Statistics*, has the rounded-off sum of 2,700.

Sources: 1632 Norwich Children's Hospital—US Bureau of the Census, *Historical Statistics*, pt. 2, Washington DC, 1975, p. 1175; 1687 St Bartholomew's Hospital—J. C. Drummond and Anne Wilbraham, *The Englishman's Food*, London, 1957, p. 104; 1699 Bristol Children's Workhouse—E. E. Butcher (ed.), *Bristol Corporation of the Poor, 1696–1834*, in *Bristol Record Society Publications*, 3 (1932), 68–9; 1725 St Albans Workhouse and Greenwich Workhouse—*An Account of Several Workhouses for Employing and Maintaining the Poor*, London, 1725; 1732 St Andrew Holborn Workhouse and Clerkenwell Workhouse—ibid., 1732 ed.; 1743 Northampton County Hospital—*Statutes . . . for . . . Hospital . . . Northampton*, Northampton, 1743; 1773 Norwich Hospital—*Norwich and Norfolk Hospital*, London, 1773, pp. 37–8; 1732 New York Poorhouse—Audit of the Account of Mr John Sebring, Keeper and Overseer of the Poorhouse, New York Historical Society; 1769 Philadelphia Workhouse and Almshouse—Almshouse Manager's Minutes, 1766–78, vol. i, Philadelphia City Archives, City Hall Annex; rest of workhouses—Eden, *State of the Poor*, ii, and iii, *passim*.

not as heavily produced in the colonies as it had been in sixteenth-century England, but milk was readily available.

The institutional diets are weakest in reflecting usage of the new commodities by the general population. The 'good' new commodities—rice, potatoes, and maize—were probably more quickly adopted by the poorhouses than by the public because of their cheapness and their ability to substitute for the traditional grains. In England, rice was routinely used in the institutions by the 1720s, while potatoes only show up regularly after mid-century.[33] In America, inmates consumed maize most extensively, although in the Philadelphia workhouse both potatoes and rice were also provided. From other evidence, it seems potatoes became common in America around mid-century.[34]

In contrast to the 'good' new commodities, the 'bad' new commodities probably appeared less often and in smaller quantities in institutions than among the population at large. Most English poorhouses forbade the use of caffeine drinks, tobacco, and spirits because they did not want to be accused of giving 'luxuries' to the indigent. As a consequence, tea almost never appears in the menus of institutions before 1800. The financial accounts are more ambiguous because they often have a general category of 'groceries' that could include these items. Where complete enumeration is given, tobacco, brandy, tea, gin, and wine occasionally do appear in the records of payment. When they do, they are usually justified as being for medicinal purposes. Complaints about inmates using the small amounts of wages earned at houses of industry to purchase tea and sugar or hoarding workhouse food to sell outside in order to buy these sinful goods suggest that individual consumption was higher than the institutional records indicate.[35]

Thus the percentage of expenditure by English poorhouses on sugar products and caffeine drinks that appears in Table 5.8 is primarily for sugar and molasses, and the reporting is probably incomplete. According to the table, sugar began showing up in the institutional records during the late seventeenth century and was in constant use by the 1720s.

In the colonies, where the main dispute over the new commodities were in reference to the taxation policies of the Crown and Parliament, rather than complaints over the consumption habits of the poor, institutions in the port towns of New York and Philadelphia spent large amounts on sugar, molasses, rum, tea, and chocolate.[36] Eliminating sugar by-products—molasses and rum—and considering only sugar itself, the consumption per inmate in the New York Almshouse during 1738 was over 7 lb. and in Philadelphia in 1769 it was more than 5 lb.

Estimates for the non-institutionalized labouring poor are two to three times higher.[37]

A Nutritional Famine?

The materials that have been put together here present a mixed picture of food consumption in the early modern period. Most of the English population, and especially that portion which migrated to America, were not subject to the kinds of famines and food crises that plagued many societies of the time. On the other hand, as starvation-related mortality seemed to decline and finally disappear, low calorific levels continued and the dietary changes that occurred may have had a less salutary effect on the health of the population, at least in England. The abysmal dietary situation of the early nineteenth-century industrialization period, focused upon in the standard of living debates, may well have had its origin a century earlier.

The examination of the proportion of household budgets and wages devoted to food has shown that it was often lower than commonly assumed. The working class in England in years of war and shortages might devote as much as 70% of their budget to food, but in more normal times the percentage was probably more often in the mid-50s. Indeed, when the proportion rose over 60% this seemed to trigger disturbances and investigations. The percentages were notably lower in America where it is unlikely that food took up more than 50% of expenditure when all types of miscellaneous outlays are included.

The fact that normally 50–60% of household budgets rather than 80% went on diet, however, does not mean that the members of the working class ate to their hearts' content. In fact food elasticities were higher than sometimes thought. When working people had extra money they often spent it on food, and when they had less income, they cut back. Food was not the only necessity—others were rent, fuel, clothing for protection from the elements, not to mention medicine, lying-in expenses, and burials. By the end of the early modern period, many English labouring families bought nearly their entire diet—apart from garden produce – on the market from the baker, the butcher, the grocer or whoever sold the tea, sugar, butter, milk, flour, bread, and meat in the locality. The more prepared the food the better, so that fuel would not have to be expended in cooking it. About 10% of the budget went on the new commodities, mainly sugar and tea. There were nutritional problems associated with these trends. In the 1780s and 1790s, the calories furnished by the shop-bought diet frequently did not provide the energy needed to perform manual labour. The question is how typical was this labourer's diet of earlier decades? As we have seen, evidence from workhouse records suggests that throughout the eighteenth century, the poor may have had to make do with a diet with a calorie level in the mid- to upper 2,000s—enough energy units perhaps for today's sedentary existence, but not for hard physical work. How can these amounts of calories be squared with the supposed sunrise-to-sunset work schedule? True, the working class did not work that schedule every day. Also, perhaps as many as a third of adult men under the age of 50 had some chronic disabilty that prevented them from fully participating in the workforce.[38] There is, too, the question of nutritional balance. As the eighteenth century progressed and the population increased, bread took up a larger and larger percentage of total outlay on food. There were meat shortages, but the steady decline in milk and cheese consumption during the eighteenth century seems of even greater significance and may help to explain the difference in growth patterns observed between the English and the colonials, who not only consumed more meat but also owned more cows and other livestock.

Why did the shift from oatmeal, milk, cheese and bread to tea, sugar, bread, and butter occur? There is no doubt that the mercantile community reaped rich rewards from promoting the new commodities, for, as has been noted before, they were what made the 'commercial revolution' a reality. In agriculture, the landed classes pushed for reductions in common rights, making household livestock-raising and planting less and less feasible.

The circumstances of pre-industrial consumers, however, should not be completely ignored unless one wants to consider them as no more than passive dupes. If they had unlimited resources no doubt they would have combined their taste for the new commodities with more cheese and meat. When forced to choose, though, they preferred the sugar, tea, butter, and bread. Some of these preferences may have been physiological—the addictive characteristic of caffeine or the energy boost of sugar[39]—and some may have been connected to changes in family work roles and investment patterns. This subject will come up again when consumer durables are discussed. Depending more on a shop-bought diet may have had its nutritional drawbacks, but the earlier mode of local and household production, which may have been associated in people's memories with frequent periods of severe want, may have seemed an even less attractive option.

Although the evidence is too sketchy to allow any certainty, the following seems to be a likely scenario for how these dietary changes developed. In the earlier part of the eighteenth century, when the use of tea, sugar, wheaten bread, and butter was growing, prices for many basic foods were relatively low. Cottagers may have been just as well off, for example, not trying to support a cow, as long as commercial dairy farming continued to grow. It is to be noted that the superior position of the North in the Davies–Eden surveys was not due to labourers possessing their own cow. They bought their milk. It was the increased amount of milk production by the dairies in the region as opposed to the emphasis on producing veal and butter or grains in the South that probably explains the difference. At the end of the century when prices rose and shortages occurred, the working-class consumers were trapped. Consumption of animal products containing protein and calcium dropped further and calorie levels declined. Whether calorific and calcium deficiencies contributed to the growth and health problems observed in some portions of the English population is not certain, for other possible causes—disease, insufficient vitamins from vegetables and fruits, and adulteration of food—could not be measured in the sources used here. Increased alcoholic intake is also sometimes mentioned as a cause, although considering the consumption of rum in America, it seems unlikely that the colonists derived their advantage by being more abstemious than their Old World counterparts.

Over ten years ago Freudenberger and Cummins raised the question of whether workers in the pre-industrial period had enough energy to raise productivity. They assumed, however, that this situation changed during the Industrial Revolution. But low levels of calories seem to have been the norm for many English workers during the later eighteenth century and for a number of decades in the nineteenth century as well. If there is a dietary change that can be documented as occurring in the eighteenth and nineteenth centuries, it is the increasing reliance on appetite appeasers such as tobacco, caffeine drinks, and sugar. Public health reports from the 1860s show that the per head calorie level of diet of indoor workers in domestic industries (silkweavers, glovers, stocking-knitters, and shoemakers) was 2,190, and that of rural labourers was 2,760. Factory operatives normally consumed more calories, although many of the added energy units came from sugar.[40]

The picture that one comes away with from looking at a wide variety of sources on diet in early modern England and America is not one of starvation among large numbers of the working class, so much as a condition of continual longing for greater quantities of the new commodities and for more—and better-quality—bread, meat, and milk. It is hard to believe that food was not constantly on the minds of a large percentage of the working population. And it is probably no accident that most of the promotional literature on America treats in great detail the plentifulness of fruit, vegetables and game and emphasizes the generous quantities of food that appeared on New World tables. Perhaps the longing for more food was less in the colonies because of this abundance, although it would seem that the thirst for the new commodities continued there as elsewhere. It was, after all, a food riot involving a tax on tea that brought on the American Revolution.

What is particularly noteworthy, considering how poorly those in the working class were fed, is the 40% or so of their expenditure that went on necessities other than food. The food percentage does not reflect a nutritionally satisfied population, but one resigned to a certain level of malnourishment. Thus one finds low-income groups with high food elasticities, ready to spend extra money on food as if it were a luxury. Pent-up food demand may also explain why nineteenth-century improvements in working-class incomes did not produce a more dramatic drop in the proportion of expenditure devoted to diet.

Chapter 5

1. In *The Population History of England, 1541–1871*, London, 1981, E. A. Wrigley, R. S. Schofield, and Ronald Demos Lee report that in the periods 1544–1640 and 1641–1745 there was a weak but positive relation between prices and mortality; between 1746 and 1834 the relation becomes negative and very weak. The major effect on mortality occurred not in the year of high prices but in the two subsequent years, implying that it was not starvation that killed the people but a slow deterioration in health and resistance to infectious disease (pp. 371–2 and 399). This finding coincides with D. J. Oddy's assertion that most death from famine is morbidity-generated and not due to outright starvation ('Urban Famine in Nineteenth-Century Britain: The Effect of the Lancashire Cotton Famine on Working-Class Diet and Health', *Economic History Review*, 36 (1983), 71). Wrigley and Schofield do not deny local or regional food shortages, of course, and scholars have found evidence of these in early modern times and later, although they are usually reluctant to state unequivocally that they produced mortality crises. Andrew B. Appleby, 'Grain Prices and Subsistence Crises in England and France, 1590–1740', *Journal of Economic History*, 39 (1979), 882, mentions that a group of Midlands parishes between 1727 and 1730 were possibly plagued by a subsistence crisis. Victor Skipp, *Crisis and Development: An Ecological Case Study of the Forest of Arden*, Cambridge, 1978, p. 38, sees the early 17th-cent. situation in the area he studied as

Malthusian, but rejects the term 'crisis of subsistence' as a description, because the vital statistics did not change in a sudden, dramatic way as in the classic cases. Oddy (in the Lancashire article) believes a nutritional famine existed during the early 1860s in some textile towns, but has trouble linking this to deaths. In England, it becomes more and more difficult to isolate diet as the cause of death after the early 17th cent.—which seems to be what Wrigley and Schofield are saying. For the extensive literature on food-related mortality crises, see the bibliography in *Population History of England*.

2. Charles Tilly, 'Food Supply and Public Order in Modern Europe', in *The Formation of National States in Western Europe*, ed. Charles Tilly, Princeton, 1975, pp. 380–455; John Walter and Keith Wrightson, 'Dearth and the Social Order in Early Modern England', *Past and Present*, 71 (1976), 22–42; Dale Edward Williams, 'Were "Hunger" Rioters Really Hungry? Some Demographic Evidence', ibid., pp. 70–5; R. B. Outhwaite, 'Death and Government Intervention in English Grain Markets, 1500–1700', *Economic History Review*, 2nd ser. 34 (1981), 389–406; and Walter James Shelton, *English Hunger and Industrial Disorder*, Toronto, 1973.

3. See Fernand Braudel, *The Structures of Everyday Life*, London, 1981, chs. 2 and 3; Immanuel Wallerstein, *The Modern World-System*, ii, *Mercantilism and the Consolidation of the European World Economy, 1600–1750*, New York, 1980, pp. 258ff.; and Redcliffe N. Salaman, *The History of Social Influence of the Potato*, Cambridge, 1949.

4. Robert William Fogel, 'Second Thoughts on the European Escape from Hunger: Famines, Price Elasticities, Entitlements, Chronic Malnutrition, and Mortality Rates', unpublished copyrighted paper, Nov. 1988, pp. 28–35; Kenneth L. Sokoloff and Georgia D. Villaflor, 'The Early Achievement of Modern Stature in America', *Social Science History*, 6 (1982), 453–581; Roderick Floud and Kenneth W. Wachter, 'Poverty and Physical Stature: Evidence on the Standard of Living of London Boys, 1770–1870', ibid., pp. 422–542; and Robert William Fogel, 'Biomedical Approaches to the Estimation and Interpretation of Secular Trends in Equity, Morbidity, Mortality and Labor Productivity in Europe, 1750–1980', unpublished copyrighted paper, Nov. 1987. On the decline in the European diet, see Bartolomé Bennassar and Joseph Goy, 'Contribution à l'histoire de la consommation alimentaire du XIVᵉ siècle', *Annales: Économies, Sociétés, Civilisation*, 30 (1975), 427, and H. J. Teuteberg, 'The General Relationship between Diet and Industrialization', Elborg Forster and Robert Forster (eds.), *European Diet from Pre-industrial to Modern Times*, New York, 1975, p. 64.

5. Robert A. Margo and Richard H. Steckel, 'The Heights of American Slaves: New Evidence on Slave Nutrition and Health', *Social Science History*, 6 (1982), 516–38, and Steckel, 'A Peculiar Population: The Nutrition, Health, and Mortality of American Slaves from Childhood to Maturity', *Journal of Economic History*, 46 (1986), 721–41; and Robert William Fogel, 'The Conquest of High Mortality and Hunger in Europe and America', unpublished copyrighted paper, Sept. 1988, pp. 34–47. (This article by Fogel and the two others cited in n. 4 are part of a forthcoming book, *The Escape from Hunger*.)

6. On Engel studies see George J. Stigler, 'The Early History of Empirical Studies on Consumer Behavior', *Journal of Political Economy*, 42 (1954), 95–113; Jeffrey

G. Williamson, 'Consumer Behavior in the Nineteenth Century: Carroll D. Wright's Massachusetts Workers in 1875', *Explorations in Entrepreneurial History*, 4 (1967), 98–135; and more recently, Steven Dubnoff, 'A Method for Estimating the Economic Welfare of American Families of Any Composition: 1860–1909', *Historical Methods*, 13 (1980), 171–80.

7. E. M. Phelps-Brown and Sheila V. Hopkins, 'Seven Centuries of the Prices of Consumables, Compared with Builders' Wage-Rates', in E. M. Carus-Wilson (ed.), *Essays in Economic History*, ii, New York, 1962, p. 180. A new version of the Phelps-Brown and Hopkins figures for 1500–1911 appears in Wrigley and Schofield, *The Population History of England*, pp. 638–44, but the weights remain the same. The other two weighted indices covering long periods of time, those of E. Gilboy and R. Tucker, use percentages for diet of 80% and 75% respectively. See their articles reprinted in Arthur J. Taylor (ed.), *The Standard of Living in Britain in the Industrial Revolution*, London, 1975, pp. 1–25. M. W. Flinn discusses the various indices produced on prices and wages in 'Trends in Real Wages, 1750–1850', *Economic History Review*, 2nd ser. 27 (1974), 395–413.

8. I calculated the percentages from data provided by King in the following way:

Households	Cost of adult diet p.a. (£)	Average no. of adults in household	Average no. of children in household	Expenditure on diet p.a. (£)	Total expenditure (£)	% expenditure on diet
Day labourers and paupers	2	2	1[a]	5	6.75	74.1
Farmers and freeholders	5	3	2	17	45	37.8
Tradesmen	6	3	2	20	47.5	42.1
Freeholders over £50 income	6	4	3	27	77	35.1
Retainers	8 }					
Noblemen, gentry, children	20[b] }	9	—	108	319.5	33.8
					Total 1%	60.7[c]

[a] King allotted infants and children £1 for diet per annum.

[b] King grouped children and adults together in diet calculations for upper classes to get household expenditure for diet per annum. I estimated that 33% of the members of the upper-class households would be eating at the nobleman–gentry rate and 2.35 eating at the retainer rate.

[c] Weighted average based on the percentage each household group contributes to the entire population.

For an evaluation of how well King estimated the income distribution of the population see Peter H. Lindert and Jeffrey G. Williamson in 'Revising England's Social Tables, 1688–1812', *Explorations in Economic History*, 19 (1982), 385–408.

9. Lynn Hollen Lees, 'Getting and Spending: The Family Budgets of English Industrial Workers in 1890', in John Merriman (ed.), *Consciousness and Class Experience in Nineteenth-Century Europe*, New York, 1979, pp. 169–86.

10. D. Caradog Jones, *The Social Survey of Merseyside*, i, Liverpool, 1934, p. 228, notes the exclusion of all but a few miscellaneous items of expenditure in the 1904 Ministry of Labour survey. Nevertheless, the weights derived from that survey were used to calculate the cost of living index during the depression. There were complaints then that the heavy weight given to food in the index (60%) made the working-class family seem better off than it actually was.

11. G. S. Holmes, 'Gregory King and the Social Structure of Pre-industrial England', *Transactions of the Royal Historical Society*, 5th ser. 27 (1977), discusses the motivation behind King's research.

12. The standard guide to wage assessment for England is W. E. Minchinton (ed.), *Wage Regulation in Pre-industrial England*, Newton Abbot, 1972.

13. Donald Woodward, 'Wage Rates and Living Standards in Pre-industrial England', *Past and Present*, 91 (1981), 28–46, presents evidence that craftsmen's wages were normally only a part of their entire income.

14. For an attempt to do just that see John Komlos, 'The Food Budget of English Workers: A Comment on Shammas', *Journal of Economic History*, 48 (1988), 149; see also my reply, *Journal of Economic History*, 48 (1988), 673–6.

15. Wrigley and Schofield, *Population History of England*, pp. 638–9. Steve Rappaport's real wage index for sixteenth-century London workers shows less of a decline between 1500 and 1600, yet the drop still amounts to 30%. See *Worlds within Worlds: Structures of Life in sixteenth-century London*, Cambridge, 1989, pp. 145–61.

16. See e.g. table 49 in Peter R. Shergold, *Working-Class Life: The 'American Standard' in Comparative Perspective, 1899–1913*, Pittsburgh, 1982. Also note the over-unity elasticity for food that Michael Haines reports for German workers in 1890 ('Consumer Behavior and Immigrant Assimilation', paper presented at the 1987 ASSA meeting, Chicago, table 1).

17. The tables in Stigler, 'Early History of Consumer Behavior', p. 97, show this clearly. Using the Eden and Davies data, I found that they yielded 193 usable observations and produced an elasticity for food of 1.069 (double log form, with the log of household size included in the regression). N. F. R. Crafts ('Income Elasticities of Demand and the Release of Labour by Agriculture during the British Industrial Revolution', *Journal of Economic History*, 9 (Spring, 1980), 157), separating the data given by Davies and by Eden and using fewer observations, obtained slightly different results, although he also stresses high elasticity. Unlike Crafts, I used expenditure rather than income, so that my figures would be comparable to those of other budget studies. For the expenditure and family-size elasticities for different kinds of food and drink see Carole Shammas, 'The Eighteenth Century English Diet and Economic Change', *Explorations in Economic History*, 21 (1984), 259.

18. Sokoloff and Villaflor, 'The Early Achievement of Modern Stature in America'; Margo and Steckel, 'The Heights of American Slaves: New Evidence on Slave Nutrition and Health'; Floud and Wachter, 'Poverty and Physical Stature: Evidence on the Standard of Living of London Boys, 1770–1870'. Joel Mokyr and Cormac O'Grada, 'Living Standards in Ireland and Britain, 1800–1850: The East India Company Army Data', unpublished paper, 1986, indicate that even Irish soldiers were taller than the British. The standard accounts of English and American diets, respectively, are J. C. Drummond and Anne Wilbraham, *The*

Englishman's Food, rev. ed. London, 1957, and Richard Osborn Cummings, *The American and His Food: A History of Food Habits in the United States*, rev. edn. Chicago, 1941.

19. The percentage allotted to miscellaneous expenditure was 6%, while the proportion given for other American samples and for European ones in the late 19th cent. was between 15% and 20%. It should be noted, too, that the calculations of Billy G. Smith ('"The Best Poor Man's Country": Living Standards of the "Lower Sort", in Late Eighteenth Century Philadelphia', *Working Papers from the Regional Economic History Research Center*, 2 (1979),), made for Philadelphia workers in 1762, did not include a miscellaneous category, so the Philadelphia percentages for food are also too high.

20. For the per capita figures here, I counted all the people in the household, including infants. In earlier work I did, infants were excluded for the Eden and Davies per capita figure. For the adult equivalent figure, however, infants were counted as 0.75, along with all other children of 16 years and younger, both in my *Explorations in Economic History* article and here. I estimated that the number of children who consumed less than 0.75 of an adult's diet should compensate for those adolescents who consumed or should have consumed as much or more than an adult.

21. Fogel, 'Biomedical Approaches', pp. 32–50 and 86.

22. Below is the age structure of the 141 people in the Davies and Eden surveys, each age-group's share of the people in the budgets, and the ratio of each age-group's calorific consumption to that of males aged 20–39. The sex of many of the children was not given, so I assumed the unknowns were half girls and half boys. The ratio of calorific consumption, which is taken from the table in Fogel, 'Biomedical Approaches', p. 6, reflects the sex composition of the age-group. If women aged 20–39 counted as consuming the same calories as men aged 20–39, then for the North, the conversation factor would be 0.77, and for the South, it would be 0.72. If, in addition, children aged 10–19 counted as consuming the

(1) Age-group	(2) % share of age-group in total sample	(3) Ratio of calorific consumption to that of men aged 20–39	(4) Product of cols. 2 and 3 (conversion factor)
North of England (30 people)			
0–4	0.23	0.44	0.10
5–9	0.27	0.69	0.19
10–14	0.13	0.85	0.12
15–19	0.03	0.90	0.03
20–39	0.20	0.87	0.17
40–9	0.03	0.70	0.02
50–9	0.07	0.78	0.03
60–9	0.03	0.70	0.02
Conversion factor for male adult equivalent			0.69

(1) Age-group	(2) % share of age-group in total sample	(3) Ratio of calorific consumption to that of men aged 20–39	(4) Product of cols. 2 and 3 (conversion factor)
South of England (111 people)			
0–4	0.21	0.44	0.09
5–9	0.28	0.69	0.19
10–14	0.15	0.85	0.13
15–19	0.04	0.90	0.04
20–39	0.28	0.85	0.24
40–9	0.01	0.95	0.01
50–9	0.04	0.78	0.03
Conversion factor for male adult equivalent			0.73

2352/0.69 = 3408 × 0.33 (population share of North) = 1,125
1734/0.73 = 2375 × 0.67 (population share of South) = 1,591
TOTAL   = 2,716

same calories as men aged 20–39, then the conversion factor would be 0.74 in the North and 0.79 in the South.

23. See Helen Andrews Guthrie, *Introductory Nutrition*, 3rd edn, St Louis, 1975, p. 496, for current recommended calorie levels. Fogel, 'Biomedical Approaches', p. 49.

24. The distinction between North and South was often remarked upon by contemporaries and has been noted time and time again by historians. See Brinley Thomas, 'Feeding England During the Industrial Revolution: A View from the Celtic Fringe', *Agriculture History*, 56 (1982), 328–42, and Charles Smith, *Three Tracts on the Corn Trade*, London, 1766, pp. 183–5. I put both the eastern and western halves of the South of England together because their patterns were similar. A few Monmouthshire households were also included under the rubric South.

25. Frederic Morton Eden, *The State of the Poor*, London 1797, p. 876. Drummond and Wilbraham, *Englishman's Food*, give similar statements from 18th-cent. critics of the working class such as Arthur Young. David Davies was more sympathetic (*Laborers in Husbandry*, pp. 31–40). He linked the changes in production and consumption together. In the Davies and Eden surveys, I have found that the elasticities for meat (1.9) and beer (2.89) are higher than for tea and sugar (1.06). Bread is below unity, but barely so (0.92).

26. J. C. Waterlow and P. R. Payne, 'The Protein Gap', *Nature*, 258 (1975), 113–17, argue that the problem is mainly one of insufficient calories, not protein. More recently, Lawrence S. Greene's review of the issue shows that the controversy continues. He concludes that 'caloric supplementation to pregnant mothers, infants, and toddlers is probably the most effective means of increasing birthweight early in life and decreasing high rates of infant and toddler mortality

and morbidity. . . . However, the data cited strongly suggest that protein intake in late childhood and adolescence is the limiting factor affecting physical growth during this period. Although mortality is not a significant risk factor at this time, the final morphological characteristics of the developing individual are molded during this period. . . . Thus attention to protein needs during adolescence may have a significant influence on worker productivity, and thus economic capability, later in life': Lawrence S. Greene and Francis E. Johnston (eds.), *Social and Biological Predictors of Nutritional Status, Physical Growth, and Neurological Development*, New York, 1980, pp. 316–17. See also A. Roberto Frisancho, 'Role of Calories and Protein Reserves on Human Growth during Childhood and Adolescence in a Mestizo Peruvian Population', ibid., pp. 49–60, for research on the enhanced protein needs of children and adolescents. What remains elusive in the debate is the question of protein quality and what mix of low-grade vegetable proteins and high-grade animal proteins is needed. Waterlow and Payne argue that cereal proteins are sufficient. Guthrie, *Introductory Nutrition*, pp. 56–7, on the other hand, seems to feel that vegetable proteins alone do not promote growth.

27. Drummond and Willbraham, *Englishman's Food*, discuss the importance of milk, cheese, and eggs more extensively than most historical treatments of diet. See *passim*, esp. pp. 75–6 and 446–7, although some of the research is now out of date.

28. Eden notes that in one Hinsworth, Herefordshire family, tea consumption was high 'as the children use much', *State of the Poor*, iii, p. ccxliii. In a Rutlandshire workhouse, breakfast every day of the week for women consisted of 'tea and bread and butter', while for men it was 'milk or broth', ibid. ii. 602. Edward Shorter, *A History of Women's Bodies*, New York, 1982, pp. 20–2, argues that European women in this era routinely received less to eat than men, even though their body size was more comparable to that of men than is the case today. He suggests this differential may have affected their energy levels and ability to resist disease. On the medieval diet and dairy products, see Christopher Dyer, 'English Diet in the Later Middle Ages', in T. H. Aston *et al.* (eds.), *Social Relations and Ideas*, Cambridge, 1983, pp. 206–7. On 20th-cent. trends, see Chris Wandle, *Changing Food Habits in the U.K.*, London, 1977, pp. 36–7.

29. T. L. Richardson, 'The Agricultural Labourer's Standard of Living in Kent, 1790–1840', in D. Oddy and D. Miller (eds.), *The Making of The Modern British Diet*, London, 1976, pp. 103–15, uses the accounts of poorhouses in Kent but they are all from the 19th cent.

30. Apparently, women and children were given less in most institutions, and the reductions given for one institution indicate that the proportions for children were far below what would be recommended today. In a Tiverton, Devon workhouse in 1782 the diet for women contained about 90% of the calories of the male allotment, 'working children' received 80%, while those not working got 60%, Eden, *State of the Poor*, ii, 144. Calorie tables today show children over 10 needing as many as or more than the fully grown male, Guthrie, *Introductory Nutrition*, p. 496. Drummond and Wilbraham, *Englishman's Food*, pp. 255–8, discuss the Tiverton diets and the problems inherent in not accounting for the calories children need for growth. The total calories they estimate for the diets are lower than my estimates.

31. Eden's estimates appear in *State of the Poor*, iii, p. ccclvi. American workhouses had more extensive gardens than most English workhouses, and probably the Philadelphia and New York inmates received substantial supplements to their diet from this source. Nevertheless it would be hard to imagine that this could amount to more than a few hundred calories a day.

32. There is an unusual unanimity found in the estimates of meat consumption by the American civilian population during the mid-18th. cent. Sara F. McMahon, 'Provisions Laid up for the Family: Toward a History of Diet in New England, 1650–1850', paper delivered at the Conference on Economic Growth and Social Change in the Early Republic 1775–1860, Chicago, Ill., Apr. 1980 (shortened version published in *Historical Methods*, 14 (1981), 4–21), shows between 0.4 and 0.5 lb. a day in Middlesex County, Massachusetts between 1730 and the Revolution. Billy G. Smith estimates the Philadelphia worker's intake at 0.48 in the 1760s ('"Best Poor Man's Country"', p. 52). David Klingaman, 'Food Surpluses and Deficits in the American Colonies, 1768–1772', *Journal of Economic History*, 31 (1971), 559, suggests 0.41 at *c*.1770. James Lemon finds that Pennsylvania farmers' widows received about 0.42 in the 1740–90 period, *Best Poor Man's Country*, Baltimore, 1972, pl 155. US Bureau of the Census, *Historical Statistics of the United States, Colonial Times to 1970*, Washington DC, 1975, pt. 1, pp. 329–30, has civilian consumption in 1900 at 0.41 and in 1965, among the lower third of income groups in urban areas, 0.57. The mid-18th-cent. levels then were rather modern. There is some evidence that in the 17th cent., though, colonial consumption of meat was 25% to 50% lower. See McMahon, 'Provisions for the Family', and Gloria L. Main, *Tobacco Colony: Life in Early Maryland, 1650–1720*, Princeton, 1982, pp. 202–5.

33. The low level of cheese manufacturing in America has been noted in Chap. 3.

34. McMahon finds in her survey of Middlesex County, Massachusetts that potatoes began appearing in a noticeable way in inventories during the 1740s, and were mentioned in 20% of those inventories where food was enumerated by the time of the Revolution ('Provisions for the Family').

35. One of the few poorhouses that admitted to using tea in its menu was in Rutland-shire: Eden, *State of the Poor*, ii, 602. In another poorhouse, in Yorkshire, women had to spend their earnings from spinning to obtain tea (ibid. iii, 822), but those who used tobacco were given 8 oz. a month. Predictably, Arthur Young complained about inmates in houses of industry being allowed to spend their paltry wages on tea and sugar; Drummond and Wilbraham, *Englishman's Food*, p. 204. In the anonymous pamphlet, *Observations on the Present State of the Poor of Sheffield*, Sheffield, 1774, p. 10, the author charged inmates with selling poorhouse food to people outside in order 'to purchase snuff, tobacco, tea, sugar and such'. Jonas Hanway, in *A Plan for Establishing a Charity-House to be called the Magdalen Charity*, London, 1758, forbade the 'apparatus of a tea table' in his proposed house. Joseph Massie (*A Plan for the Establishment of a Charity-House for Exposed or Deserted Women*, London, 1758) would have restricted tea drinking to 'those of the First Class'. Spirits are mentioned in the acounts of the Bristol Poorhouse and that of the Isle of Wight: Eden, *State of the Poor*, ii, *passim*. The amounts were not large and the prime justification was undoubtedly 'medicinal'.

36. Liberal amounts of chocolate appear. In the New York accounts, and the

quantities of tea and rum consumed in the Philadelphia almshouse and work-houses far exceeded, it would seem, those required for medicinal purposes. In Virginia, William Dabney's account of 'Necessarys delivered to the Poor of St. Martin's Parish Hanover County during my Wardship', Charles Dabney Papers, 1744–8, Research Department of Colonial Williamsburg, microfilm, shows that Dabney dispensed not only corn, bacon, and pork to the indigent but rum as well.

37. Smith, ' "Best Poor Man's Country" ', p. 51, estimates that 16.8 lb. of sugar were consumed annually by a Philadelphia worker in the 1760s. It may be that the rate of sugar consumption after its early 18th-cent. jump did not rapidly increase again until the later 19th cent. See Appendix B on p. 236 in Cummings, *The American and His Food*.
38. Fogel, 'Biomedical Approaches', p. 74.
39. There is a substantial literature in experimental psychology that shows infants' preference for liquids that have been sweetened. See e.g. J. A. Desor, Owen Maller, and Kathryn Andrews, 'Ingestive Responses of Human Newborns to Salty, Sour, and Bitter Stimuli', *Journal of Comparative Physiological Psychology*, 89 (1975), 966–70. I owe this reference to Eugene Eisman. On the appeal of sugar generally see Sidney Mintz, *Sweetness and Power*, New York, 1985.
40. Herman Freudenberger and Gaylord Cummins, 'Health, Work, and Leisure Before the Industrial Revolution', *Explorations in Economic History*, 13 (1976), 1–12. D. J. Oddy, 'Urban Famine, in Nineteenth-Century Britain: The Effect of the Lancashire Cotton Famine in Nineteenth-Century Britain', *Economic History Review*, 36 (1983), 78–80.

6

Housing, Consumer Durables, and the Domestic Environment

THE severity of the domestic environment in pre-modern society has often been commented on by historians. 'It is abundantly clear where the heart of the medieval housekeeper lay', writes Dorothy Davis in her history of shopping,

If he had little money he spent it all on his stomach; if he had plenty, he lavished most of it on his stomach and the rest of it on his back. Far below these in importance came the beauty and comfort of his surroundings, which seem to have made little claim on his purse ... such things as silver and porcelain, sculpture and carving, tapestry and stained glass were considered more suitable for the house of God than the house of man.[1]

In other words, the houses of ordinary individuals were not sites for consumption. The home did not function as much as a social centre for the family because few could afford to create a comfortable environment. Instead villagers gathered in the parish church, the alehouse, and, occasionally, the estate of the local great man. Scarcity imposed a regimen of collective consumption on the community. Diaries, letters, travel accounts, and advice books have provided the basis for most of the generalizations made about the spareness of the domestic environment.[2]

Literary evidence from the end of the Tudor period, however, suggests that things changed in England during the course of the sixteenth century and that the housing of those living in the countryside greatly improved. An Elizabethan clergyman, William Harrison of Essex, is often quoted in regard to this development. He wrote in *The Description of England* that the old men in the village where he lived 'noted three things to be marvelously altered in England within their sound remembrance'. The first was the increased number of chimneys:

(I)n their young days there were not above two or three, if so many, in most uplandish towns of the realm (the religious houses and manor places of their lords always excepted, and peradventure some great personages), but each one made his fire against a reredos [back of an open hearth] in the hall, where he dined and dressed his meat.

The second was the replacement of mats by beds:

for (said they) our fathers, yea, and we ourselves also, have lien full oft upon straw pallets, on rough mats covered only with a sheet, under coverlets, made of dagswain or hapharlots (I use their own terms), and a good round log under their heads instead of a bolster or pillow.

The pillow was thought only appropriate for women in 'childbed'. After many years of marriage, Harrison contended, the head of the household considered himself well-off if he could purchase a flock mattress. Lords might not have feather beds, and servants lacked even a sheet to protect them from the straw irritating their skin. Finally, the old men remarked upon the substitution of pewter for wooden eating equipment: 'for so common were all sorts of treen stuff in old time that a man should hardly find four pieces of pewter (of which one was peradventure a salt) in a good farmer's house.'[3] Richard Carew, writing only a few years later, reported similar improvements in West Country standards of living, even in the remote areas of Cornwall. Once the Cornish husbandman had earthen walls in his house, no plank floors, no glass windows, and no chimneys, but now he 'conformeth himselfe ... to the Easterne patterne'.[4]

Theory of the Great Rebuilding

Historians began to appreciate the comments of these sixteenth-century writers when they saw the early results of a systematic cataloguing of traditional farmhouses and cottages that had survived in the English countryside. It turned out that the first sizeable number of extant dwellings that might be termed vernacular (common to a given area at a given time) dated from the Tudor period. W. G. Hoskins identified the years 1575–1625 as particularly crucial and referred to the phenomenon as the 'Great Rebuilding' of rural England. Villagers, it was argued, converted their houses from one to two storeys by replacing the open-hearth multi-purpose hall, adding chimneys, ceilings, more specialized rooms, and glass windows. Animals sheltered in a byre—a space walled off from the family quarters, but sharing a roof with the main part of the house—were removed to stables and barns. Also builders laid founda-tions rather than placing wall posts into earth-holes, and they used sturdier materials. Instead of timber and mud, brick and stone became more common, and houses lasted at least several generations. More rooms meant more separation of work from the social side of family life and more privacy. With brick chimneys and fireplaces replacing open fires, stairways replacing ladders, and glass replacing paper or shutters in windows, dwellings became more comfortable, lighter, and less smoky.[5]

Over thirty-five years have elapsed since the theory of a Great Rebuilding was initially advanced, and during that time a number of qualifications have been added to its propositions. A close examination of the construction dates for surviving houses has cast doubt on the notion that the crucial period nationwide was in the late sixteenth and early seventeenth centuries or that most of the rebuilding took place in one particular period.[6] Rather, there were cycles of increased building activity at various points in early modern times, with construction in the 1690s being particularly heavy. Parts of south-eastern England fit comparatively well into the old Rebuilding chronology, but that is not true of the rest of the country, particularly the North-east, where few surviving farmhouses antedate the eighteenth century.

Questions have also been raised concerning the switch from timber-frame (with some mixture of earthen or stone infilling) to brick and stone structures. Apparently, not everywhere did the same evolutionary process take place. Regions relied on local materials for vernacular housing and in some areas stone was more plentiful than wood. In those places timber-frame construction had never been dominant. Furthermore the widespread use of bricks did not occur until after the alleged heyday of the Great Rebuilding (1575–1625). The reason that both bricks and stone grew in popularity and timber-frame housing began to disappear after 1650 seems to be related to a sharp jump in the price of wood during the seventeenth century, causing cost of a timber-frame farmhouse to increase fivefold. In other words, husbandmen and yeomen switched to brick and stone because wood-frame houses had lost their price advantage, not because they suddenly decided they wanted permanent rather than impermanent dwellings. As long as timber-frame houses were cheaper to build, householders accepted the higher maintenance costs and shorter life expectancy but, when the price differential began to disappear, brick and stone seemed the better investment.[7]

Finally, there is the problem of how far down the economic ladder these changes in housing extended. The theory asserts that it was peasant housing that was rebuilt, but in early modern England the designations of occupational status were changing. Yeomen and husbandmen comprised the sixteenth-century peasantry, and during most of that century, they probably constituted a majority of English household heads. As one moves into the seventeenth century, though, fewer and fewer husbandmen appear in the record. Many apparently joined the ranks of labourers or identified themselves by their part-time trade rather than by their agricultural work. If these housing improvements were only carried out in the houses of yeomen and those farmers who had substantial leaseholds, then the rebuilding affected no more than a third of all rural families, according to Gregory King's portrayal of the social structure in *c*.1690. Alternatively, one could include as peasants all those on land that retained some common rights, whether called husbandmen or cottagers or some type of craftsman. The problem with that approach is the improbability that these people could have afforded to construct the Rebuilding theory's permanent dwellings, those of the type described in the surveys of surviving houses. If landlords put them up, there would still be a substantial rent to pay. By the late seventeenth century, a multi-storey brick, stone, or timber-frame house of four rooms or more cost from £40 to £100, an amount that, based on King's schedule of income by class, represented six to seven years of the total household income of labourers and cottagers. Only with difficulty could these families devote more than a tenth of their expenditure to shelter.[8]

There are examples of surviving seventeenth-century houses built by lords for their tenants and workers. They are frequently rows of attached cottages in stone or brick. There are also examples of stone and timber-frame cowhouses and stables converted to shelter for humans.[9] On the other hand, documentary evidence on the kind of housing those in the 'Great House' erected for their 'people' suggests that one-room to two-room semi-detached or detached dwellings made of unbaked earth may have predominated. Such structures were cheaper than houses made out of other materials. A house with one and a half or two storeys constructed out of 'mud and stud' and thatch on a Lincolnshire estate in 1684 cost £12. It had glazed windows and presumably a clay and timber chimney, for no bricks were mentioned. This was the same price as a Yorkshire cottage of the 1660s made from the same materials. Glass was not mentioned but the chimney, again of clay and timber, was listed. In the eighteenth century, a mud and stud cottage could be built for £20 to £30. A mud and stud cottage could endure, if contructed properly and repaired frequently. Probably some of these dwellings disappeared, not because they fell apart but to make way for a more lucrative use of the land. In the eighteenth century, plans for cottages in the South of England seem to have had more than one room, but in the North most of what has survived in stone or has been excavated shows that families continued to live in a single multi-purpose hall.[10]

When landlords did not erect enough low-rent housing, people had to build their own shelters. The products were usually rather crude and very impermanent. A document from the County of Wiltshire listing thirty-three squatters' dwellings constructed in one locality between 1606 and 1639, a period of rapid demographic growth, indicates that settlers put up these dwellings themselves and that they were quite small, 12 ft. × 10 ft. on average, with two being no larger than 80 sq. ft. This, of course, was the lowest level of rural housing.[11]

Comparison of the number of rooms listed in inventories from Oxfordshire, Worcestershire, and East London (Table 6.1) supports the view that English houses in the southern half of England grew larger over time, or at least that domestic space in them became more differentiated. Many households at the lower end of the income scale, however, experienced little improvement. Using inventories to indicate house size is, of course, fraught with danger. In some places at some time periods, appraisers did not enumerate the goods in a way that makes it possible to determine the number of rooms. That is why only four of the ten inventory samples used in this study could be analysed for rooms. Second, in samples where appraisers did describe the contents of houses by room, not all inventories list the rooms. Sometimes it is because the deceased did not live in his or her own house, but it could also be due to the fact that the house had only one room. That is why it is important not just to discard those observations that contain no enumeration of rooms. Finally, the number of rooms is a rough gauge of the total living-space available to families, but even those houses with many rooms could be very small. For example, in an urban area such as East London the ground floor could be no larger than 200 sq. ft., but the house could contain eight rooms distributed over two floors, as well as a cellar and an attic.[12] Finally, some control for wealth is needed in order to adjust for the fact that some samples had more affluent people in them than others. The deceased, therefore, were divided into a low-wealth group (£40 or less in inventoried wealth, 1660–9 prices) and a medium- to high-wealth group (over £40). Most households in the population, perhaps two-thirds, fell into the former category.

Table 6.1 suggests that there was a big difference between the two

TABLE 6.1 Number of rooms enumerated in inventories: percentage of each wealth group possessing given no. of rooms

No. of rooms[b]	Oxfordshire 1530–90		S. Worcestershire 1669–70		E. London 1661–4		E. London 1720–9		Essex Co., Massachusetts 1660–73	
	Low[a] wealth (No. = 125)	Med./High wealth (No. = 126)	Low wealth (No. = 131)	Med./High wealth (No. = 144)	Low wealth (No. = 90)	Med./High wealth (No. = 39)	Low wealth (No. = 35)	Med./High wealth (No. = 142)	Low wealth (No. = 94)	Med./High wealth (No. = 206)
Not indicated	61.6	31.7	47.3	34.0	45.6	30.8	34.3	22.5	97.9	87.4
1	2.4	7.9	6.1	3.5	3.3	0.0	8.6	0.7	0.0	0.0
2	12.0	8.7	3.8	4.2	11.1	12.8	8.6	3.5	2.1	1.5
3	9.6	14.3	10.7	3.5	15.6	5.1	14.3	3.5	0.0	1.5
4	7.2	10.3	13.0	5.6	8.9	10.3	8.6	7.0	0.0	7.3
5	2.4	7.1	5.3	8.3	6.7	7.7	14.3	10.6	0.0	1.0
6–10	4.8	19.0	13.7	31.3	8.9	28.3	11.4	34.7	0.0	1.5
10+	0.0	0.8	0.0	9.7	0.0	5.1	0.0	14.8	0.0	0.0

[a] Those in the low-wealth group had £40 sterling or less, 1660–74 prices. That amount equalled £20 sterling in 1550–90 and £45 in the 1720s. In 1660s Massachusetts currency it equalled £48.

[b] Barns, stables, and other structures that were clearly outbuildings not included.

Source: See Appendix L.

wealth groups in terms of number of rooms. While over time, the number of rooms occupied by those in both wealth groups increased, a majority of those in the low-wealth group still lived in 1–3 rooms in the late seventeenth and the early eighteenth centuries. Between the sixteenth and the late seventeenth century, however, a majority of those in the medium- to high-wealth category moved from living in houses with fewer than four rooms to houses with four or more (four here signifying the minimum needed to have a house that could be considered to meet the Rebuilding criteria).

In late sixteenth-century Oxfordshire, 64% of the inventories in the low-wealth group gave no indication of rooms or listed only one room, while if those with two rooms are included, the proportion was 76%. A sample of 300 labourers' inventories gathered from all over England and covering the years 1560–1640 indicates that Oxfordshire was not an anomaly. In 73% of those 300, there was no indication that the deceased lived in more than one room. In both the later seventeenth-century samples displayed in Table 6.1, the inventories show more evidence of multi-room living for those in the low-wealth group. The proportions of those living in one room or where there was no indication of rooms had dropped to about 50% in both Worcestershire and in East London. By the 1720s in East London, the proportion was down to 43%, but still, it was a distinct minority of those in the low-wealth group that lived in four or more rooms in all of the samples.[13]

That was not the case with those in the medium- to high-wealth group. While only 37% of the Oxfordshire inventories in that category specify four or more rooms, by the 1660s the proportion was 55% in Worcestershire. The growth in proportion of those listing six or more rooms was especially significant, increasing from 20% to 41%. It seems likely, at least in the Midlands, that a majority of yeomen and farmers' families were by that time ensconced in larger, multi-storeyed houses. With more service rooms, such as kitchens and butteries, and more chambers, less work and less sleeping went on in halls and parlours, freeing space for other kinds of activities.[14]

These conclusions seem somewhat at odds with what Ursula Priestley and Penelope Corfield found in their impressive study of housing and room use in Norwich between 1580 and 1730. Drawing on a sample of over 1,400 inventories, they concluded that house size changed very little over the period, with 80% of the deceased living in dwellings with more than three rooms. If one reworks their data, however, and includes those inventories with no room enumeration and puts them in the one- to three-category, then a different picture emerges. The proportion of the deceased who lived in houses with four or more rooms rises from 33% in the period 1580–1604 to 67% in the years 1705–30. Interestingly enough, that percentage is very near what the 1720s East End of London figures would be if in Table 6.1 the sample had not been broken down by wealth group. It is, therefore, quite possible that if wealth controls had been applied to the Norwich data, a majority of those of modest means would have been found to have been living in dwellings of one to three rooms.[15]

What lay behind the addition of rooms? Wealth, as Table 6.1 reveals, was certainly important, but there might be other factors as well. Was it affected by increases in family size? Did it occur more often among those in agriculture or in trade? Did urban living reduce the number of rooms because women engaged in less household production and, therefore, fewer service rooms were needed, or did the more intense social life in towns require more rooms? A comparison of the percentages in Table 6.1 for Worcestershire and East London in the 1660s suggests that the urban factor had a slightly negative effect, but the other variables were not held constant, and the Worcestershire sample contained both rural and urban observations. To investigate these questions, I ran a regression on the determinants of the number of rooms mentioned in the Worcestershire 1669–70 inventories, excluding those observations where there was no room enumeration. Apart from wealth, I ran household size (as measured by number of beds owned), town residency, and occupation. The latter two test whether some aspect of rural life or farming was producing the increase. Household size could be measuring the effects of larger families—there was an increase in fertility in the later sixteenth and earlier seventeenth century. Unfortunately, household size contains a lot of measurement error. Consequently, the results of the regression analysis shown in Table 6.2 have to be interpreted with care. Household size is positively related to number of rooms and strongly significant ($p < 0.001$). The trouble is that wealth had an impact on household size through enabling people to marry earlier, raise more children, and have relatives and servants to live with them. Furthermore, with beds serving as a proxy, wealth is even more of a confounding variable, explaining about a quarter of the variation in household size. It is difficult, therefore, to put forward without many qualifications the notion that demographic change led to room differentiation.

Neither town residency (whether one lived in Worcester or one of the three smaller market towns) nor the occupational categories played a

TABLE 6.2 The determinants of the number of rooms in a house,[a] southern Worcestershire, 1669–1670 (OLS Regression; No. = 134)

Independent variables[b]	Coefficients	Significance level
Household size (ln)	0.498	0.000
Wealth (ln)	0.101	0.044
Town residency	−0.220	0.104
Occupational status		
élite	0.259	0.118
farmer	−0.033	0.773
tradesman	0.124	0.389
Constant	0.249	
Adjusted R^2	0.355	

[a] The dependent variable is the natural log (ln) of the number of rooms. Observations with no room enumeration were eliminated.

[b] Independent variable transformations: those with (ln) have been transformed into natural logs; household size was computed as the number of beds times 2, with those inventories having no beds coded as 1; town residency is a dummy variable coded 1, 0, with Worcester, Evesham, Pershore, and Droitwich coded 1 and the rural parishes, the reference category; and occupational status is a dummy variable coded 1, 0, with labourers, widows and occupation missing as the reference category.

Source: see Appendix 1.

very large role in determining the number of rooms in a house once wealth and household size were controlled for. Town residency had a mildly negative effect, with a probability level that does not meet the standard $p < 0.05$ cut-off. Also, whatever towns may have contributed to reducing the number of rooms inhabited by their residents, this did not seem to be the result of occupational differences between rural and urban settings. There was no significant difference between any of the occupational categories in terms of number of rooms. Perhaps the fact that towns often charged higher rents has more to do with whatever differences appear. In short, the affluent added rooms and did so primarily for reasons other than occupational ones.

Whatever the shortcomings of domestic dwellings in England, it appears that the situation was worse in America, at least for the middle- and upper-wealth groups. Table 6.1 indicates that only about 10% of the inventories from 1660–73 Massachusetts sample gave indications that more than one room was being lived in, which might lead one to believe that appraisers were not enumerating rooms, were it not that inspections of surviving New England houses from the seventeenth century reveal that almost all houses began their existence as basically one-room structures with dimensions of about 25 ft. × 20 ft. Despite the fact that the average number of persons in the household was 50% greater than in England, the houses in Massachusetts did not grow accordingly and featured fewer rooms. One multi-purpose hall with a chamber or loft above comprised the living-space of most families. Lean-tos provided added storage and service area. Eventually most families added on to this basic structure. What is rather surprising, however, is that substantial two-storey homes, two rooms deep, do not seem to have been common for more affluent people outside Boston until after the 1720s, and in the interior of the colony, until the 1750s.[16] Furthermore, almost all inhabitants, even in the eighteenth century, continued to live in wooden dwellings, where both the frame and the walls were made from clapboard. Apart from the problem of impermanence, wooden housing posed a greater safety risk, particularly when the chimneys were part timber as well.

Wood and limited square footage also appear to have been the most salient characteristics of housing in the South. Extensive excavations of seventeenth-century Chesapeake dwellings indicate, moreover, that the wooden dwellings there seldom included foundations. The colonists put the frames into the ground or into postholes.[17] It had been believed that earthfast structures of this type were no longer being built in early modern England, but their prominence in America suggests that there may also have been more non-foundation domestic building in the Mother Country than has so far been acknowledged by architectural historians.

Most houses in early Maryland and Virginia were single-storey dwellings with one or two rooms and seldom a full second floor. Instead of larger houses, outbuildings became popular in the South, where the heat made hall cooking unbearable in the summer and where the servants were slaves with their own families. It was also easier to put up a lot of separate structures of primitive design rather than to build one big, complex house. The plans of these houses, regardless of the income of the owner, remained extremely simple for a very long time. Even as late as the 1720s, surviving room inventories indicate that 80% of the *wealthiest* Virginia decedents lived in houses with only two ground-floor rooms. Another study, of Lancaster County, Virginia in 1710–40, reveals that only one out of every ten decedents had an inventory that clearly indicated they lived in more than one room. By the 1750s, sturdily built, two-storied houses, two rooms deep, had become more common among the planter class. The hall became a public room and the chambers and parlours were more for the family, while the dining-room was used not only for dining but also for family and social purposes.[18]

Improvements at mid-century for those white Southerners at the lower end of the economic scale are less certain. One of the best sources of information about the houses of small planters in the Chesapeake during the pre-Revolutionary period is a 1767–8 survey of several hundred tenants with houses on proprietary land in Maryland. In America, tenants frequently constructed their own dwellings. In this case, the proprietors had specified that houses should be 20 ft. wide and 30 ft. long and have brick chimneys, but more often than not the square footage was 100 to 200 sq. ft. less. It also seems that over 70% of tenants did not comply with the requirements that their chimneys be made out of brick. Given the dimensions of the houses and the fact that none was listed as having two stories, most tenants would have had no more than one or two rooms on the ground floor and a loft. Nor did the tenants compensate for the smallness of their dwellings by building detached kitchens; only one in five houses had these. The sides of the houses were covered in clapboard, planks, or logs, and dirt floors seem to have been the norm.[19]

A national survey of the family dwellings of free persons done for taxation purposes in 1798 suggests that only about 15% of the US housing stock had a high enough value to have met the Great Rebuilding criteria of a two-storey structure fashioned out of permanent materials with differentiated rooms, a stairway, a brick chimney, and glazed windows. In a frontier area such as Mifflin County, Pennsylvania, 67% of the dwellings were less than 400 sq. ft. in area, and 90% of the houses were of log, a form of construction that grew quite popular in the mid-Atlantic region in the eighteenth century and then spread down to the South and out to the Midwest and beyond.[20]

It was not just frontier conditions, however, that produced crude and cramped shelter for a majority of inhabitants. In a Maryland county that had been settled since the early seventeenth century, probably 75% of all late eighteenth-century families (if both slave and free are counted) lived in structures that were no bigger than those in Mifflin. In pre-Revolutionary Philadelphia, the rent paid by 33% of the population indicates that they could not have been living in anything much more than a single-storey dwelling with dimensions of about 12 ft. by 18 ft., while another 20% to 30% in colonial America's largest city were living in only slightly larger abodes.[21]

Where, then, does this leave us as far as the theory of a Great Rebuilding is concerned? Clearly at the start of the early modern period certain portions of the English population embarked upon housing improvements, most notably the placement of animals in outbuildings and the installation of ceilings, chimneys, and glass windows. A significant portion of the general population eventually adopted these improvements during the course of the seventeenth century and they were transferred to America. A certain proportion of English households, perhaps a third, managed to go further. They switched to brick and stone, erected sturdy houses of two full storeys with rooms that allowed work, sleep, and leisure activities to be more spatially separated. In America, it seems, an even smaller percentage of families made these additional improvements to their domestic structures. The vast majority of families seem to have lived in one- to three-room wooden houses that continually left them at the mercy of the elements. Their houses may have been cleaner, warmer, and brighter than in the past but their own life expectancy still outdistanced that of their dwelling.

One can only speculate as to why reasonably well-off colonists adhered to such low standards of construction in the eighteenth century. Certainly, the demographic growth of America contributed to a chronic shortage of good housing. Also, the élites in America—the group with some capital—apparently did not have much interest in investing in tenant or worker housing. The institution of slavery made it necessary for masters to furnish quarters for bound servants, but that only ensured that a significant portion of the southern population would be housed in flimsy, sub-standard structures. Additionally, the scarcity of skilled artisans in America may account for some of the problem. House carpenters, brickmakers, bricklayers, plasterers, and glaziers only very slowly increased their numbers in the colonies. Initially, skilled craftsmen might come to a new settlement, but insufficient demand for their services often led them to leave or change occupation. Later in the eighteenth century, when the market for houses built by craftsmen may have improved, fewer skilled artisans were migrating from Britain. In a detailed study of craftsmen in an Eastern Shore county of Maryland, Jean Russo found that not until 1750, over 100 years after settlement, did house carpenters begin to appear as a specific trade. At the same time, bricklayers and plasterers increased in number. However, there were fewer brickmakers and glaziers at mid-century than there had been *c*.1700. Moreover, the percentage of inventoried households that stocked their own carpentry tools grew to over 25% by the 1750s.[22] Essentially, most colonial American householders were responsible for constructing their own shelter without much help from landowners or trained professionals.

Consumer Durables and Semi-durables

What about interior furnishings? Contemporaries cited big improvements in this area, too, during the sixteenth century. The evidence from inventories strongly reinforces their comments in at least one category of expenditure, that of bedding. In fact the figures in Table 6.3 encourage one to believe that the entire early modern period should be relabelled the Age of the Bed. In nine of the ten inventory samples from England and the colonies, from the sixteenth to the eighteenth century, bedding constituted over 20% of the total value of consumer goods. The one exception was in the 1720s East End of London sample in which the plate and jewellery accumulations of the wealthy distorted the percentages. Much of what was expended on beds was for textile products. While in some cases the deceased owned ornate bedsteads and frames, most often their money had been spent on better mattresses, pillows, blankets, curtains, and valances.

Extra expenditure on bedding, moreover, was generalized among the population and continued right up to the end of the eighteenth century. There is evidence, for example, that bed curtains became more popular over time, perhaps to obtain greater privacy in crowded houses with few rooms.[23] Table 6.4 shows the percentage of the deceased in each period and place who had bedding as the most expensive category of good in their inventory. Apart from the 1720s East London sample, already referred to, from 50% to 80% of the deceased in all the samples had spent the most on it. This proportion is high, especially considering that some of the deceased, usually the poorer ones, did not have their own households or household goods: in their case, clothing was often the item that constituted the largest part of their total consumer goods. Plate and jewellery tended to be the most valuable category for the wealthiest deceased.

In the last samples, those from 1774, fine furniture and carriages also made an appearance as the most valuable category of goods. The only other time furniture showed up as even marginally important as a

TABLE 6.3 Percentage of the total value of consumer goods in major categories

Time and place	Bedding	Household linen	Brass and pewter	Plate and jewellery	Clothing clothing
1550–90, Oxfordshire	25.5	14.9	11.7	4.3	12.8
1669–70, S. Worcestershire	23.7	7.9	8.2	4.5	9.6
1661–4, East London	22.7	8.7	10.3	10.3	14.9
1660–73, Essex Co., Massachusetts	26.5	11.2	6.1	1.1	16.7
1660–76, Virginia	28.7	4.6	6.1	3.4	12.3
1720–1, S. Worcestershire	22.2	9.2	7.9	3.6	10.5
1720–9, East London	11.4	7.4	2.2	33.1	9.2
1724–9, Virginia	27.9	2.8	8.4	6.0	6.7
1774, Massachusetts	21.1	6.7	4.7	14.8	16.8
1774, Virginia and Maryland	39.2	4.0	4.0	6.8	20.1

Source: see Appendix 1.

TABLE 6.4 The percentage of inventories with a particular category of goods as most expensive

Category of goods	Oxford., 1550–90 (No.=238)	S. Worcestershire, 1669–70 (No.=268)	E. London, 1661–4 (No.=123)	Essex Co., Massachusetts, 1660–73 (No.=292)	Virginia, 1660–76 (No.=132)	S. Worcestershire, 1720–1 (No.=271)	E. London, 1720–9 (No.=153)	Virginia, 1724–9 (No.=282)	Massachusetts, 1774 (No.=294)	Virginia and Maryland, 1774 (No.=141)
Bedding	50.8	77.3	65.9	67.8	68.9	73.4	47.1	78.7	56.1	79.4
Household linen	14.3	1.9	4.1	2.1	0.8	3.3	0.7	0.0	0.7	0.7
Brass and pewter	12.2	5.6	4.1	0.3	5.3	4.1	0.7	3.5	1.4	2.1
Plate and jewellery	1.7	3.0	7.3	1.0	3.0	4.8	37.3	3.2	9.2	1.4
Clothing	11.8	10.4	18.7	26.4	20.5	14.0	11.1	12.8	21.8	13.5
Furniture	8.0	0.0	0.0	0.0	0.0	0.4	1.3	0.0	10.2	0.7
Carriages	0.0	1.5	0.0	0.0	0.0	0.0	0.7	0.0	0.3	0.7
Other	1.3	0.4	0.0	2.4	1.5	0.0	1.3	1.8	0.3	1.4

Source: see Appendix 1.

category was in the 1550–90 Oxfordshire sample, and then it was the most expensive category for the poorest deceased, those householders who did not have the resources to acquire proper bedding.[24] In the later eighteenth century it was the affluent who had begun investing in decorative pieces. The trade of cabinetmaking grew more common in English market towns and colonial capitals.[25] Among the richest 10% of the 1774 Massachusetts inventories, over half listed mahogany furniture, as did a majority of Boston inventories. More and more of the rich or those in comfortable circumstances in cities emptied one or both of their two front rooms of beds and household production materials, and proceeded to decorate their homes with fine wood pieces, upholstered leather chairs, window curtains, and even floor coverings. The vast majority of owners of rural English and American houses, even those who were relatively affluent, just did not decorate rooms. Early modern men and women decorated movables, specifically their beds and their tables. Perhaps there was a special chair for the head of the household, more and more frequently rush or cane seats for others, and a picture or wall hanging, but not cabinetry, stuffed chairs, wallpaper, floor carpets, or sufficient lighting for night-time entertainment. These acquisitions were more often found in the nineteenth century.[26]

Both Tables 6.3 and 6.4 chart the decline in the importance of household linen and brass and pewter. Sixteenth-century commentators remarked upon the adoption of bed linen and the substitution of brass and pewter for wooden tableware. In the Oxfordshire sample, linens comprised nearly 15% of the total value of consumer goods, and brass and pewter constituted 11.7%. It was all downhill after that, however. In the 1720s sample from Worcestershire, the two had dropped to 9% and 8% respectively. In the 1770s, they each made up only 4% of the total value of Chesapeake consumer goods, while in Massachusetts the percentages were 6.7% and 4.7% respectively. These goods also less frequently fell into the category of most expensive. In Tudor Oxfordshire, household linens were the most expensive category of consumer good for 14.3% of the deceased, and for another 12.2%, this category comprised brass and pewter. Over 25% of the inventories had one or the other as most expensive. In the seventeenth- and early eighteenth-century samples, the *combined* percentage rose no higher than 8%, and in the last two colonial samples from 1774, neither reached 3%. In other words, both household linens and brass and pewter seem to have peaked in the late sixteenth century, and after that became gradually less prominent as an object of expenditure.

In Chapter 4 it was hypothesized that some of the decline in the proportion of wealth in linens was due to a drop in price and the availability of cheaper fabric, because there is every indication that the ownership of bed and table linen grew rather than diminished. With brass and pewter, however, it seems an actual drop in usage may have come about at some time after the mid-seventeenth century, as those wanting an investment chose plate and those wanting cheapness and utility chose tin, glass, or ceramics, the latter emerging in the early eighteenth century as an appropriate material for hot caffeine drinks.[27] This substitution was part of a more general transformation in tableware and, presumably, in mealtimes as well.

What made one household stock up on linens or brass and pewter while another accumulated bedding, plate, or clothing? One way to gain some insight into consumer decisions is to compare the characteristics of the deceased with their holdings in these five categories of goods which for most households constituted most of their wealth in consumer goods both at the beginning and at the end of the early modern period. Tables 6.5 to 6.9 show the results of the regressions. Because missing data were a problem with some of the categories of goods and with some of the predictor variables, I eliminated from the analysis several of the smaller data sets (Virginia and the East End of London in the 1660s, and the East End in the 1720s). The dependent variables were the £ value of the particular category in the inventory transformed into natural log (ln) form. Because every one of the deceased must have owned some clothing, I restricted the analysis of the value of wealth in clothing to those observations in which clothing was listed. For the other consumer goods, I analysed all inventories regardless of whether they had a zero amount for that good or not.

It is important, of course, to use multivariate techniques when analysing ownership differences among probated deceased, because variables such as wealth, occupation, and urban residency are almost always intercorrelated. That is, more of the wealthy live in towns and are gentlemen or merchants. Studies can overestimate the importance of occupation or townlife, if they do not first control for wealth.[28]

In almost all the time periods and places, wealth was the most important determinant of the value of the various categories of goods. Because both the dependent variables and the wealth variables were logged, the wealth coefficient takes the form of an elasticity. In all cases there was a positive effect on the value of the good owned. That is, the value went up as wealth went up. But the relationship was also always

TABLE 6.5 Determinants of the £ (ln) value of bedding in inventories, England and the Colonies (OLS Regression)

Variables	Oxfordshire, 1550–90	S. Worcestershire, 1669–70	S. Worcestershire, 1720–1	Essex Co., Massachusetts, 1660–73	Massachusetts, 1774	Virginia, 1724–9	Virginia and Maryland, 1774
No. of inventories	247	216	216	267	268	298	137
Variables							
Wealth (ln)	0.245 (0.000)	0.206 (0.000)	0.115 (0.002)	0.461 (0.000)	0.080 (0.034)	0.374 (0.000)	0.280 (0.000)
Household size (ln)	1.592 (0.000)	1.419 (0.000)	1.292 (0.000)	1.449 (0.000)	1.534 (0.000)	1.223 (0.000)	1.520 (0.000)
Book-ownership	n.a.	−0.156 (0.300)	0.074 (0.526)	0.092 (0.471)	0.004 (0.966)	0.006 (0.950)	0.190 (0.225)
Town residency	−0.103 (0.518)	−0.235 (0.083)	0.176 (0.074)	−0.125 (0.315)	0.143 (0.096)	n.a.	n.a.
Trade or craft	0.137 (0.446)	0.040 (0.784)	−0.190 (0.080)	0.130 (0.496)	0.008 (0.928)	0.164 (0.181)	0.169 (0.390)
Woman	0.289 (0.102)	0.195 (0.121)	0.046 (0.669)	0.448 (0.034)	0.202 (0.208)	0.064 (0.633)	0.050 (0.828)
Constant	0.893	−1.675	−1.062	−1.860	−1.162	−1.665	−2.234
Adjusted R^2	0.658	0.725	0.690	0.624	0.745	0.780	0.809

Source: see Appendix 1.

TABLE 6.6 Determinants of the £ (ln) value of household linens in inventories, England and the Colonies (OLS Regression)

	Oxfordshire, 1550–90	S. Worcestershire, 1669–70	S. Worcestershire, 1720–1	Essex Co., Massachusetts, 1660–73	Massachusetts, 1774	Virginia, 1724–9	Virginia and Maryland, 1774
No. of inventories	247	212	215	263	268	297	137
Variables							
Wealth (ln)	0.335	0.434	0.630	0.550	0.447	0.423	0.379
	(0.001)	(0.000)	(0.000)	(0.000)	(0.000)	(0.000)	(0.000)
Household size (ln)	1.345	0.889	1.368	1.390	1.035	0.438	0.294
	(0.000)	(0.000)	(0.000)	(0.000)	(0.000)	(0.001)	(0.119)
Book-ownership	n.a.	−0.139	0.547	0.466	0.214	0.208	0.210
		(0.635)	(0.229)	(0.009)	(0.246)	(0.192)	(0.457)
Town residency	0.016	0.434	0.632	0.099	0.511	n.a.	n.a.
	(0.948)	(0.103)	(0.099)	(0.560)	(0.003)		
Trade or craft	0.161	−0.570	−0.312	0.491	−0.118	0.241	0.006
	(0.564)	(0.049)	(0.462)	(0.064)	(0.508)	(0.265)	(0.986)
Woman	0.289	0.162	0.791	0.597	0.531	−0.065	0.811
	(0.290)	(0.515)	(0.057)	(0.033)	(0.092)	(0.786)	(0.047)
Constant	−1.803	−3.234	−2.992	−3.855	−4.002	−3.910	−3.905
Adjusted R^2	0.405	0.333	0.292	0.540	0.462	0.312	0.224

Source: see Appendix 1.

TABLE 6.7 Determinants of the £ (ln) value of brass and pewter in inventories, England and the Colonies (OLS Regression)

	Oxfordshire, 1550–90	S. Worcestershire, 1669–70	S. Worcestershire, 1720–1	Essex Co., Massachusetts, 1660–73	Massachusetts, 1774	Virginia, 1724–9	Virginia and Maryland, 1774
No. of inventories	246	212	211	264	268	295	138
Variables							
Wealth (ln)	0.632	0.325	0.060	0.285	0.256	0.130	0.045
	(0.000)	(0.000)	(0.524)	(0.003)	(0.000)	(0.068)	(0.600)
Household size (ln)	0.901	0.754	1.707	1.097	1.063	1.031	0.925
	(0.000)	(0.000)	(0.000)	(0.000)	(0.000)	(0.000)	(0.000)
Book-ownership	n.a.	0.020	−0.746	0.415	0.136	−0.052	0.080
		(0.929)	(0.019)	(0.010)	(0.338)	(0.729)	(0.727)
Town residency	−0.070	−0.142	0.607	0.220	0.326	n.a.	n.a.
	(0.793)	(0.481)	(0.020)	(0.150)	(0.012)		
Trade or craft	0.359	−0.093	−0.109	0.082	−0.022	−0.598	−0.420
	(0.237)	(0.671)	(0.702)	(0.729)	(0.871)	(0.003)	(0.146)
Woman	−0.525	−0.121	0.344	−0.020	0.469	0.121	0.140
	(0.077)	(0.523)	(0.222)	(0.935)	(0.053)	(0.596)	(0.672)
Constant	−3.071	−2.034	−0.047	−2.538	−2.924	−1.604	−2.093
Adjusted R^2	0.382	0.372	0.330	0.421	−0.499	0.401	0.348

Source: see Appendix 1.

TABLE 6.8 Determinants of the £ (ln) value of plate and jewellery in inventories, England and the Colonies (OLS Regression)

	Oxfordshire, 1550–90	S. Worcestershire, 1669–70	S. Worcestershire, 1720–1	Essex Co., Massachusetts, 1660–73	Massachusetts, 1774	Virginia, 1724–9	Virginia and Maryland, 1774
No. of inventories	246	214	214	271	270	296	140
Variables							
Wealth (ln)	0.246 (0.004)	0.457 (0.000)	0.304 (0.000)	0.139 (0.094)	0.750 (0.000)	0.520 (0.000)	0.382 (0.003)
Household size (ln)	0.211 (0.128)	−0.012 (0.931)	−0.090 (0.526)	0.131 (0.335)	0.178 (0.314)	0.118 (0.494)	−0.026 (0.908)
Book-ownership	n.a.	0.446 (0.030)	0.643 (0.004)	0.141 (0.303)	0.320 (0.165)	0.247 (0.159)	0.710 (0.034)
Town residency	0.012 (0.955)	0.876 (0.000)	0.928 (0.000)	0.072 (0.586)	1.342 (0.000)	n.a.	n.a.
Trade or craft	0.307 (0.181)	−0.273 (0.279)	0.185 (0.357)	0.225 (0.272)	0.368 (0.097)	−0.293 (0.227)	1.144 (0.007)
Woman	0.332 (0.143)	−0.037 (0.864)	0.207 (0.305)	0.264 (0.229)	1.293 (0.001)	0.068 (0.795)	1.644 (0.001)
Constant	−3.876	−3.786	−3.348	−2.854	−5.260	−3.971	−3.821
Adjusted R^2	0.082	0.245	0.241	0.044	0.409	0.249	0.172

Source: see Appendix 1.

TABLE 6.9 Determinants of the £ (ln) value of clothing in inventories, England and the Colonies (OLS Regression)

	Oxfordshire, 1550–90	S. Worcestershire, 1669–70	S. Worcestershire, 1720–1	Essex Co., Massachusetts, 1660–73	Massachusetts, 1774	Virginia, 1724–9	Virginia and Maryland, 1774
No. of inventories	168	158	0	242	224	170	84
Variables							
Wealth (ln)	0.609	0.375	n.a.	0.359	0.514	0.422	0.480
	(0.000)	(0.000)	n.a.	(0.000)	(0.000)	(0.000)	(0.000)
Household size (ln)	−0.153	0.007	n.a.	−0.049	−0.170	−0.051	−0.595
	(0.123)	(0.909)	n.a.	(0.518)	(0.020)	(0.619)	(0.000)
Book-ownership	n.a.	0.204	na.	0.155	0.158	−0.137	0.441
		(0.137)	n.a.	(0.040)	(0.114)	(0.298)	(0.077)
Town residency	0.029	0.345	n.a.	−0.100	0.385	n.a.	n.a.
	(0.847)	(0.006)	n.a.	(0.169)	(0.000)		
Trade or craft	0.149	−0.333	n.a.	0.079	0.085	0.339	0.621
	(0.378)	(0.015)	n.a.	(0.478)	(0.359)	(0.035)	(0.024)
Woman	0.360	0.110	n.a.	0.382	0.623	0.516	0.022
	(0.016)	(0.298)	n.a.	(0.002)	(0.000)	(0.028)	(0.964)
Constant	−0.806	−0.709	n.a.	0.216	−0.694	0.709	−0.407
Adjusted R^2	0.416	0.421	n.a.	0.324	0.525	0.317	0.278

Source: see Appendix 1.

inelastic (coefficients below 1.0 or unity). The percentage increase in bedding or linens or some other commodity did not increase as much as the proportion that wealth rose. Inventories included both production or capital assets as well as consumer goods. As people got wealthier, a higher proportion of their wealth took the form of livestock, equipment, and financial assets and a smaller percentage took the form of things such as bedding. Most of the elasticities, therefore, fall into the range of 0.200 to 0.650. In other words, as wealth went up 1%, the value of these goods went up between 0.2% and 0.65%.

The most interesting relationship between wealth and a particular category of consumer good involved brass and pewter. In the sixteenth century this category exhibits a relatively high elasticity, 0.632, when compared to the other four classes of goods, suggesting that as Tudor wealthholders became richer they accumulated stocks of drinking vessels, plates, and other consumer objects made of these metals at a faster rate. This pattern of expenditure did not continue, however, and, by the eighteenth century not only do the elasticities drop but in several of the samples wealth is no longer a statistically significant predictor of the value of brass and pewter in the inventory. Only in the Massachusetts 1774 sample is wealth still a clear determinant. Perhaps these results indicate the inroads that ceramics and other metals had made into both the higher and lower end of the brass and pewter market.

The other most important predictor of the stocks of these particular consumer goods owned by the deceased is a proxy for household size, the number of beds found in the inventories. Whatever shortcomings this proxy may have, it does act as a good discriminator between personal consumer goods and household consumer goods. As the five tables show, the household size proxy is either negatively related to the value of clothing and of plate and jewellery or has no statistically significant relationship in all the samples. Usually the only clothing and jewellery that appeared in an inventory was that worn by the deceased. Conversely, the bedding, bed and table linens, and brass and pewter that appraisers listed were the whole household accumulation. As household size increased, the stocks of these goods increased, while the stocks of clothing and jewellery did not. Consequently the effect of household size on the stocks of bedding, linen, and brass and pewter was universally positive. Objects made of silver plate could be either household or personal goods, but only the very wealthy had significant amounts of household silver. More common was the individual cup or watch. Consequently the value of jewellery and plate is not positively related to the number in the household.

The regressions in Tables 6.5 to 6.9 also attempt to measure the effects of education (as indicated by book ownership) and market accessibility. Presumably those living in cities, market towns, or towns of over 2,500 inhabitants would have better exposure to consumer commodities than those living in strictly rural surroundings. One might also hypothesize that those in trades or in merchandizing would be closer to the source of consumer goods.

It is difficult to evaluate the impact of education, especially as book ownership might not be a good proxy for the kind of educational experience that influenced the accumulation of particular consumer goods. The tables show that it had only a mildly positive and statistically insignificant impact on the ownership of bedding, linens, and brass and pewter, and only a slightly greater effect upon stocks of clothing and plate and jewellery. Of course, the consumption that might be most influenced by education is that of new commodities, and the general categories of consumer goods do not capture that dimension.

The two indicators of market accessibility do not behave similarly over all the samples. Instead, town residency in the sixteenth and seventeenth centuries only has a statistically significant and positive effect on personal consumer goods, not on bedding, linens, or brass and pewter. By the eighteenth century, though, all the categories of expenditure are positively influenced, some quite strongly. On the other hand, being in a craft or trade discouraged or had no impact on the accumulation of any category of good. The sole exception was in the eighteenth-century Chesapeake samples where there was no town variable. In these southern colonies, craft and trade occupations positively influenced the value of clothing and of plate and jewellery. The results suggest, therefore, that a market accessibility effect existed, although in the sixteenth and seventeenth centuries it only promoted personal consumer goods and only later did it extend to household goods. Also it seemed to be associated more with an urban lifestyle than with mercantile networks.

Because of women's close identification with work within the household, and the gender specific nature of dress in the early modern period, it is important to try to measure the influence of sex on accumulations of consumer goods. The common-law property system, unfortunately, puts considerable barriers in the way of investigation. Almost no inventories exist for married female decedents because their personal property became their husband's upon marriage. Any influence they may have exerted on consumer decisions, therefore, is reflected in their husbands' inventories, not in inventories of their own. Furthermore, the inventories of widows—and nearly all inventories for females fall into this category—reflect not only their own consumption behaviour but the type of possessions their husbands considered appropriate for them to inherit. Finally, women were so seldom wealthholders that they comprised no more than 5–10% of the American samples and 20% of those from England. Such small numbers mean it is more difficult to establish sex differences. In a number of the samples the value of widows' stocks of clothing and linens exceeded those of men, if all other variables are held constant. Also, in the 1774 samples from Massachusetts and the Chesapeake, women's holdings of plate and jewellery (after controlling for all other influences) exceeded those of men. Considering that widows tended to inherit more household goods than productive capital, the negative or insignificant results on bedding and brass and pewter are a little surprising. I suspect part of the answer has to do with the strong and inverse correlation between widowhood and wealth. The two variables battle for much of the same variance, and what should be attributed to which gets confused. In all of the regressions the simple (zero order) correlation between the value of a particular consumer good and being a woman is negative. After controlling for wealth in a multiple regression, the coefficient for woman usually turns positive, but not always to the point of statistical significance.

Innovations in Tableware

Although the equipment promoting rest—the bed and its accessories—consistently claimed the lion's share of those resources devoted to consumer goods, it was another function, eating, that seemed to inspire the most change in consumer durables or semi-durables during the early modern period. Inventories are the best source of information about this transformation, which affected all economic groups. While there is the problem that English inventories were no longer being taken in sufficient numbers for statistical use much after the 1720s, colonial samples are available for the rest of the eighteenth century. The colonies, of course, had a direct link with London, and they may have acquired some goods before the North of England did so. It is difficult to imagine, however, that, all other things being equal, manufactured goods such as cutlery, glassware, and pottery were in much wider circulation in Massachusetts or the Chesapeake than in most English counties.

Table 6.10 shows how frequently tableware appeared in the English samples used in this study and in two other studies, one by Lorna

TABLE 6.10 Percentage of inventories with new tableware commodities, England, 1550–1729

Tableware	Oxford., 1550–90 (No. = 253)	S. Worcestershire, 1669–70 (No. = 272)	E. London, 1661–4 (No. = 123)	Gloucestershire 1660–99 (No. = 480)	England 1675 (No. = 520)	S. Worcestershire, 1720–1 (No. = 235)	E. London, 1720–9 (No. = 168)	England, 1725 (No. = 390)
Knives and forks	0.0	0.7	0.0	0.0	1.0	2.6	18.5	10.0
Glassware	0.0	1.1	1.6	2.9	n.a.	3.0	16.7	n.a.
Ceramics[a]	0.0	0.0	0.8	0.0	0.0	1.7	38.7	9.0
Tea equipment	0.0	0.0	0.0	n.a.	0.0	1.7	31.6	15.0
Coffee equipment	0.0	0.0	0.0	n.a.	0.0	2.1	23.2	
Consumer goods median (£)[b]	10.0	17.0	14.0	n.a.	n.a.	17.0	32.0	n.a.

[a] This includes all ceramic dishes designed for table use as opposed to cooking and storage, except in the England 1675 and 1725 samples where only dishes described as 'china' are counted.

[b] Median wealth in consumer goods is in constant £ sterling, 1660–74 prices.

Sources: For the Vale of Berkeley, Gloucestershire 1660–99 figures, see James Horn, 'Everyday Life in Seventeenth Century England and the Chesapeake', unpublished paper, 1984; for England 1675 and 1725 see Lorna Weatherill, *Consumer Behaviour and Material Culture in England, 1660–1750*, London, 1988, p. 26; and for all other figures see Appendix 1.

Weatherill for all of England in 1675 and 1725, and another by James Horn for the Vale of Berkeley section of Gloucestershire from 1660 to 1669. The mean wealth in consumer goods for each sample is listed, but it was not possible from the information available to divide the observations into uniform wealth categories. This was not too much of a disadvantage, because the main purposes of the table are to discover, first, when these goods begin to appear and second, when they spread to more than just the élite. The items in the table were all relatively new to early modern consumers: knives and forks for eating; glassware for table use; china or any kind of ceramics, such as English made queenware and delftware, made into plates, cups, saucers; and tea and coffee equipment, including pots, cups, spoons, chests, tables. What Table 6.10 reveals is that these goods did not begin to appear much before 1720. At that point the incidence suggests that possession of these goods was confined to the élite, except in London, where it extended to some of the middle class. Peter Earle has found that among the group of London men of trade he studied, about half had tea equipment mentioned in their post-mortem inventories by 1710.[29] While in the Worcestershire 1720–1 sample no more than 3% owned any of these tableware items, in the East End of London—which had a larger proportion of wealthy decedents than the other samples—31.6% owned tea equipment, and 23.2% even had coffee-pots. Comparing the percentages of ownership in England in 1675 with England in 1725 shows a real growth in demand, but still only about one in ten people possessed any of the new commodities.

Table 6.11 on tableware ownership in the colonies continues the story. On the whole, its percentages and provincial England's look a lot alike in the 1720s. Tidewater Virginia had a slightly higher proportion of inventoried decedents with knives and forks and glassware than Worcestershire at the same period, but that may be due to the fact that less detail is found in the Midlands inventories. At any rate, it is with the 1770s Massachusetts and Chesapeake samples that the surprise comes. Clearly at that time there was mass consumption of these goods by all classes. Even among the low-wealth group in the 1774 Massachusetts sample (those with £60 of inventoried wealth or less), nearly 50% had tea equipment and glassware, 39.6% had knives and forks, while 24.2% had ceramic dishes of some sort. Considering this was a group whose members often did not have their own household, these percentages seem quite high.

A very careful study of consumption patterns by decade in four Chesapeake counties by Lois Green Carr and Lorena Walsh provides

TABLE 6.11 Percentage of inventories with new tableware commodities, the Colonies, 1660–1774

Tableware	Virginia, 1660–76 (No. = 133)	Essex Co., Massachusetts 1660–73 (No. = 300)	Virginia, 1724–9 (No. = 278)	Virginia and Maryland 1774 (No. = 141)	Massachusetts, 1774 (No. = 294)	Massachusetts, 1774 low-wealth group[a] (No. = 149)
Knives and forks	0.0	0.3	15.8	70.7	52.7	39.6
Glassware	0.0	0.0	9.0	45.5	55.9	45.6
Ceramics[b]	0.0	0.0	2.3	35.5	35.0	24.2
Tea equipment	0.0	0.0	2.7	48.9	55.4	49.7
Coffee equipment	0.0	0.0	1.3	19.1	23.5	18.8
Consumer goods median (£)[c]	14.0	28.0	18.0	15.0	17.0	10.0

[a] Those at or below the median in personal wealth.
[b] This includes all ceramic dishes designed for table use as opposed to cooking and storage.
[c] Median wealth in consumer goods is in constant £ sterling, 1660–74 prices.

Source: see Appendix 1.

more precise information about when the change occurred among different wealth groups in that area. Their work shows that knives and forks, ceramic dishes, and tea equipment were being widely used by those in the upper half of the wealth distribution by the 1730s, and by those in the lower half by the 1750s or 1760s, depending on the commodity. In towns such as Annapolis and Williamsburg, usage soared a decade or so earlier. Another equally exhaustive study, this time of colonial New England inventories, identifies the second third of the eighteenth century as the critical time of change in consumption patterns in that region as well. Again, an important part of the change was the mass consumption of new tableware.[30]

Just how far down the wealth distribution these goods penetrated has been a point of contention.[31] The inventory evidence suggests that by 1700 all groups in England and white groups in America had upgraded their stocks of bedding, linens, and pewter. The new tableware, however, did not make many inroads into households of those other than the élite until after 1730. By mid-century in the colonies, one finds in most samples of inventories that about 50% of the deceased in the middle-wealth groups owned these commodities, and 20% to 25% of those in the lower-wealth categories. Eighteenth-century demand, therefore, was not generated simply by those in the top 10% or even the top 30% of American wealthholders, nor, by implication, by that segment in England.

Moreover, recent research by Cissie Fairchilds indicates that the kinds of changes in consumption patterns that we have been discussing were not confined to the English-speaking world. Analysing the inventories of lower-income Parisians c.1725, she finds that they were just as likely (or more likely) to possess ceramic dishes and tea- or coffee-drinking equipment as their English counterparts, 44% owning ceramic dishes and 19% owning tea or coffee equipment. In the metropolis, then, France was hardly behind England in ownership of these goods, and of many other types of personal goods that Fairchilds traces.[32] At what time possession of these goods became commonplace in the French country-side, and whether this happened more quickly in England or on the Continent, remains to be established.

Although none of the new commodities we have discussed were essential, they could not be considered luxury goods, because they became a part of nearly everyone's daily life. There were certainly luxury versions of glassware, tea-sets, china, and knives and forks, but there were cheap plebeian editions as well. Like so many of the new consumer commodities of the eighteenth century, they did not require a big outlay. As discussed in Chapter 4, mean wealth in consumer durables does not seem to have risen during the eighteenth century, and it seems that households may have purchased the impermanent and innovative objects with the money that was saved by not buying so much of the older, more traditional metalware. The fact that so many of the new commodities were more easily destroyed, however, raises the question of whether the lifetime outlay was not comparable or greater. Inventories cannot answer this question.

Changes in the Domestic Environment

Nearly ten years ago, I wrote an article entitled, 'The Domestic Environment in Early Modern England and America' in which I discussed in detail what material changes in housing and furnishings implied about social life within the household. I noted the increased comforts available in the sixteenth and seventeenth centuries brought about by chimneys, glass windows, partitioning of rooms, and superior bedding. At the same time, I argued that by and large most homes remained undecorated and supplied with few tools to promote family sociability or neighbourhood entertaining. There was little about the home that distinguished it as a place for social interaction. I even remarked that the ordinary household interior looked as if the occupants expected a flash flood to sweep away their belongings at any moment. In fact, all the valuables in the house—plate, brass and pewter, linens, and clothing—could be quickly grabbed and stuffed into chests, which apart from benches and table boards were the main pieces of household furniture.

The first sign that things might be changing, I suggested, was the explosion in tableware after 1720. The proliferation of knives and forks, glassware, ceramic dishes, and tea equipment throughout all social classes implied more sociability accompanying the taking of food and drink in the home. I suggested that women whose work kept them more closely tied to the house and who because of their sex were less accepted in public places were a major force in promoting these enhancements to the domestic environment. Contemporaries associated women with the jump in tea consumption, and statistical analysis of inventories does show that the female deceased were more likely to own tea-drinking equipment.[33] In Chapter 4, I found that women in both the 1774 samples of inventories had a higher proportion of their wealth in consumer goods, although for earlier dates no statistically significant relationship existed. When one analyses the major categories of consumer goods, however, inventories for females more often differed from those for males in the personal goods categories of clothing and plate and jewellery than in household goods, where only in ownership of linens was sex an important variable, and then not in every sample. The ability of early modern women below élite status to change their domestic environment may have been limited to the table and to meal-taking.

The research that has appeared in the intervening years has improved our understanding of why certain changes in the domestic environment occurred and why others did not. When I wrote the article in 1980, I stressed the impact tea-drinking had made on the material culture of the English and the Americans, but I did not fully appreciate the close association between the dietary changes occasioned by the new groceries and the transformation in eating and drinking utensils—specifically the boost to ceramic commodities provided initially by tobacco, which was usually smoked in clay pipes in the seventeenth century. These pipes were mass produced in England and shopkeepers stocked them by the gross. It was this white pipe-clay that was soon to be used also for delftware and stoneware dishes.[34] Caffeine drinks laced with sugar popularized ceramic tableware because that material was the most appropriate for the hot liquids. The diffusion of tableware almost perfectly mimics the rise in tea consumption during the first half of the eighteenth century. There also seems to be a connection between the acceptance of new tableware and the stagnation in brass and pewter products and the fall in the use of treen (wooden) ware. This shift involved the replacement of quite sturdy durables with more decorative but more disposable crockery and glass. Households prized these new commodities for their utility in everyday life, and less for their investment value. It may be that as financial assets became more available, the necessity for using consumer goods as articles of saving declined.

Work on the nineteenth- and twentieth-century domestic environment has also served as a reminder of what did *not* happen in the eighteenth century. The emergence of a parlour as a room decorated by women and one which they could properly use for the visits of other women and men was, for all but the élite, a post-1800 development, only discarded in the twentieth century by which time women had invaded the entire dwelling, pushing men into the basement, den, or garage. The emphasis on cleanliness and the development of the bathroom were also post-1800 developments for most households. It seems evident that many of the nineteenth- and twentieth-century alterations in household space and technology were connected to alterations in women's work and status. The sewing-machine, and the cooking-stove and other kitchen innovations, went along with women spending more and more time on such things as baking and sewing, the part of home production that one might term the finishing processes. This change also freed areas of the home for entertainment purposes.[35]

The early modern changes to the domestic environment, then, should be put into perspective. In some ways it is amazing that so many innovations did occur, given the flimsy and unsafe housing in colonial America, and the very limited abilities of women everywhere to control family capital.[36] It is also useful to remember that contemporaries considered the transformations in housing and, later, in mealtimes and tableware to be monumental ones. Social critic Frederic Eden, in a burst of cultural pride, observed that in late eighteenth-century England 'not only the lowest peasant eats his meal at a table, but also has his table covered with a table cloth'. 'Sitting together at a table', he declared, 'is perhaps one of the strongest characteristics of civilization and refinement.'[37]

Chapter 6

1. Dorothy Davis, *Fairs, Shops, and Supermarkets: A History of English Shopping*, Toronto, 1966, p. 39.
2. On this literary evidence see Carole Shammas, 'The Domestic Environment in Early Modern England and America', *Journal of Social History*, 14 (1980), 1–24.
3. William Harrison, *The Description of England*, ed. George Edelen, Ithaca, 1968, pp. 200–1. Bracketed material in the quotation was added by the editor of the volume.
4. Richard Carew, *Survey of Cornwall*, London, 1602, p. 66.
5. W. G. Hoskins, 'The Rebuilding of Rural England, 1570–1640', *Past and Present*, 4 (1953), 44–59.
6. M. W. Barley, 'Rural Housing in England', in Joan Thirsk (ed.), *The Agrarian History of England and Wales*, iv, 1500–1640, Cambridge, 1967, pp. 734–60, and v. 2, 1640–1750, Cambridge, 1985, pp. 653–4, and R. Machin, 'The Great Rebuilding: A Reassessment', *Past and Present*, 77 (1977), 33–56. The situation in cities is not well researched, but see Alan Dyer, 'Urban Housing: A Documentary Study of Four Midland Towns, 1530–1700', *Post-Medieval Archaeology*, 15 (1981), 207–18, and Ursula Priestley and P. J. Corfield, 'Rooms and Room Use in Norwich Housing, 1580–1730', *Post-Medieval Archaeology*, 16 (1982), 93–123.
7. Eric Mercer, *English Vernacular Houses: A Study of Traditional Farmhouses and Cottages*, London, 1975, pp. 113–36; R. Machin, 'The Mechanism of the Pre-industrial Building Cycle', *Vernacular Architecture*, 8 (1977), 815–18; Barry

Harrison and Barbara Hutton, *Vernacular Houses in North Yorkshire and Cleveland*, Edinburgh, 1984, p. 9.

8. Machin, 'Pre-industrial Building Cycle', pp. 815–18. King estimated the annual household income of labourers at £15 and cottagers at £16. 10s. 0d., Gregory King, 'A Scheme of the Income and Expense of the Several Families of England Calculated for the Year 1688', in *Seventeenth-Century Economic Documents*, ed. Joan Thirsk and J. P. Cooper, Oxford, 1972, pp. 780–1. In previous chapters I have suggested that the proportion of expenditure that working-class families spent on food and drink has probably been exaggerated. Still, it would be difficult for them not to have spent between 50–60% on diet. If clothing took up 15–20% (15% is very low for the early modern period, but cloth prices were declining), fuel and transportation 5%, and miscellaneous expenses including health cost 10%, then that would leave, at best, 20% for shelter and, at worst, 5%.

9. Mercer, *English Vernacular Houses*, pp. 75–7.
10. Machin, 'Pre-industrial Building Cycle', pp. 815–18; Harrison and Hutton, *Vernacular Houses in North Yorkshire*, pp. 8–9; Barley, 'Rural Housing', p. 677; Stuart Wrathmell, 'The Vernacular Threshold of Northern Peasant Houses', *Vernacular Architecture*, 15 (1984), 29–33; and Lucy Caffyn, *Workers' Housing in West Yorkshire, 1750–1920*, Royal Commission on the Historical Monuments of England, supplementary ser. 9, London, 1986, p. 1.
11. J. H. Bettye, 'Seventeenth Century Squatters' Dwellings: Some Documentary Evidence', *Vernacular Architecture*, 13 (1982), 28–30.
12. M. J. Power, 'East London Housing in the Seventeenth Century', in Peter Clark and Paul Slack (ed.), *Crisis and Order in English Towns, 1500–1700: Essays in Urban History*, London, 1972, p. 250.
13. Alan Everitt, 'Farm Labourers', in Thirsk (ed.), *Agrarian History*, iv, 442–3. Everitt finds that one-room cottages were much more prevalent in the North and North-west. Harrison and Hutton, *Vernacular Houses in North Yorkshire*, p 49, report that in the area of Yorkshire they studied, 'storeyed construction [apart from houses of higher status] does not seem to have got under way until well into the 18th century'. Caffyn, *Workers' Housing in West Yorkshire*, p. 1, is also of this opinion. Sarah Pearson, *Rural Houses of the Lancashire Pennines, 1560–1760*, Royal Commission on the Historical Monuments of England, London, 1985, p. 108, associates the period c.1700 with improved housing for copyhold tenants in the Pennines.
14. On the proliferation of service rooms, chambers, and parlours and changes in the function of rooms see P. Garrard, 'English Probate Inventories and their Use in Studying the Significance of the Domestic Interior', in *AAG Bijdragen*, 23 (1980), pp. 67–8; Christopher Husbands, 'Standards of Living in North Warwickshire in the Seventeenth Century', *Warwickshire History*, 4 (1981), 208; Barley, 'Rural Housing', pp. 644–5; and Priestley and Corfield, 'Rooms and Room Use in Norwich', pp. 101–23.
15. Priestley and Corfield, 'Rooms and Room Use in Norwich', tables 1 and 2, pp. 99–100.
16. Mean household size in early modern England is frequently cited as being around 4.75, Peter Laslett and Richard Wall, *Household and Family in Past Time*, Cambridge, 1972. In the Chesapeake and New England it tended to fall between 6 and 7, Robert Wells, *The Population of the British Colonies in America before*

1776, Princeton, 1975, pp. 299–300. On the early housing see Abbott Lowell Cummings, *The Framed Houses of Massachusetts Bay, 1625–1725*, Cambridge, Mass., 1979, p. 23, and Cary Carson and Lorena Walsh, 'The Material Life of the Early American Housewife', paper delivered at the Conference on Women in Early America, 5 Nov. 1981, Williamsburg, Va., n. 32. On the slowness of change see Kevin M. Sweeney, 'Mansion People: Kinship, Class, and Architecture in Western Massachusetts in the Mid-Eighteenth Century', *Winterthur Portfolio*, 19 (1984), 231–56, and Michael Peter Steinitz, 'Landmark and Shelter: Domestic Architecture in the Cultural Landscape of the Central Uplands of Massachusetts in the Eighteenth Century', unpublished Ph.D. dissertation, Clark University, 1988. Jack Michel (p. 31), studying Pennsylvania housing from 1685 to 1735, estimates that perhaps 67% of the rural inhabitants lived in houses of three rooms or less, 'In a Manner and Fashion Suitable to their Degree': A Preliminary Investigation of the Material Culture of Early Rural Pennsylvania', *Working Papers from the Regional Economic History Research Center*, 5, 1981. Bernard Herman (*Architecture and Rural Life in Central Delaware 1700–1900*, Knoxville, Tenn., 1987) also finds that in a restricted small proportion the eighteenth century Delaware population experienced significant improvements in housing.

17. Cary Carson, Norman F. Barka, William M. Kelso, Garry Wheeler Stone, and Dell Upton, 'Impermanent Architecture in the Southern American Colonies', *Winterthur Portfolio*, 16 (1981), 135–67.

18. Gloria L. Main, *Tobacco Colony: Life in Early Maryland, 1650–1720*, Princeton, 1982, ch. 4; William M. Kelso, *Kingsmill Plantations, 1619–1800: Archaeology of Country Life in Colonial Virginia*, Orlando, 1984, ch. 3; Carter Hudgins, 'Exactly as the Gentry do in England: Culture, Aspirations, and Material Things in the Eighteenth Century Chesapeake', paper delivered at the Conference on the Eighteenth-Century Chesapeake, Peabody Library, Baltimore, Sept. 1984, table 1; and Dell Upton, 'Vernacular Domestic Architecture in Eighteenth Century Virginia', *Winterthur Portfolio*, 17 (1982), 95–119.

19. Gregory A. Stiverson, *Poverty in a Land of Plenty: Tenancy in Eighteenth Century Maryland*, Baltimore, 1977, pp. 56–84. Stiverson characterizes the tenants on proprietary lands as poor. Some of them clearly were, and certainly few of those whose prime holding was a tenancy were very rich. Still the probate inventories of the tenants (pp. 46–7) show a mixture of low wealth and medium to high wealth that was not too different from a lot of other communities in England and the colonies.

20. Lee Soltow, 'Egalitarian America and its Inegalitarian Housing in the Federal Period', *Social Science History*, 9 (1985), 202, gives the number of houses and how that housing was valued in 1798 for taxation purposes in the fourteen states with complete records. I assumed that a stone or brick building of two storeys or more would be valued at $500 or above, and such buildings amounted to 13.3% of all housing. On Mifflin County, see Lee Soltow, 'Housing Characteristics on the Pennsylvania Frontier: Mifflin County Dwelling Values in 1798', *Pennsylvania History*, 47 (1980), 57–70. On the different types of wooden houses built in America, see Fred B. Kniffen and Henry Glassie, 'Building in Wood in the Eastern United States: A Time Place Perspective', *Geographical Review*, 56 (1966), 40–66. Warren E. Roberts in 'The Tools Used in Building Log Houses in

Indiana', in Dell Upton and John Michael Vlach (eds.), *Common Places*, Athens, Ga., 1986, pp. 182–203, argues that log houses made from hewn wood were constructed by craftsmen and could be permanent dwellings. The haste with which structures were put up in Mifflin County, however, suggests that they were the temporary, self-contructed variety of log building.

21. On St Mary's, see Carson and Walsh, 'Early American Housewife', p. 25. On Philadelphia, see Sharon V. Salinger and Charles Wetherell, 'Wealth and Renting in Prerevolutionary Philadelphia', *Journal of American History*, 71 (1985), 836.

22. Jean B. Russo, 'Occupational Diversification in a Rural Economy: Talbot County, Maryland, 1690–1759', paper presented at the 45th Conference on Early American History, Baltimore, 13–15 Sept. 1984.

23. Kevin Sweeney, 'Furniture and the Domestic Environment in Weathersfield, Connecticut, 1639–1800', *The Connecticut Antiquarian*, 36 (1984), 31.

24. I have listed below the various categories of goods, and the mean wealth of those Tudor Oxfordshire deceased for whom a particular category was the most valuable one in their inventory. The values are in current sterling.

> Plate and jewellery: £201.9.
> Bedding: £37.5.
> Other: £34.0.
> Pewter and brass: £32.4.
> Household linen: £32.1.
> Clothing: £17.8.
> Furniture: £8.2.

25. Sweeney, 'Domestic Environment in Weathersfield', p. 23, cites 1730 as the date of the first cabinetmaker's appearance in that town. In Talbot County, Md., the trade begins to be noted in the 1740–59 period, Russo, 'Occupational Diversification', table 1. Obviously other woodworkers could do cabinet work; still, the fact that artisans identified themselves as cabinetmakers indicates a new demand for the product.

26. Only among the élite (the top 10% in most communities and perhaps the top 20% in London) does one see these kind of changes occurring during the early modern period. See, for London, Peter Earle, 'The Domestic Possessions of the London Middle Classes, 1665–1720', paper delivered at the Clark Library Workshop, Los Angeles, 22 Oct. 1988. On early modern colonial interiors see Susan Prendergast Schoelwer, 'Form, Function, and Meaning in the use of Fabric Furnishings: A Philadelphia Case Study, 1700–1775', *Winterthur Portfolio*, 14 (1979), 27, 30, 31; John E. Crowley, 'Artificial Illumination in Early America, and the Definition of Domestic Space and Time', paper delivered at the 3rd International Conference of the Centre de recherches sur l'histoire des États-Unis, Paris, 2–4 June 1987.

27. On the consumption of linen see Margaret Spufford, *The Great Reclothing of Rural England: Petty Chapman and their Wares in the Seventeenth Century*, London, 1984, ch. 7. In addition to the data presented in Chap. 4, above, there is evidence in a study done of Lancaster County, Va., inventories from 1680 to 1740 that the mean amount invested in cloth and clothing declined over time. See Hudgins, 'Exactly as the Gentry do', table 9. The mean amount for pewter in Lancaster County rose throughout the 1720s, and then declined in the 1730s.

Furniture, bedding, ceramics, and utensils all increased in mean value. Lorna Weatherill, *Consumer Behaviour and Material Culture in Britain*, London, 1988, pp. 26–9, finds usage of pewter dishes beginning to wane in English inventories of the 1720s.

28. E.g. Lorna Weatherill, in her fine study of consumption trends in England between 1675 and 1725, *Consumer Behaviour and Material Culture*, closely examines the effects of townlife and occupational class on ownership of new consumer goods (chs. 4 and 8). Because wealth is not held constant, it is impossible to know whether greater incidence of ownership should be attributed to urban residency or occupation, or whether those occupations and urban residents are just richer. Similarly, Weatherill (ch. 3) argues that the deceased in the North-east of England (Durham and Northumberland) had a higher incidence of ownership of new consumer goods than those in most other provincial areas, including Hampshire, the North-west, and the north-west Midlands. The North-east sample, however, had a disproportionate number of inventories from urban areas: 59% came from towns, while in the samples from the other regions apart from London, the proportion was between 10% and 20%. When in ch. 4 (table 4.3), Weatherill breaks down the regions into rural and urban zones, the differences between the areas in question largely disappear.

29. Earle, 'Possessions of London Middle Classes', n. 14.

30. Lois Green Carr and Lorena S. Walsh, 'Changing Lifestyles and Consumer Behavior in the Colonial Chesapeake', tables 1.A–1.F, forthcoming in Ronald Hoffman and Cary Carson, *Of Consuming Interest*, and Gloria L. Main and Jackson Turner Main, 'Standard and Styles of Living in Southern New England, 1640–1774', forthcoming in *Journal of Economic History*. Also on ceramics see George L. Miller, 'Marketing Ceramics in North America: An Introduction', *Winterthur Portfolio*, 19 (1984), 1–6, and Regina Lee Blaszczyk, 'Ceramics and the Sot-Weed Factor: The China Market in a Tobacco Economy', ibid., 7–19.

31. Weatherill, *Consumer Behaviour and Material Culture*, ch. 9, takes issue with the statements of Joan Thirsk, Margaret Spufford, and D. E. C. Eversley which include the working class as consumers of the new commodities. 44% of Weatherill's sample of the probated deceased had less than £50 of inventoried wealth, but she seems reluctant to consider this group as of low income or as working class. What I suspect bothers Weatherill is the assumption that working-class buyers of the new commodities were doing so because all their more basic needs—food, clothing, and shelter—were completely taken care of. As is argued in this book, no such assumption should be made.

32. Cissie Fairchilds, 'The Production and Marketing of Populuxe Goods in Eighteenth Century Paris', paper presented at the Clark Library, Los Angeles, 6 Jan. 1989, pp. 6–7.

33. See table in the appendix of Shammas, 'Domestic Environment', for results of a probit analysis of tea-drinking equipment. Female inventoried deceased were more likely to have owned such things as teacups, tea kettles, tea tables, and so forth, even if variables such as wealth are held constant. Lorna Weatherill compares the percentage of inventoried males and females in England who owned various consumer items in 'A Possession of One's Own: Women and Consumer Behavior in England, 1669–1740', *Journal of British Studies*, 25

(1986), 131–56. The differences are few, though there remains a possibility that some might become apparent if wealth were held constant.

34. Lorna Weatherill, 'The Growth of the Pottery Industry, in England, 1660–1815', unpublished Ph.D. thesis, University of London, 1981, ch. 2, discusses the use of white pipe-clay for delft and stoneware.

35. Sally McMurry, 'City Parlor, Country Sitting Room: Rural Vernacular Design and the American Parlor, 1840–1900', *Winterthur Portfolio*, 20 (1985), 261–80, and Katherine Grier, *Culture and Comfort: People, Parlors, and Upholstery, 1850–1930*, New Haven, 1988. Ruth Schwartz Cowan, *More Work for Mother*, New York, 1983, has argued that women's work increased as a result of improved household technology. I am uncertain about that argument, but clearly the proportion of time women devoted to finishing processes (e.g. cooking, sewing, decorating, and cleaning) rose. I suspect that is the phenomenon that Cowan's book is really describing. Recent research by Martha Olney seems to indicate that there was a slight tendency for early 20th-cent. households that had full-time housewives to spend more on household technology durables than those in which the wife brought in earnings. See Olney, 'Credit Financed Consumption of Durable Goods', paper presented at the 1988 Social Science History Association meeting in Chicago, 6 Nov. The gender implications of another domestic development, the rise of the bathroom, are unclear. See Richard L. Bushman and Claudia L. Bushman, 'The Early History of Cleanliness in America', *Journal of American History*, 74 (1988), 1213–38.

36. On the long history of American's reliance on wood construction see Michael J. Doucet and John C. Weaver, 'Material Culture and the North American House: The Era of the Common Man, 1870–1920', *Journal of American History*, 72 (1985), 560–88. In discussing the fall in real housing costs between 1870 and 1910, they note that wood remained the largest single cost factor in housing construction, ranging between 40% and 50%. Fire laws forbade the use of wood on the exteriors of city dwellings, but elsewhere wood houses continued to be popular. On the degree of control women had over capital in early America see Carole Shammas, Marylynn Salmon, and Michel Dahlin, *Inheritance in America, Colonial Times to the Present*, New Brunswick, 1987, chs. 1–3 and 5.

37. Frederic Eden, *The State of the Poor*, London, 1797, i, 524.

III

DISTRIBUTION

Hierarchically Structured Demand and Distribution

IN sixteenth- and seventeenth-century England, most shopping took place in market towns. There were over 700 of these centres spread around the country. Each held one or more market-days during the week, and sometimes sponsored annual fairs. Practically all market towns contained a few craft shops to serve customers.[1]

In some respects, the system seems ideal. People could buy fresh food, cloth, and consumer durables from the producers themselves in their stalls. There are other indications, however, that buying at the market or from producers had its drawbacks, especially for labouring people. Markets only operated on set days and featured a limited variety of goods. Being within an 8-mile radius of a market town enabled a person on foot to go marketing and return the same day, but 8 miles was a long way to go if one had only a few shillings or less to spend. The closest market town might not have a full array of services and it would then be necessary to go further to shop. In one study, from 60% to 80% of those going to markets in the South, East, and West of England had journeyed under 10 miles to get there, but in the more thinly populated North, half of the market-goers had travelled 20 miles or more. In times of shortages, commodities would be scooped up by the bigger buyers. Large purchases at the market or ordering goods from an artisan required a substantial pre-payment, unless the customer was of sufficient importance to be allowed credit.[2] Market buying became even more complicated when, like the American colonists, one lived on the fringes of the English commercial world and market towns did not operate in the same ways as they did in the Mother Country.[3] So barriers to consumer sovereignty were considerable, and they grew as one moved from perishable to durable goods and as the value of the product increased.

The English labouring people, from the Middle Ages on, had relatively little trouble shopping for small quantities of food. Cheap meals could be purchased in the alehouses that existed in every small village. Apart from a pot of beer and a pipe of tobacco, one could procure a 'pennyworth of eggs', bread and cheese, and some broth or meat. The quality of the fare, of course, often left something to be desired. Contemporaries complained of 'twice baked bread', 'withered costive cheese', and beer that would kill a horse. Gentlemen found the environment dirty and smoky.[4] Yet like the Burger Kings and McDonalds of today, these institutions provided food for those who had neither the time nor the resources to cook at home. They also offered credit to their customers and kept track of the debts by making chalk marks on the wall or on a slate. The probate inventories of publicans record these tallies along with book debts, bills, bonds, and other credits.

In addition to visiting the weekly or semi-weekly town markets, people could buy food, for home preparation or ready to eat, at the shops of butchers, bakers, millers, brewers, and maltsters. Occupational surveys (see Chapter 8 below) indicate that these shops were sufficiently numerous to make it probable that if one's own village lacked a particular type of shop, a neighbouring village would have one. And in addition to the markets and food shops, higglers, regraters, and 'travelling market folks' furnished households with door to door service. Many of these pedlars were women, and almost all of them were poor.[5]

Still, buying food was far from problem-free for the labouring classes. Not the least of the difficulties faced by consumers of modest means concerned the medium of exchange. Tradespeople might be reluctant to offer credit and small coins were in short supply—and not just in America. A mid-seventeenth-century political controversy provides insight into the dilemmas faced by those making small cash purchases.

In 1644 the English Parliament abruptly withdrew $\frac{1}{4}d$. and $\frac{1}{2}d$. pieces from mass circulation. These coins of small denomination had been manufactured by Crown favourites who obtained a profit from the minting and distribution of them. During the Civil War, when the smouldering resentment against patents, monopolies, and special privileges developed into a full-fledged fire, Parliament revoked all coinage rights and recalled the coins. These actions, as might be expected, created chaos within the commercial community, and soon towns and retailers began producing trade tokens to fill the vacuum. Redeemable for regular money from the issuer, they were marked with his or her name and trade as well as the place of origin. Most issuers sold some type of food or drink. It has been estimated that over 12 million (just how much over is debated) tokens circulated among the 5 million inhabitants of mid-seventeenth-century England. They functioned as a major medium for exchange from the 1640s to 1672, when the Restoration government of Charles II finally took over responsibility for issuing farthings.[6]

The tokens indicate two things about early modern shopping. First, the volume of the coins and the fact that they were issued from so many towns and villages throughout England and Wales suggest the importance of the small transaction in retail business. Amidst the furore caused by the withdrawal of the farthing in 1644, it was revealed that the heaviest users of the $\frac{1}{4}d$. and $\frac{1}{2}d$. were the large numbers of working poor and the tradesmen they patronized. The tokens also serve as a reminder of what a tenuous hold on consumer sovereignty the 'common sort' had. Without a second thought, Parliament could remove small coins from circulation and leave the average consumer entirely at the mercy of the local town corporations and shopkeepers for the means to make his or her purchases. The tokens confined the buyer to one area and even to certain shops much more than regular farthings had, and one remonstrance for the restoration of the old coins accused the retailers of using the token system to restrict the consumer's freedom of choice in shopping. Urban workers in the colonies lodged similar kinds of complaints when, nearly a hundred years later, they received half of their wages in shop notes.[7]

When one moves to consider clothing, the issue of exchange is replaced by one of credit. Small accessories sold at fairs and markets by pedlars and producers—ribbons, stockings, looking-glasses, and short pieces of linen—posed little problem, but purchasing a broadcloth coat, a gown, or a pair of boots, standard items of clothing in the early modern period, caused real difficulties for many labourers. It was not that English villages did not have skilled persons to do the work: in the sixteenth and early seventeenth centuries, occupational surveys indicate that tailors and weavers resided in most of the larger villages.[8] Rather, it was that the garments were made to order and required substantial expenditure of time and money before the product was finished. The diaries and account books of the élite of England and America are replete with examples of how involved this requisitioning could be.

In 1712 Nicholas Blundell, a Catholic gentleman living in the North of England, decided to have a suit made for himself out of wool from his own flock instead of buying the cloth from a merchant, as he usually did. Because he had repaired an old wheel and a tenant had made a new bobbin for it, the spinning could be done by one of the servants, but outsiders had to be found for the other tasks: the weaving, dyeing, and fulling. Then buttons, silk, and shammy cloth had to be purchased to finish it. Although in the end the suit only cost £1. 15s. 7d., the recruiting of the workforce and the overseeing of the activities entailed considerable effort.⁹ Making clothing involved many steps that tended to be done by different people; and clothing had to be provided not only for family members but for servants as well. The late seventeenth-century disbursement book of Sir Thomas Haggerston, also from the North, contains entries such as the following: 'to a spinner woman for 8 weeks spinning for my wife'; 'to William Bell for 30 yards cloath weaving for my wife'; 'to Robert Simmons for my wife's blew cloath dyeing at Anwick with charges'; 'to Mrs. Ashley for knitting a paire of cotton stockens'; 'to young Wilson Tayler Barwick for the pypers livery coat'; 'to an Old Scotch woman for bleatching 2 webbs cloath att Greyden'. Haggerston even used an outsider to do the spinning. Around the same time, Timothy Burrell, a member of the gentry from Sussex, recorded similar items of expenditure in his accounts: 'for carding 13 lbs. of wool'; 'for weaving 21 yards of cloth'; 'for scouring and fulling', and so on.¹⁰

Often the workers would stay in the household while they did their work. 'Catharine Frazakerly helped my wife to make some Head Cloths,' wrote Blundell in his diary, 'and she Lodg'd here because she is to sew for my wife for some time.'¹¹ Tailors and shoemakers also resided with the family when they made or repaired articles of dress.

The requisitioning process could be simplified if the household purchased cloth on the market, and, in fact, almost all families did buy some ready-made textiles, particularly those that would be used in making clothes for the head of the household and his wife. Of course, buying cloth required some time and special knowledge also. Sometimes the fabrics would come from small producers, sometimes from pedlars, at other times from local merchants, and sometimes all the way from London. In his manuscript farming book, apparently intended as a guide for his heirs, Henry Best included, along with his advice on farming and animal husbandry, sections on buying food, clothing, and fuel. One of these was entitled 'buying all sorts of linen cloath', in which he detailed all the different qualities of linen and stated from whom they might be bought. First there was 'such linnen cloath as here made in England and commonly call huswife cloath', which cost 14d. or 15d. a yard and 'which our mayd servants usually buy for holyday aprons, and crosse-cloaths, and necke-cloathes'. Linen costing 16d. to 17d. was 'exceed-inge good, and much used for table-cloathes'. A still higher grade, priced at 2s., was 'used of gentle-folkes for shirts' and could be obtained from pedlars who purchased it in provincial towns. Otherwise, 'att Newe

Malton live many att whose houses one may att all times furnish themselves with this kind of cloath.' Linen from Scotland could also be procured: 'the worst sorte of Scotch-cloth is 18*d.* a yard, and the best sorte of all 2*s.* 6*d.* and eight groates a yard; it is spunne by their Lards [Lairds'] wifes, and brought into England by the poore Scotch-merchants and much used here for womens handkerchers and pockett-handkerchers.' The finest linen, however, came from overseas:

There is holland from 2*s.* 6*d.* an ell to 6*s.* 8*d.* an ell, for Holland is (most commonly) solde by the ell; wherof one sorte is called flezy-Holland; it is sayd to bee spunne by the nunnes in the Lowe Countryes, brought over by our merchants and solde to our linnen drapers att whose shoppes our countrey-pedlers furnish themselves; it is a strong cloath, and much used by mens bands, gentlewomens handkerchers, and cross-cloathes and halfe shirts &c.[12]

Best concluded by discussing the most expensive foreign linens, cambrics, used for ruffs.

I quote from these passages in Best's mid-seventeenth-century farming book at length because they reveal the kind of knowledge the head of a large early modern household possessed about the materials that went into the making of consumer goods.

Obtaining housewares demanded the same care and expense as did requisitioning cloth and clothing. Craftsmen had to be found and then often provided with food and lodging while they did the work. In the early seventeenth century, the Shuttleworth family of Gawthorpe Hall in Lancashire paid a 'disshe-thrower' and 'his man' for twelve days of 'felling, cutting, and dewinge of disshes, bassenes, and cheese fattes [vats]' and another nine days for actually making them.[13] Sometimes the dish-thrower made furniture too, although the family usually hired a joiner for that job. For other types of work, carpenters, wrights, or coopers would be engaged, depending on the type of product needed. To produce some of their metal ware, the family bought iron and paid a smith to make hooks, pothooks, and handles for some pans they had purchased.[14]

Later in the seventeenth century, the Fell family of Swarthmoor Hall, also in Lancashire, were still hiring wrights to saw down trees for planks that, under family supervision, would be made into beds.[15] The Blundells, however, when in 1704 they needed a new bed, chose to purchase it from a Liverpool craftsman. On 9 March Blundell recorded: 'My wife and Aunt went to Leverpoole & discursed Aldridg about making a new Bed for the Garden Chamber.'[16] A month and a half later

Blundell had a servant travel the 6.5 miles to Liverpool to collect the bed from the upholsterer. Three days later, on 27 April, Aldridge sent 'his man' out to set up the bed, 'but not all to content'. The next day Blundell went to the city, paid Aldridge £10, and probably complained, for a week later Mrs Aldridge came out to Blundell's residence with a joiner to 'mend the faults' in the new bed. After providing her with a meal, Blundell had to send a man and horse to accompany the woman back to Liverpool. Thereafter, Blundell stopped at Aldridge's shop when in Liverpool, making payments on his bill and, on a couple of occasions, dining with him. The account was finally settled in September 1706, about two and a half years after the order was initiated.

Occasionally one comes across people much lower down the economic scale engaged in the requisitioning of goods. Formerly a small shopkeeper in Scotland, John Harrower had failed in business and migrated to Virginia. In 1776 he was serving out his indenture as a schoolmaster on a plantation. He and the housekeeper Lucy Gaines pooled their resources and purchased 3 lb. of cotton that they calculated would be enough to make a gown for her and two vest coats for him. If it had not been for the hostilities with Great Britain, both servants would probably have bought the cloth ready-made, but the fear of war had affected the supply of British textiles. Gaines could spin but she had to do it at night after her chores were over, and so she favoured small jobs such as spinning yarn for knitted gloves. Consequently, one Saturday in January, Harrower walked 'six miles into the Forrest to one Daniel Dempsies to inquire if his wife would spin the cotton'. She accepted the work if he would carry the cotton to her house, informing him the yarn would be ready by the end of May, some four months later! In the middle of June, Harrower brought his share of the yarn to the weaver and noted proudly that the vest coats and two handkerchiefs to be made from it had been 'all prepared at my own expense'. As the diary comes to an end, he was setting about requisitioning the labour and supplies for another article of clothing—but it seems he found a new spinner.[17]

Obviously if Harrower had headed his own household and had had to order every consumer item for it in the manner in which he obtained his cotton clothes, he would have had time to do little else. Obtaining custom-made products required time that gentry like the Fells or Blundells could afford because they had stewards or housekeepers, and because they had no manual farm labour or other employment to perform. Often the craftsman who supplied their goods also made the tools they needed for production, as was the case with the Shuttleworth's dish-thrower. In addition, the gentry had the space and the extra food to lodge the crafts people while they did their work, and the labour to fetch the finished products if they were made in the shop. Finally, the standing of these families in the community reassured an artisan embarking upon the creation of a piece of furniture or formal suit that compensation would eventually follow. I say eventually, because customers ran up big bills with those in trade and commonly paid them at about the same pace as Blundell discharged his debt to the Liverpool upholsterer.

All these conditions helped make hierarchically structured consumer demand an inevitability. Many people in early modern England and America simply had to let others do the shopping for them. This aspect of distribution, however, has been largely ignored, or confused with straight bartering. I would argue that the value of exchanges between those of unequal economic standing in which one side offered goods and the other offered labour far exceeded the value of exchanges of goods between equals or near-equals. The head of the family, the master or employer, and on some occasions, when the other two did not seem to be performing their job, government authorities made a lot of consumer choices for those under their control. It is important to explore the restraints placed on consumer sovereignty by this system in order to understand the receptivity of many people to the gradual expansion in retailing.

The Patriarch and Inheritance

What did the head of the family have to do with consumption? Obviously, being at the helm of a household, he requisitioned goods for the unit's workforce, both family members and hired or bound labour. In this role he was interchangeable with the master whose buying operations are discussed in the next section. What I want to analyse first, however, relates more exclusively to family consumption: the inheritance of consumer goods from the patriarch. Pre-industrial England and America were patrilineal societies, and although women could be heirs, they had no power to devise their wealth if married. Since most women ultimately wed, men's decisions about the transmission of property tended to be the crucial ones. Even the property a widow bequeathed to her heirs depended upon what portion of family wealth her husband had seen fit to leave her.

Currently, the kind of wealth the dead transfer to the living is often of the easily alienable variety—insurance policies, realty, savings accounts, and so forth. The bulk of inherited consumer items are usually sold, given to charity, or discarded. Very few testators bequeath specific goods in their wills. One study showed that only about 3% of wills contained such legacies, and they were largely bequests of keepsakes that merely added a personal touch to a cold legal document. While wills do not record the keepsake gifts bestowed prior to death, it is noteworthy that people today do not usually find it necessary to certify the gift in their wills, as people often did in the past. Keepsake items aside, most of the physical objects that have made up the environment in which a family has lived disappear with the death of the couple, and sometimes before, when the 'senior citizens' move from their house to a retirement community or rest home. A study of contemporary consumer behaviour does not need to be much concerned with inheritance.[18]

This is not true of consumer studies of early modern societies, for two reasons. First, the portions of children and widows often included consumer durables and semi-durables. Second, some husbands chose to leave their widows room and board rather than the outright ownership of property. By this device, lineal heirs could gain control of the entire estate immediately upon the death of the father. The widow was assured maintenance, but her autonomy was restricted as both a producer and a consumer. Testators differed in the degree of specificity they used to describe the housespace she could occupy, the utensils she could borrow, and the type and quantity of food she would be provided with each year. In New England and Pennsylvania these bequests-in-kind showed up frequently, while in England and Virginia the custom seems to have been much rarer.[19]

Wills are the obvious place to look for evidence about the role inter-generational transmission of wealth played in distributing consumer goods to widows and lineal descendants. Table 7.1 indicates the nature of the settlements given to the primary heirs of testators in one area of England, the southern half of Worcestershire, and one American region, Tidewater Virginia. Samples from the latter extend into the mid-nineteenth century, revealing something about long-term trends. Relatively few testators left their legacies totally in the form of cash or other financial assets, the inheritance arrangements that made liquidation of the estate mandatory. The overwhelming majority in all periods left at least a part of their heirs' portions in kind—food, livestock, and durables. The proportion who specified particular goods ('I leave my daughter Mary one feather bed, six pewter dishes, and a cow'), however, varied. When testators bequeathed actual items instead of just shares of their estates, one can be more certain that they expected the heirs to

TABLE 7.1 Type of portion given to principal heirs in wills (by percentage)

Type of portion	Worcestershire, 1669–70 (No. = 193)	Worcestershire, 1720–1 (No. = 221)	Virginia, 1660–76 (No. = 217)	Virginia, 1720s (No. = 239)	Virginia, 1780s (No. = 116)	Virginia, 1840s (No. = 138)
Financial assets only	11.9	17.6	2.8	0.8	0.9	9.4
Shares of estate only[a]	6.7	5.9	20.3	8.8	36.2	30.4
Cash and shares of estate	13.5	14.9	0.5	2.5	10.3	17.4
Specific goods with or without cash and shares of estates	67.9	61.5	76.5	97.9	52.6	42.8
TOTAL[b]	100	100	100	100	100	100

[a] This category includes divisions of personalty, realty, and slaves.
[b] Rounding up of figures may result in totals which are not precisely 100.

Sources: Worcestershire—wills from central and southern Worcestershire parishes and peculiars probated in 1669, 1670, 1720, and 1721, Worcestershire and Herefordshire Record Office, St Helens, Worcester and PRO; Virginia—Wills from York, Henrico, Westmoreland, Isle of Wight, and Northumberland Counties, 1660–76; York, Henrico, Westmoreland, and Isle of Wight, 1724–9; York, Westmoreland, Isle of Wight, 1784–88; and York, Henrico, and Richmond (city), 1784–88; and York, Henrico, and Richmond (city), 1842–6, Virginia State Library, Richmond.

retain the legacies and not liquidate them. In the English samples, specific goods as portions initially appear in 67.9% of the cases, dropping to 61.5% in the 1720s as the number of heirs who were paid off in cash rose (11.9% to 17.6%).

The sharply higher percentage of Virginia testators leaving all or some of heirs' portions in specific goods furnishes a clue as to why this option was in the majority until the nineteenth century. The colonies had a currency problem and commodities such as tobacco or sugar often served as a medium of exchange. The value of this 'money' could fluctuate considerably, so transforming goods into cash involved a certain amount of trouble and risk.

The trend observed in Virginia is an interesting one. The percentage of testators leaving specific goods rose between 1660 and 1720, probably because the high mortality rates in the seventeenth-century Chesapeake resulted in many testators having no adult children. These heads of household gave all shares of their estates to their widows during the minority of their sons and daughters. The post-colonial samples—those for the 1780s and 1840s—show a movement away from specifying goods and towards giving financial assets and shares of estates. In the early part of the nineteenth century, Virginia legislators passed a law requiring the sale of goods in cases of intestacy. Clearly by that time, liquidating estates had become a much more acceptable operation.

What kind of goods did testators in Worcestershire and Virginia leave? As mentioned above, in neither area did room and board feature often in the portions left to widows. Livestock, which could furnish dairy products and meat, was of more importance in legacies to both wives and children, especially in early Virginia, but slaves, who could function as servants or be hired out, soon came to replace them in the legacies of the tidewater planters. Consumer durables, however, continued to be of importance for some time. Table 7.2 indicates the kinds of personal effects and household goods testators most commonly bequeathed. About one in four testators specified jewellery, weapons, books, and most often, clothing in their bequests. One in five specified articles of clothing such as suits, petticoats, and the like. Men gave to men and women to women, so, due to a lack of children of the proper sex and age, the clothes often went to distant kin or friends. The frequency of clothing bequests declined sharply over time in Virginia. Other personal effects passed much more exclusively from parent to children, particularly from a man to his son or grandson. Only weapons registered a noticeable drop after 1720, going from 18.5% to 6% in the 1780s and 1% in the 1840s.

TABLE 7.2 Percentage of testators bequeathing various types of goods as portions or mementoes

Type of Wealth	Worcestershire, 1669–70 (No. = 199)	Worcestershire, 1720s (No. = 248)	Virginia, 1660–76 (No. = 233)	Virginia, 1720s (No. = 248)	Virginia, 1780s (No. = 116)	Virginia, 1840s (No. = 138)
Personal Effects (total)[a]	25.1	27.0	27.0	38.7	21.6	17.4
Clothing	17.1	20.6	17.6	19.0	11.2	3.6
Jewellery	5.0	11.7	7.8	12.1	6.0	10.9
Weapons	1.0	0.0	8.1	18.5	6.0	1.4
Books	5.5	5.6	1.3	6.4	5.2	6.5
Household Goods (total)[a]	48.0	40.0	25.8	58.0	36.2	38.4
Bedding	32.2	24.0	17.5	44.7	24.1	21.7
Plate	7.5	10.1	5.0	7.7	2.6	7.2
Brass and pewter	19.1	13.7	6.4	24.6	6.0	0.0
Linens	12.1	12.9	3.0	3.6	0.0	4.3
Other and general	34.2	33.5	13.7	42.3	15.5	26.8

[a] The various categories will not add up to the total because some testators left more than one type of item. Often household goods or household furniture were bequeathed without the individual items being enumerated.

Sources: See Table 7.1 and Appendix 1.

This trend is Virginian, for in England the bequeathing of weapons was always extremely rare, probably because a limited number of individuals owned them in the first place.

Basically, though, it was not through clothing or other personal effects that inheritance had the strongest influence on the consumption of the lineage. It was through household goods. A study of late sixteenth-century wills from East Anglia reveals that about 40% of testators left domestic equipment as legacies.[20] As Table 7.2 shows, in five of the six samples, a similar or higher proportion of will makers specified who should get household goods. Only in seventeenth-century Virginia, where so few testators had grown children or any children at all among whom to divide their belongings, did the percentage fall below that level. These goods frequently constituted part or all of an heir's portion, and one is often struck by the careful manner in which the testator divided them. William Roper, a yeoman from Pirton parish in Worcestershire, gave to his grandson Thomas Knight £5, three napkins, a chair, and a pewter dish, and to another granddaughter, Anne Meadows, £5 and his second-best bed. It is unlikely that too many people today would be gratified or touched to receive a parent's second-best bed. In fact, such a bequest by Shakespeare to his wife, Ann Hathaway, has been interpreted by scholars as a sign that all was not well between the couple. It is impossible to know whether the playwright intended a slight or not, but such legacies appeared regularly in wills of the time and what they seem to be are efforts to make exact identification of a particular good so that the value of the legacy would be what the testator wanted and the beneficiary expected.

In the seventeenth- and early eighteenth-century samples, the specified household goods went primarily to the widow and the lineage (sons, daughters, and grandchildren), with female offspring receiving them no more frequently than the male. Those in agriculture as opposed to testators in the professions, commerce, and trade more often gave these family members commodities as legacies. Emphasizing the fact that they considered not only land, livestock, and cash, but household items as proper goods for the patrimony, early modern testators, 10–15% of them (depending on the area and time), restricted the legatee's possession of some household goods to his or her lifetime or until remarriage (if the recipient was the widow). This percentage is almost the same as that for restriction on livestock. Another measure of the value of household goods is the listing of contingency heirs, people who would inherit the property if the named legatee died before the testator. One would expect contingency heirs for realty—between 20% and 40% of land devises had such provision—but certainly not for household goods. Yet between 5% and 18% of testators in these early modern samples named contingency heirs for their household goods bequests—again, about the same proportion as made legacies of livestock.

In the Virginian wills the percentage of testators bequeathing household goods declined from 58% in the 1720s to under 40% in the 1780s and 1840s, in spite of the fact that in the latter two samples the proportion of female testators, who often had nothing more than consumer items to bequeath, increased. Household objects also became more likely to be keepsakes rather than part of an heir's portion. Slowly changes took place.

Table 7.2 also furnishes a breakdown of the kinds of household goods bequeathed. A good number of testators simply bequeathed all their household belongings to one or more legatees instead of enumerating the particular items, but among those who mentioned specific commodities, bedding appeared most frequently, followed by brass/pewter and linens.[21] Silver plate surfaced quite often considering the limited number of deceased who possessed any. Occasional mentions of furniture and tableware also occurred in wills. Apart from beds, households before the middle of the eighteenth century seldom invested much in furnishings. Daniel Defoe, writing in 1727 (at about the time the testators in two of my samples were dying), noted that houses and furniture had just begun to go in and out of style in the same manner as clothing:

It is because a policy in Trade, to alter Fashions and Customs: not only in Cloths, that part was always variable, at least in these parts of the World; but it never went such a length in other things as it does now: For the fashions alter now in the more durable kinds of things, such as Furniture of Houses, Equipages, Coaches, nay even of Houses themselves: and Houses built twenty or thirty years ago, are now old fashion'd and must be pulled down.[22]

The fact that consumer durables, unlike food and clothing, had previously not been modish objects fits in well with an inheritance system of successive generations recycling home furnishings.

A higher valuation of furniture is apparent in the later Virginian samples. Frequent references to particular pieces of furniture—desks, bureaus, tables—begin in the wills from the 1780s, while the more traditional household commodities—bedding, linens, brass, and pewter—register declines.

From this examination of wills, it appears inheritance played a major, though gradually diminishing, role over time in determining the specific consumer goods owned by early modern men and women. So many legacies were particularly or wholly paid in kind and not converted into cash. Household commodities, in particular, continued to find their way into legacies and usually into the homes of the heirs. One recent study of colonial Chesapeake inventories found that the value of consumer goods owned by native-born deceased amounted to no more than the value of consumer goods owned by immigrant decedents, if wealth and other relevant variables are held constant.[23]

The Master and Payment in Food, Clothing, and Shelter

The master, whether father or employer, bore the primary responsibility for ordering goods for the early modern household. Wives might actually do the marketing for food and choose some of the durables, but, as they had no legal control over the money needed to pay for purchases, the ultimate authority over these requisitions rested with husbands. The power of these heads of household over the consumption of their workforce was especially marked in America, because of the heavy reliance there on live-in labour. By the time of the Revolution, slaves constituted about 40% of the population in the British mainland colonies below Pennsylvania.[24] Among the white population, indentured servitude prevailed in all provinces except New England, it being estimated that over half of the immigrants in this period financed their passage by selling the profits of their labour for a set length of time. The normal stint lasted four to five years, although minors, prisoners, and some other special cases served longer.[25] This massive resort to unfree labour meant that substantial portions of the colonial population lacked consumer sovereignty and depended heavily upon the consumption decisions of the master. The slave and the servant had food, drink, clothing, and shelter provided. Planters in the West Indies and some parts of the South, anxious to obtain white indentured servants, competed with one another over the amount of meat and clothing to be allowed to their charges under statute. The Barbados government in 1682 ended up promising 6 lb. of flesh weekly and four shirts, three pairs of drawers, two jackets, one hat, four pairs of shoes, and wages of 25s. per annum— assuming that the servant survived. This situation was unusual, though. Black and Indian slaves everywhere, and white servants in the other colonies, had little bargaining power and had to accept what the master provided. Certainly, both servants and slaves might supplement their allotments with purchases financed by tips, or by produce grown on garden plots, or in some other way, but the master usually furnished the staples.[26]

Even after the term of service expired, the employer guided the servant's consumption. Freedom dues were usually paid in kind rather than money, and the most frequent commodities specified in the laws of the mainland colonies were grain and clothing. In Pennsylvania the statute directed that 'two complete suits of clothes, one of which is to be new, be given, and in Maryland one good cloth suit of Kersey or broad cloth a shift of white linen, one new pair of stockings and Shoes'. North Carolina promised 'two new suits of a value of at least £5', while South Carolina mandated 'one new hat, a good coat and breaches either of kersey or broadcloth, one new shirt of white linen, one new pair of shoes and stockings', and for women, a 'waist coat and Petticoat of new Half-thicks or Pennistone, or blue Apron and two Caps of white Linnen'. The heavier garments, if mended regularly, could last several years, even though worn constantly.[27]

When a craftsman did some work for a colonial household payment often took the form of goods rather than cash, although the 'exchange rate' was always specified. For example, Thomas Minor, one of the leading citizens of Stonington, Connecticut, agreed in 1662 to pay a shoemaker who had done work for the family 'in pease or Indian Coren 3s. per bushel, wheat at 4s. per bushel butter and good merchantabell cheese at 6d. per pound if the cheese be all new milke if not at 5 pence per pound'.[28]

England had no slaves, and its apprenticeship system involved a much smaller proportion of the workforce than did the system of indentured servitude in America; but the live-in servants, those who did domestic or agricultural labour, received much of their payment in kind, and so did some of the craftsmen and day labourers who came to do work for the household.

During the early modern period, it has been estimated that live-in servants, usually young unmarried men and women, constituted between 33% and 50% of hired agricultural workers.[29] Whether they functioned as domestics or field labourers, servants commonly received not only bed and board but also clothing. Male servants, such as coachmen or footmen, might be dressed up in uniform, but the rest apparently got ordinary attire regardless of whether or not it was referred to as livery. Some of the garments, shoes, and hats were new. In that case the employer had either to buy the woollens and linen or have the raw materials spun, woven, dyed, and fulled before the tailor could fashion them into clothing. Shoemakers might be called in to the residence, but hats were usually bought ready made.[30] Sometimes, though, the employer could fob off old clothing on his workforce. In 1642 the Yorkshire estate owner Henry Best recorded in his account book that he was giving his servant, Christopher Pearson, £4 and 'a pair of my boots which are to strate for mee and a pair of old shoes'. All of the payments in kind, even the used clothing, however, were given a monetary value, and the form of payment had been agreed to ahead of time. For example, on another occasion Best noted that a servant, one 'Robert Gibson to have £3 wages, an old hatt or else 3s. in money whether he will'.[31] In other words, the employer did not simply give away good clothes to poor servants as a charitable gesture, the way today's affluent families offer last year's fashions to the 'cleaning lady'. In many respects these handouts are in lieu of a decent wage, but the 'deal' is unspoken. In the early modern period, everything was spelled out because the stakes were higher. A good suit of wool clothes could cost £4 to £5—as much as or twice as much as a servant's yearly wage, and about the cost of the furnishings in a labourer's cottage.

In addition to the regular servants who received a yearly salary that might be paid in annual, semi-annual, or, if they were lucky, quarterly instalments, most landowners also hired occasional labour during harvest or shearing-time. Often tenants or neighbouring cottagers, these men and women worked on a piece or per diem basis for a few weeks a year and usually received, besides their wages, the following: (1) harvest gloves; (2) food and drink; (3) a feast at the end of the season. In the diaries and account books of the time one also finds special agreements made between the employers and their regular or occasional labourers whereby the former agreed to feed pigs and sheep for the latter or furnish bushels of wheat and barley. The cottagers with insufficient acreage to grow grain or provide forage for livestock managed through these arrangements to supplement the diet of their household.

Apart from the servants and part-time hired hands, workmen— smiths, carpenters, tailors, shoemakers, weavers, spinners, indeed, all types of craftsmen—might stay in the household while they performed their tasks, receiving meals and even lodging from the employer. The local grandee also ordered goods for workers and neighbours from tradesmen who would not want to bother directly with a small purchaser whose creditworthiness was an unknown.

The fixing or assessing of maximum wages by the local authorities in every county provides quantifiable information about the proportion of wages paid in kind. These sources were used in Chapter 5 to investigate food consumption. The schedules listed the top wage that could be awarded 'with meat and drink' and 'without meat and drink'. For workers paid by the day, the wage could be from 33% to 60% less if the employer provided diet. Generally, workers receiving an annual wage— bailiffs, serving-men, husbandry servants, shepherds, and so on—lived with the master, and the Justices of the Peace did not draw up a 'without meat and drink' rate for them. But on the rare occasion when they did supply the figures, about a 50% differential was apparent. The rates for servants paid annually would usually contain a ceiling for the amount to be spent on livery: normally 10–20% of the total wage. Thus in the sixteenth century a servant in husbandry commonly had a maximum wage of 20s. and a 5s. ceiling on clothing expenditure. In effect, then, we may assume that out of the total remuneration received by a live-in servant, about 67% was in kind, including meals and livery. For day labourers, the percentage amounted to about 50%, if the master provided diet.[32]

Who benefited from this part wage, part payment-in-kind system? According to Robert Loder, an affluent Berkshire yeomen of the early seventeenth century, his servants did. At the end of his accounts each year, Loder seldom missed an opportunity to complain about his expenses, and the outlay he most resented was that for his servants' diet. He vowed annually to try to get them on 'bord wages', that is, 'wages without meat and drink', but for his house servants and dairymaids that solution appeared impracticable. Loder also regretted the money for clothing he expended on one servant, declaring that 'the apparel cost more than the wages would have'.[33] While peculiarities in Loder's personality might account for some of his discontent over payments in kind to his servants—he appears to have been a close man with a penny—the inflation in prices during the first decades of the seventeenth century, particularly grain prices, probably had more to do with it. In times of extremely high food prices, labourers obviously derived some advantage from the system, even if their employers found ways to skimp on food allocations.

The disadvantages to servants of payments in kind however, were considerable. Receiving board and clothing from the master meant workers had little choice, little sovereignty, in consumption. They more or less ate and wore what was put before them. In one early eighteenth-century account book, there are references to servants requesting that livery be excused: that is, they wanted more money instead of a new set of clothes. Usually the master agreed to the change, although in one instance he refused because he believed the servant would spend all the additional cash on drink.[34] Payments in kind encouraged and supported this type of paternalism.

Wages paid in food and clothing also possessed a vagueness and room for manœuvring on the part of the employer that cash payment would not allow. Who could say where the master might choose to economize? Some, in sending grain to the mill, distinguished between the grade of flour to be ground for family use and that for the 'folks' (the work-force).[35] Servants usually drank small beer while master got strong,[36] and the amount and kind of meat provided farm labourers varied markedly. The same inconsistency occurred in clothing. Robert Lowe, apprenticed to a shopkeeper in the 1660s, might well have wished for a wage rather than clothing from his master when disagreements cropped up over whether each outfitting entailed a full suit or just a coat. Lowe spurned the coat and received nothing.[37] Masters tended to have the last word in such disputes.

Still, Henry Best noted, 'Some servants will (at their hyringe) condition to have an olde suite, apayre of breeches, and olde hatte, or a payre of shoes; and mayde servants to have an apron smocke, or both, but it is sometimes and with some servants that such things are desired.'[38] Clothing was expensive and not easy to obtain for those without a credit rating. Consequently, a servant might have no other choice than to 'condition' for a garment with his or her master.

The above-mentioned wage assessments that authorities drew up from medieval times up until the eighteenth century suggest that over the course of the early modern period changes in the master–servant relationship occurred and that the employer came to pay more of the wage in cash. Table 7.3 shows the percentage of assessments that contained livery provision for annual wage-earners and diet options for day labour from 1560 to 1760. Two trends can be detected. Livery provision for servants began to disappear in the seventeenth century, first among women and then among men. After the 1650s, only bailiffs and personal servants , as opposed to those who did farm work, continued to have livery written into the schedule after their wages. A later change affected workers paid on a per diem basis. In the eighteenth century some assessments started to drop food from the dietary provisions, restricting the option to drink only. As with livery, this alteration did not necessarily mean that employers never provided a full diet, but only that the practice

TABLE 7.3 Percentage of English wage assessments that include option of partial payment in kind

| Time period | No. of assessments | % with option of livery | | | % with option of diet | |
		Farm servants, male	Farm servants, female	Craftsmen	Food and drink	Drink only
1561–1600	20	95	79	40	100	0
1601–40	9	33	11	33	100	0
1641–80	12	8	0	8	100	0
1681–1720	11	0	0	0	100	0
1721–60	11	0	0	0	64	36

Note: Regardless of the number of assessment schedules extant, each county and town was counted no more than once in each time period.

Source: See Table 5.2.

of giving only cider or ale was firmly established. When evidence about the eighteenth-century substitution of day labourers for live-in husbandry servants is added to these findings, it becomes clear that employers' control over the consumption of English workers lessened over the three centuries we have been considering.[39] However, because of slavery, heavy dependence on the master continued longer for much of the American workforce.

The State and Sumptuary Laws

The head of household functioning as patriarch and master placed considerable constraints on the consumer sovereignty of those under his government. Public authorities, in turn, engaged in sporadic efforts to limit his budgetary freedom and also to correct the consumer excesses of those in his household over whom he had lost control. These efforts largely consisted of passing sumptuary laws against over-indulgence in the two biggest areas of pre-industrial consumer expenditure—food and clothing.

The earliest-known English sumptuary law on the national level was enacted in 1336 and concerned restraints on diet.[40] It regulated the number of courses and the kinds of meat allowed in dishes. By the sixteenth century, the legislative emphasis had definitely shifted to the policing of dress, the food battle perhaps being recognized as a lost cause. A shower of proclamations and statutes concerning clothing rained down on Tudor England, and these orders and laws reflected the mixed motivations behind their creation. The Crown worried about the negative effects of increased importation of foreign goods on the domestic economy. The monarch, members of Parliament, and other officials also disliked the confusion in the social order produced by commoners wearing fabrics and trimmings believed to denote nobility, gentility, or an official position in society. In the days before universal literacy, photographs, and mass communications, clothing informed people instantly of someone's political, social, or economic importance. First and foremost, however, the ruling-class simply did not trust the judgement of ordinary consumers.

One group of Tudor regulations aimed at stopping relatively affluent men and women from dressing the same as those in social stations directly above them. The central government concocted elaborate specifications of what could and could not be worn by those of various socio-economic levels. For example, according to a 1533 statute, only the peerage could wear textiles with gold and silver mixed into the thread; and only the peerage and knights could don red or blue velvet, foreign woollens, and certain types of furs. Other types of furs, outward garments of silk, taffeta, satin, and damask, as well as gold, silver, and silk ornaments, were forbidden to men with per annum incomes under £200; and finally, the law required of persons to earn at least £100 a year to wear anything velvet on outer garments. At the time, even the lowest of the above cut-off points represented the top 10% or so of the population.

Enforcement of the sumptuary legislation was patchy and seldom directed at anyone of any social or economic substance. Reading the 1533 law, one might assume the authorities dragged gentlemen into court routinely for wearing the garb of peers. Most prosecutions, however, occurred in the lowest courts of the realm, the constables' petty sessions or the court leets held on manors.[41] These bodies tried violations by craftsmen, husbandmen, labourers, and servants. They disciplined ordinary people for wearing breeches made with too many yards of material, for sporting hose woven from expensive fabrics, and for parading around with showy boots. The manorial courts punished a large number of tenants for infringement of a 1571 statute requiring those below gentry status to wear caps instead of hats on Sundays and feast-days. Unlike some of the other statutes, the Cap Act awarded half of the fine to the lord of the manor, and thus provided some incentive for enforcement. Usually the entire inhabitants of a village were fined, and jointly paid the modest sum. Because the statute was so universally violated and only applied to non-gentry, no unpleasant distinctions between upper-middle-class types had to be made. The lesson of the Tudor sumptuary laws is that officials tended only to prosecute violators who belonged to social classes far below their own. The prime targets were servants. For example, when the Privy Council under Elizabeth issued in 1559 an order regarding the enforcement of the sumptuary laws, it directed every master to take a census of his servants' clothing and to see that they were giving up the forbidden items.[42]

In 1604, the Crown and Parliament threw in the towel and repealed the existing sumptuary legislation, largely because no agreement could be reached on just what groups should be allowed to wear what. Efforts to reinstitute regulation of clothing occurred from time to time, but the threat such regulations posed to the expansion of commerce doomed most of them from the start. Only the disciplinary apparatus of various religious sects seriously attempted to continue sumptuary regulation for purposes of social control.[43]

In the hemisphere of the Great Experiments, sumptuary laws continued to be passed throughout the seventeenth century. At one point or another, most of the mainland colonies tried to limit excesses in dress. Like the Tudor enactments, these laws turned out to be rearguard actions, even though the colonists abandoned all efforts to draw distinctions between the upper levels of the population and confined themselves in their legislation almost exclusively to the modest householder and the working class.

Massachusetts, as one might guess, passed the greatest number of regulations—nearly a new law every decade from the 1630s up to the 1680s—and enforced the provisions for at least a year or two after each enactment. Of course, the Puritans informally encouraged sombre dress on the part of the inhabitants, and, judging by the letters of merchants during the seventeenth century, they succeeded to a certain extent in narrowing the spectrum of available colours in cloth.[44] Their actual legislation, however, related to 'men or women of mean condition' who took upon themselves 'the garb of Gentlemen'. For example, in 1651 the Massachusetts legislature prohibited the wearing of gold or silver lace, gold or silver buttons, bond lace, silk hoods and scarfs, great boots, ribbons, and points (decorations worn above boots) by those worth less than £200. By the mid-seventeenth century, £200 in wealth (as opposed to yearly income) did not separate a small élite group from everyone else in the way most of the Tudor legislation did. The £200 could be in both goods *and* realty, and thus a larger number of middle-income householders exceeded the amount. Furthermore, the law exempted those with estates worth below £200 who held public office, possessed an education or employment 'above the ordinary degree', or had once owned considerable property. Although some members of the small propertied class could not meet any of these requirements, the law essentially pertained to labourers and servants. A 1662 addition to the regulation was even more pointed. It specified that servants and children 'under government in Families' should be prosecuted for wearing 'any Apparel exceeding the quality and condition of their persons or Estate'. Tailors who made the offending garments for them could also be charged.[45]

In the two years following the passage of the 1651 law, thirty-four persons came before the Essex County Court to answer charges made against them. During 1652, the fourteen men brought to court for their own offences or for those of their wives or daughters tended to be the neighbourhood 'bad boys', the same fellows whom the constables charged with drunkenness, swearing, fighting, minor thefts, and so forth. A whole group of them seem to have been labourers in the Hammersmith ironworks. None of the defendants requested a dismissal of charges on the grounds that they were of an estate or condition above that specified in the law.[46]

In the following year, something rather strange happened. A larger proportion of those presented were on grand juries, were constables, or were clerks of the court. While not the élite of the colony, they did occupy positions of respect in the locality. What appears to have happened was that the law, not a very popular one in the first place, was being used in communities to get even with enemies. One of the letters sent to the court on behalf of a deacon in the church whose wife had been charged with wearing a silk hood alleged the man had been presented because 'of ignorance or willfulness by some Neighbor'. Due to this situation, twelve of the twenty persons charged in 1653 had their cases dismissed because they had sufficient wealth or status to wear the garments in question. New England residents resented the regulation as much as the Tudor villagers had. While the social classes that escaped supervision had dropped down several notches, the consumption of finery had gone even further. Neither servants nor labourers any longer wanted to be told that they could not wear silk ribbons.

'Trickle-down' Consumers and their Discontents

From what we have seen, the average consumer in the early modern period resorted constantly to market goods, but the choice of commodities might often be made by the head of the household or employer. Consumer demand was hierarchically structured, with many people obtaining food, clothing, and shelter from their masters or employers and inheriting consumer durables from their relatives. The problems of exchange and liquidity as well as the limits to how much credit and time for shopping those with capital would allow labouring people kept this arrangement in place despite complaints from both sides.

Signs of deterioration in the system, however, did appear during the course of the early modern period. The rash of sixteenth-century sumptuary laws regulating dress tell us that the English state felt heads of household were losing control over the clothing being bought by their workforce. Other legislation passed during the reign of Elizabeth sought to restrict all but the wealthiest portions of the population from patronizing shops selling foreign textiles or articles of clothing.[47] During the early seventeenth century, a big drop occurred in the proportion of wage-asssessment schedules that included an option for a servant's livery in lieu of cash, and by the end of the century that option had entirely disappeared. In the eighteenth century, the practice of providing full meals for day labourers seems to have been on its way out at the same time that the proportion of live-in servants in husbandry began a long secular decline.

In America, bound servitude kept many more eighteenth-century heads of household functioning as shoppers for their workforce than was the case in England. One of the things that may have made indentured and slavery systems seem such peculiar institutions in the Revolutionary era was this long-term authority of masters over the consumption needs of their workers. Once village shops and general stores invaded the rural landscape the restrictions on consumer sovereignty may well have been felt much more keenly.

Chapter 7

1. Dorothy Davis, *Fairs, Shops, and Supermarkets: A History of English Shopping*, Toronto, 1966; Alan Everitt, 'The Marketing of Agricultural Produce', in Joan Thirsk (ed.), *The Agrarian History of England and Wales*, iv, 1500–1640, 1967, pp. 446–592; J. A. Chartres, 'The Marketing of Agricultural Produce', in Joan Thirsk (ed.), *The Agrarian History of England and Wales*, v. 2, 1640–1750, Cambridge, 1985, pp. 406–502; T. S. Willan, *The Inland Trade*, Manchester, 1976, pp. 52–4; and A. D. Dyer, 'The Market Towns of Southern England', *Southern History*, 1 (1979), 123–34. On the spread of shops into villages, see Chap. 8 below. On medieval market towns, see R. H. Hilton, 'Medieval Market Towns and Simple Commodity Production', *Past and Present*, 109 (1985), 4–23.

2. Alan Everitt, 'Farm Labourers', in Thirsk (ed.), *Agrarian History*, iv. 451–2; Everitt, 'Marketing of Agricultural Produce', p. 498; and Dyer, 'Market Towns of Southern England', p. 132.

3. Max George Schumacher, *The Northern Farmer and His Markets during the Late Colonial Period*, New York, 1975, pp. 88–104; Karen Friedman, 'Victualling Colonial Boston', *Agricultural History*, 47 (1973), 189–205; and Winifred B. Rothenberg, 'The Market and Massachusetts Farmers, 1750–1855', *Journal of Economic History*, 41 (1981), 312.

4. Peter Clark, *The English Alehouse: A Social History, 1200–1830*, London, 1983, pp. 39–63; R. F. Bretherton, 'Country Inns and Alehouses', in Reginald Lennard (ed.), *Englishmen at Rest and Play: Some Phrases of English Leisure, 1558–1714*, Oxford, 1931, pp. 147–201; Anon., *The Humble Petition and Remonstrance for the Restoring of Farthing Tokens*, London, 1644; Worcester County Records. *The Quarter Session Rolls, 1591–1640*, comp. J. W. Willis Bund, Worcester,

1899, p. 530; and J. R. S. Whiting, *Trade Tokens: A Social and Economic History*, Newton Abbot, 1971, p. 60.

5. On regratresses see Alice Clark, *The Working Life of Women in The Seventeenth Century*, London, 1919; W. Thwaites, 'Women in the Marketplace: Oxfordshire *c.* 1690–1800', *Midland History*, 9 (1984), 23–42; and Carole Shammas, 'The World Women Knew: Women Workers in the North of England during the late Seventeenth Century', in Richard S. Dunn and Mary Maples Dunn (eds.), *The World of William Penn*, Philadelphia, 1986, pp. 103–9.

6. On trade tokens see Willan, *The Inland Trade*, pp. 83 ff.; and E. Thurlow Leeds, 'Oxford Tradesmen's Tokens', in Revd. H. E. Salter (ed.), *Surveys and Tokens*, Oxford Historical Society, 75 (1920), 357–453. 18th-cent. businesses, particularly industrial concerns in growing provincial areas, from time to time issued tokens to supplement government coins. See Peter Mathias, *English Trade Tokens: The Industrial Revolution Illustrated*, London, 1962.

7. Anon., *The Humble Petition and Remonstrance . . . for the Restoring of Farthing Tokens*, London, 1644, n.p., and Gary Nash, *The Urban Crucible: Social Change, Political Consciousness, and the Origins of the American Revolution*, Cambridge, Mass., 1979, p. 115.

8. A. J. Tawney and R. H. Tawney, 'An Occupational Census of the Seventeenth Century', *Economic History Review*, 5 (1934–5), 41, indicates that in 1608, out of Gloucestershire manors with 30 or more men 80% had tailors and 76.3% had weavers or some type of textile worker. These were about the most common trades represented. John Patten, *English Towns, 1500–1700*, Hamden, Conn., 1978, pp. 244–64, found that in the years 1500–1700 more East Anglian market towns had tailors than any other trade. The representation of weavers in towns, however, had begun to decline in the 17th cent.

9. *Blundell's Diary and Letter Book, 1702–1728*, ed. Margaret Blundell, Liverpool, 1952, pp. 123–4.

10. *Selections from the Disbursements Book (1691–1709) of Sir Thomas Haggerston, Bart*, ed. Ann M. C. Forster, Surtees Society 180 (1965), *passim*; 'Extracts from the Journal and Account-Book of Timothy Burrell, Esq. Barrister-at-Law . . . 1683–1714', ed. Robert Willis Blencowe, *Sussex Archaeological Collections*, 3 (1850), *passim*.

11. *The Great Diurnal of Nicholas Blundell*, Record Society of Lancashire and Cheshire, 1 (1968), 248.

12. *Rural Economy in Yorkshire, in 1641, Being the Farming and Account Books of Henry Best*, ed. C. B. Robinson, Surtees Society, 33 (1857), 105–6. *Accounts of the Roberts Family of Boarzell, Sussex*, ed. Robert Tittler, Sussex Record Society, 71 (1977–9), 64–5, 134–5, 138–9, 148–51, contain other examples of the requisitioning of cloth and tailoring.

13. *The House and Farm Accounts of the Shuttleworths of Gawthorpe Hall . . . 1582–1621*, ed. John Harland, Chetham Society, 35 (1857), 159.

14. Ibid., p. 204.

15. *The Household Account Book of Sarah Fell of Swarthmoor Hall, 1673–1678*, ed. Norman Penney, Cambridge, 1920, p. 11.

16. *Blundell Diurnal*, pp. 53, 55, 56.

17. 'Diary of John Harrower, 1773–6', *American Historical Review*, 6 (1900–1), 105–7.

18. See Carole Shammas, Marylynn Salmon, and Michael Dahlin, *Inheritance in America, Colonial Times to the Present*, New Brunswick, NJ, 1987, Introduction, and Marvin Sussman, Judith N. Cates, and David T. Smith, *The Family and Inheritance*, New York, 1970, p. 156.

19. Shammas, Salmon, and Dahlin, *Inheritance in America*, chs. 2 and 5. R. J. Bernard, 'Peasant Diet in Eighteenth Century Gevaudan', in Elborg Forster and Robert Forster (eds.), *European Diet from the Pre-industrial to Modern Times*, New York, 1975, p. 20 contains information about the use of these portions in France. Comments about England are based upon my analysis of Worcestershire and East London wills.

20. Rachel P. Garrard, 'English Probate Inventories and Their Use in Studying the Significance of the Domestic Interior, 1570–1700', in *AAG Bijdragen*, 23 (1980), 55–81. The 138 wills were from Suffolk in 1584.

21. This was true in Elizabethan Suffolk, too: ibid.

22. Daniel Defoe, *The Complete English Tradesman*, New York, 1969, reprint of 2nd edn. of 1727, ii. 2. 6.

23. Lois Green Carr and Lorena S. Walsh, 'Changing Life Styles and Consumer Behavior in the Colonial Chesapeake', forthcoming in Ronald Hoffman and Cary Carson (eds.), *Of Consuming Interest*, tables 1.A–1.F.

24. US Bureau of the Census, *Historical Statistics of the United States, Colonial Times to 1970*, Washington DC, 1970, p. 1168.

25. Abbot Emerson Smith, *Colonists in Bondage: White Servitude and Convict Labor in America, 1607–1776*, Chapel Hill, 1947, pp. 3–4; David Galenson, *White Servitude in Colonial America*, New York, 1981, pp. 102–6; and Sharon Salinger, *'To Serve Faithfully and Well': Labor and Indentured Servants in Pennsylvania, 1682–1800*, New York, 1987, p. 80.

26. Smith, *Colonists in Bondage*, p. 237, and Allan Kulikoff, *Tobacco and Slaves*, Chapel Hill, 1986, pp. 392–3.

27. Smith, *Colonists in Bondage*, pp. 239–40, and Frederic Morton Eden, *The State of the Poor*, London, 1797, i, 557.

28. *The Diary of Thomas Minor 1653 to 1684*, ed. Sidney H. Miner and George D. Stanton, jun., New London, 1899, pp. 54–5.

29. Ann Kussmaul, *Servants in Husbandry in Early Modern England*, Cambridge, 1981.

30. These observations and some of the following remarks about the payments in kind made by employers to their servants and workmen are based upon: *The House and Farm Accounts of the Shuttleworths of Gawthorpe Hall*, ed. Harland, Chetham Society, 35, 41, 43, 46 (1856, 1857, 1858); *Robert Loder's Farm Accounts, 1610–1620*, ed. G. E. Fussell, Camden Society, 3rd ser. 53 (1936); *The Account Book of a Kentish Estate, 1616–1704*, ed. Eleanor C. Lodge, London, 1927; *Rural Economy in Yorkshire in 1641*, ed. Robinson; *The Household Account Book of Sarah Fell*, ed. Penney; 'Journal and Account Book of Timothy Burrell', ed. Blencowe, pp. 117–72; *Disbursements Book (1691–1907) of Sir Thomas Haggerston, Bart.*, ed. Forster; *The Diary of Roger Lowe ... 1663–74*, ed. William L. Sachse, New Haven, 1938; *Blundell Diurnal*, 2 vols., 1968 and 1970; and *The Journal of Giles Moore*, ed. Ruth Bird, Sussex Record Society, 68 (1971).

31. *Rural Economy*, ed. Robinson, pp. 158, 164. For additional examples of

employers clothing servants see Revd. R. G. Griffiths, 'Joyce Jeffreys of Ham Castle: A Seventeenth-Century Business Gentlewoman', *Transactions of the Worcestershire Archaeological Society*, 10 (1933), 1–32, and 11 (1934), 1–13.

32. These statements are based upon an analysis of the wage assessments listed in the source note to Table 5.2, above. A list of extant wage assessments can be found in W. E. Minchinton (ed.), *Wage Regulation in Pre-industrial England*, Newton Abbot, 1972, pp. 206–25.

33. *Loder's Farm Accounts*, ed. Fussell, p. 172.

34. 'Journal and Account Book of Timothy Burrell', ed. Blencowe, pp. 122, 150.

35. *Rural Economy*, ed. Robinson, p. 104.

36. William Cobbett, *Rural Rides*, New York, n.d., p. 266.

37. *Diary of Lowe*, ed. Sachse, p. 80.

38. *Rural Economy*, ed. Robinson, p. 134.

39. Kussmaul, *Servants in Husbandry*, chs. 2 and 7, discusses the decline of servants. K. D. M. Snell, 'The Standard of Living, Social Relations, the Family and Labour Mobility in Southeastern and Western Countries *c*.1700–1860', unpublished doctoral dissertation, Cambridge University, 1979, finds (ch. 2) a shortening of servants' and apprentices' terms of service too. Although she does not print the assessment documents, so they could not be included in Table 7.3, Elizabeth Gilboy (*Wages in Eighteenth Century England*, Cambridge, Mass., 1934, pp. 19, 88–90, 125, 197, 202) presents evidence that indicates drink rather than diet was what many employers provided in the 18th cent.

40. Frances Elizabeth Baldwin, *Sumptuary Legislation and Personal Regulation in England*, Baltimore, 1926, p. 28. See also Wilfrid Hooper, 'The Tudor Sumptuary Laws', *English Historical Review*, 30 (1915), 433–49; and N. B. Harte, 'State Control of Dress and Social Change in Pre-industrial England', in D. C. Cole an and A. H. John (eds), *Trade, Government and Economy in Pre-industrial England: Essays Presented to F. J. Fisher*, London, 1976, pp. 132–65. The French continued to issue sumptuary regulations until the 1720s. See Cissie Fairchilds, 'The Production and Marketing of Populuxe Goods in Eighteenth-Century Paris', paper presented at the Clark Library, 6 Jan. 1989, pp. 8–9.

41. On the sumptuary prosecutions in the petty constable sessions see F. G. Emmison, *Elizabethan Life: Disorder*, Chelmsford, 1920, pp. 30ff. For examples from manorial records see *Court Leet Records*, tr. and ed. F. J. C. Hearnshaw and D. M. Hernshaw, Southampton Record Society, 1.1 (1905), 138–9, 161; G. Eland, *At the Courts of Great Canfield, Essex*, London, 1949, p. 75; *Court Rolls of the Manor of Acomb*, ed. Harold Richardson, Yorkshire Archaeological Society Record Series, 131 (1969), 1. 92, 96, 98, 101; *The Court Leet Records of the Manor of Manchester*, Manchester, 1884, i. 155, 185, 191, 200, 201, 205; *The Coventry Leet Book or Mayor's Register*, tr. and ed. Mary Dormer Harris, London, 1907–13, pp. 600–1, and *Records of the Manor of Henley in Arden, Warwickshire*, tr. and ed. Frederick C. Wellstood, Stratford upon Avon, 1919, p. 28.

42. *Tudor Royal Proclamations*, ed. Paul L. Hughes and James F. Larkin, New Haven, 1969, ll. 136.

43. Paul Hair (ed.), *Before the Bawdy Court*, London, 1972, p. 56.

44. Linda R. Baumgarten, 'The Textile Trade in Boston, 1650–1700', in Ian M. G.

Quimby (ed.), *Arts of the Anglo-American Community in the Seventeenth Century*, Charlottesville, 1975, p. 224.

45. Massachusetts Colony, *Colonial Laws of Massachusetts*, Boston, 1887, pp. 5–6. On sumptuary legislation in New England see David H. Flaherty, *Privacy in Colonial New England*, Charlottesville, 1972, 184–8 and Norman H. Dawes, 'Social Classes in Seventeenth Century New England', unpublished dissertation, Harvard University, 1941, ii. 340–8 and 357–60.

46. Massachusetts Colony, *Records and Files of the Quarterly Courts of Essex County, Massachusetts*, Salem, 1916, i. 278–304.

47. 5 Elizabeth c. 6. This legislation will be discussed in more detail in the next chapter.

The Rise of the English Country Shop

FOR English households to have continual and direct access to a wide variety of commodities, they needed to have permanent retail establishments in their local communities. The question is, when did such shops for processed and ready-made goods on credit become common? The old answer: in the nineteenth century when the Industrial Revolution urbanized the working class, has been challenged by a number of scholars working on retailing in the eighteenth, seventeenth, and even sixteenth century. Using occupational surveys and probate inventories, historians have demonstrated that many communities with fewer than 2,500 people, the usual cut-off point for urban status, had shops in the early modern period.[1]

The most comprehensive study of early modern retailing, Hoh-cheung and Lorna H. Mui's *Shops and Shopkeeping in Eighteenth Century England*, argues persuasively that the ratio of population to shops fell dramatically during the eighteenth century, dropping down to levels never to be seen again. Put another way, there were more shops per capita in the 1750s than in the industrial era. They estimate that there was one shop for every 42 persons in 1759, while in 1950 the reported ratio had risen to one for every 92. Other data I have collected (see Table 9.4) shows somewhat higher eighteenth-century ratios, but supports the Muis' main contention. The trend in the number of shops per capita over the past three centuries has been curvilinear rather than linear, and eighteenth-century shopkeepers were comparatively thick on the ground.[2]

What explains the apparent explosion in shops during the eighteenth century? The Muis attribute it to (1) improvements in transportation, (2) increased urbanization, and (3) the demand effects of population growth, more wage-earners, and larger incomes. Questions can be raised, however, about the validity of all these explanations. While some have argued that road-carrying services multiplied in the seventeenth century and grew even faster in the eighteenth, others chart a much slower growth, one that failed to keep pace with industrial output. Increased urbanization cannot very easily explain the multiplication of shops nationally in the period prior to the 1750s because much of the urban growth can be traced to London. The population of most English provincial towns stagnated between 1650 and 1750. Likewise, England's total population increased very little during that 100-year period, casting suspicion on demand explanations. Nor is it certain that the early eighteenth century, as opposed to the early seventeenth century, witnessed any particular spurt in the number of people earning a wage. There may have been an improvement in relative income due to lower prices for certain commodities, but the reason why that directly benefited shops as opposed to other modes of distribution remains obscure.[3]

Before we can isolate the factors that led increasingly to shops taking over the distribution of goods, it is necessary to know something about the location of these outlets, their merchandise and the nature of their transactions not only during but prior to the eighteenth century. To what extent was the growth in shops an early eighteenth-century phenomenon? Did the new shops primarily utilize the traditional market-town network, or did they forge another network? Did they supplement or replace itinerant traders? What about the merchandise shops stocked? Did specialization accompany the expansion, and, if so, was it specialization in retailing itself or in the selling of a particular type of commodity? Also very little is known about the suppliers of these shops, the customers, and the terms of trade. Unfortunately no one source tells us all we want to know. Rather, it is necessary to examine different types of materials—occupational surveys, probate inventories, merchant account books, and tax records—to piece together the evolution of retailing during the early modern period.

Occupational Listings and the Location of Shops

Good occupational listings for English towns and villages are few and far between. Guild records do not furnish very reliable figures because fewer and fewer tradesmen belonged and those who did might not be practising the trade of their guild. Even in the sixteenth century, town authorities complained about numerous country traders illegally selling wares within city limits and impoverishing the resident members of merchant guilds. A 1552 Parliamentary statute confined outsiders who retailed goods that they did not make themselves to selling only at town fairs, but the effectiveness of that legislation is doubtful. By the later seventeenth century, according to one source, no more than a quarter of towns still had guild organizations, and contemporary reports alleged that shopkeepers set up business without any apprenticeship. Business directories only began in the late eighteenth century, and they seldom cover more than market towns. Because of these shortcomings in the records of trades, T. S. Willan resorted to using trade tokens in order to study mid-seventeenth-century retailing.[4]

Of the lists that are most useful for discovering the prevalence of retailers in early modern communities, the majority, in fact, were compiled for purposes other than trade. Muster rolls for identifying able-bodied men eligible for military service offer one of the most complete enumerations of occupations. Historians have also employed probate records, parish registers and tax lists.[5]

The lists suggest that at the beginning of the early modern period many artisan retailers routinely resided in rural communities. Tailors, weavers, smiths, shoemakers, carpenters, and butchers are all identified as being in most sixteenth- and early seventeenth-century market towns in the South of England and in 25% or more of the medium-sized villages. The main interest here, however, is not in producer- or artisan-sellers, but in retail shopkeepers who distributed goods manufactured or processed by others, often products made in another region or country: those called merchant, shopkeeper, mercer, grocer, haberdasher, draper, chapman, ironmonger, stationer, bookseller, apothecary, tobacconist, and the like.[6]

Table 8.1 shows what can be learned about those who engaged exclusively in retail trade in the smaller market towns of East Anglia and Gloucestershire. By smaller, I mean those with fewer than 2,500 inhabitants. Nationally, 85–90% of the 700 or so market towns fell into this category.[7] Only two areas, East Anglia (the counties of Norfolk and Suffolk) and Gloucestershire are amenable to this kind of analysis because the other occupational lists relate to only one town or a very small number of towns. The table indicates that during the sixteenth and early seventeenth century, 75% of these smaller market towns had at least one distributive retailer, and the presence of such a trader may have become universal by the end of the seventeenth century. The evidence for that is the change in East Anglia between 1600–49 and 1650–99, when the percentage of towns having one or more retailer rose from 75% to 92%. Of course, East Anglia was probably more commercialized than most areas.

Table 8.1 also reveals what kinds of retailers were being added. The increase came primarily among those trading in groceries—grocers, apothecaries, and tobacconists. East Anglia always appears to have had

TABLE 8.1 Percentage of market towns with fewer than 2,500 inhabitants having various types of retailers

Retailer	East Anglia			Gloucestershire
	1500–99 (39 towns)	1600–49 (40 towns)	1650–99 (37 towns)	1608 (29 towns)
Grocer	41.0	47.5	75.7	0.0
Mercer	28.2	20.0	21.6	72.4
Merchant	20.5	20.0	27.0	0.0
Draper	33.3	35.0	40.5	13.8
Haberdasher	10.3	10.0	16.2	6.9
Chapman	0.0	0.0	0.0	10.3
Ironmonger	2.6	0.0	0.0	3.4
Apothecary	7.7	15.0	37.8	3.4
Tobacconist	0.0	0.0	8.1	0.0
Bookseller	0.0	0.0	0.0	0.0
None of above	25.6	25.0	8.1	24.1

Sources: Derived from data in John Patten, *English Towns, 1500–1700*, Folkestone, 1978, and John Smith, *Men and Armour for Gloucestershire in 1608*, Trowbridge, 1980, reprint of 1902 edn.

more market-town grocers than most other regions, where the most common designation for a retailer was the mercer, a person who dealt in both cloth and groceries as well as other goods (note Gloucestershire in Table 8.1).[8] Whether it was the increasing importance of groceries that accounted for growth in shops, however, can only be settled by consulting the inventories of the tradespeople.

It would be good to know the increase in the average number of retailers per town, but probate records (which only count retailers when they die) are of no use for that purpose, and it is hard to find muster rolls for several time periods. For instance, there is evidence that the twenty-nine smaller market towns of Gloucestershire in 1608 averaged 2.0 shopkeepers each, but there is no figure for the late seventeenth or early eighteenth century with which to compare this average. One can make a comparison for the small market town of Colyton, Devon. In 1608–12, parish registers reveal two shopkeepers: a draper and a mercer, while in 1765–79 they show five: two grocers, two drapers, and a mercer. Unfortunately, Colyton is not the world. Also, population growth alone may account for the difference. The number of retailers, moreover, does not reveal the whole picture, because the size of the stock of these retailers, many of whom traded in a wide variety of goods, is also of importance. Predictably, occupational surveys for non-market communities are even less reliable. None extend into the eighteenth century. East Anglian villages did increase their shopkeeping class over time, but even so, at the end of the seventeenth century less than 15% had one or more retailers. Essentially, Table 8.2 implies that prior to 1700 few non-market rural communities had distributive retail shops. The occupational listings demonstrate the importance of market-town status in shopkeeping. For example, if the communities of c. 500 inhabitants in the 1608 Gloucestershire muster roll are compared, it turns out that all of the six that had markets had distributive retailers, but only three out of the eleven without markets had such traders. Shopkeepers apparently depended on the market and fair days for much of their business.[9]

TABLE 8.2 Percentage of rural non-market communities with retailers[a]

Year	Place	No. of communities	% with trades
1522	Rutland	all in county	0.0
1522	Babergh Hundred, Suffolk	29	3.6
1500–99	East Anglian parishes	1,125	4.9–6.5[b]
1600–40	East Anglian parishes	1,133	6.3–9.0[b]
1650–99	East Anglian parishes	1,129	8.5–14.8[b]
1608	Gloucestershire manors	401	3.0
1660–99	Gloucester area villages	72	2.8
1649–72	England	c. 8,500	4.7[c]

[a] Unless otherwise noted, the only retailers counted as such are those listed in Table 8.1.
[b] Includes victuallers and clothiers but excludes apothecaries and booksellers.
[c] Includes butchers, bakers, chandlers, and merchant taylors.

Sources: Julian Cornwall, 'The People of Rutland in 1522', *Transactions of the Leicestershire Archaeological Society*, 37 (1961–2), 7–28; John Patten, 'Village and Town: An Occupational Study', *Agricultural History Review*, 20 (1977), 1–17; ibid., 'Changing Occupational Structures in the East Anglian Countryside, 1500–1700', in H. S. A. Fox and R. A. Butlin (eds.), *Change in the Countryside*, London, 1979, pp. 103–22; John Smith, *Men and Armour for Gloucestershire in 1608*, Trowbridge, 1980, reprint of 1902 edn.; Peter Ripley, 'Village and Town: Occupations and Wealth in the Hinterland of Gloucester, 1660–1700', *Agricultural History Review*, 32 (1984), 170–8; T. S. Willan, *Inland Trade*, Manchester, 1976, pp. 83–9.

Probate Inventories and Merchandise

Evidence like that in Table 8.2 makes it difficult to understand who was reading the handbooks addressed to country shopkeepers and pedlars that were being printed and reprinted in the later seventeenth century, and why contemporaries believed shops were springing up everywhere. The often quoted statement by a pamphlet writer in 1681 that shop-keepers were to be found in 'every country village where is . . . not above ten houses' seems not merely an exaggeration, but a serious delusion.[10]

Some of the discrepancy between perception and reality, however, may be accounted for by omissions in the occupational listings. That is, the muster rolls, parish registers, and probate inventories did not identify as merchandisers all those villagers who in fact sold retail goods. Those with honorific titles such as alderman, gentleman, or esquire are one such group. Another is women. Women were left out of muster rolls entirely, and in the other records they were most often designated by marital status, not occupation. Finally, retailers with dual occupations—farmers and traders or manufacturers and traders—sometimes have the other vocation listed, or have no occupation after their name. It is logical, moreover, to suspect that those with dual occupations would be more prevalent in villages than in market towns. This certainly seems to be a possible explanation for why so few people called alehouse-keepers or innkeepers or victuallers show up in occupational lists, yet licensing records indicate that in the late sixteenth century about every thirtieth dwelling in the realm was a public house.[11] The same could be true about the reporting of retail shopkeepers. Sellers of ale and sellers of wares, of course, could be the same individuals as well.

The best way to test whether omissions of this sort resulted in a gross undercounting of distributors is to examine the contents of probate inventories for evidence of retailing. Also inventories allow one to gauge the scale of the enterprise. As in the chapter on household production, printed collections of inventories will be used, plus the inventories I gathered for the Worcestershire sample. In the various inventory collections for the provinces (London area retailers were excluded), I selected those that at least had an evaluation for the total amount of wares owned. In other words, inventoried persons who were identified as retailers but whose property included no wares were omitted. Table 8.3 breaks down the seventy-nine eligible inventories by where the retailer lived. In the late sixteenth and early seventeenth century most resided in the larger market towns—60.0% and 52.9%, respectively. But

TABLE 8.3 Where inventoried provincial retailers lived

Years	No. of inventories	% living in non-market communities	% living in market towns <2,500 population	% living in market towns >2,500 population
1560–99	15	13.3	26.7	60.0
1600–59	17	11.8	35.3	52.9
1660–99	31	22.6	58.1	19.4
1700–40	16	18.8	50.0	31.2

Sources: *Nottinghamshire Household Inventories*, ed. P. A. Kennedy, Thoroton Society Record Series, 12 (1963); *Household and Farm Inventories in Oxfordshire, 1550–1590*, ed. M. A. Havinden, London, 1965; Margaret Spufford, *The Great Reclothing of Rural England*, London, 1984; *Banbury Wills and Inventories, 1591–1620*, ed. J. S. W. Gibson, Banbury Historical Society, 13 (1985); *Banbury Wills and Inventories, 1621–1650*, ed. E. R. C. Brinkworth and J. S. W. Gibson, Banbury Historical Society, 14 (1976); *Chesterfield Wills and Inventories, 1521–1603*, ed. J. M. Bestall and D. V. Fowkes, Derbyshire Record Society, 1 (1977); *Wills and Inventories . . . : Archdeaconry of Richmond*, ed. James Raine, Surtees Society, 26 (1854); *Durham Wills and Inventories*, ed. William Greenwell, Surtees Society, 38 (1860); A. D. Dyer, 'Probate Inventories of Worcester Tradesmen, 1545–1614', *Worcestershire Historical Society*, n.s. 5 (1967), 1–67; *Stockport Probate Records, 1578–1619*, ed. C. B. Phillips and J. H. Smith, Record Society of Lancashire and Cheshire, 124 (1985); J. J. Bagley, 'Matthew Markland, a Wigan Mercer: The Manufacture and Sale of Lancashire Textiles in the Reigns of Elizabeth 1 and James 1', *Lancashire and Cheshire Antiquarian Society*, 68 (1958), 45–68; D. G. Vaisey, 'A Charlbury Mercer's Shop, 1623', *Oxoniensia*, 31 (1966), 107–16; Revd. R. G. Griffiths, 'An Inventory of the Goods and Chattels of Thomas Cowcher, Mercer of Worcester', *Transactions of the Worcester Archaeological Society*, 14 (1937–8), 45–60; *Edgley Probate Inventories, 1614–1787*, ed. John S. Roper mimeo, Dudley, n.d.; *Newmarket Inventories, 1662–1715*, ed. Peter May, mimeo., Newmarket, 1976; *Probate Inventories of Lichfield and District, 1568–1680*, ed. D. G. Vaisey, Staffordshire Record Society, 4th ser. 5 (1969); *Yorkshire Probate Inventories, 1542–1689*, ed. Peter C. D. Brears, Yorkshire Archaeological Society Record Series, 134 (1972); *Devon Inventories of the Sixteenth and Seventeenth Centuries*, ed. Margaret Cash, Devon and Cornwall Record Society, n.s. 11 (1966); *Farm and Cottage Inventories of Mid-Essex, 1635–1749*, ed. Francis W. Steer, Colchester, 1950; *Yeoman and Colliers in Telford: Probate Inventories for Dawley, Lilleshall, Wellington, and Wrockwardine, 1660–1750*, ed. Barrie Trinder and Jeff Cox, London, 1980; *Selby Wills*, ed. Dr F. Collins, Yorkshire Archaeological Society, 47 (1912); G. H. Kenyon, 'Petworth Town and Trades, 1610–1760', pt. 2, *Sussex Archaeological Collections*, 98 (1960); and Hereford and Worcestershire Record Office, Consistory Court Probate files for the Diocese of Worcestershire, 1669–1670 and 1720–1.

inventories from retailers in towns with under 2,500 inhabitants came to dominate in the two later periods, when over 50% are derived from the smaller market towns, and about 20% lived in villages. If cities such as London or even Bristol or Norwich had been included in the samples, the small market towns would have claimed a lesser proportion. Still, the late seventeenth-century increase, whatever the proper proportion may be, is noticeable.

Table 8.4 gives detailed information about the forty-seven inventories from the smaller market towns and the non-market communities. The

TABLE 8.4 Characteristics of provincial retailers in inventories, 1560–1740

Date	Place	Occupational designation	Second occupation	Method of retailing	Value of wares (£)	% in cloth	% in haber-dashery	% in garments	% in groceries	% in provisions	% in other
MARKET TOWNS UNDER 2,500 INHABITANTS											
1560	Southwell, Notts.	Mercer	Farmer	Shop	32	n.a.	n.a.	n.a.	n.a.	n.a.	n.a.
1588	Winslow, Bucks.	None	—	Shop	10	80	10	—	10	—	—
1588	Chesterfield, Derby.	Draper	Farmer	Stall	15	100	—	—	—	—	—
1591	Stockport, Ches.	Linen Draper	Farmer	?	10	100	—	—	—	—	—
1606	Stockport, Ches.	Linen Draper	—	Pack-horse	20	100	—	—	—	—	—
1607	Stockport, Ches.	None	—	Shop	24	79	21	—	—	—	—
1609	Stockport, Ches.	Mercer	—	Shop	8	87	—	—	13	—	—
1617	Wigan, Lancs.	Mercer	Farmer	Shop	343	63	22	—	13	—	2
1619	Stockport, Ches.	None	—	Shop	19	—	100	—	—	—	—
1623	Charlbury, Oxon.[a]	Mercer	—	Shop	97	19	55	—	10	7	8
1663	Selby, Yorks.	Grocer	—	Shop	75	19	48	—	21	5	7
1663	Newmarket, Suffolk	Haberdasher	—	Stall	23	48	52	—	—	—	—
1654	Dartmouth, Devon	Merchant	—	Shop	22	4	4	—	—	—	18
1669	Alcester, War.	Mercer	—	Shop	1,145	n.a.	n.a.	n.a.	n.a.	n.a.	n.a.
1669	Pershore, Worcs.	Mercer	—	Shop	442	n.a.	n.a.	n.a.	n.a.	n.a.	n.a.
1670	Stratford-upon-Avon, War.	Chapman	—	?	30	83	17	—	—	—	—
1674	Doncaster, Yorks.	None	Farmer	Shop	256	—	4	—	85	1	10
1679	Grantham, Lincs.	Chapman	—	On foot	7	29	71	—	—	—	—
1680	Bury, Lancs.	None	—	On foot	3	—	100	—	—	—	—

1681	Petworth, Sussex	Draper	Maltster	Shop	801	n.a.	n.a.	n.a.	n.a.	n.a.	n.a.
1687	Wellington, Salop.	Mercer	—	Shop	55	27	53	—	18	—	2
1688	Donnington, Lincs.	None	—	Stall	38	79	21	—	—	—	—
1689	Selby, Yorks	Mercer	—	Shop	231	4	16	—	26	45	9
1690	Great Chart, Kent	Chapman	—	Pack-horse	20	100	—	—	—	—	—
1692	Petworth, Sussex	None	—	?	88	68	32	—	—	—	—
1692	Petworth, Sussex	Chapman	—	?	162	n.a.	n.a.	n.a.	n.a.	n.a.	n.a.
1693	Petworth, Sussex	Mercer	—	Shop	359	48	5	—	18	27	1
1695	Barnstaple, Devon	Apothecary	—	Shop	15	n.a.	n.a.	n.a.	n.a.	n.a.	n.a.
1700	Wellington, Salop.	Mercer	Farmer	Shop	90	64	14	1	17	8	2
1704	Sittingbourne, Kent	Salesman	—	Shop	205	61	5	34	—	—	—
1711	Petworth, Sussex	Mercer	—	Shop	900	78	9	—	1	5	7
1712	Petworth, Sussex	Mercer	—	Shop	373	92	4	—	—	—	4
1716	Congleton, Ches.	Chapman	—	Shop	20	—	15	—	65	20	—
1721	Tonbridge, Kent	Salesman	—	Shop	217	69	20	11	—	—	—
1725	Wellington, Salop.	Mercer	Tallow chandler	Shop	3	—	—	—	—	100	—
1729	Downham Market, Norfolk	Chapman	—	Shop	224	77	14	—	1	—	7
NON-MARKET COMMUNITIES											
1581	Kidlington, Oxon.	None	—	?	2	n.a.	n.a.	n.a.	n.a.	n.a.	n.a.
1595	Linge, Norfolk	Chapman	—	Pack-horse	6	83	17	—	—	—	—
1613	Sutton St James, Lincs.	Chapman	Farmer	Shop	6	33	—	—	50	—	17
1658	Sedgley, Staffs.	Petty Chapman	—	?	13	23	77	—	—	—	—
1665	Monkland, Her.	Chapman	—	On foot	6	—	100	—	—	—	—
1668	Slaithwaite, Yorks.	Chapman	Farmer	Shop	83	5	—	—	80	15	—

TABLE 8.4 (cont.)

Date	Place	Occupational designation	Second occupation	Method of retailing	Value of wares (£)	% in cloth	% in haber- dashery	% in garments	% in groceries	% in provisions	% in other
1683	Roxwell, Essex	None	—	?	19	100	—	—	—	—	—
1687	Writtle, Essex	None	—	Shop	1	—	30	—	—	70	—
1691	Randwick, Glos.	Petty Chapman	—	Shop	71	45	46	1	7	1	1
1692	Roxwell, Essex	None	†	Shop	67	39	13	3	31	4	9
1695	Stableton, Cumb.	Chapman	—	On foot	15	50	43	—	—	—	7
1714	Caythorpe, Lincs.	Chapman	—	Pack-horse	12	75	25	—	—	—	—
1721	Inkberrow, Worcs.	None	Farmer	Shop	10	—	—	—	—	100	—
1721	Great Malvern, Worcs.	None	Farmer	Shop	13	15	15	—	38	31	—

a No market, but had a fair and so counted as a market town.

Source: See Table 8.3.

occupational designation refers to what was included on the will or inventory as the occupation. Over 80% of the inventories from the smaller market towns had a designation, about half of them mercer, with the other half divided between chapman, draper, salesman, grocer, and haberdasher. Drapers were more common in the first half of the period, while salesmen do not appear until the early eighteenth century. In the sixteenth century, the tradesmen tended to farm as well, later this became rarer. Two-thirds definitely seemed to have shops, the rest had market stalls or peddled from a horse or on foot. The range of the value of the wares ranged from £3 to £1,145, but only one of the inventories prior to 1669 had a value above £100. There were usually small shops and pedlars based in these towns, but in the later seventeenth century the value of the stock carried by most shops moved upward. So not only does the number of shops seem to have increased in these smaller market towns, but the value of their stock grew as well.

What stock did these shops carry? I have separated the wares listed into six categories. Cloth, haberdashery (thread, ribbons, lace, buttons, etc., and clothing accessories such as gloves, scarves, hats, and stockings), garments (gowns, shifts, petticoats, suits, breeches, jackets, coats), groceries (imported plant foodstuffs such as sugar, tobacco, tea, coffee, chocolate, rice, spices, dried fruits, dyes, and medicines), provisions (regionally obtained foodstuffs such as grains, cheese, butter, meat, salt, beer, plus types of fuel such as candles and coal), and other (mostly tableware, other metalware, stationery, books, and gunpowder). Some of what I put under provisions contemporaries considered to be groceries, but it is useful to separate items which had to come from abroad from those which could be obtained closer to home. Nearly all of the thirty-six retailers stocked goods in more than one category. Only prior to 1660 was it common to stock a single type of merchandise, usually cloth. After 1660 only two pedlars and a shopkeeper with wares amounting to £3 had such limited inventories. Of the specialized traders who sometimes showed up in the occupational surveys of the smaller market towns—ironmonger, stationer, tobacconist, apothecary—only the latter is represented among these inventories, and no breakdown of his wares was possible.

Cloth and haberdashery dominated these inventories, but as the seventeenth-century progressed the shopkeepers invested more and more in groceries and provisions, and in the eighteenth century, ready-made garments other than mere accessories started to show up.

Out of the fourteen inventories in Table 8.4 from non-market

communities, nearly 50% give no occupational designation, a much
higher proportion than was true of traders in the market towns. Eliminating the four that indicated peddling on foot or by pack-horse, exactly
50% were not identified as retailers. This suggests that the figures
derived from occupational listings should perhaps be doubled in order to
compensate for undercounting. This would mean, if we use the figures
cited in Table 8.3, that at the end of the seventeenth century, at least 17%
of East Anglia's non-market parishes and 6% of Gloucestershire's had
shops.

There is also some reason to believe that these village retailers, unlike
those in market towns, were sometimes among the poor and were under-
represented in probate records. A study of village traders at the end of the
eighteenth century found that 20% of families in larger parishes
concerned themselves with retailing, mainly of groceries and provisions.[12] Most of these people were cottagers. They had some common
rights, but not enough property to make a living entirely off the land. Of
the village traders in Table 8.4, none had stock worth £100, and of those
with shops, most farmed. In the sixteenth century these were the kinds of
people who might have had an alehouse. By the eighteenth century, they
had increased the variety of their stock, and along with selling beer,
cheese, and candles they stocked imported goods—sugar as well as
tobacco—and also haberdashery items and a little cloth. Groceries and
provisions played an even more important role in the trade of village
retailers than in that of market-town traders. For those with shops, these
categories of goods were dominant, not cloth and haberdashery, which
were more the stock of the itinerants. Village shopkeepers with their
small inventories needed constant turnover, which groceries and
provision provided.

About 25% of the sixteenth- and seventeenth-century inventories in
Table 8.4 were of itinerants or people who had market stalls rather than
shops. They are still there in the eighteenth-century inventories, although
the proportion has dropped to 10%. As Margaret Spufford has shown,
pedlars continued to operate in conjunction with country shops,
dispensing cloth and haberdashery items to rural residents. The
inventories, however, suggest that they declined in relative importance
during the eighteenth century. If we want to know how many of them
there were, in absolute numbers or in per capita numbers we need to look
at data on licensing.

A pedlar's licensing fee was levied in 1697–8 (8 and 9 William III, *c.*
25). Any 'Hawker, Pedler, Petty Chapman or other trading Person or

Persons going from Towne to Towne or to other Mens houses & travelling either on foot or with Horse' had to buy a £4 licence if he or she intended to trade elsewhere than at markets and fairs. Those selling food, newspapers, or wares of their own making were exempted, so the act largely tapped the resources of people peddling manufactured goods, not regraters and regratresses. Even so, the tax seems rather stiff considering that according to our inventory analysis itinerants usually carried wares worth under £25, and some, under £10.

In England and Wales, 2,559 people—2,243 men and 316 women—paid the fee in 1697. Of these, 25% listed the London area (London, Middlesex, or Surrey) as their place of abode. Among women, the proportion was much higher, over 80%. An additional 67% resided in provincial market towns, and a mere 7% lived in non-market towns and villages.[13] The county of Worcestershire was typical. Forty pedlars were licensed there, 1.6% of the total, about the same percentage as the county represented of the total population of England and Wales. Thirty-nine came from the city of Worcester and one from Evesham, a small market town. The government collected the fee again in 1698–9, but the number who paid nationwide dropped by 40%.[14] Again, Worcestershire followed the pattern. There were twenty-four licensees, 40% less than the year before, and about a third of them were new names.

The cost of the licence and the number involved, at least in the 1697–8 registration, is evidence of a substantial travelling merchant class dealing in textile products, not too different in size relative to the population from what is recorded for the nineteenth century.[15] Table 8.5 compares the number of persons per pedlar in 1697 with later registration years in the decades of the 1780s, 1820s, 1830s, and 1840s. To make the figures comparable, I had to exclude Wales from the calculations. There were 2,016 people for every licensed English itinerant at the end of the seventeenth century, roughly one pedlar for every 425 households. The raw figure dropped dramatically in 1783 to 1,296 licensed pedlars. The number of people per pedlar soared to nearly 5,500. In the 1820s and 1830s, the number of registered pedlars rebounded, exceeding the growth in population and producing lower people per pedlar ratios (1,788 and 1,752 per pedlar) than in 1697–8. Then in the 1840s, pedlars once again failed to keep pace with the population and on a per capita basis began dropping below the late seventeenth-century figure, although not in the dramatic way they had in 1793.

It is quite possible that the sharp drop recorded in the 1780s was simply an artefact of the licensing system. The fees were very stiff, and

TABLE 8.5 The ratio of people to registered
pedlars in England

Year	No. of registered pedlars	People per pedlar
1697	2,469	2,016
1783	1,296	5,499
1820	6,319	1,788
1830	7,479	1,752
1840	7,057	2,097
1843	5,762	2,662

Sources: Great Britain, Public Record Office, AO 3/370; Hoh-
cheung and Lorna H. Mui, *Shops and Shopkeeping in Eighteenth
Century England*, Kingston, Canada, 1989, pp. 99–100; David
Alexander, *Retailing in England During the Industrial Revolution*, London, 1970, p. 63; E. A. Wrigley and R. S. Schofield,
The Population History of England, 1541–1871, London, 1981,
pp. 533–5.

differences in enforcement or compliance could have resulted in severe
under-reporting. The problem with assuming that under-reporting is the
sole explanation, however, is that data on revenues collected from the
licensing of pedlars from the 1720s to the 1750s suggests an eighteenth-
century decrease in numbers. If one leaves out the eighteenth century and
just looks at 1697–8 and the nineteenth century, then it appears that
there was a certain stability over the period at least until the 1840s. In
order to investigate this question of a major discontinuity in the
eighteenth century, it is necessary to compare more closely the county
totals in 1697–8 with those in 1783 and look for differences in the
factors that explain the presence or absence of large numbers of pedlars
in an area. Such an analysis will be done later in the chapter.

Shop Accounts, Suppliers, and Clientele

As we have seen, small market towns had the edge over non-market small
towns of similar size as sites for the early country shops. Undoubtedly the
advantages they offered in terms of pre-existing trade networks and
pools of customers explains much of this popularity. What remains to be
discussed is how the supply network actually worked in both market and
non-market towns and villages, and the role of London, the outports,

provincial centres, and the locality, respectively, in keeping these shops stocked. Of equal significance is the problem of who bought the goods and to what extent the country shop broke down the hierarchically structured demand and distribution system discussed in the preceding chapter. Both of these issues can best be explored through using shop-keeper account books. Merchant account books of any type are relatively rare in the early modern period, and those of provincial retailers, who occupied a lowly position on the mercantile ladder, are about as frequently encountered as the family papers of seventeenth-century agricultural labourers. One can only do one's best with the few that have survived.

Table 8.6 gives a profile of the suppliers to five provincial shopkeepers who carried a variety of wares and who have left behind usable accounts. The first, William Wray, lived in Ripon, Yorkshire, a market town with less than 2,500 inhabitants during the Elizabethan period. He stocked cloth and haberdashery items, including stockings and hats, plus groceries and provisions. Over a century and a half later, another small market-town shopkeeper in the North of England, Abraham Dent of Kirkby Stephen, Westmorland, featured a similar generalized inventory. Nevertheless, the amount of stock ordered by this Georgian tradesman, even allowing for a doubling or tripling in price due to inflation and an incomplete record of purchases by Wray, far exceeded what his Elizabethan counterpart bought annually. About the same time that Dent began his business, there was an anonymous Cambridgeshire merchant, probably based in Ely, whose accounts show an operation about the same size as the Westmorland shopkeeper's, although with more of an emphasis on provisions, groceries, and ironmongery than on cloth. Ely was a smaller market town, and in addition, like Ripon, the site of a cathedral.

Table 8.6 also includes two mid-eighteenth-century shopkeepers from provincial centres that were market towns with well over 2,500 inhabitants: John Webb, mercer of Stafford, and Thomas Dickenson, a Worcester grocer. The stock of both of these men was not as comprehensive, yet both sold more than one type of ware.

The difference between the supply patterns of North and South are marked. Neither Wray nor Dent bought much directly from London or even from the outports. Instead they relied on regional market towns. Wray's suppliers were nearly all from small market towns in his home county of Yorkshire. Two of the four men he ordered most from lived in Beverley, one lived in Ripon, and the location of the last is not known.

TABLE 8.6 Stock and suppliers of English provincial shops

	Shopkeepers				
	Wray, Ripon, Yorks. 1588–98	Webb, Stafford, Staffs. 1738–44	Dickenson, Worcester, Worcs. 1740–7	Anon., Ely(?) Cambs. 1750	Dent, Kirby Stephen, Cumbria, 1756–77
Stock					
Amount ordered annually (£)	48[a]	n.a.	646	820	821
Type of stock	Cloth, provisions, groceries, haberdashery	Cloth, haberdashery	Groceries, provisions, stationery	Groceries, provisions, cloth, haberdashery, stationery	Groceries, provisions, cloth, haberdashery, stationery

Suppliers					
No. of suppliers	21	30	37	30	185
% from London	0	40	32	70	6
% from outports	0	0	46	0	20
% from large market towns	14	50	16	23	44
% from small market towns	72	10	5	7	22
% from villages	14	0	0	0	7
% from home county or adjacent county	90	23	24	20	81
% giving credit >3 months	55	n.a.	78	88	n.a.

a Suppliers of most groceries and some haberdashery are not given, so, based on customer sales, the total was adjusted.

Sources: 'The Account Book of William Wray', ed. Revd J. T. Fowler, *Antiquary*, 32 (1896–7), 55–7, 76–81, 117–20, 178–80, 212–14, 242–4, 278–81, 346–7, and 369–75; William Salt Library, Stafford, HM 28/10–11, John Webb, Stafford mercer 1738–44, accounts; William Salt Library, Stafford, HM 27/5 and 29/1–4, Thomas Dickenson, Worcester grocer, 1740–7, accounts; Cambridge Record Office, Cambridge Shire Hall, R65/42, Ely [?], provision merchant accounts, 1749–56; T. S. Willan, *An Eighteenth-Century Shopkeeper: Abraham Dent of Kirkby Stephen*, Manchester, 1970, pp. 28–49.

Wray also appears to have obtained provisions to sell—soap, starch, linen yarn—from local producers, often women. Because not all the suppliers have a place after their name, it is possible that there were Londoners among them, but they could not have been a very considerable part of his supply network. Wray kept his orders below £10 and did not seem to rely a great deal on long-term credit. Of those purchases for which the date of payment was recorded, many were paid for when received, and payment for the others usually took place within three months. At one time or another 55% of the suppliers had extended over 90-days' credit to Wray, but those instances represented a small proportion of the total number of purchases made.

   Although the exact figures are not available, long-term credit played a larger role in the eighteenth-century business of Abraham Dent, who obtained some stock from merchants in Newcastle as well as from shopkeepers in larger market towns. Provincial merchants in larger market towns of the North, however, the people who supplied shopkeepers like Wray and Dent, moved goods by water and dealt more directly with London. The first thing William Stout of Lancaster did in 1688 when he set up a shop was to journey to London to order £200 of merchandise, which was sent to him by sea.[17] Sheffield, an interior market town and one of the growing centres of manufacturing, received orders worth £20 from him. The further south, the more likely it became that shopkeepers in market towns would place orders with London merchants. Dickenson, the Worcester grocer, used Bristol a lot, but still 32% of his suppliers came from the metropolis. The degree to which they used interior market towns depended upon how much cheaper cloth, haberdashery, and other manufactured goods figured in their inventories. Webb of Stafford, who basically traded in cloth and haberdashery, conducted half of his trade with industrial towns in the Midlands, while Dickenson and the anonymous Ely shopkeeper emphasized groceries and provisions and had relatively few suppliers from the interior. Nor did people in the surrounding localities provide them with much. Less than 25% of their suppliers came from their own or an adjacent county. In contrast, 90% of Wray's suppliers and 82% of Dent's did. Interestingly, shopkeepers in the more southern parts of the country even sent to London for items like soap. They obtained credit from the majority of those with whom they did business. Most accounts were settled within six months to a year, with a few running over into a second year. Seldom did they pay the entire amount upon receipt of goods. The likelihood of dealing with London directly, then, depended on several factors: the size of the market town in which one was located and the size of the stock, the distance from the metropolis, and the commodities sold—groceries being particularly likely to be ordered from London.

To whom a shopkeeper sold and how egalitarian he or she was about clientele depended not only on the size of the market town and of the shopkeeper's inventory, but also on the time at which he or she was operating. Sixteenth-century shopkeepers normally dealt with a much smaller and wealthier stratum of society than did their eighteenth-century counterparts. Those provincial merchants who had a restrictive trade in the eighteenth century usually operated out of large market towns and derived much of their profits from supplying other tradesmen. This can be seen by analysing the list of customers in their daybooks or accounts. These same records show something about the socio-economic level of their clientele, because they include honorific titles such as 'Sir', 'gent. esquire', or 'Mr'. Some in the sixteenth and seventeenth centuries used the term 'goodman' or 'goodwife', which usually connotes a house-holder of intermediate status, a small farmer or a tradesman. These records frequently leave out cash transactions, but they are informative about who received credit and for how much.

Table 8.7 shows the size of transactions and the socio-economic level of the customers for shopkeepers in two larger market towns, Cambridge in the late sixteenth century and Worcester in the mid-eighteenth century, and they can be compared with William Wray's in Elizabethan Ripon, and with those of John Poyser, a Staffordshire village grocer, in 1778. At neither date did the two larger market-town shopkeepers, one a draper and the other a grocer, display much interest in giving credit for small purchases. Sometimes, when historians refer to general store account books, they comment on the miniscule sums charged, without noting the contemporary value of what they find to be 'small'. Small is defined here as 1s. or less in the Elizabethan period, and 2s. or less in the eighteenth century, by which time prices had about doubled. Late sixteenth-century Justices of the Peace in the counties set 1s. a day as the most a skilled craftsman could earn. Labourers' wages fell below that. By the mid-eighteenth century, craftsmen's daily wages in the provinces were around 2s. Consequently, to working-class people 1s. or 2s. was not a trivial amount, and to have to produce such an amount or more in cash to purchase sugar, a small piece of cloth, or stockings might not always be easy. A sign that such people were frequenting a shop is a constant stream of these small purchases in accounts, with an occasional larger amount for several yards of cloth or a garment. Less than a quarter

TABLE 8.7 Customers of provincial shopkeepers, and the value of transactions

	Shopkeepers in large market towns		Shopkeepers in small market towns	
	Anon., Cambridge, June–Oct. 1580	Dickenson Worcester, 1–31 Jan. 1743	Wray, Ripon, 1588–98	Poyser, Yoxall, 1–31 Jan. 1778
Status of customers				
Honorific titles[a] (%)	50.0	75.0	34.9	31.7
Goodman and goodwife (%)	30.4	—	—	—
Retailers (%)	6.1	25.0	3.8	0.0
Other (%)	19.5	—	61.3	68.3
Small[b] purchases as % of transactions	23.1	24.5	9.5	69.1

[a] 'Esquire', 'Sir', 'Mr.', 'Mistress', and all servants and family members making their own purchases.
[b] Small is 1s. and under in the late 16th cent. and 2s. and under in the 18th cent.

Sources: Cambridge University Library, Manuscript Room, Additional MS. 3309 (9), Anon., Cambridge draper Daybook, 1580; William Salt Library, Stafford, HM 27/5 and 29/1–4, Thomas Dickenson, Worcester grocer, 1740–7, accounts; 'The Account Book of William Wray', ed. J. T. Fowler, *Antiquary*, 32 (1896–7), 55–7, 76–81, 117–20, 178–80, 212–14, 242–4, 278–81, 346–7, 369–75; and William Salt Library, Stafford, M603, John Poyser, grocer of Yoxall, Staffordshire, daybooks, 1775–1804.

of the transactions of both the Tudor draper in Cambridge and the Georgian grocer in Worcester were for small amounts, as defined here. The former catered for the residents of the colleges in the University town who had honorific titles, and also sold to Cambridge tradesmen, many of whom were designated 'goodmen'. (A few of these tradesmen, 6.1% of the customers, were drapers and tailors who were probably buying supplies for business purposes.) Altogether these types of customer constituted over 80% of the clientele. Even though the draper sold small haberdashery items such as thread and lace as well as yardage, most of his wares went to the more substantial citizens of Cambridge.[18]

A hundred and sixty years later, Thomas Dickenson had a similarly restricted trade. He dealt a lot with other retailers, providing Worcestershire bakers, apothecaries, and innkeepers with groceries. Nearly 25% of his clientele was of this type. By the eighteenth century the term 'goodman' had ceased to be used and the usage of 'Mr.' had expanded; all the customers who received a place in the account book had that title or an even more elevated one. This did not mean that all inhabitants had (as they do in the twentieth century) an honorific title attached to their name. It was just that Dickenson did not deal with those who were not so referred to—at least, not on a credit basis. Merchants on Dickenson's level were leading citizens of provincial centres, frequently serving as mayors and dominating the city councils.[19]

If we come down to the level of a mercer like William Wray, in a small Elizabethan market town such as Ripon, one might expect a broader clientele. And indeed he had fewer customers with honorific titles, but that appears to be because he did not use the designation 'goodman'. Consequently, a lot of the local town worthies, people who were designated by the Cambridge draper as 'goodman' and by the Worcester grocer in the eighteenth century as 'Mr.', are thrown into the 'other' category in Table 8.7. The percentage of Wray's transactions that were small purchases is more revealing—only 9.5%. Wray was in business during the late sixteenth century selling a small stock, probably worth under £50 annually, of mainly imported cloth and groceries. He had agricultural holdings, and also engaged in money-lending. As already discussed, Wray was near the end of the supply line, and seems to have only acted as a supplier himself to itinerants and one local tailor.[20] HIs biggest customers were the gentry in and around Ripon.

Wray's failure to deal with a broader class of people is probably a reflection of the age in which he lived. The idea that the ordinary person should not buy goods in shops like Wray's, where foreign commodities composed a large part of the stock, was still strong in the sixteenth century. In 1563 the English Parliament passed an act that basically tried to stop shopkeepers from selling foreign cloth, clothing, and accessories on credit to anyone but the élite. It directed sellers to get ready money or payment within 28 days from all persons buying these wares, unless their annual income exceeded £3,000. Probably less than 1% of the English population fell into this category, yet the law prohibited merchants from using the legal system to recover money promised in payment from anyone whose income was less. No provincial shopkeeper could have restricted credit sales to the £3,000-plus group and still have remained in business. It was also unrealistic, because shopkeepers commonly performed many of the functions later taken over by banks in the community. Not surprisingly, an attempt to renew the legislation later in

Elizabeth's reign failed. Still, the law indicates that the ruling class of this period did not believe anyone but themselves could be trusted with consumer sovereignty.[21]

Although Wray's business dealings were considerably more egalitarian than was Elizabethan legislation, they differed markedly from the kind of trading in which John Poyser of Yoxall, Staffordshire, engaged 180 years later. Poyser was an example of one of those shopkeepers listed in Table 8.4 as retailers in non-market communities. His books for the 1770s, written in a poor hand with many misspellings, indicate sales worth about £10 a month. In addition, he seems to have been engaged in some agricultural pursuits, and he also lent out money. Poyser sold everything—sugar, tobacco, candles, soap, mustard, bacon, cheese, peas, coals, cloth, yarn, buckles, nails, books, shot, gunpowder. He, like Wray, occasionally bought products such as hemp and flax from a local supplier, usually a woman. He did not stock more expensive goods, however, but ordered them for customers. Thus the entry 'send for a fine hat for Wm Bentley with crown' appears, along with the measurements, with a price of 12s. 6d.[22] The majority of Poyser's transactions fell into the small purchases category (69.1%), and less than 33% of his customers had any honorific title associated with their names.

Evaluating the role of English women in making purchasing decisions is hampered by the fact that a married woman, as a feme covert, could accumulate no debts of her own. Also, in daybooks, it is often difficult to tell whether women who are listed had ordered the goods, or were just collecting them. Married women were invariably referred to as, for instance, 'John Doe's wife' or 'Goodwife Doe'. Élite women received the appellation 'Mistress', and widows were 'Widow Doe'. Very seldom is the first name of a woman recorded. Females comprised between 5% and 20% of the entries, depending on the merchant: the village shopkeeper Poyser had the highest proportion.[23]

Because no ledgers, only daybooks, have survived for these shop-keepers, we do not know the medium of payment they accepted for their wares. Given the clientele of the shopkeepers in Cambridge and Worcester, it is likely they received mostly cash, notes, and bills. As we know that in the country shops of Wray and Poyser, the shopkeepers purchased some products from locals, we may assume that some of their customers satisfied their debts with goods or services. T. S. Willan notes that Abraham Dent, the storekeeper in Kirkby Stephen, credited two carriers for their work, and set this against their bill. Another man brought in seeds and vegetables, and yet another brought coal. The diary of an eighteenth-century shopkeeper, Thomas Turner of Sussex, also indicates that he occasionally accepted goods as payment. What none of these merchants seemed involved in, however, was in trading their shop stock for the major crops, products, and manufactures of the region. Dent was involved in the wholesale stocking trade of the area, merchandise whose ultimate buyer was the military; but this was largely a separate operation from his shopkeeping.[24] In other words, the collection and export of commodities out of a region and the importation and distribution of commodities within the region did not necessarily involve the same people.

There was less contrast between the shopkeepers in the geographical location of their customers than in the location of their suppliers. In the records of a shopkeeper in a non-market community such as Yoxall, the residence of customers is not even listed, as nearly everyone came from the community itself. What is more surprising, perhaps, is that the shopkeepers in market towns, regardless of size, seldom attracted customers from further than 10 miles away. Table 8.8 shows that only 2% or 3% of customers lived that far away, or further. However, where customers lived is not always specified; if one confines consideration to those customers whose location is identified, then the percentage rises to around 5% or 6%. Someone like Dickenson, the grocer from Worcester, survived with so limited a radius of customers because he supplied local

TABLE 8.8 Percentage of customers living further than 10 miles from provincial shops

Shopkeeper	All customers	Customers identified specifically by place
Anon., Cambridge,	2.2	5.1
June–Oct. 1580	(88)[a]	(39)
Wray, Ripon,	2.8	6.5
1588–98	(107)	(46)
Webb, Stafford	3.1	5.4
1738–44	(163)	(93)
Dickenson, Worcester,	0.0	0.0
Jan. 1743	(28)	(28)

[a] The figures in parentheses are the number of observations.

Sources: see Tables 8.6 and 8.7.

tradesmen and dealt with the gentry from the surrounding area. The size of his marketing area resembled that laid out in a study of late sixteenth-century Worcester. It had not grown during the entire early modern period. Other research on the customers of market-town shopkeepers in both the South of England (Winslow, Buckinghamshire, and Downham Market, Norfolk) and the North (Abraham Dent of Kirkby Stephen, Westmorland) indicates a similar pattern of confining one's trade to the area the town had always served as a marketplace.[25] The size of the stock of some of these merchants grew over time as more people bought their wares, and regions might differ as to the length of the shopping radius, but they depended upon the same area for their business as earlier retailers had done.

Explaining the Growth in Shops

Up to this point, we have looked primarily at retailing and shopkeeping in specific places, wherever detailed records exist. These sources suggest a long, slow growth in the number of retail shops. During the seventeenth century more and more of the small market towns added shops, particularly outlets selling groceries. Virtually every town of this sort had a shop by 1700. But in villages which were not designated as market-places, the addition of shops was primarily an eighteenth-century phenomenon, made possible by selling small amounts of a wide variety of goods.

There is not really any good nation-wide indicator of how deeply shops had penetrated into the countryside until the Shop Tax enumerations of 1785.[26] The government levied this tax on all retailers (apart from victuallers and bakers) whose shops had a rent of £5 or more: the greater the rent, the higher the tax. Some of the smaller shopkeepers, types like Poyser, for example, might be omitted, while artisan shopkeepers such as butchers, tallow chandlers, and tailors, who only sold what they made themselves, were included if their rent was above the limit.[27] The listings cannot be used to give absolute numbers of shopkeepers. Indeed, most of the counties do not list the number of shops, but only what, if any, tax money was collected in a parish. The enumeration, therefore, is best used to indicate the relative importance of shopkeeping in each county.

Figure 8.1 shows the percentage of non-borough parishes in each county that had at least one shop paying the tax. Predictably, the counties surrounding London—Surrey, Essex, Kent-had about every

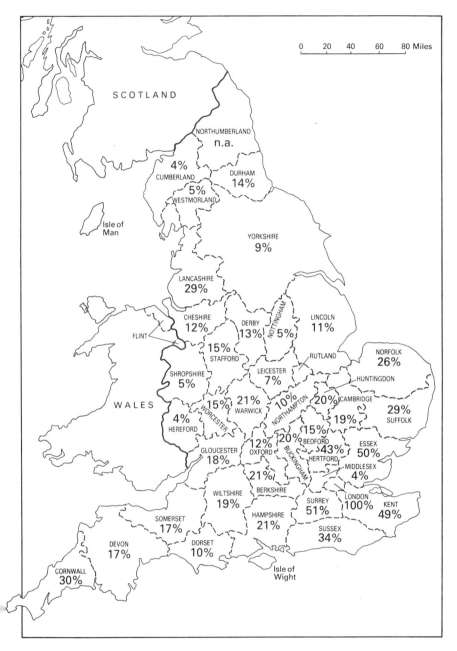

FIG. 8.1. Percentage of non-borough parishes in each county of England paying the 1785 Retail Shop Tax. Public Record Office, E/192, Retail Shop Tax 1785

other parish paying. Slightly further away, the proportion fell to between 34% and 20%. Certain counties in the North and the West had under 10%. There were exceptions, though. About 30% paid in Lancashire and Cornwall, so proximity to the metropolis cannot have been the only factor in operation.

In an attempt to identify those factors that led to (1) a growth in country shops, as measured by the percentage of non-borough parishes with at least one shop paying the tax, and (2) the growth in shop trade altogether, as measured by the amount of tax a county paid per 1,000 inhabitants, I collected county-level data of several sorts. I wanted to test, as best I could, all the standard explanations for a growth in shop trade mentioned at the beginning of this chapter. As an indicator of improved transportation, I took the number of road carrying services weekly between London and destinations in each county for 1765 (the nearest year to 1785 for which there are reasonably reliable figures). Another factor that allegedly had an effect on shopkeeping was urbanization. I used the change in the number of market towns listed in a county between 1693 and 1792 for that variable.[28] The impact of increased demand is measured by population density (number of persons per square mile) which taps both population growth and economic changes. If the fact that people are living closer together in towns or in more crowded village communities prompted consumers to patronize shops, then the density variables should be of significance in explaining both the percentage of non-borough parishes in a county that had at least one shop and the amount of tax a county paid per 1,000 people. I also included the geographical size of each county as a separate variable. We know that customers were reluctant to travel far to shop. In a large county with some parishes covering a big area, even a sparse population might attract a shop, whereas the same size population in a smaller district would patronize a shop in a neighbouring parish. Geographical size, measured here as the number of square miles in a county, should not affect the per capita value of the shop tax, however. It should only affect the percentage of parishes having shops. In an effort to gauge the effect of the metropolis, distinct from the issue of transportation, I put in the distance between London and the centre of each county. The assumption might be that proximity to London afforded more opportunities to learn of new commodities, and thereby increased demand in the local shops. Finally, I attempted to detect regional differences in consumption, particularly diet, by including dummy variables, North and West.

The results of the multivariate analysis appear in Table 8.9. There are four regressions in all. The first two include the transportation variable, the number of road carrying services from London, and so there are only thirty-three counties included in the analysis. The far north seldom used a land route to obtain goods from London, and so the counties above Lancashire and York are excluded, as is Cornwall in the far west. Obviously, the regional dummies, North and West, could not be used.

Population density, clearly, was the most important determinant of shop growth. Its coefficient was positive and statistically significant for both the proportion of parishes with shops and the amount a county paid in tax per 1,000 people. For every additional person per square mile the proportion of rural parishes with a shop went up by almost 0.1%. Counties (Middlesex excluded), or more accurately their shopkeepers, paid on average about £2 in shop tax per 1,000 inhabitants—a little less than a ½d. per person—to the central government in 1785. Each additional person per square mile raised the amount by about 3½d. per 1,000 inhabitants. Geographical size mattered in the spread of shops, but it did not have an effect on the shop tax paid. This variable is very highly correlated with distance from London and may be over-influenced by one or two outliers.

The urbanization variable behaved as one might expect. An increase or decrease in the number of market towns in a county did not seem related to a change in the percentage of non-borough parishes with shops, but it did increase the amount of shop tax paid, presumably because more shops, and certainly more merchandise, could be found in urban areas— the more urban areas, the more to tax. Unfortunately one cannot be too certain that this was what was happening because of the way the shop tax was levied. The tax was based on the amount of rent a shopkeeper had to pay. It may simply be that rents were higher for shops in market towns, so the greater the number of market towns, the greater the number of shops with higher rents. Whatever the case, the more interesting finding with this variable is the lack of effect that market-town growth had on the diffusion of shops into the countryside.

In both regressions, the effects of better transportation on shop growth are minimal. In spreading shops into the countryside, the impact is modestly positive (0.275), but not significant at the standard 0.05 level. In terms of the amount of shop tax paid, the coefficient is insignificant. There is collinearity between the transportation variable and the variable, distance from London. When the former is run in the shop tax regression without the latter, however, it is still insignificant.

That the distance from London was quite important in limiting the

TABLE 8.9 Determinants of shop growth in English counties, 1785[a] (OLS regression)

	Dependent variables			
	Amount of shop tax per 1,000 population	% of non-borough parishes taxed	Amount of shop tax per 1,000 population	% of non-borough parishes taxed
No. of observations	33	33	37	37
Independent variables				
No. of road carrying services weekly, 1765	−0.031 (0.320)[b]	0.275 (0.136)	—	—
Size of county (sq. mls)	0.000 (0.517)	0.004 (0.051)	0.000 (0.953)	0.002 (0.356)
Miles from London	−0.015 (0.085)	−0.152 (0.004)	−0.000 (0.988)	0.014 (0.718)
Population density of county, 1801	0.014 (0.003)	0.099 (0.000)	0.011 (0.003)	0.094 (0.001)

Change in no. of market towns, 1693 to 1792	0.235 (0.032)	−0.038 (0.951)	0.236 (0.019)	0.222 (0.743)
Region[c]				
North	—	—	−1.159 (0.159)	−19.187 (0.002)
West	—	—	−0.030 (0.965)	−13.689 (0.007)
Constant	1.143	9.213	0.301	10.166
Adjusted R^2	0.363	0.612	0.419	0.513

[a] London/Middlesex is excluded from analysis, and data on shops was unavailable for Northumberland. In addition the first two regressions do not have data for Cornwall, Cumberland, Westmorland, and Durham.

[b] Significance levels are in parentheses.

[c] North and West are dummy variables for Region and are coded (1, 0). North covers the far north, the Pennines, and the north-eastern Midlands. West covers the South-west and the west Midlands. The reference category includes the other regions: East Anglia, south-eastern Midlands, and the South-East.

Sources: Public Record Office, E 182, Retail Shop Tax 1785; Dorian Gerhold, 'The Growth of the London Carrying Trade, 1681–1838', Economic History Review, 2nd ser. 41 (1938), 392–410; J. A. Chartres, 'The Marketing of Agricultural Produce', in Joan Thirsk (ed.), The Agrarian History of England and Wales, v. 2, 1640–1750, Cambridge, 1985, pp. 410–11; Great Britain, 1841 Census, Enumeration Abstract, pt. 1, London, 1843; Wrigley and Schofield, Population History of England, p. 622; and Gazetteer of the British Isles, Edinburgh, 1966. See Appendix 3 for a breakdown by county of the amount of shop tax paid in 1785, the percentage of non-borough parishes paying the shop tax, and the number of pedlars registered in 1697 and 1783.

spread of shops, and even had a slightly negative effect on the amount of shop tax paid, is interesting given the fact that transportation itself was being controlled. It seems worth investigating this further, using the counties excluded from the first two regressions. This means dropping transportation, but that variable was insignificant anyway. Also, the new specification that one sees in regressions three and four tests the robustness of some of the results in regressions one and two.

In Table 8.9's last two regressions, population density continues to be of prime importance for both the spread of shops and the amount of tax collected per 1,000 inhabitants. In the latter regression the urbanization effect, as measured by the change in the number of market towns in a county during the eighteenth century, also remained significant. The effects of geographical size and distance from London, both significant in the first regression, lose their explanatory power once the dummy variables, North and West, are entered into the equation. The spread of shops into rural areas was still much less advanced in the West and even more so in the North according to these coefficients. It was not just remoteness from the metropolis or sparseness of population that accounted for this; there seems to have been something else going on.

Interestingly enough, region exerted less of an effect on the amount of shop tax paid. The West actually behaved no differently from the Southeast. All in all, though, shop-trading in the North and the West was concentrated in a smaller number of towns and villages. People travelled further to make shop purchases in these regions.[29] There was something about demand in these places that mandated a different type of distribution system.

Before we speculate more on that point, it might be well to examine growth or the lack of it among the other sources of retail goods, marketplaces and pedlars. We already know from the previous regressions that shops did not cause market towns to decay. There was a positive relationship between the value of the shop tax per 1,000 inhabitants and change in the number of market towns, and no relationship between the latter and the spread of shops. In Table 8.10, the first two regressions have as their dependent variables the number of market towns in 1693 and in 1792. These years were chosen because lists exist of the towns operating markets in those years and they closely coincide with the years for which we have estimates from the pedlar's register and the shop tax. The regression results show that in 1792 as in 1693 what mainly determined the number of market towns was the geographical size of the county. Nothing else was significant, and yet 70% or more of the variance was explained. Market towns were spaced so as to serve a local clientele.[30] Apparently in more densely populated areas, the number of retailers or the amount of inventory they stocked was what usually increased, not the number of market centres. With these variables, there is no way to judge the vitality of the trade in the marketplace on market-day. Shops could have been sapping the strength of the market tradition, but the status of the town as a trading centre clearly remained. Market towns were not hurt by the spread of shops into rural areas.

The results from the two regressions on the number of licensed pedlars in 1697 and 1783 are more complicated. In 1697, the only independent variable of importance was geographical size. These pedlars seemingly served a country clientele, the greater the area, the greater the number. The regression equation predicts that with every additional 34 square miles, another pedlar would join the ranks of the county corps, all other variables held constant. In 1783 the area had increased to 42 square miles. Geographical size was still the prime determinant, but density also seems of some importance. As discussed earlier in the chapter, the number of licensed pedlars and the number per capita fell sharply between 1697 and 1783. The numbers recovered in the early nineteenth century, but the question remains as to whether the nature of peddling changed in the eighteenth century as shops expanded into rural areas. The percentage of shops in non-borough parishes was negatively related to the number of pedlars in 1783, but the coefficient was not significant ($p = 0.343$) at an acceptable level. The Muis have established that there was some rivalry between pedlars and shopkeepers. The itinerants, however, were not locked in battle with village shopowners, but instead with the larger market-town merchants. These businessmen charged the pedlars with coming into town, renting a space for a few days, and selling goods at a price much lower than that which shopkeepers, with their higher overheads, could match. In exchange for agreeing to a shop tax in 1785, the shopkeepers had Parliament pass an act forbidding pedlars from selling goods in market towns other than in the marketplace itself on the appointed day or days of the week. In the legislative battles between the two types of retailers, another group weighed in on the side of the itinerants—manufacturers of textile products. There appears to have been a much more formal system of distribution through hawkers than had been the case in 1697. There were even firms that advertised themselves as suppliers of licensed hawkers. Supposedly the use of pedlars was greater in the North and in the

TABLE 8.10 Determinants of non-shop retailing activity in English counties[a] (OLS regression)

| | Dependent variables | | | |
	No. of market towns, 1693	No. of market towns, 1792	No. of pedlars, 1697	No. of pedlars, 1783
No. of observations	38	38	38	37
Independent variables				
Size of county (sq. mls)	0.008 (0.001)[b]	0.009 (0.001)	0.029 (0.001)	0.024 (0.014)
Miles from London	−0.020 (0.314)	−0.022 (0.254)	−0.187 (0.282)	0.059 (0.732)
Population density of county, 1700	0.031 (0.373)	—	0.353 (0.246)	—
Population density of county, 1801	—	0.015 (0.240)	—	0.281 (0.075)

No of pedlars in ≈697	—	—	—	− 0.024 (0.903)
% of non-borough parishes paying shop tax, 1785	—	—	—	−0.789 (0.343)
Region[c]				
North	−1.412 (0.648)	−2.756 (0.359)	−4.127 (0.879)	−26.718 (0.379)
West	3.260 (0.208)	2.333 (0.343)	−11.661 (0.604)	0.258 (0.991)
Constant	3.602	5.650	−4.945	−28.475
Adjusted R²	0.700	0.755	0.211	0.190

[a] Excluding Middlesex county.

[b] Significance levels are in parentheses.

[c] North and West are dummy variables for Region and are coded (1, 0). North covers the far north, the Pennines, and the north-eastern Midlands. West covers the South-west and the west Midlands. The reference category includes the other regions: East Anglia, south-eastern Midlands, and the South-East.

Sources: Public Record Office, E 182, Retail Shop Tax 1785; Public Record Office, AO 3/370, 'Register of Licenses Granted . . . from June 24th, 1697 to Hawkers and Pedlers'; Hoh-cheung Mui and Lorna H. Mui, Shops and Shopkeeping in Eighteenth Century England, Kingston, Canada, 1989, pp. 99–100; Chartres, 'The Marketing of Agricultural Produce', pp. 410–11; Great Britain, 1841 Census, Enumeration Abstract, pt. 1; Wrigley and Schofield, Population History of England, p. 622; and Gazetteer of the British Isles.

Midlands, except that one notices that in the regression, North has a negative (though insignificant) coefficient. So apparently, not everywhere in the North did pedlars thrive.[31]

It is particularly interesting that the number of pedlars in 1697 is such a poor predictor of the 1783 figures. The coefficient is negative, with $p = 0.903$. More than anything else, this suggests that there was a change underway in the organization of the hawking profession. The continued importance of geographical size indicates that some pedlars still made their living by furnishing the more remote areas with goods, but the influence of density on the number of pedlars in 1783 also indicates that some were interested in the discount trade around more heavily populated areas.

An Alternative to Hierarchically Structured Demand and Distribution

So how does one explain the decline of the old hierarchical system and the rise of the country shop and the discount trader? Population density was of course crucial. It certainly explains why certain places had shops and sold lots of merchandise and others did not, but it leaves something to be desired as far as a complete explanation goes. After all, the growth in shops situated in small market towns, a phenomenon of the later seventeenth century, did not occur during a period of population growth or great provincial urbanization. And the expansion of shops indicated by the very low ratio of population to these outlets recorded in the 1759 excise survey preceded any big population boom. There was no great increase in population in this period, so greater population density in one spot would result in greater sparseness in another. No net gain would occur; one county's increase would be another county's decrease. Obviously simple population growth does not explain the increase in shops.

Judging by the 1785 shop tax regressions, improved transportation was not the key to change, either. Urbanization, as measured by a growth in market towns, explains some of the increase in the shop tax payments, but does nothing to illuminate the spread of rural shops. For that, the one lead is the slower growth in shop outlets throughout the North and West, all the variables held constant. This cannot be explained as simple provincialism, for distance from London is controlled. Moreover, these regions were not significantly different from the other parts of England in the amount of shop tax paid. That is, the inhabitants of these regions apparently spent similar amounts in shops to inhabitants of other areas, if the tax is a good proxy for inventory and if other variables are held constant. They just did not have the same number of local village shops to patronize.

Some hint of what might have been going on can be gleaned from the information gathered in this chapter about what was sold in rural shops. In city and village, textiles and textile products were the single most valuable portion of the aggregate inventory. Elizabethan shops, as has been seen, catered to a very limited clientele, and the government tried to keep it that way by constantly rewriting the sumptuary laws. While the sixteenth-century artisan–seller was still of some importance, a transformation of the cloth industry occurred in the seventeenth century, the full ramifications of which are still not understood.[32] Clearly, though, the artisan–seller lost out to those with larger-scale operations, those supplying outworkers, and foreign manufacturers. These cheaper textiles found their way into the market-town shops of mercers, drapers, haberdashers, and others with a generalized trade and a credit line. Of course, itinerants handled a lot of the distribution of cloth and haberdashery, coexisting in most places with the small shops they supplied and with the large provincial centre establishments which supplied them.

By the eighteenth century, shops moved beyond cloth and haberdashery, and some even sold ready-made garments. Military orders for clothes during the French wars of the 1690s seem to have stimulated the pre-à-porter trade,[33] and then civilians continued to fuel the demand after the hostilities had ceased by purchasing this mass-produced clothing, new or secondhand, from 'salesmen'.

If village shops sold only cloth and cloth products, however, there would not have been as much need for permanent outlets in non-market towns and villages, because they were occasional purchases that could wait for a trip to the market town or a visit from a pedlar. The demand for groceries only obtainable from abroad and not traditionally sold in the public market stimulated the mercantile community to set up country shops. Once shopkeepers stocked tobacco, sugar, and caffeine drinks that were bought frequently but in small amounts, it made sense to stock other provisions purchased in the same way, such as salt, soap, starch, candles, butter, cheese, flour and bacon. The importance of groceries in the inventory of shops is clear. It has been estimated that *c.* 1760, every fourth shop had a licence to sell tea.[34] Textile products cost more, but the profit margin was usually greater and the turnover faster with groceries. It was the selling of goods that people had to buy constantly that made shop retailing attractive. By the mid-eighteenth century domestic economy handbooks assumed rural housewives would have country shops available to them.[35] It is not clear, though, that the dietary shifts and the trade networks that made these shops viable had taken hold as strongly in the North and West, where meals of tea, sugar, and white bread were less well entrenched.

At this point it is probably not possible to give a complete answer to the question posed at the beginning of this chapter—what produced the growth in shops during the eighteenth century. The effects of population density, land transportation, and distance from London appear to be more problematic than is sometimes assumed, while the growing fondness of English households for groceries, a factor previously neglected but one that has come up continually in this book, seems of undeniable importance.

Chapter 8

1. For the older view, see J. B. Jeffreys, *Retail Trading in Britain, 1850–1950*, Cambridge, 1954, pp. 1–9; David Alexander, *Retailing in England during the Industrial Revolution*, London, 1970, p. 231; and Janet Blackman, 'The Corner Shop: The Development of the Grocery and General Provisions Trade', in Derek Oddy and Derek S. Miller (eds.), *The Making of the Modern British Diet*, London, 1976, p. 150. For the challenge to this position, see T. S. Willan, *The Inland Trade*, Manchester, 1976; John Patten, *English Towns, 1500–1700*, Hamden, Conn., 1978, ch. 6; and Margaret Spufford, *The Great Reclothing of Rural England: Petty Chapmen and their Wares in the Seventeenth Century*, London, 1984. Also there is research showing an increasing number of corner shops in the bigger market towns during the 18th cent.: Roger Scola, 'Food Markets and Shops in Manchester, 1770–1870', *Journal of Historical Geography*, 1 (1975), 153–68 and Ian Mitchell, 'The Development of Urban retailing, 1700–1815', in Peter Clark (ed.), *The Transformation of English Provincial Towns*, London, 1984, pp. 259–83.
2. Hoh-cheung Mui and Lorna H. Mui, *Shops and Shopkeeping in Eighteenth Century England*, Kingston, Canada, 1989, pp. 45, 297.
3. Ibid., p. 12. See J. A. Chartres, 'Road Carrying in England in the Seventeenth Century: Myth and Reality', *Economic History Review*, 2nd ser. 30 (1977), 73–94 and J. A. Chartres and G. L. Turnbull, 'Road Transport', in D. H. Aldcroft and M. J. Freeman (eds.), *Transport in the Industrial Revolution*, Manchester, 1983, pp. 64–99 for the expansionist view on transport. For an assessment of more limited growth, see Dorian Gerhold, 'The Growth of the London Carrying Trade, 1681–1838', *Economic History Review*, 2nd ser. 41 (1988), 392–410. On urbanization, see Jan de Vries, *European Urbanization, 1500–1700*, Cambridge, Mass., 1984, ch. 4, and E. Anthony Wrigley, 'Urban Growth and Agricultural Change: England and the Continent in the Early Modern Period', *Journal of Interdisciplinary History*, 15 (1985), 688, 693.

4. 1 and 2 Philip and Mary, c. 7. Spufford, *Great Reclothing*, pp. 12–13 on town authorities trying to crack down on pedlars. Alan D. Dyer, *The City of Worcester in the Sixteenth Century*, Leicester, 1973 and Michael Reed, 'Economic Structure and Change in Seventeenth Century Ipswich', in Peter Clark (ed.), *County Towns in Pre-industrial England*, Leicester, 1981, pp. 88–141, are two examples of town studies that find Tudor–Stuart guilds to be in rather anaemic condition. J. R. Kellett and Steve Rappaport assess the situation in the metropolis in 'The Breakdown of Gild and Corporation Control over the Handicraft and Retail Trade in London', *Economic History Review* 2nd ser. 10 (1958), 381–94, and *Worlds Within Worlds: Structure of life in sixteenth-century London*, Cambridge, 1989, pp. 110–17. David Harris Sacks, *Trade, Society, and Politics in Bristol, 1500–1640*, New York, 1985, pp. 137, 508–25, indicates the problems guilds had in the second city of the realm. Christopher Hill, *The Century of Revolution*, New York, 1961, p. 205, has the figure on guild organization in late 17th-cent. towns. Anon., *The Trade of England Revived*, London, 1681, reprinted in *Seventeenth Century Economic Documents*, ed. Joan Thirsk and J. P. Cooper, London, 1972, p. 397, contains the complaint about unapprenticed shopkeepers. About the earliest comprehensive tradesmen's directory was that published in the 1790s by Peter Barfoot and John Wilkes under the title *The Universal British Directory*, T. S. Willan, *Inland Trade*, pp. 83–90 examines the evidence from trade tokens.

5. John Smith, *Men and Armour for Gloucestershire in 1608*, Trowbridge, 1980, reprint of 1902 edn.; A. J. Tawney and R. H. Tawney, 'An Occupational Census of the Seventeenth Century', *Economic History Review*, 5 (1934–5), 25–64; Patten, *English Towns*, ch. 6; id., 'Village and Town: An Occupational Study', *Agricultural History Review*, 20 (1977), 1–17; id., 'Changing Occupational Structures in the East Anglian Countryside, 1500–1700', in H. S. A. Fox and R. A. Butlin (eds.), *Change in the Countryside*, London, 1979, pp. 103–22; Willan, *Inland Trade*, pp. 83–90; E. A. Wrigley, 'The Changing Occupational Structure of Colyton over Two Centuries', *Local Population Studies*, 18 (1977), 4–21; D. Avery, 'Male Occupations in a Rural Middlesex Parish', *Local Population Studies*, 2 (1969), 29–35; Phillip Styles, 'A Census of a Warwickshire Village in 1698', *University of Birmingham Historical Journal*, 3 (1951–2), 33–51; id., *Studies in Seventeenth Century West Midlands History*, Kineton, War., 1978, pp. 205–12; Julian Cornwall, 'The People of Rutland in 1522', *Transactions of the Leicestershire Archaelogical Society* 37 (1961–2), 7–8; Peter Ripley, 'Village and Town: Occupations and Wealth in the Hinterland of Gloucester, 1660–1700', *Agricultural History Review*, 32 (1984), 170–8; and C. W. Chalkin, 'A Seventeenth-Century Market Town: Tonbridge', in Margaret Roake and John Whyman (eds.), *Essays in Kentish History*, London, 1973, pp. 89–100.

6. In the muster of 1608 in Gloucestershire, the Tawneys found tailors to be the most numerous, about 75% of medium-sized manors having them, and they were followed in popularity by textile-workers (mainly weavers), woodworkers, smiths, butchers, and shoemakers: Tawney and Tawney, 'Occupational Census', p. 41. Patten, *English Towns*, p. 254, found that East Anglian market towns in the 16th cent. almost always had a weaver, 75% had a tailor, next in frequency were carpenters, then shoemakers, smiths, and butchers. In the villages of East

Anglia (Patten, 'Village and Town', pp. 12–13), clothiers, tailors, smiths, butchers, carpenters, tilers, and shoemakers, in declining order, appeared most often in the 1522 muster roll. Clothiers were in 50% of the villages, tailors in 40%, and the rest in about 33%. I omitted chandlers from the list of distributive retailers becuse they were usually tallow chandlers. In some parts of the country, however, 'chandler' did become a name for a generalized shopkeeper, and some tallow chandlers combined their craft with selling other wares. Mui and Mui in *Shops and Shopkeeping* use chandler as a term for petty shopkeeper, pp. 59 and 201.

7. Population estimates for large and small market towns can be derived from the figures in Jan de Vries, *European Urbanization, 1500–1800*, Cambridge, Mass., 1984, pp. 270–1; Patten, *English Towns*, ch. 3; and Penelope Corfield, *The Impact of English Towns, 1700–1800*, Oxford, 1982, pp. 12–14.

8. In 16th- and 17th-cent. Lincolnshire, Worcester, and the Oxford area, mercers predominated over grocers in the probate records. See L. B. and M. W. Barley, 'Lincolnshire Shopkeepers in the Sixteenth and Seventeenth Centuries', *The Lincolnshire Historian*, 2. 9 (1962), 7–8; B. A. Holderness, 'Rural Tradesmen, 1660–1850, A Regional Study in Lindsey', *Lincolnshire History and Archaeology*, 7 (1972), 77–83; Dyer, *Worcester*, ch. 7; and D. G. Vaisey, 'Probate Inventories and Provincial Retailers in the Seventeenth Century', in Philip Riden (ed.), *Probate Records and the Local Community*, Gloucester, 1985, pp. 104–7. The reason why some of those who handled groceries chose to be mercers and others grocers may in part have to do with the guild structure in the county town. For example, in Worcester the mercers' company included grocers, haberdashers, and upholsterers: Revd. R. G. Griffiths, 'An Inventory of Goods and Chattels of Thomas Crowther, Mercer of Worcester', *Transactions of the Worcestershire Antiquarian Society*, 14 (1937–8), 46. In Coventry grocers also belonged to the mercers' company, Charles Phythian-Adams, 'Ceremony and the Citizen: The Communal Year at Coventry, 1450–1550', in Peter Clark (ed.), *The Early Modern Town*, London, 1976, p. 125.

9. The Gloucestershire muster roll of 1608 gives names and occupations by manor. I considered manors that reported having 100–20 men to be communities of *c.* 500 people. On the importance of market and fair days to shopkeepers see Mui and Mui, *Shops and Shopkeeping*, p. 9.

10. Willan, *Inland Trade*, p. 99; Spufford, *Great Reclothing*, p. 12; Patten, *English Towns*, p. 150, all refer to this statement, which is from Anon., *The Trade of England Revived*, London, 1681. Spufford, *Great Reclothing*, p. 10, also notes the appearance of provisional retailer literature, items such as *The City and Country Chapman*, London, 1685, and *The Merchant's Warehouse Laid Open*, London, 1696. Another such reprinted book of the period was N. H., *The Compleat Tradesman*, London, 1684.

11. Peter Clark, *The English Alehouse: A Social History, 1200–1830*, London, 1983, p. 43, estimates from the 1577 licensing survey that there was an alehouse for every 142 inhabitants. If we assume households comprised 4.75 people, then, that would mean an alehouse for every 29.9 households.

12. J. M. Martin, 'Village Traders and the Emergence of a Proletariat in South Warwickshire, 1750–1851', *Agricultural History Review*, 32 (1984), 179–88.

13. Great Britain, Public Record Office, AO 3/370; 90 out of the 2,559 came from

Wales. Spufford, *Great Reclothing*, pp. 14–20, also discusses this register, noting the small number who had pack animals. We differ in our estimates of the proportion of the traders based in market towns. She finds 'just over half'. I included the Surrey pedlars in the London area because they were overwhelmingly from the London suburbs and usually a parish or street was mentined as their residence, not a town. The fact that only 12.3% of the total were female is not surprising considering the legal status of women and the problems that might confront them in travelling freely. Occasionally one sees a male with the same name before or after a female in the register, but not usually. One study of stall-keepers and licensed higglers in Oxford market also found few women. Where women retailers were found was as regratesses, peddling from door to door. See W. Thwaites, 'Women in the Market Place: Oxfordshire *c.* 1690–1800', *Midland History*, 9 (1984), 23–42.

14. Great Britain, Public Record Office, AO 3/371.

15. Some itinerants carried expensive stock. *The Journal of Giles Moore*, ed. Ruth Bird, Sussex Record Society, 68 (1971), 19, records Moore paying one itinerant upholsterer from Lewes nearly £3 for bedding, and another itinerant from Chichester £8.

16. Mui and Mui, *Shops and Shopkeeping*, p. 99.

17. Willan, *Inland Trade*, pp. 93–4.

18. On wages, see the sources listed in Table 5.2 and Elizabeth Gilboy, *Wages in Eighteenth Century England*, Cambridge, Mass., 1934, pp. 250–87. I included 'the man' or 'son' etc. of a person with an honorific title in the honorific category because the identification of the person in that way implies credit was being extended by virtue of the relationship, and the charge was probably going on the account of the person with the title.

19. Gwen Talbut, 'Worcester as an Industrial and Commercial Centre, 1660–1750', *Transactions of the Worcestershire Archaeological Society*, 10 (1986), 98.

20. These were a 'peddler', John Wilson; a 'petty chapman' from Bedfordshire, Thomas Marshall (who must have been peddling in the neighbourhood when supplied by Wray, or have had some other connection with him); and a tailor, Marmaduke Wildeman. Alexander Cooper may also have been a tailor, although he is not designated as such. See 'The Account-Book of William Wray', ed. Revd. J. T. Fowler, *Antiquary*, 32 (1896–7), 55–7, 76–81, 117–20, 178–80, 212–14, 242–4, 278–81, 346–7, 369–75. Ripon in this period probably had under 1,000 inhabitants. Somewhat earlier in the century it had only 118 tax-paying households. See R. B. Smith, *Land and Politics in the England of Henry the Eighth: The West Riding of Yorkshire, 1530–1546*, Oxford, 1970, p. 108.

21. 5 Elizabeth, c. 6. See Frances Elizabeth Baldwin, *Sumptuary Legislation and Personal Regulation in England*, Baltimore, 1926, pp. 208–9.

22. There are several account books for Bedfordshire village shopkeepers in the University of London Library, Additional MSS. 625 and 626, in which the clientele and trade seem similar to that of Poyser: (1) an anonymous grocer and draper in Westoning, Bedfordshire, whose account books cover the years 1785–1800; and (2) John Goodman of Eversholt, Bedfordshire, with an account book for 1786. Both sold small amounts of cloth, garments, haberdashery, alcohol, flour, and other provisions.

23. The exact percentage of female customers for each shopkeeper are: Cambridge draper, 6.8%; Wray, 16.0%; Webb, 4.9%; Dickenson, 17.9%; Poyser, 20.0%.

24. T. S. Willan, *An Eighteenth-Century Shopkeeper: Abraham Dent of Kirkby Stephen*, Manchester, 1970, pp. 24–5. Willan on pp. 46–8 explains in detail how bills worked. David Vaisey, *The Diary of Thomas Turner, 1754–1765*, Oxford, 1984, p. 341.

25. Dyer, *Worcester*, pp. 68–9; Spufford, *Great Reclothing*, pp. 74–5, 78; Willan, *Dent*, p. 20.

26. The 1759 survey of shops analysed by Mui and Mui in *Shops and Shopkeeping*, is aggregated by tax district. It is impossible to tell whether the shops were in towns or villages. Also the tax districts were different from the county boundaries, and so the other county level variables cannot be related to the tax district shop numbers. Another source, business or trade directories with good coverage of all regions of the country do not begin until the 1790s and only list retailers in market towns.

27. Public Record Office, E 182, boxes arranged by county. Most counties have several boxes covering a few years and giving returns for a number of different taxes including those on land, servants, and windows. The 1785 shop tax returns for Northumberland were misplaced and could not be located. Consequently, that county could not be included in the regression analyses that used shop tax data. On the shop tax, see Ian Mitchell, 'Pitt's Shop Tax in the History of Retailing', *Local Historian*, 14 (1981), 348–50. Some city totals taken from Home Office records are used by Mui and Mui, *Shops and Shopkeeping*, but they seem unaware of the parish level data in the Exchequer files.

28. J. A. Chartres, 'The Marketing of Agricultural Produce', in Joan Thirsk (ed.), *The Agrarian History of England and Wales*, v. 2, *1640–1750*, Cambridge, 1985, p. 409.

29. Because of the disparate size of the counties, heterogeneity in the error terms might be expected. Consequently I tried a Generalized Least Squares specification in which all variables were multiplied by the square root of the population in 1801. The results, however, were so similar to the OLS version that I left the coefficient in Table 8.9 in their original form.

30. The market town regressions run with the variables transformed into natural log form gave almost the same results. About the only difference worth noting is that in the 1792 regression, the negative coefficient for distance from London attained a significance level of 0.09. When the number of market towns in 1693 and 1792 were put in per capita form and regressions run, geographical size was no longer significant and population density was. However, the effect of density was *negative*. That is, counties with higher population density had a lower ratio of market towns per capita, all other things being equal. Essentially, this says something similar to what was found in the regressions in Table 8.9: market towns did not spring up in response to population growth, although the size and the value of their trade was no doubt affected by such growth.

31. Mui and Mui, *Shops and Shopkeeping*, ch. 4, discuss the fights between shopkeepers and peddlers during the drafting of the shop tax legislation. They assume peddling was more important in the North.

32. Much has been written about the New Draperies, and Eric Kerridge has recently produced a book, *Textile Manufactures in Early Modern England*, Manchester,

1985, describing the new products. The effects on prices, wages, employment, and the occupational structure over the course of the 17th-cent., however, require further study. Specifically, we need to know if the reorganization of production resulted in the drop in cloth prices that appears to have occurred (see Chap. 4), and what was the impact of the change on the working population.

33. Acc. 985 in The Victoria Library, London, Westminster Archives Department, is an account book for Joseph Ashley, citizen and draper of London, for the period *c*.1692–1703. It includes the purchases of London customers, probably other shopkeepers, who were buying cloth. However, Ashley also sold ready-made clothing to the military in partnership with someone identified as 'citizen and salesman of London'. It is not too difficult to imagine how this production and distribution network might have shifted to the private sector in peacetime. On the secondhand trade, see Beverly Lemire, 'Consumerism in Preindustrial and Early Industrial England: The Trade in Secondhand Clothes', *Journal of British Studies*, 27 (1988), 1–24.

34. Mui and Mui, *Shops and Shopkeeping*, pp. 190–1.

35. William Ellis, *The Country Housewife's Family Companion*, London, 1750, pp. i–viii.

9

Colonial Retailing

THE market town system played an important role in the expansion of retail distribution in early modern England, surviving the reduced importance of marketplaces and the increased resort to fixed shops. There is little sign, however, that the colonists created anything comparable to that system in America. Proprietors might designate a community as a county town or grant a charter that permitted markets, but that was no guarantee that the town would flourish or that a market-place would be established.[1] Some colonists, imbued with republican sympathies, associated market charters with Crown monopolies. Their belief in the inevitability of special interests insinuating themselves into State-controlled operations clearly worked against regulated market-places.

The best-known markets were in the provincial capitals of Philadelphia and New York, but even there controversies tended to arise over their operations.[2] During most of the colonial period, hawkers going from door to door victualled much of Boston. Inhabitants wrote disparagingly of the marketplace system, claiming it cost too much to set up and simply allowed the richer citizenry to keep prices high. These critics managed to stop the building of a permanent marketplace until the late eighteenth century.[3] Once erected, the Boston market only provided an opportunity for trading, not a mandatory place that all sellers of provisions had to use. This appears to have been the form of marketplace that eventually developed in a number of communities. Consequently, the establishment of a market was more a recognition of the size to which a town had grown than the conferring of a special trading status on the locality that would assure it a regular clientele.[4]

Contemporary travellers' guides and almanacs, the kind of literature that in England listed market towns, remained silent on the subject in America, confirming that colonials did not recognize such a system.[5] If a seventeenth-century almanac writer thought it was important to note anything about a community, it was the date when the court met. In seventeenth-century Massachusetts and Connecticut, the court dates given in almanacs were associated with a town name, but elsewhere only the county name appeared.[6] We know from impressionistic evidence that court days were occasions when various political, social, and economic activities occurred. At some point, pedlars began to descend on a community during the days a court was in session, but the exact volume of trading that went on is unclear, nor is it known how influential these proceedings were in attracting more fixed marketing centres.[7]

Almanacs—mainly those for the Middle Colonies—also listed towns having fairs and Quaker or Baptist meetings, but those events occurred between two and four times a year and may not have been very important in establishing market centres, either. These listings, moreover, cropped up a lot less often for parts of colonial America outside the Middle Colonies.

Not until the 1720s did descriptions of roads with mileage between principal places in the colonies commonly appear.[8] For New England, all places noted were towns. Once New York was reached, however, river crossings, mills, and individual residences, presumably taverns or estates, frequently replaced the names of communities. Beginning with locations in Maryland, all entries were of this variety except the final destination, usually a capital city. In the Chesapeake, planters living near ferries sometimes requested a tavern licence, citing the frequent demands of travellers for food, drink, and shelter. From the 1750s, stopping-places in the Middle Colonies were towns, but in the South they continued to be crossings.[9] There were towns in the Chesapeake by this period.[10] Yet, apart from the colonial capitals, few towns appeared on the road listings of books published in New York, Philadelphia, Boston, or even Williamsburg. During much of the colonial period, it seems, retailers outside of New England did not necessarily situate themselves in towns or villages.

The Role of the Staple in Retail Distribution

Most market towns in England had been chartered in the medieval period to serve the surrounding communities. Even in the eighteenth century the geographic size of a county rather than population density determined the number of its market towns. Essentially, they seemed spaced to serve a clientele from 5 to at the most 10 miles away, more or less without regard to how many people lived in the community or how economically important it was to the national economy. That was why so many market towns were so small.

In America, it seems, retail distribution was more tightly integrated with the export trade, particularly in terms of personnel. The Chesapeake area is probably the place where this integration had proceeded the furthest. The effect of the tobacco staple on settlement patterns in Virginia and Maryland is well known. Inhabitants settled far from one another on plantations along the navigable portions of rivers so that their crops could be easily shipped overseas. Ship captains who came for the staple sold goods to the planters, as did factors and agents representing English firms who had, at least temporarily, settled in the country. The other primary source for wares, initially, seems to have been the local great planter who ordered goods for himself from London merchants and kept stores of goods to sell to smaller operators.[11] It is no accident that colonists began calling retail outlets 'stores', a usage unfamiliar to the British.[12] Until the end of the seventeenth century, few year-round shopkeepers operated in the Chesapeake.

Most historians see the 1730s, with the beginning of the tobacco inspection acts, as a watershed in the general organization of Chesapeake trade. To export tobacco, planters had to have their crops checked. Everyone converged on the inspection stations with their staple product in tow, and this convergence plus greater population density encouraged the formation of towns and also, allegedly, increased the size of the merchant and shopkeeper community. One study of Prince George's County has found that in the 1760s, there were approximately twenty-one general stores in the county, and all but one were located in towns or at crossroads that had tobacco inspection warehouses. London merchant firms, it is believed, began shifting away from direct trade with planters and dealt more with Virginia merchants who bought on credit bundles of groceries and manufactured goods. Consequently, fewer planters distributed goods from their stores, and more merchants opened permanent outlets.[13] The most striking development in this period, however, involved the establishment of chainstores by Scottish and English mercantile houses along the rivers and in the interior of Maryland and Virginia. Planters could obtain merchandise on credit, paying off the store with their crops when they were ready for shipment.[14]

The chainstore phenomenon was so important to the mid-eighteenth-century commercial development of the Chesapeake and was so unusual an institution that it is worth investigating its operation in more detail. One of the biggest firms involved in the business was John Glassford and Company of Glasgow, and one of their many tidewater stores was at Colchester in Fairfax County, Virginia. Accounts for a two-year period, 1758–60, reveal an inventory of about £1,900 available for sale at any one time, with a couple of shipments of stock coming in from Britain each year, plus groceries shipped in from other parts of the New World. The store had a branch in Quantico and seemed to supply one tavern and two other retailers, possibly pedlars. There were 387 customers listed in the ledger, 10% with honorific titles. Only 5.7% of the customers were women, and no more than two accounts belonged to slaves. The store dealt principally with the white male population, but within that group few distinctions seemed to be made. Over 80% of the amount sold was on credit, with customers usually paying within a year, most often with part or all of their tobacco crop.[15]

Table 9.1 lists what they bought. Unlike the transactions in English shops, one of the main commodities was cash. Slightly over 33% of the total debits involved customers receiving money rather than products. Sometimes Glassford and Company made the cash payments to third parties who were creditors of their customers. The store supplied much of the currency for the community, giving ready money for crops or occasionally as a loan.

Rivalling cash as a commodity was cloth, which also constituted 33% of purchases. When the percentages for cloth, haberdashery, and

TABLE 9.1 Goods and cash received by customers, Glassford Company store, Colchester, Virginia 1758–1760 (No. of customers = 40[a])

Category	% of total	% excluding cash
Cloth	33.1	50.3
Haberdashery	18.3	27.8
Garments[b]	2.8	4.2
Groceries	4.0	6.1
Provisions	0.5	1.0
Other goods	7.2	10.9
Cash[c]	34.2	—
TOTAL (£)	521	343

[a] A sample of every tenth name in the ledger index.
[b] Includes main articles of clothing and finished textile-house products such as blankets and rugs.
[c] Includes all instruments of exchange, and debts paid directly by Glassford and Company to the creditors of customers.

Source: Library of Congress, John Glassford and Company Papers, containers 184 and 216.

garments are combined, they equal over 50% of the total. Groceries and provisions—essentially sugar, rum, brandy, salt, and a little tea—made up less than 5% of trade. Planters came to these stores for British manufactured goods and for money. Most of what came under the 'Other' category in Table 9.1 was tableware and leather products, also manufactures. Colonists acquired some commodities, notably shoes and saddles, through retail stores that the English normally obtained from craftsmen. The array of manufactured goods was much more comprehensive than in an English country shop, but groceries and particularly provisions did not occupy as important a place in the stock. This may have been due in part to colonists supplying more of their own foodstuffs, but probably the main reason was that British chainstores left a lot of the grocery and provisions trade to local Chesapeake merchants and ordinaries. The emphasis in the inventory might differ, then, from store to store, yet almost every outlet, whether in a chain or independent, contained some mix of food and dry goods.[16]

In frontier areas that grew little tobacco, shopkeepers set up stores confined largely to small transactions and unrelated to any major export business. The work of Robert Mitchell on the Shenandoah Valley enables us to make some comparisons between stores there and two tidewater merchants (the Glassford operation and Charles Ridgely's store in Baltimore County), in regard to the kind of payments customers made. Table 9.2 gives this information, and also includes data from a New England store studied by Margaret Martin. The Glassford chainstore in Colchester, Virginia, received only 21% of its receipts in cash (about the same proportion that it paid out to customers wanting ready money for their tobacco). Tobacco constituted 73%, and another 5% came in the form of other goods, mainly provisions for use by the store and its employees. Labour services made up merely 1%, even though slaves rather than the account-holders were available to do the work. In Baltimore County, Ridgely also took the bulk of his payments in tobacco and accepted little in labour. In contrast, customers in the Shenandoah Valley and in Springfield, Massachusetts, relied much more on cash payments, and when that was not convenient, they resorted to labour services as compensation.

The frontier was also where the local 'great man' continued to play an important retailing role. A figure similar to the old tidewater planter with a store appeared in sparsely settled areas, the fellow who, in addition to selling consumer goods, owned the gristmill, the forge, a brewery, and so forth.[17] Like many enterprises, he could make productive use of the

TABLE 9.2 Customers' means of payment at eighteenth-century general stores

Store, place, and date	% of total receipts[a]		
	Cash and notes	Goods	Labour
Tidewater Virginia			
Glassford, Colchester, 1758–60	21.0	78.0	1.6
Tidewater Maryland			
Charles Ridgely Sr., Baltimore Co.[b]	39.0	50.0	7.0
Interior of Virginia			
Read & Johnston, Staunton, 1761–70	73.2	17.7	9.9
Anderson, Rockbridge, 1775–85	62.7	28.0	9.3
Reid, Rockbridge, 1776–97	40.0	28.6	31.4
Interior of Massachusetts			
Dwight, Springfield, 1755–67	59.1	31.4	9.5

[a] Rounding up of figures may result in totals which are not precisely 100.

[b] The 4% of Ridgely's receipts not accounted for in this table were classified by Steffen as miscellaneous.

Sources: Library of Congress, John Glassford and Company Papers, containers 184 and 216; Charles G. Steffen, 'The Rise of the Independent Merchant in the Chesapeake, Baltimore County, 1660–1769', *Journal of American History*, 76 (1989), Robert D. Mitchell, *Commercialism and Frontier: Perspectives on the Early Shenandoah Valley*, Charlottesville, 1977, p. 212; and Margaret E. Martin, *Merchants and Trade of the Connecticut River Valley, 1750–1820*, in Smith College Studies, 24, Northampton Mass., 1938–9.

labour and provisions payments that Table 9.2 indicates sometimes came his way in lieu of cash. In some instances, particularly with ironworks, it appears that stores were more or less required in order to retain a labour force.

What about trade in the North? Was retail distribution, according to shop accounts, tied in any way to collection of products for export, or did it more closely resemble the southern frontier pattern? Did a sizeable shopkeeper class develop as in England?

In the Middle Colonies, particularly in the largest, Pennsylvania, there certainly seems to have been a period in which general storekeepers took in wheat and sold farmers manufactured goods and groceries in return for their staple.[18] After 1750 in mature areas, the two functions may have become more separated,[19] but in the newer settlements the dual-purpose store continued. The proprietor could be someone like John Harris of Harrisburg: the 'great man' of the locality who also owned the mill or the transportation system. Furthermore, as in the Chesapeake, forge-owners operated general stores to furnish employees and the surrounding community with supplies.[20]

Thomas Doerflinger has studied the supply of rural Pennsylvanian shopkeepers by Philadelphia dry goods merchants. Most of these country stores relied primarily on these merchants for their British manufactured goods, but obtained most of their food products from traders identified as provision merchants and grocers. In analysing 52 separate shipments from those in the dry goods trade, he found that 70% of the value was in cloth, about 16% in what contemporaries called haberdashery (sewing materials, combs, and accessories such as hats, hose, and handkerchiefs), 4% in groceries, and 10% in other goods including stationery, hardware, eating utensils, and gunpowder. As with the Glassford accounts, the heavy dominance of cloth is somewhat misleading, because these merchants were not the main source of groceries and provisions. Still they found it necessary to keep a supply on hand. While people bought small amounts of groceries at a time, purchases were frequent. Doerflinger gives quotations from shopkeepers attesting to the importance of groceries and alcohol in building up a clientele.[21]

In the accounts of early Massachusetts shopkeepers, there is evidence of the local 'great man' phenomenon as well. John Pynchon of Springfield in Hampshire County is the most famous example. Many of his customers in the 1660s were also his tenants.[22] From other account books that remain, it seems that a more average class of shopkeepers did eventually emerge even in smaller communities, but the role these people played in the collection of goods, as opposed to their distribution, is uncertain.[23] The best study of New England shopkeeping was written fifty years ago by Margaret Martin, who examined the records of a group of late eighteenth-century merchandisers living in the Connecticut River Valley. Her work and the recent analysis by Winifred Rothenberg of the marketing of agricultural produce in Massachusetts suggests customers paid the storekeeper they patronized less often in goods and more frequently in cash, and when produce was the payment, the shopkeeper may have kept it for his own use or to sell to other customers rather than forwarding it. Also the fact that farmers travelled on average 25 miles or more to sell their crop or livestock means they were accustomed to dealing with more than just the local merchandiser and relied on different people for selling and for buying.[24]

At this point there does not seem any way to estimate the degree to which the collection and distribution networks in Massachusetts were integrated, but there is a data source that demonstrates just how ubiquitous retail outlets were in Pre-Revolutionary Massachusetts: a 1771 tax evaluation list that has recently been put into machine-readable form.[25] Even though it is a superficial accounting of internal trade, it does provide a fairly comprehensive look at the distribution of retailers and merchandise in one of the most important colonies.

Massachusetts Merchandising in 1771

The tax valuation list of 1771 contains approximately 38,000 names. Although lists for some towns are lost or incomplete, there is a good sampling of people from communities in all regions of what was then Massachusetts, including Maine: 62% of the colony's towns and 54% of rateable polls are covered.[26] The individuals with whom we are concerned are the approximately 1,700 who owned stock-in-trade. Fortunately, the valuations were made at a time when there was a lull in the reprisals being taken against Britain, and non-importation was not in effect.[27] Occupations were rarely noted, so merchandising and all other economic activities must be surmised from the type of wealth owned. Possessors of stock-in-trade could be wholesalers, retailers, or artisans selling the products of their own labour. The number of merchants who engaged solely in wholesale operations, however, was miniscule, and so it seems valid to refer to the group as retailers.[28] Some manufactured their own goods, although many producer-sellers—butchers, weavers, tailors, carpenters, for example—did little stockpiling of the wares they made. The merchandisers being assessed for stock-in-trade, therefore, were mainly storekeepers, owners of taverns and public houses, or in selected trades such as candlemaking, distilling, tanning, and jewellery-making where stocks tended to build up.[29]

Table 9.3 shows the distribution of Massachusetts retailers and merchandise in relation to the people paying taxes in the colony, who were mainly heads of households. In Suffolk County, where Boston was located, there were 7.6 taxpayers per retailer, yet in one interior county the number rose to 369.7. The average for all regions was 21.4 per retailer. The value of stock per taxpayer also varied greatly, from £30 to less than £1, with a mean for Massachusetts as a whole of £9. If each taxpayer represented five people, then the per capita figure for stock in

TABLE 9.3 Prevalence of retailers and merchandise, Massachusetts, 1771

Counties	No. of taxpayers[a] per retailer	Value of merchandise per taxpayer ($£$[b])
North coastal		
Suffolk	7.6	30.3
Essex	10.7	23.0
Midland		
Middlesex	29.1	4.2
Interior		
Worcester	60.6	1.6
Hampshire	46.7	1.5
Berkshire	369.7	0.3
South coastal		
Bristol	65.4	1.7
Plymouth	36.0	2.3
Barnstaple	74.1	0.8
Dukes	160.0	0.3
Maine		
Cumberland	59.6	0.4
Lincoln	72.8	1.4
York	58.9	1.4
All counties[c]	21.4	9.0

[a] Non-resident and deceased taxpayers have been removed.

[b] In $£$ sterling. To reconvert to Massachusetts currency, multiply by 1.33.

[c] The total number of taxpayers was 36,297, and of retailers, 1,698. The total value of merchandise was $£325,877$.

Sources: Massachusetts Tax Valuation List of 1771, Inter-University Consortium for Political and Social Research tape, Ann Arbor, Michigan. Data was prepared by Bettye Hobbs Pruitt.

1771 was $£1.80$ or 15% of per capita income, which has been estimated at $£12$ per annum.[30]

These figures become more meaningful when compared with the situation elsewhere at the time and with that of later periods in English and American history. Table 9.4 shows, in addition to the Massachusetts figure, the ratio of people to retailers in England in 1759; in Prince George's County, Maryland in 1760–5; Worcestershire, England in

Colonial Retailing 275

TABLE 9.4 The ratio of population to retail establishments

Date	Place	No. of retail establishments*	Population per retail establishment
1759	England	137,611	42
1760–5	Prince George's Co., Maryland	64	234.4
1771	Part of Massachusetts	1,698	106.9
1785	Worcestershire, England	1,070	112.1
1929	United States	1,342,072	90.7
1950	England	n.a.	92.0
1967	United States	1,415,434	139.5
1982	United States	1,541,500	150.4

Sources: Hoh-cheung Mui and Lorna H. Mui, *Shops and Shopkeeping in Eighteenth Century England*, Kingston, Canada, 1989, pp. 45 and 297; Allan Lee Kulikoff, 'Tobacco and Slaves: Population, Economy and Society in Eighteenth Century Prince George's County, Maryland', unpublished dissertation, Brandeis University, 1976, pp. 349–50; Massachusetts Tax Valuation List of 1771; Great Britain, Public Record Office, E182, Retail Shop Tax; Bureau of the Census, *Historical Statistics of the United States, Colonial Times to 1970*, Washington DC, 1975, p. 843; Bureau of the Census, *Statistical Abstract of the United States in 1986*, Washington, DC, 1985, pp. 5, 438, 776, 779.

1785; and in twentieth-century England and the United States. Eating and drinking places are excluded from the analysis.

Ironically, the lowest ratio, 42, is associated with the earliest date, England in 1759. The excise survey appears to have been very complete and that may explain why it is quite a bit lower than the figures for other places in the eighteenth century. But surprisingly, most of the other late eighteenth-century figures are no higher than the ratios for the first half of the twentieth century and, generally, they are lower than the ratios for contemporary times. The eighteenth-century Worcestershire ratio (112.1 people per retailer), and especially the Massachusetts ratio (106.9) compare quite favourably with those for modern America, where the ratio has increased over the course of the century, rising from 90.7 in 1929 to 150.4 in 1982. In other words, the population has been growing at a faster rate than retailers. This may reflect the emergence of more high-volume sellers. Still, it does mean that not only were there fewer outlets per capita in 1982 than in 1967 and in 1929, but also that there were *fewer* retail shops per capita than in eighteenth-century Massachusetts and England. Only in the eighteenth-century South were there larger numbers of people per retailer, and that of course was in a Maryland county that had a substantial slave population. Similarly, the percentage of per capita income represented by retail stock in 1982 was 6.2%, substantially less than the approximately 15% of per capita income that retail stock represented in Massachusetts *c.* 1771.[31] All of this demonstrates the importance and ubiquity of retail business in the early modern period. There were a lot of outlets and the stock they sold constituted a significant proportion of what people spent annually.

How did a primarily rural society such as Massachusetts manage to support so many retailers? Table 9.5 suggests that one answer is that most of them had very small stocks of merchandise. The proportion of merchandisers with small stocks, of course, varied according to the size of the settlement. Boston with a population of between 15,000 and 20,000 was clearly in a class by itself. The cut-off point for considering a place to be urban is 2,500 inhabitants, so all towns of that size or larger have been grouped together. The remainder, those smaller than 2,500, are the most numerous.[32] In the smaller towns nearly half of the retailers (47.4%) carried merchandise worth no more than £20, and even in the larger towns, those with populations over 2,500, 30% held that little. Although turnover might have been more rapid than we sometimes suppose and some of these tradesmen may have been producer-sellers, it is difficult to believe that most retailers with such modest amounts of merchandise could support themselves solely from their shop activities. It is also interesting to note the small percentage of retailers with stock worth over £500. The Colchester, Virginia chainstore with its inventory

TABLE 9.5 The value of the merchandise held by Massachusetts retailers

Value of merchandise	% of retailers		
	In Boston	In towns >2,500[a]	In towns <2,500
	(No. = 510)	(No. = 635)	(No. = 557)
£1–20	18.2	30.2	47.4
£21–100	32.0	32.1	32.3
£101–500	34.9	28.8	18.0
£500+	14.9	8.8	2.3

[a] The towns in the list with an estimated population of over 2,500 are Salem, Wrentham, Ipswich, Newburyport, Marblehead, Lynn, Gloucester, Plymouth, Bridgewater, Taunton, Rehobeth, Dartmouth, York, Kittery, Berwick, Sherburn, Lancaster, Springfield.

Source: Massachusetts Tax Valuation List of 1771.

of £1,900 would have been a highly unusual establishment in provincial Massachusetts.

An analysis of the probate inventories of several hundred eighteenth-century Connecticut traders supports the generalization that New England merchandisers stocked relatively modest amounts of goods. Jackson Turner Main, who studied these inventories, reports that the median value of their merchandise was £53, with the highest value well under £500. According to Main these traders hoped to turn over their stock three times a year.[33]

The other way so many merchandisers survived in a place like colonial Massachusetts was by engaging in a number of other activities apart from retailing. Table 9.6, using information from the tax list, gives the percentages of retailers doing other things in addition to selling wares. Only in Boston was it common for a shopkeeper to be simply a shopkeeper: there 44% were in that category, and if they had supplementary employment it was commercial in nature, wholesaling or shipping. Of the 22% who had an industrial occupation, some were producer-sellers,

TABLE 9.6 Percentage of Massachusetts retailers with other occupations, 1771

Nature of other occupation	Retailers in Boston (No. = 510)	Retailers in towns >2,500 (No. = 635)	Retailers in towns <2,500 (No. = 557)
None	44.1	25.4	22.1
Wholesale trade and shipping[a]	28.4	21.6	3.6
Industrial[b]	22.4	18.1	20.3
Farming[c]	0.2	6.6	17.2
Farming, wholesale trade, and shipping	0.0	5.8	3.6
Farming, industrial	0.0	8.0	25.5
Wholesale trade and shipping, and industrial	4.7	9.6	3.4
All	0.2	4.9	4.3

[a] Those in valuation list with warehouses, vessels, wharves, or commissions for factoring.
[b] Those in valuation list with mills, distilleries, tanneries, or ironworks.
[c] Those in valuation list with more than three cows or producing grain.
Source: Massachusetts Tax Valuation List of 1771.

while others both practised a trade and were also distributive retailers of goods unassociated with what they manufactured.

In the other major towns, there was also a lot of commercial activity; about 40% of shopkeepers combined selling merchandise with some form of wholesaling or shipping. However, a much smaller percentage (25.4%) just sold wares. Over 20% of the retailers engaged in farming and many had not just dual but multiple occupations. That was even more true in the smaller towns, where half were farmers, half followed industrial activities, and 30% did both. Very few, of course, were involved in wholesaling and shipping. All in all, it seems fair to say that the versatility of Yankee traders far exceeded that of their counterparts in English villages.

To probe further into the characteristics of retailers in Boston, in the larger towns, and in the smaller towns, I ran three separate regressions with the value of merchandise being the dependent variable in each. The results appear in Table 9.7. Some of the most significant variables, engaging in wholesale trade and/or shipping and the amount of income from realty (which is actually a proxy for wealth) are there more for control purposes than for purposes of enlightenment. Obviously those involved in commercial supply would have greater amounts of merchandise, as would wealthier people.

What is more informative is that in all towns, regardless of size, the value of merchandise owned by a person had nothing to do with the importance of pastoral holdings and was inversely related to the amount of land in tillage. In other words, the bigger the merchandiser the less he or she engaged in cultivation. As noted in Table 9.6 many retailers did some farming, but the regression results suggest this was more often the ones with smaller amounts of commodities to sell. Affluent traders in the larger towns clearly did not bother with agriculture.

The variable industrial activity (which is a dummy variable that merely indicates whether a person owned a mill, foundry, or other manufacturing site, not how much was owned) shows that producers of goods held smaller inventories than those in distributive trades. This may be what the negative coefficients in the regressions for Boston and for towns of 2,500 or above reveal. In the smaller towns, however, the coefficient is positive and statistically significant. Perhaps it reflects the phenomenon of the local 'great man': the general storekeeper who owned the mill or the ironworks. Significantly, the coefficient for the number of acres in tillage, as in the larger towns, registered a negative, supporting the notion that these types were businessmen first and farmers second.

TABLE 9.7 Determinants of the value of merchandise[a] held by Massachusetts retailers, 1771 (OLS regression)

	Retailers in Boston	Retailers in towns >2,500	Retailers in towns <2,500
No. of retailers	510	635	557
Independent variables[b]			
Wholesale trade and shipping	1.186	1.104	1.323
	(0.000)[c]	(0.000)	(0.000)
Industrial activities	−0.233	−0.077	0.257
	(0.123)	(0.540)	(0.037)
Acres in pasturage (ln)	0.034	0.043	0.029
	(0.883)	(0.197)	(0.486)
Acres in tillage (ln)	−0.370	−0.255	−0.256
	(0.618)	(0.000)	(0.000)
Money at interest (ln)	0.041	0.027	−0.003
	(0.240)	(0.219)	(0.871)
Income from realty (ln)	0.170	0.258	0.286
	(0.000)	(0.000)	(0.000)
Region			
Midland	——	−0.669	0.381
		(0.284)	(0.013)
South coastal	——	−0.555	0.248
		(0.001)	(0.303)
Interior	——	0.459	1.038
		(0.118)	(0.000)
Maine	——	−0.314	−0.490
		(0.281)	(0.101)
Constant	3.334	3.105	2.298
Adjusted R^2	0.193	0.252	0.219

[a] The variable is in ln or natural log form.

[b] The following variables are dummied: wholesale trade and shipping—coded 1 if retailer had warehouses, vessels, wharf-space, or received factorage commissions, and coded 0 if retailer did not; industrial activities—coded 1 if retailer had mills, distilleries, tanneries, or ironworks, and coded 0 if retailer did not; region—each area coded 1 if the retailer was a resident of that area, and 0 if the retailer was not. The reference category is north coastal, which includes the counties of Suffolk and Essex.

[c] Numbers in parentheses are significance levels.

Everywhere, the amount of money at interest was resolutely unrelated to the value of merchandise. Big merchandisers and big money-lenders were not necessarily synonymous. Retailers offered goods on credit rather than cash loans.

The effects of region are rather complicated. The reference category in each regression is the north coastal area of Massachusetts, towns in Suffolk and Essex. Considering the wide divergence in Table 9.3 between the different areas, particularly between the north coastal and the other four areas, one would expect region to be very important, with midland, interior, south coastal, and Maine all having negative coefficients. The zero order correlations (with each category regressed on the value of merchandise) in the analysis of retailers in towns with more than 2,500 inhabitants are all negative. Those selling wares in towns of that size in Suffolk and Essex handled more merchandise than their counterparts in large towns in other counties of Massachusetts. After controlling for all the other variables (being in wholesaling or shipping and having income from realty), however, only the difference between retailers in the big north and south coastal towns remained significant. Boston, of course, was not included in this analysis, yet there was enough disparity between retailers in the big Essex ports and places such as Plymouth to retain statistical significance.

In the smaller towns the effect of region was different. Apparently, retailers in the small towns in Middlesex and even in the interior counties possessed more merchandise than did traders in the small towns of Suffolk and Essex. After controlling for the other variables, the shopkeepers in Middlesex and the interior counties still had more merchandise, and the difference is statistically significant. The large inventories of the merchandisers in the major ports of Suffolk and Essex apparently limited the sales opportunities for retailers in the small towns nearby. Perhaps some of these retail outlets were merely branches that a port merchant set up in partnership with a person who ran the store.

If we move to the aggregate level and consider the total trading stock available in each community, excluding the provincial capital of Boston, the variables behave differently because the question has changed. The issue becomes, what made a place a merchandising centre?

Table 9.8 shows the results of the regression analysis. Population density, as measured by polls (basically, all adult males) per improved acre, was, as might be expected, of importance, but what is even more interesting is what did *not* have an impact. Neither industrial nor agricultural production seem to have been very influential in boosting the

TABLE 9.8 Determinants of the total value of merchandise[a] 1771, Massachusetts towns except Boston (OLS Regression; No. = 150)

Independent variables	Coefficient	Mean	Standard deviation
Money at interest per poll (ln)	0.500 (0.000)[b]	0.950	1.567
Inequality index[c]	0.172 (0.006)	2.514	1.956
Income from realty per poll (ln)	0.554 (0.009)	1.200	0.585
Polls per improved acre (ln)	0.626 (0.005)	−2.526	0.572
Ratio of pasturage to tillage	0.082 (0.005)	3.184	4.114
Industrial sites per poll (ln)	0.388 (0.066)	−1.626	0.527
Region[d]			
Midland	0.389 (0.302)	0.220	0.416
South coastal	−0.245 (0.529)	0.160	0.368
Interior	0.684 (0.078)	0.387	0.489
Maine	0.743 (0.129)	0.087	0.282
Constant	−0.446		
Adjusted R^2	0.432		

[a] Per poll and put in ln (natural log) form. The mean is −0.447 and the standard deviation is 1.663.
[b] Numbers in parentheses are significance levels.
[c] The skewness of yearly income from real property within each town.
[d] Each category of region was coded 1 if the town was in the area and 0 if it was not. The reference category is north coastal, which includes the counties of Suffolk and Essex.

Source: Massachusetts Tax Valuation List of 1771.

amount of merchandise per poll in a community. The number of mills, distilleries, and other manufacturing establishments correlated less strongly with the value of merchandise than might be expected and missed the conventional cut-off point of 0.05 for statistical significance. While one would not anticipate that a farming community would have been a big merchandising centre and would possibly predict a strong negative relationship between both acres in tillage and pasturage and the value of merchandise, the actual results are more puzzling. In preliminary analysis, tillage was negatively related—pasturage had a positive sign— and neither was statistically significant at an acceptable level. As we know from the examination of individual retailers, agricultural pursuits did go on in most Massachusetts towns apart from Boston. What seems to have been the case is that the level of agricultural activity did not matter one way or another. The only form of these two variables that did achieve significance was the one appearing in Table 9.8, the ratio of pasturage to tillage. Perhaps this indicates that merchandising was conducted on a greater scale in the pastoral areas of the colony because livestock was more of a marketable commodity, although that seems to be stretching the suppositions one can make from the data further than advisable.

Equally interesting is the fact that region had such a small impact upon the value of merchandise in a community. Table 9.3 revealed a great discrepancy between the value of merchandise per taxpayer, and presumably per capita, in the north coastal counties of Suffolk and Essex and the other areas. While the regression analysis in Table 9.8 does not include Boston, it does have other large towns with much trading stock, such as Salem. None of the areas, however, is statistically different from the Suffolk and Essex towns which are the reference category. Moreover, the signs of the coefficients in three out of the four areas are positive. In other words, the vast differences between the areas in the value of merchandise per person can more or less be accounted for by differences in population density and in the economic variables. After these are put in the equation and thereby held constant, the midland, interior, and Maine communities had *more* merchandise per poll than the north coastal area, although the spread was not statistically significant at the 0.05 level. Proximity to Boston in itself was plainly of little consequence. There was no simple metropolitan effect.

What economic variables were of importance? Money at interest, inequality, income from realty, and ratio of pasturage to tillage were all statistically significant at 0.05 level, and the number of industrial sites per poll was very near that conventional cut-off point. Basically, most of these variables identify wealth in the community. That generalization is even true of the pasturage/tillage ratio because of the poor soil in New England and the tendency for more affluent farmers to raise livestock rather than cultivate arable land. It also clears up a rather confusing finding about money-lending in Table 9.7. While the big retailers were not necessarily the big money-lenders, it does appear money-lending and retailing tended to occur in the same places.

Colonial Retailing in Perspective

There was no system of market towns in America, and initially colonists seemed even more dependent on a type of hierarchically structured demand and distribution than were the English. The 'great man' or planter in the community might operate a store and integrate production and consumption. This integrated system is most associated with the plantation South, but it could also be found in parts of the wheat-producing Middle Colonies, where ironworks or other major industrial enterprises were established, or in very recently settled areas.

Later a merchandiser of more modest means and with a permanent shop became more important in trade. In the case of the Chesapeake, some of these people were actually the employees of big British chain-stores set up to buy tobacco and sell dry goods. These stores had large inventories, engaged in a small number of big transactions with their customers, and offered a choice of goods or cash for the staple. They did not usually engage in planting, but in terms of functions performed and in terms of variety of stock they could not exactly be called specialized. Throughout the eighteenth century, the staple continued to exercise an influence on shopping that exceeded the influence of large towns. Lois Green Carr and Lorena Walsh found that Chesapeake town dwellers owned more consumer goods than those in the countryside, but the towns had no coat-tails. Living near a town did not raise the amount of consumer goods possessed, implying that rivers, not a town network, still dominated the mercantile system.[34]

The kind of retailing revealed by the Massachusetts tax evaluation of 1771 was of a different variety, more comparable to the English situation, but specialization was not one of its prime characteristics, either. By the time of the Revolution, the number of Massachusetts retailers compared well, in per capita terms, with the Mother Country and with twentieth-century America. The multitude of merchandisers supported themselves through a diversification in stock and in occupation that even exceeded that of their English counterparts. One of the interesting findings from the regression on the value of an individual retailer's stock-in-trade is that the amount of money being lent out was not highly correlated with how much merchandising a person did. Scholars looking at account books often draw attention to the money-lending activities of shopkeepers. Most of them did lend out money, but in the pre-bank era and with securities at a nascent level of development it turns out that most people with capital lent out money. Or at least, that is what the regression results suggest.

As in England, population density was very important in determining the value of the merchandise in a particular Massachusetts town. Also, indicators of wealth in the community such as a lot of money out on loan or being collected in rents increased the amount of stock-in-trade. Controlling for those variables, however, left no regional effect. Being a town close to the coast did not in itself matter.

When the historical development of trade is discussed, the process of specialization is always assumed to be a key element.[35] It is associated with growth. The big merchants of early American ports, in contrast to their counterparts in later periods, seem to have been unspecialized, seldom confining themselves to wholesaling or selling a single kind of commodity,[36] and for that reason, in historical surveys, the early American period is seen as one in which little commercial growth took place—unspecialized, ergo undeveloped. The main way this picture of stagnation has been challenged has been to focus on specialization in port towns. For example, a recent student of Philadelphia merchants in the last half of the eighteenth century has pointed out how their trading stock increased during the Revolutionary era and how some differentiation between merchants had occurred. Specifically, all but the largest merchant houses tended to specialize in either the importation of manufactured goods (dry goods) or the provisions/groceries trade.[37] Of course these types of goods had, traditionally, been handled by separate trading groups, and it is only because on the retail level they were so often combined in the merchandise offered by American shopkeepers that this division has been obscured.

Rather than trying to argue that colonial American merchandisers were relatively specialized, I would question the assumption that there has been a linear trend towards specialization and that it should automatically be equated with growth in trade. Very seldom have traders in a community not diversified their activities at all, but limited their business to the retailing or wholesaling of a particular commodity, or even just to commerce. Today, for example, many retail chains are part of conglomerates. Not even in the classic case of the nineteenth century, when an expansion in the wholesaling function led to a complex network of differentiated traders, is the story simply one of specialization, because on the retailing level this was also the period when department stores and sales by catalogue emerged. What has varied historically is the kind of diversification merchandisers pursued. In medieval trade, wholesaling and retailing tended to be fairly distinct occupations and shops were devoted to specific commodities. The production and selling of goods, however, was not well differentiated. In the early modern period growth was achieved by the proliferation of retail outlets in the countryside, the small towns and villages, and by merchandisers carrying a more generalized stock than had been the practice formerly. In both England and the colonies, the increasing demand for groceries and provisions and the proliferation of semi-durable, more easily damaged goods posed problems for itinerants and encouraged the establishment of shops. Producer-sellers declined, but they were often replaced by shopkeepers with dual occupations selling a variety of goods. This phenomenon, observed in England, characterized American retail trade from the beginning. Growth did occur, but it was not a product of occupational or commodity specialization.

Chapter 9

1. See *The statutes . . . of Virginia*, comp. William W. Hening, i, Richmond, 1809, pp. 362 and 392 on legislation for James City markets, and also Darrett B. Rutman and Anita H. Rutman, *A Place in Time: Middlesex County, Virginia, 1650–1750*, New York, 1984, pp. 210–11. James Lemon, *The Best Poor Man's Country: A Geographical Study of Early Southeastern Pennsylvania*, Baltimore, 1972, pp. 130–1, has information on Pennsylvania county towns and markets. For Massachusetts, see Winifred B. Rothenberg, 'The Market and Massachusetts Farmers, 1750–1855', *Journal of Economic History*, 41 (1981), 312–13.

2. See for New York, New York [City] Laws, *A Law for the Better Regulating of the Publick Markets*, New York, 1774, a law banning butchers from the eastward market because householders in the vicinity complained about them slaughtering animals there. Two broadsides from Philadelphia supported and opposed the construction of market shambles in High Street: *To the Freeman . . . of Philadelphia*, 1773 and *You are Earnestly Requested to Meet . . .*, 1773. Those in opposition complained about the cost and resented the obstruction to traffic.

3. Karen Friedman, 'Victualling Colonial Boston', *Agricultural History*, 47 (1973), 189–205, and Gary B. Nash, *The Urban Crucible: Social Change, Political Consciousness, and the Origins of the American Revolution*, Cambridge, Mass., 1979, pp. 130–6. The contemporary debate appears in [Benjamin Colman], *Some Reasons and Arguments Offered to the Good People of Boston . . . for the Setting up of Markets in Boston*, 1719, and Anon., *Some Considerations against the Setting up of a Market in this Town . . .*, 1733. Rules for a 1734 market that failed are in *Meeting of Freeholders . . . for Setting up and Regulating a Public Market*, 1734.

4. Lemon, *Best Poor Man's Country*, p. 138.

5. There are few extant colonial trader's and chapman's handbooks that go beyond tables for the calculation of interest, values, and quantities. One that does have more is [Thomas Prince], *Vade Mecum*, Boston, 1732. The almanacs that most towns with printers published, however, often provided some local information for travellers.

6. The earliest almanac that I have found that lists court days is [Samuel Danforth], *An Almanack for 1646*, Cambridge, Mass., n.d.; fairs in Dorchester, Salem, and Watertown are also recorded, although such listings became less common later in New England almanacs.

7. Richard R. Beeman, 'Trade and Travel in Post-Revolutionary Virginia: A Diary of an Itinerant Peddler, 1807–1808', *Virginia Magazine of History and Biography*, 84 (1976), 174–88, discusses the journal of an early national period pedlar who visited an area on the day of monthly meetings of the county court. In the 18th cent., most counties required that pedlars going from town to town pay a licensing fee.

8. John Jerman, *An Ephemeris for the Year 1721*, Philadelphia, 1720; Felix Leeds, *American Almanack*, Philadelphia, 1727; [Prince], *Vade Mecum*. On planters taking out licences see Alan Kulikoff, *Tobacco and Slaves: The Development of Southern Cultures in the Chesapeake, 1680–1800*, Williamsburg, 1986, p. 222.

9. Anon., *The Virginia Almanac for 1749*, Williamsburg, n.d.; Roger Sherman, *An Almanack for . . . 1750*, New York, n.d. Information on posts comes later. See e.g. Anon., *The Philadelphia Newest Almanac for . . . 1776*, Philadelphia, n.d., and Anon., *The New York and Country Almanack for 1776*, New York, n.d.

10. Kulikoff, *Tobacco and Slaves*, pp. 225–8, finds that in Prince George's County by the 1730s there were four small towns, but at that point merchants did not necessarily live in them. Piedmont residents, even in the 1770s, went to crossroads not towns to find a tavern and a store. See also Carville Earle and Ronald Hoffman, 'Staple Crops and Urban Development in the Eighteenth-Century South', *Perspectives in American History*, 10 (1976), 60–1.

11. Lois Green Carr, 'The Metropolis of Maryland', *Maryland Historical Magazine*, 69 (1974), 124–45; Edmund Morgan, *American Slavery, American Freedom: The Ordeal of Colonial Virginia*, New York, 1975, p. 177; Lorena Seebach Walsh, 'Charles County, Maryland, 1658–1705', unpublished Ph.D. dissertation, Michigan State University, 1977, pp. 54, 222–3; 290; Paul G. E. Clemens, *The Atlantic Economy and Colonial Maryland's Eastern Shore: From Tobacco to Grain*, Ithaca, 1980, pp. 92–7; Gloria L. Main, *Tobacco Colony: Life in Early Maryland, 1650–1720*, Princeton, 1982, pp. 231–6; Rutman and Rutman, *A Place in Time*, pp. 205–7.

12. See the *Oxford English Dictionary* under 'store'.

13. Calvin Brewster Coulter, jun., 'The Virginia Merchant', unpublished Ph.D. dissertation, Princeton University, 1944; Robert Polk Thomson, 'The Merchant in Virginia, 1700–1775', unpublished Ph.D. dissertation, University of Wisconsin–Madison, 1955; Alan Kulikoff, 'Tobacco and Slaves: Population, Economy, and Society in Eighteenth Century Prince George's County, Maryland', unpublished Ph.D. dissertation, Brandeis University, 1976, pp. 349–50; and Charles G. Steffen, 'The Rise of the Independent Merchant—the Chesapeake, Baltimore County, 1660–1769', *Journal of American History*, 76 (1989), 9–33.

14. J. H. Soltow, 'Scottish Traders in Virginia, 1750–1775', *Economic History Review*, 12 (1959), 83–98; James H. Soltow, *The Economic Role of Williamsburg*, Charlottesville, 1965; Aubrey C. Land, 'Economic Behavior in a Planting Society: The Eighteenth-Century Chesapeake', *The Journal of Southern History*, 33 (1967), 469–85; Peter Victor Bergstrom, 'Markets and Merchants: Economic Diversification in Colonial Virginia, 1700–1775', unpublished Ph.D. dissertation, University of New Hampshire, 1980; Jacob M. Price, *Capital and Credit in British Overseas Trade: The View from the Chesapeake, 1700–1776*, Cambridge, Mass., 1980; id., 'The Last Phase of the Virginia–London Consignment Trade: James Buchanan and Company, 1758–1768', *William and Mary Quarterly*, 3rd ser. 43 (1986), 64–98. There is much less published on the structure of internal trade in South Carolina, but see *The Letterbook of Robert Pringle, 1737–1742*, ed. Walter B. Edgar, Columbia, South Carolina, 1972.

15. Library of Congress, John Glassford and Company Papers, containers 184 and 216. There were a total of 409 accounts in the index, but that included a number of internal accounts and some for Scottish merchants. Kulikoff, *Tobacco and Slaves*, found (pp. 225–6) in the records of a Glassford store in Piscataway, Maryland, that under 10% of customers were women. Regina Lee Blaszcyzk, 'Ceramics and the Sot-weed Factor: The China Market in a Tobacco Economy', *Winterthur Portfolio*, 19 (1984), 11, discusses the accounts of another Chesapeake shopkeeper who was also an agent of a Glasgow merchant house. In 1772 the stock in the store was worth £2,300, supporting the generalization that these outlets carried unusually large amounts of merchandise.

16. See Steffen, 'Rise of the Independent Merchant', p. 31; Library of Congress, Edward Dixon, Caroline County, Virginia, store ledger, 1743–7; John Lee Webster, Bushtown, Maryland, store journals, 1765–8; Crenshaw and Company, Amelia County, Virginia, ledger 1770; and James Ritchie and Henry Ritchie, Brooksbank, Essex County, Virginia, store inventory, 1776.

17. Robert D. Mitchell, *Commercialism and Frontier: Perspectives on the Early Shenandoah Valley*, Charlottesville, 1977, p. 212.

18. Historical Society of Pennsylvania, Philadelphia, Richard Hayes, Chester County, Pennsylvania, store ledger, 1708–40. Most of the research on Pennsylvania commercial transactions has focused upon the overseas aspect. See, however, Wilbur C. Plummer, 'Consumer Credit in Colonial Philadelphia', *The Pennsylvania Magazine of History and Biography*, 66 (1942), 385–407, and ch. 6 in Grace Hutchinson Larsen, 'Profile of a Colonial Merchant: Thomas Clifford of Pre-Revolutionary Philadelphia', unpublished Ph.D. dissertation, Columbia University, 1955. I owe the latter reference to Thomas Doerflinger.

19. American Philosophical Society, Philadelphia, John Williams, Middletown, Lancaster County, Pennsylvania, store daybook and ledger, 1773–4, and Historical Society of Pennsylvania, Thomas Scully, Christiana Bridge, Delaware, store daybook, 1773.

20. The Historical Society of Pennsylvania has numerous general store journals and ledgers from the mid-18th cent. to the Revolution for John Harris, Harrisburg, Pennsylvania, and for the Potts family who had stores and ironworks in Berks. County, Pennsylvania. On the former see John Walzer, 'Transportation in the Philadelphia Trading Area', unpublished Ph.D. dissertation, University of Wisconsin, Madison, 1968, pp. 41–2 and 307–8, and on the latter see Linda

McCurdy, 'The Potts Family Iron Industry in the Schuykill Valley', unpublished Ph.D. dissertation, Pennsylvania State University, 1974. Another ledger at the Historical Society of Pennsylvania, that of William Bird, involves a general store connected with a forge in Amity Township, Berks. County, 1741–7.

21. Thomas M. Doerflinger, 'Farmers and Dry Goods in the Philadelphia Market Area, 1750–1800', in Ronald Hoffman *et al.*, *The Economy of Early America: The Revolutionary Period 1763–1790*, Charlottesville, 1987, pp. 168–78.

22. Connecticut Valley Historical Museum, Springfield, Mass., Pynchon papers, 1652–1702, microfilm at the Van Pelt Library, University of Pennsylvania. On the Pynchons, see Stephen Innes, *Labor in a New Land: Economy and Society in Seventeenth-Century Springfield*, Princeton, 1983.

23. American Antiquarian Society, Richard and Jonathan Champney, Cambridge and Southborough, accounts 1746–83, and John Child, jun. [?], Holden, Worcester County, daybook and ledger, 1770–89; Baker Library, Harvard University, Elisha Ford, Marshfield, Plymouth County, store daybook, 1771–95.

24. Margaret E. Martin, *Merchants and Trade of the Connecticut River Valley, 1750–1820*, South College Studies, 24, Northampton, Mass., 1938–9, pp. 1–284, and Rothenberg, 'The Market and Massachusetts Farmers', p. 291.

25. The data from the Massachusetts Tax Valuation of 1771 were originally collected and coded by Bettye Hobbs Pruitt and made available through the Inter-University Consortium for Political and Social Research, Ann Arbor, Mich. The list has also been edited in book form by Pruitt, *The Massachusetts Tax Valuation List of 1771*, Boston, 1978. In addition to the use made of it by Pruitt in her dissertation, 'Agriculture and Society in the Towns of Massachusetts, 1771: A Statistical Analysis', unpublished Ph.D. dissertation, Boston University, 1981, and in an article, 'Self-Sufficiency and the Agricultural Economy of Eighteenth-Century Massachusetts', *William and Mary Quarterly*, 3rd ser. 41 (1984), 333–64, this list has been an important source for a number of other scholars. See James A. Henretta, 'Economic Development and Social Structure in Colonial Boston', ibid. 22 (1965), 75–92; Allan Kulikoff, 'The Progress of Inequality in Revolutionary Boston', ibid. 28 (1971), 375–412; Edward M. Cook, jun., *The Fathers of the Town*, Baltimore, 1976; Gary B. Nash, 'Urban Wealth and Poverty in Pre-Revolutionary America', *Journal of Interdisciplinary History*, 6 (1976), 545–84; and G. B. Warden, 'Inequality and Instability in Eighteenth Century Boston: A Reappraisal', ibid. 585–620.

26. Pruitt, 'Self-Sufficiency and Agricultural Economy', pp. 335–6. The percentage distribution of taxables in each county is very similar to the county by county distribution of the entire population in 1772: Evarts B. Greene and Virginia D. Harrington, *American Population Before the Federal Census of 1790*, Gloucester, Mass., 1966, p. 30. Only the south coastal counties may be under-represented, Nantucket being excluded completely and Plymouth and Barnstaple having less than their percentage of the population. The aggregate analysis on the town level includes those towns with incomplete lists, the assumption being that the exclusion was random and that what has survived is representative of the entire population of the community.

27. Out of the entire listing of 37,938 taxpayers, 1,702 had merchandise (stock-in-trade). For some calculations, those who had died by the time the tax was collected or who were non-residents were removed, leaving 36,297 taxpayers

and 1,698 with merchandise. On the non-importation agreements see Arthur Meier Schlesinger, *The Colonial Merchants and the American Revolution*, New York, 1939, reprint of 1918 edn.

28. This was my conclusion after comparing the advertisements of merchants in the Boston newspapers and the *Essex Gazette* during 1771 with those possessing stock-in-trade in the tax valuation list. Out of 136 merchandisers who appeared in both advertisements and the tax list, less than 10% indicated that they sold only wholesale or acted solely as suppliers to business. As these were almost entirely Boston and Salem merchants, one can only assume that the percentage was considerably lower in other towns.

29. I checked through those in the tax list identified as owning industrial establishments—tanneries, slaughterhouses, blacksmith's forges, and so on—and noted those who did and did not also have stock-in-trade. Generally, it seemed that craftspeople who dealt in ephemeral goods such as meat or bakery goods were not assessed for stock-in-trade, nor were those who had primarily a bespoken trade—weavers, tailors, cabinetmakers, and carpenters.

30. I used a multiplier of 5 rather than 4 with those on the tax valuation list because the total seemed to correspond best with other estimates of Massachusetts' population c. 1771. See Greene and Harrington, *American Population*, p. 17. The source of the estimate of per capita income in the 1770s is discussed in Chap. 3, above.

31. Bureau of the Census, *The Statistical Abstract of the United States, 1986*, Washington DC, 1985, pp. 5, 438, 776. The objection might be raised that omitting wholesale prices in the later periods distorts the figures because the figure for 1771 clearly includes some stock that was being wholesaled. There are figures for 1967 for both retail and wholesale inventories, and when combined they still amount to only 9.7% of personal income: Bureau of the Census, *Historical Statistics of the United States, Colonial Times to the Present*, Washington DC, 1975, p. 842.

32. A number of historians have worked on classifying New England towns: see Cook, *Fathers of the Town*; Pruitt, 'Agriculture and Society'; Douglas Lamar Jones, *Village and Seaport: Migration and Society in Eighteenth Century Massachusetts*, Hanover, NH, 1981; and Bruce C. Daniels, *The Connecticut Town: Growth and Development, 1635–1790*, Middletown, Conn., 1979, pp. 140–70.

33. Jackson Turner Main, *Society and Economy in Colonial Connecticut*, Princeton, 1985, p. 283. Main gives the median as £70 in constant Connecticut currency, base years 1756–76. I divided that amount by 1.33 to obtain the £ sterling figure of £53. £449 in Connecticut currency was the value of the trading stock of the biggest merchandiser in the inventory sample, which would convert to £338 sterling. Turnover of three times a year was also the rate estimated for Pennsylvania country shops by a late 18th-cent. Philadelphia merchant: see Doerflinger, 'Farmers and Dry Goods', p. 169.

34. Lois Green Carr and Lorena S. Walsh, 'Changing Lifestyles and Consumer Behavior in the Colonial Chesapeake', in Cary Carson, Ronald Hoffman, and Peter Albert (eds.), *Of Consuming Interest: The Style of Life in the Eighteenth Century*, Charlottesville, forthcoming.

35. See e.g. James E. Vance, jun., *The Merchant's World: The Geography of*

Wholesaling, Englewood Cliffs, 1970, p. 61. He writes, 'Perhaps the central condition in the development of trade over the centuries has been the slow emergence of consistency and specialization.'

36. See Bernard Bailyn, *The New England Merchants in the Seventeenth Century*, Cambridge, Mass., 1955, pp. 99–101; Stuart Bruchey, *The Roots of American Economic Growth, 1607–1861*, New York, 1968, pp. 48–54; and Daniels, *The Connecticut Town*, pp. 147–8.

37. Thomas M. Doerflinger, *A Vigorous Spirit of Enterprise*, Chapel Hill, 1986, ch. 2.

Conclusion: Economic History, Economic Theory, and Consumption

HISTORICAL writing on consumption has been criticized for being too full of declarations about revolutions. 'Historians are forever using and then debasing their own coinage,' complains one fellow-practitioner of the trade, 'and so we now have consumer societies and even consumer revolutions, dating from 1780, 1760, 1700, and even 1560.'[1] The situation is actually worse than this critic indicates, because he excludes all the literature on nineteenth- and twentieth-century consumer culture in which 'revolutions' also abound. Michael Schudson in his recent book on advertising has summarized the arguments of some of these historians.[2] One of them sees the United States transformed into a consumer culture in the late nineteenth century with the development of the department store and national advertising; another cites the 1920s, when instalment buying, the automobile, movies, and the radio came into the lives of many Americans; and a third considers the rapid rise in real family income, suburban home-ownership, two cars in the garage, and television during the 1950s as the real watershed. Each have different criteria, or the same criteria but different indicators.

Historians are encouraged by a well-entrenched sociological tradition, which includes the theories of both Marx and Weber, to dichotomize their subjects into a before and an after with some transforming event or process falling in between.[3] The demands of narrative also still weigh heavily on most of those in the discipline, which means that the historian needs a beginning, a climax, and an end. As a result, there is tremendous pressure to locate origins and revolutions in whatever time period one is studying.

This book is an example of the alternative approach. It begins rather uncertainly in mid-sixteenth-century England, primarily because probate inventories, an important source for the study of consumption, become plentiful at that point. Perhaps the decision to require an enumeration of the personal property of deceased persons for the benefit of creditors was coincident with some major economic development, but as is so often the case when linking the study of a subject to the beginnings of a statistical series, the antecedent situation cannot be investigated because there are no comparable data to use. In this case, no origins of the market system are uncovered. At the point at which inventories commence in England, a large proportion of households and localities had to go outside to obtain two of the most important commodities they consumed, grain and textiles. If there was any big change in household production for many English rural households, any proletarianization, during the centuries under consideration here, this change was not so much the loss of control over arable land: most English households did not have such control to begin with. Rather, it was the decline in livestock ownership. In addition to cyclical trends, lower-wealth groups, over the long term, lost their cows and with them the ability to practise dairying, and sheep-raising became concentrated among a smaller number of households.

Under a household mode of production, families had to be wealthy and large to be able to take care of their own consumption needs. Even then they might not choose to do so. The colonial Chesapeake in the seventeenth century provides a good example of a place where the planters had plenty of land, considerable capital, and comparatively large households, yet they channelled their labour into tobacco production and away from such activities as the cultivation of English grains, brewing, dairying, sheep-raising, and cloth-production. Later, as the profits from staple production declined, household production in some of these abandoned activities picked up once again. In England, one can also identify certain home-production processes—brewing for example—that became more common as time went on. Household production for home consumption should not be regarded totally as following a downward linear trend.

The consumption habits of the American colonies, both plantation and non-plantation, demonstrate how well developed the international trade networks were. By the time of the American Revolution, I estimated that perhaps as much as 30% of per capita income in a given colony was spent on goods imported from outside that colony, and about 75% of those goods would be classified as consumer commodities. It is hard to believe that the percentage coming in from outside a state became much higher in America during most of the nineteenth century. Great quantities of sugar, rum, tea, textiles, clothing, and in some places, grain flooded in.

The two big growth areas in consumption appear to have been

groceries—tobacco, sugar products, and caffeine drinks—and semi-durables. The groceries all became items of mass consumption in England and America between 1650 and 1750 and provoked what may have been, in England at least, a very deleterious change in the content of the human diet. The proliferation of manufactured goods mainly involved what I have labelled semi-durables—lighter, cheaper textile products, pottery, glass, and paper. More and more of these goods were used to enhance the domestic environment. Bedding became more elaborate over the entire period studied, and tableware grew prominent as an area of consumer expenditure during the eighteenth century. In England, this enhancement seemed to coincide or follow closely on the heels of structural improvements in the housing of at least middle-income groups. They adopted chimneys, second storeys, and more differentiated rooms, stairways, glass windows, and brick or stone rather than wood and earthen exteriors. In America, however, the acquisition of many durables seemed to proceed in many households without a concomitant upgrading in housing.

There were other characteristics of dietary and durables consumption that do not appear to have changed much in either England or the colonies. People altered the content of their diet, but the proportion of household expenditure devoted to food and drink did not seem to move a great deal over the long term, staying at an average of between 50% and 60% for English labouring people, and in times of crisis climbing up to 70%. American figures were most likely 10% lower, with few or no crisis periods. While budget studies have often exaggerated the percentage which families in the past had to expend on diet, some seeing a steady 80% to 85% going on food, they were not wrong about the secular flatness of the trend until the end of the nineteenth or the beginning of the twentieth century. Likewise the trend in the consumption of major durables—furniture, carriages, what later became known as appliances—remained decidedly unexciting for all but the very affluent throughout the eighteenth century.

This book has also examined the problem of distribution in what were basically rural societies. So much of what people ate, drank, wore, and otherwise consumed during the centuries under consideration came to them through a hierarchical system of distribution. The patriarch made bequests, the master offered payments in kind, and the state acted as an oversight committee with its sumptuary laws. By the latter part of the seventeenth century, however, consumers seem to have had much more direct access to retailers selling pre-processed or ready-made goods on credit. Not that the hierarchical system disappeared. The practice of keeping farm servants, for example, tended to fluctuate with the cost of feeding them. Indentured servitude and then slavery grew in importance over time. Still, the secular trend seems to have been away from payment of wages in kind.

The growth in the trade in groceries and the relatively inexpensive semi-durables for which there was fairly constant demand made it much more feasible for pedlars and shopkeepers to operate in the countryside. In England, the market-town system provided a pre-existing network for these merchandisers, who often carried very small amounts of stock and engaged in other occupations as well. In some parts of America, however, the retail distribution system was closely intertwined with the collection of exports, and that combination produced distinctive patterns of retailing. For example, Sears-like outlets became entrenched in the Chesapeake colonies. These chainstores run by British mercantile firms had an impressive array of merchandise of every sort and also—for a price and for their crops—functioned as financial institutions for planters. In a sense, these merchants replaced the local 'great man' or the employer, although they differed in that they offered more choice in goods and would more readily pay in cash rather than commodities if the planter requested it.

The distribution system in these basically non-urban societies was made possible through the dual occupations of merchandisers and the generalized nature of their stock. Estimates of numbers of retail outlets per capita for eighteenth-century England and Massachusetts compare quite favourably with those for twentieth-century America. The difference of course comes in the value of merchandise per retailer. These early merchandisers were everywhere, but they did not carry a large stock. In the Chesapeake there were fewer stores, but by eighteenth-century standards they maintained big inventories.

So there you have an example of the alternative approach. The author uncovers changes, variations, and trends, but no Origins of the Market, no Great Transformations in Consumer Consciousness. The book ends rather raggedly *c.* 1780–1800 because the objective was to study consumption prior to the advent of factories, power-driven machinery, and mass urbanization. The end is of course not a proper end at all, because one of the main points of this book is that there is no organic unity to pre-industrial life and that the Industrial Revolution, at least as far as consumption is concerned, is not the watershed it was once thought to be.

Whatever the 'story' may lack in terms of dramatic excitement, however, I like to think it makes up for by what is discovered in using early modern data to test theories of economic behaviour derived from twentieth-century experience. Principal among those theories are the ones concerning the determinants of demand. Price and income are traditionally considered to be the most important contributors to the level of demand in a society. In the case of both England and the colonies, price obviously did play an important role in the growth in the consumption of groceries and in demand for at least one of the semi-durables, textiles. A significant drop in the prices of tobacco, sugar, and tea occurred at various points in the seventeenth and eighteenth centuries, and that change seemed to account for the soaring demand as a commodity like sugar moved from being a luxury to a commonly consumed good. The fact that in the eighteenth century groceries (particularly sugar and tea) claimed an ever greater share of the total value of imports, however, suggests that more than just a price decline was involved.

It also seems from the evidence available on textile prices that they nosedived from the mid-seventeenth century on. This price decline, plus the substitution of lighter and cheaper textiles, may have eventually resulted in smaller outlays made for greater amounts of household linen and clothing. If indeed there was such a sharp decline, that raises the question of what exactly happened to textile production during the seventeenth century. Could a reorganization of the labour force have produced a drop of this apparent magnitude, and was this in any way comparable to the transformation of textile manufacturing in the nineteenth century? Historians have known for some time that there was a crisis among English clothiers due to the introduction of the lighter woollens, the 'New Draperies', but the long-term implications for textile-workers, the largest group in the manufacturing sector, as well as for consumers have never been fully understood.[4]

Unfortunately, there is not enough information on the prices of other semi-durables to indicate trends. The only additional area investigated where price seemed to result in a change in demand was in construction. The high price of wood in England during the seventeenth century may have been responsible for the shift to using more brick and stone in housing.

Price, then, seems to have been undeniably important in boosting demand, especially during the seventeenth and early eighteenth centuries in England and in the eighteenth century in America. Assessing the impact of income was more troublesome because I had to work mainly with wealth stocks which could not give information about expenditure on diet and which underestimated lifetime outlays on semi-durables; nor does the wealth figure include realty. There were also problems in controlling for the rampant inflation of the late sixteenth and early seventeenth centuries and in determining the degree to which the wealth biases of the samples were constant over time. Because of these factors, about the most one can say is that there may have been an increase in real £ sterling 'invested' in the category of consumer durables (both the semi and the permanent variety) between the late sixteenth century and the 1660s, a time of hardship for many in England. But after that there is no evidence of growth. It can also be said with some confidence that the proportion of wealth in consumer durables did not rise *vis-à-vis* producer goods (both physical and financial wealth) over the time period studied, and may in fact have declined, although most of the decline can be attributed to higher mean wealth. This happened despite the fact that in England holdings in one of the major components of producer wealth, livestock, fell for many households. Interestingly enough, the proportion in consumer durables in a contemporary estimate of household wealth in America corresponds very closely to the percentage found in many of the early modern samples, once the figures have been made comparable by excluding realty and making a few other adjustments.

Complicating this attempt to measure demand shifts is the problem of including the time allocations of households in the equation. As Gary Becker and the New Home Economists as well as historians of women's work have pointed out, households do not just spend money, they spend time.[5] If there was any trend in the early modern period, it seems to have been in the direction of household members allocating less time to food production for home consumption, although that trend seems more clear-cut in England than America. The reliance of early settlements on imported food and the disruption of trade networks during the Revolutionary era render trends in the colonies less linear. If on the whole households in England and British America did spend less time on food production, then presumably more of their total resources went into other categories of expenditure or savings, all other things held constant. Which categories the resources went into, however, remains an open question.

Does the fact that one cannot prove that there was any increase in either the proportion of wealth devoted to diet or in that spent on consumer durables mean that probably no real demand shifts occurred, that is, shifts that cannot be attributed to either changes in price or changes in income levels? Yes, if one confines oneself to making comparisons between the three categories of producer wealth or savings, food and drink, and consumer durables. If outlay on diet and durables is disaggregated, however, there do seem to be important shifts *within* standard expenditure categories that require explanation, specifically the adoption of groceries and the substitution of semi-durables for durables.

As mentioned above, existing evidence about the proportion of the budget early modern households devoted to food and drink suggests that there was little change over time. In fact, it is unclear whether there were substantial drops in this proportion until the early twentieth century in America and even later in Britain. What did change was the composition of the diet, so much so that the eighteenth-century ingredients resemble the twentieth-century ones more than those of the early seventeenth century. The changeover made by so many people completely reorganized trade and promoted colonization and slavery. In trying to analyse the reasons for this change in intake it is important to remember that it occurred after grain prices had risen considerably and milk and cheese consumption was on the decline. In other words, the English population was already having problems with its traditional diet, and the calorific content of that diet for the poorer elements in society was apparently very low: insufficient, it seems, for completing a full day's manual work. Under these conditions, the appetite-abating and energizing properties of tobacco, sugar, and caffeine drinks might well have been especially attractive. Tobacco and the hot tea, coffee, and chocolate beverages in turn stimulated the consumption of clay pipes and pottery dishes. Our understanding of how calories were distributed between and within households is, of course, very limited. Who sacrificed—the labouring poor in general? Women? Children? The old? The disabled?[6]

One other characteristic of early modern consumer behaviour in regard to diet that is worth noting, because it conflicts with modern data, is the fact that within the working class food sometimes behaved like a luxury. That is, as income rose there is evidence of households defying Engel's law and spending a *greater* proportion of their budget on food. Considering what is now being discovered about calorie levels, these findings make some sense.

There is also some need to explain the shift away from consumer durables made from more permanent materials to semi-durable, more disposable goods. For example, by the eighteenth century the £ sterling amount invested in brass and pewter actually declined while objects made from pottery and glass proliferated. Many of these were tableware objects and some owed their popularity to dietary trends, particularly the consumption of hot caffeine drinks. The increased interest in dressing the table and in decorating the bed marked the beginning of a long-term movement to invest in the domestic environment. Women being confined largely to this environment and, with a change in household work roles, the most responsible for it, may have had some influence on these items of expenditure. Certainly, tea-drinking and its accompanying equipment was associated particularly with women in the eighteenth century. Whether this means they gained more power over actual expenditure, however, is difficult to prove. Building patterns in America suggest that if women did increase their authority in the home, their influence stopped when it came to the structure itself. Colonials seemed to keep up quite well with trends in British semi-durable furnishing, but no one at this point seems to have succeeded in pressuring American men to erect better housing. The legal system, particularly feme covert status, ensured that husbands had the ultimate say in consumer decisions.

In the area of distribution, early modern data also indicates that the traditional association of specialization with an expansion of retailing and non-specialization with primitive, non-growth situations is misleading. In the later seventeenth and eighteenth centuries, there was certainly specialization in mercantile occupations in the metropolis of London. The proliferation of retailers elsewhere, however, was accomplished through broadening the kind of merchandise offered for sale and through the practice of combining multiple occupations. In terms of number of outlets and proportion of income of the population expended on imports, it is difficult to label this unspecialized system undeveloped. Actually, what seems to vary over time is not so much degree of specialization as the type of diversification chosen by those involved in distribution.

Then there is the relationship between the state and early modern consumption to consider. Since Keynes, it has been customary to ask about the impact of the state on consumer demand. But in the seventeenth and eighteenth centuries, the causal order was the reverse: consumer demand's effect on the state. England abandoned sumptuary legislation in the first part of the seventeenth century and the colonies eventually followed suit. Guilds had little power over the price and quality of goods. Republican ideology decried the resort to consumer 'luxuries', but also considered less as more when it came to state inter-

vention. Consequently, Crown awards of monopolies largely disappeared, leading to a race for market share among the 'enterprising'.
Although there were protectionist measures for certain industries, and
through military expenditures, an inadvertent boost given to the ready-
made clothes industry, very little surfaced in the area of what might be
termed consumer protection or expenditure on material well-being that
had not been in place from almost the beginning of the period.[7] In
contrast, it appears that the French government struggled much longer
and harder to regulate the consumption of its population.[8]

The British government used trade, the bulk of it being in consumer
goods, as the justification for the expansion of the state into an empire.
Moreover, the continued operation of the state came to depend more and
more on revenues generated from import duties, excises, and taxes on
carriages, windows, and shops. While these heavy, and often very regres-
sive, taxes must have somewhat lowered demand, their effects on politics
and policy are even more demonstrable, the American Revolution
perhaps being the most graphic example. In that sense the period covered
in this study does have some unity, extending as it does from the creation
of an empire built on consumer goods to its dismemberment.[9]

In the final analysis, the single most surprising aspect of the spread of
new consumer commodities during the early modern period is that it
occurred among a broad spectrum of people, at least some of whom were
malnourished and/or poorly housed. The kinds of compromises made by
lower-income households in the realm of consumption, as well as the
various limits and restrictions imposed on their choices by masters,
employers, markets, and the government, are more complicated than
previously imagined. Paradoxically, the individual who drank tea in a
teacup, wore a printed cotton gown, and put linen on the bed could be
the same person who ingested too few calories to work all day and lived
in a one-room house.

Chapter 10

1. David Levine, *Proletarianization and Family History*, Orlando, 1984, p. 117.
2. Michael Schudson, *Advertising, the Uneasy Persuasion: Its Dubious Impact on
   American Society*, New York, 1984, pp. 178–9.
3. Not that I have totally escaped the old way of thinking, either. The liberal use of
   the term 'early modern', which is part of a trilogy, 'modern' and 'post-modern'
   being the other components, and the occasional use of 'pre-industrial', including
   its appearance in the title of the book, reveal how dependent we all are on this kind
   of conceptualization.

4. The recent book by Eric Kerridge, *Textile Manufactures in Early Modern England*, Manchester, 1985, has much useful information on the making of cloth in its heavily footnoted text, but the evidence for the basic contention of the author, that English freedoms and ingenuity made England the clothier of the world, is not analysed in a systematic fashion and consequently is of limited use in discriminating between various explanations for 17th-cent. developments.

5. See George J. Stigler and Gary S. Becker, 'De Gustibus Non Est Disputandum', *American Economic Review*, 67 (1977), 76–90, for the new home economics approach. Ruth Schwartz Cowan, *More Work for Mother*, New York, 1983, is an example of the interest of historians in the time women spend on housework.

6. Nancy Folbre and Heidi Hartmann, 'The Rhetoric of Self-Interest: Ideology and Gender in Economic History', unpublished paper, 1986, discuss the problem with assuming that market relations are self-interested but family relations are governed by an altruism from which all household members benefit equally.

7. Robert William Fogel, 'Second Thoughts on the European Escape from Hunger: Famines, Price Elasticities, Entitlements, Chronic Malnutrition, and Mortality Rates', unpublished copyrighted paper, November 1988, draws attention to the importance of late 16th-cent. English legislation that required local authorities rather than charitable organizations to assume responsibility for poor relief. Fogel also argues that efforts by the Crown to relieve food shortages grew more effective in the early 17th cent. but were abandoned after the Civil War. John Brewer in *Sinews of Power: War, Money and the English State 1688–1783*, New York, 1989, discusses the widespread effects of military expenditures on English society.

8. Cissie Fairchilds, 'The Production and Marketing of Populuxe Goods in Eighteenth-Century Paris', unpublished paper presented at the Clark Library, Los Angeles, Jan. 1989.

9. This is the theme of a book in progress by T. H. Breen.

Inventory Samples Used in Statistical Analysis

Probate inventories are probably the single most valuable source of information about the consumption of semi-durables and durables during the sixteenth, seventeenth and eighteenth centuries. According to English law all decedents whose personalty or personal wealth (all property apart from realty, including financial assets, leases, slaves, livestock, crops, equipment, household goods, and personal items) exceeded £5 in value were to be inventoried and their estates probated in local ecclesiastical courts. Those who had property in more than one ecclesiastical jurisdiction (usually the wealthier decedents) had their estates probated at a higher court, most often the Prerogative Court of Canterbury. In the American colonies the county court normally handled probate. Probate coverage, however, differs from community to community, and seldom does it extend to as much as 50% of all decedents. Urban areas usually have much lower coverage rates. See Carole Shammas, 'The Determinants of Personal Wealth in Seventeenth-Century England and America', *The Journal of Economic History*, 37 (1977), 675–89, on how Worcestershire, the East End of London, and Virginia compare as far as coverage is concerned.

The routine taking of inventories ended in England c. 1730, but it continued in the colonies up to the Revolution. After the Revolution, the states adopted the practice, although in the nineteenth century the enumerations in some jurisdictions became less detailed.

The inventory samples that I computerized and submitted to statistical analysis came both from data I gathered myself in local record offices and from printed collections of probate inventories gathered by others. Collecting, coding, and cleaning an inventory sample of approximately 300 observations with perhaps 50 variables takes one person, working continually, anywhere from three to six months, depending on the condition of the original records. Consequently, the only way I could possibly get much variation over time and region in inventory samples was to rely when I could on data collected by others. Below is a list of the different data sets, the archive or printed collection from which I obtained them, and a brief description of what they cover. Dates are according to the new calendar, with the year beginning in January. I copied all complete inventories extant for the time periods listed.

Sources of Inventory Samples

1. **Oxfordshire, 1550–90.** Printed in Michael Ashley Havinden (ed.), *Household and Farm Inventories in Oxfordshire, 1550–1590*, London, 1965. The sample covers Oxford and some market towns as well as agricultural villages. A

few inventories that were incomplete were omitted. Havinden did not include Oxfordshire decedents whose estates were proved at the Prerogative Court of Canterbury; nor did he print wills, so information about literacy was based on book ownership rather than signatory ability.

2. **Southern Worcestershire, 1669–1670.** I took down information from probate files in Worcestershire Consistory Court, County of Hereford and Worcestershire Record Office, St Helens, Worcester and in the Prerogative Court of Canterbury, Public Record Office, London. The area covered was the 128 parishes that make up the southern two-thirds·of Worcestershire, beginning with the parishes of Feckenham, Hanbury, Droitwich, Ombersley, Shrawley, Martley, Witley, and Shelsley Beauchamp. The provincial capital of Worcester was included, as were all the peculiars that fell into the region. The area, unlike the north of Worcestershire, was heavily agricultural. Information about age and signatory ability was taken down for those inventories decedents who left wills. About 51% of adult male decedents were inventoried.

3. **Southern Worcestershire, 1720–1.** See 2, above.

4. **East End of London 1661–4.** All completed inventories for the parishes of Stepney, Whitechapel, Stratford-Le-Bow, and St Leonard Bromley filed in the Commissary Court, whose records now reside at the London Guildhall. The Consistory Court records at the Greater London Record Office only had a few additional inventories. The Prerogative Court of Canterbury, Public Record Office, also contributed a few. Information on age and signatory ability was collected for those inventoried decedents who left wills. This area was around the docks and contained a lot of paid labourers, seamen, and foreign artisans. As might be expected, the probate coverage was very limited, only about 16% of adult male decedents left an inventory.

5. **East End of London, 1720–9.** See 4 above. There were more inventories in the Prerogative Court of Canterbury for this period than for the period 1661–4. Partially that may reflect a richer element residing in the dockside parishes, but mainly, I suspect, it is an artefact of the uneven cataloguing procedure for the Prerogative Court records. When I was copying inventories, there were more available for the early eighteenth century than for the seventeenth century. Because wealth was so distorted in London and because the probate coverage of the ordinary East End inhabitants was so incomplete, this sample is the most unreliable of all those I collected. Wealthy decedents dominate the means and percentages, and give the area a more affluent cast than it should have. On the cataloguing of the Prerogative Court of Canterbury, see J. S. W. Gibson, 'Inventories in the Records of the Prerogative Court of Canterbury', *Local Historian*, 14 (1980–1), 222–5.

6. **Tidewater Virginia, 1660–77.** Inventories from the county courts of York, Isle of Wight, Westmorland, Northumberland, and Henrico available on microfilm from the Virginia State Library, Richmond. Virginia had a tobacco

economy in this period and most of the probated decedents were white male planters. I copied information on age and signatory ability for those inventoried decedents who had left wills. Because of the use of bound labour, colonial inventories include as assets the time left to serve for those on indentures and the value of slaves. This is a substantial part of Virginian inventoried wealth.

7. **Tidewater Virginia, 1724–9.** See 6 above. The same county courts were used except that there are no inventories in this sample from Northumberland. This sample has few peculiarities except that the coverage of financial assets, such as debts owed to the decedent, do not seem very complete.

8. **Virginia and Maryland, 1774.** These inventories are printed in Alice Hanson Jones (comp. and ed.), *American Colonial Wealth*, 3 vols., New York, 1977. Jones also took down information about age for those decedents who had made wills. I did not use Jones's tape. Instead I made up my own coding-sheet to correspond to those for the other samples.

9. **Essex County, Massachusetts, 1660–April 1673.** These inventories are printed in *The Probate Records of Essex County, Massachusetts*, i and ii, Salem, 1916–17. The sample reflects the fact that the seventeenth-century migration to New England was largely of middle-class households. New England inventories include realty as a part of inventoried wealth. For calculations in this book, I subtracted realty to make the Massachusetts samples comparable with the others.

10. **Massachusetts, 1774.** These inventories are also printed in Jones, *American Colonial Wealth*.

Conversion of Currencies to Pounds Sterling, Base Years, 1660–1674

Unless otherwise stated, all of the values of the inventories mentioned above were converted to pounds sterling, base years 1660–74, before being reported in the text. This involved two operations: (1) adjusting colonial pounds current to British pounds sterling using the conversion rates in John J. McCusker, *Money and Exchange in Europe and America, 1600–1775*, Chapel Hill, 1978; and (2) adjusting the samples from the sixteenth and the eighteenth century for inflation over time by using the price index in E. H. Phelps Brown and Sheila V. Hopkins, 'Seven Centuries of the Prices of Consumables, Compared with Builders' Wage Rates', in E. M. Carus-Wilson (ed.), *Essay in Economic History*, ii, London, 1962, pp. 193–6. The years 1660–74 in the index were averaged for the base; the years 1551–90 were averaged for the Oxfordshire deflation rate; the years 1720–9 were averaged for the 1720s samples of Worcestershire, the East End of London, and Virginia; and the years 1772–6 were averaged for the Chesapeake and Massachusetts 1774 samples. This resulted in the Oxfordshire values being multiplied by 2.00 after being rounded off for inflation over time. The 1774 samples were divided by 1.33 to account for inflation over time. (This should not be confused with those samples that also had to be divided by 1.33 to correct for inflated colonial values.) The Phelps Brown and Hopkins index indicated that the 1720s samples should be multiplied by 1.03, but that seemed too small an amount, given the degree of error in the conversion tool, to bother with. The Phelps Brown and Hopkins index seems artificially low in the early eighteenth century, perhaps because the index is very dependent on grain prices which were relatively low in that period.

Below are the transformations performed on all ten of the data sets.

1. Oxfordshire, 1550–90: values multiplied by 2.00.
2. Worcestershire, 1669–70: no transformations.
3. Worcestershire, 1720–21: no transformations.
4. East End of London, 1661–4: no transformations.
5. East End of London, 1720–9: no transformations.
6. Tidewater Virginia, 1660–76: tobacco pounds divided by 2.00 to convert to pounds sterling.
7. Virginia, 1724–9: Virginia currency divided by 1.2 to convert to pounds sterling.
8. Virginia and Maryland, 1774: Chesapeake values divided by 1.33 to convert to pounds sterling, and then divided by 1.33 to deflate for inflation of pound sterling over time.
9. Essex County, Massachusetts, 1660–73: Massachusetts values divided by 1.2 to convert to pounds sterling.
10. Massachusetts 1774: same conversion process as for Virginia and Maryland in 1774.

Cut-off Points for Low-Wealth, and Medium- to High-Wealth Groups

In certain tables in Chapters 2, 3, and 6 of this book, I have divided the inventory samples into low-wealth and medium- to high-wealth groups. The wealth being referred to is personal wealth or personalty (realty excluded). Low-wealth does not necessarily mean poverty-stricken. Rather, it probably represents anywhere from over half to two-thirds of the population in a community. The medium- to high-wealth group represents the affluent or truly propertied element. Wealth here means wealth in personalty. For England, I chose the median for the Oxfordshire 1550–90 sample, £20 sterling, current, and tried to keep to that amount, controlling for inflation. Therefore the cut-off point for the English 1660s samples was £40 sterling (2.00 times £20), which turned out to be almost exactly the median of the Worcestershire 1669–70 sample, although it was at the 70th percentile of the impoverished London 1661–4 sample. In the 1720s, the cut-off point was moved up to £45 current. The Phelps Brown and Hopkins index did not show any upward movement because it was, as mentioned above, closely tied to cereal prices. The durables in inventories did seem somewhat more expensive, and that is why I increased the cut-off point by 12.5%. £45 sterling was at the 42nd percentile of the Worcestershire 1720–1 sample, but it only reached the 20th percentile of the unusually rich East End of London inventory sample.

The cut-off points for all the colonial samples were at the median, except in Table 6.1 where I had the low-wealth group for Massachusetts conform to the English samples norm of £40 sterling in 1660–74 prices for purposes of comparison. Below are the pound sterling medians that were used as cut-off points for all the colonial samples:

1. Tidewater Virginia, 1660–76: £60.
2. Essex County, Massachusetts, 1660–73: £60.
3. Tidewater Virginia, 1724–9: £47.
4. Virginia and Maryland, 1774: £157 (£82 if slaves omitted).
5. Massachusetts, 1774: £73.

APPENDIX 2

Descriptions, Means, Standard Deviations, and Zero Order Correlation Matrices for Variables Used to Determine the Value of Consumer Goods

A. Oxfordshire 1551–1590 Regression, N = 247

Variable	Mean	Standard Deviation
1. Consumer goods (ln)	4.669	1.081
2. Wealth (ln)	5.840	1.219
3. Household size (ln)	1.480	0.766
4. Town residency	0.348	0.477
5. Farmer	0.449	0.498
6. Trades	0.239	0.427
7. Widow	0.174	0.380
8. Book-owner	0.012	0.110

Correlation Matrix

	1	2	3	4	5	6	7	8
1	1.000	0.777	0.749	0.117	0.177	0.043	−0.069	0.195
2		1.000	0.560	−0.080	0.394	−0.137	−0.076	0.152
3			1.000	0.236	0.089	0.141	−0.155	0.134
4				1.000	−0.302	0.487	−0.067	0.074
5					1.000	−0.506	−0.415	−0.026
6						1.000	−0.257	0.025
7							1.000	−0.051
8								1.000

B. Southern Worcestershire 1669–1670 Regression, N = 217

Variable	Mean	Standard Deviation
1. Consumer goods (ln)	2.828	1.014
2. Wealth (ln)	3.882	1.192
3. Household size (ln)	1.581	0.725
4. Town residency	0.184	0.389
5. Élite	0.106	0.309
6. Farmer	0.341	0.475
7. Trades	0.157	0.364
8. Widow	0.203	0.403
9. Book-owner	0.290	0.766

Correlation Matrix

	1	2	3	4	5	6	7	8	9
1	1.000	0.780	0.627	0.096	0.385	−0.049	−0.007	0.225	0.282
2		1.000	0.463	0.037	0.355	0.137	−0.068	−0.237	0.267
3			1.000	0.068	0.166	0.049	0.124	−0.266	0.165
4				1.000	0.068	−0.217	0.384	−0.092	0.255
5					1.000	−0.248	−0.148	−0.174	0.261
6						1.000	−0.310	−0.363	−0.159
7							1.000	−0.217	0.168
8								1.000	−0.162
9									1.000

C. Southern Worcestershire 1720–1721 Regression, N = 219

Variable	Mean	Standard Deviation
1. Consumer goods (ln)	2.907	1.027
2. Wealth (ln)	4.100	1.374
3. Household size (ln)	1.643	0.628
4. Town residency	0.283	0.452
5. Élite	0.055	0.228
6. Farmer	0.507	0.501
7. Trades	0.210	0.408
8. Widow	0.201	0.402
9. Book-owner	0.155	0.363

Correlation Matrix

	1	2	3	4	5	6	7	8	9
1	1.000	0.782	0.650	0.158	0.204	0.201	−0.117	−0.069	0.154
2		1.000	0.484	0.101	0.153	0.390	−0.124	−0.186	0.117
3			1.000	0.058	0.041	0.264	−0.092	−0.175	0.101
4				1.000	0.160	−0.353	0.298	0.014	0.094
5					1.000	−0.244	−0.124	−0.121	0.285
6						1.000	−0.523	−0.440	−0.056
7							1.000	0.021	−0.066
8								1.000	0.037
9									1.000

D. *East London 1661–1664 Regression, N = 120*

Variable	Mean	Standard Deviation
1. Consumer goods (ln)	2.587	1.070
2. Wealth (ln)	3.236	1.180
3. Household size (ln)	1.550	0.766
4. Book-owner	0.325	0.688
5. Élite	0.067	0.250
6. Trades	0.392	0.490
7. Widow	0.200	0.402

Correlation Matrix

	1	2	3	4	5	6	7
1	1.000	0.754	0.559	0.176	0.044	0.289	0.006
2		1.000	0.444	0.111	0.095	0.261	−0.008
3			1.000	0.014	−0.002	0.226	0.048
4				1.000	−0.029	0.168	−0.055
5					1.000	−0.214	−0.134
6						1.000	−0.401
7							1.000

E. *East London 1720–1729 Regression, N = 161*

Variable	Mean	Standard Deviation
1. Consumer goods (ln)	3.379	1.374
2. Wealth (ln)	5.373	1.857
3. Household size (ln)	1.548	0.810
4. Book-owner	0.373	0.485
5. Élite	0.087	0.283
6. Trades	0.578	0.495
7. Widow	0.174	0.380

Correlation Matrix

	1	2	3	4	5	6	7
1	1.000	0.752	0.673	0.426	0.229	0.189	−0.059
2		1.000	0.494	0.330	0.117	0.204	−0.064
3			1.000	0.368	0.144	0.189	−0.139
4				1.000	0.036	0.087	−0.015
5					1.000	−0.361	−0.142
6						1.000	−0.271
7							1.000

F. Virginia 1660–1676 Regression, N = 129

Variable	Mean	Standard Deviation
1. Consumer goods (ln)	2.758	1.079
2. Wealth (ln)	4.160	1.263
3. Household size (ln)	1.509	0.789
4. Book-owner	0.698	0.973
5. Farmer	0.643	0.481
6. Élite or Trades	0.140	0.348

Correlation Matrix

	1	2	3	4	5	6
1	1.000	0.841	0.723	0.389	0.308	0.039
2		1.000	0.605	0.245	0.335	0.123
3			1.000	0.317	0.325	−0.088
4				1.000	−0.065	0.172
5					1.000	−0.541
6						1.000

G. Virginia 1724–1729 Regression, N = 299

Variable	Mean	Standard Deviation
1. Consumer goods (ln)	2.955	1.120
2. Wealth (ln)	4.029	1.221
3. Household size (ln)	1.490	0.757
4. Book-owner	0.532	0.500
5. Élite	0.080	0.272
6. Farmer	0.605	0.490
7. Trades	0.120	0.326
8. Widow	0.114	0.318

Correlation Matrix

	1	2	3	4	5	6	7	8
1	1.000	0.890	0.698	0.420	0.324	0.168	−0.071	−0.127
2		1.000	0.648	0.389	0.371	0.225	−0.104	−0.202
3			1.000	0.450	0.280	0.221	−0.128	−0.095
4				1.000	0.203	0.147	−0.065	−0.192
5					1.000	−0.366	−0.109	−0.106
6						1.000	−0.458	−0.444
7							1.000	−0.133
8								1.000

H. *Virginia and Maryland 1774 Regression,* N = 139

Variable	Mean	Standard Deviation
1. Consumer goods (ln)	3.018	1.059
2. Wealth (ln)	4.943	1.425
3. Household size (ln)	1.661	0.797
4. Coastal residency	0.504	0.502
5. Élite	0.072	0.259
6. Trades	0.129	0.337
7. Farmer	0.640	0.482
8. Widow	0.094	0.292
9. Book-owner	0.705	0.458

Correlation Matrix

	1	2	3	4	5	6	7	8	9
1	1.000	0.784	0.648	−0.053	0.158	−0.016	0.153	−0.045	0.443
2		1.000	0.621	−0.060	0.104	−0.159	0.304	−0.129	0.372
3			1.000	0.10	−0.079	−0.078	0.364	−0.117	0.378
4				1.000	0.054	−0.003	−0.145	0.072	−0.137
5					1.000	−0.107	−0.371	−0.089	0.180
6						1.000	−0.515	−0.124	−0.173
7							1.000	−0.429	0.238
8								1.000	−0.172
9									1.000

I. *Massachusetts 1660–1673 Regression,* N = 263

Variable	Mean	Standard Deviation
1. Consumer goods (ln)	3.422	0.899
2. Wealth (ln)	4.265	1.023
3. Household size (ln)	1.129	0.614
4. Town residency	0.483	0.501
5. Book-owner	0.487	0.501
6. Élite	0.027	0.161
7. Trades	0.125	0.332
8. Farmer	0.555	0.498
9. Widow	0.103	0.304

Correlation Matrix

	1	2	3	4	5	6	7	8	9
1	1.000	0.824	0.678	0.053	0.368	0.220	0.165	0.225	−0.143
2		1.000	0.623	0.002	0.336	0.215	0.194	0.316	−0.156
3			1.000	0.162	0.271	0.191	0.224	0.200	−0.156
4				1.000	0.003	−0.065	0.185	−0.176	0.049
5					1.000	0.123	0.090	0.014	−0.004
6						1.000	−0.063	−0.185	−0.056
7							1.000	−0.423	−0.128
8								1.000	−0.378
9									1.000

J. Massachusetts 1774 Regression, N = 269

Variable	Mean	Standard Deviation
1. Consumer goods (ln)	3.119	1.003
2. Wealth (ln)	4.127	1.321
3. Household size (ln)	1.552	0.689
4. Town residency	0.409	0.493
5. Élite	0.119	0.324
6. Trades	0.338	0.474
7. Farmer	0.320	0.467
8. Widow	0.071	0.257
9. Book-owner	0.714	0.453

Correlation Matrix

	1	2	3	4	5	6	7	8	9
1	1.000	0.813	0.696	0.236	0.251	0.147	−0.122	0.067	0.312
2		1.000	0.576	0.032	0.270	0.074	0.068	−0.146	0.291
3			1.000	−0.019	0.150	0.141	−0.003	−0.166	0.284
4				1.000	−0.049	0.284	−0.457	0.007	−0.126
5					1.000	−0.263	−0.252	−0.101	0.055
6						1.000	−0.490	−0.197	0.105
7							1.000	−0.189	0.099
8								1.000	−0.050
9									1.000

APPENDIX 3

County Breakdown on Shop Tax and on Pedlars' Licences

County	Amount of tax (£)	% non-borough parish shops	No. of pedlars 1697	No. of pedlars 1783
Bedfordshire	47	14.685	2	7
Berkshire	382	20.541	108	9
Buckinghamshire	110	19.545	84	21
Cambridgeshire	183	18.939	10	8
Cheshire	260	11.506	97	10
Cornwall	230	29.630	8	15
Cumberland	65	4.167	11	14
Derbyshire	131	12.766	20	37
Devonshire	876	16.750	43	85
Dorset	187	10.039	50	1
Durham	175	13.534	8	1
Essex	421	49.882	71	13
Gloucestershire	290	18.110	188	7
Hampshire	995	20.968	65	64
Herefordshire	117	3.623	64	3
Hertfordshire	185	43.382	35	11
Huntingdonshire	55	20.388	20	1
Kent	1,080	46.556	83	50
Lancashire	1,163	29.095	71	65
Leicestershire	137	6.706	10	6
Lincolnshire	213	11.356	42	9
Middlesex (incl. London)	28,040	100.000	441	221
Norfolk	518	26.389	55	36
Northamptonshire	128	10.119	15	26
Northumberland	n.a.	n.a.	75	14
Nottinghamshire	129	4.746	8	8
Oxfordshire	236	12.329	8	6
Rutland	8	3.571	0	1
Shropshire	318	4.796	68	20
Somerset	1,926	17.009	39	43
Staffordshire	148	14.835	82	242

County	Amount of tax (£)	% non-borough parish shops	No. of pedlars 1697	No. of pedlars 1783
Suffolk	340	28.743	38	15
Surrey	2,274	51.534	185	32
Sussex	253	34.266	49	12
Warwickshire	620	20.755	48	14
Westmorland	19	4.959	12	12
Wiltshire	347	19.196	8	15
Worcestershire	312	15.111	41	12
Yorkshire	963	8.564	184	130

Sources: Public Record Office, E 182, Retail Shop Tax 1785; Public Record Office, AO 3/370, 'Register of Licences Granted . . . from June 24th 1697 to Hawkers and Pedlars'; and Hoh-cheung Mui and Lorna H. Mui, *Shops and Shopkeeping in Eighteenth Century England*, Kingston, Canada, 1989, pp. 99–100.

Index